Keith Ansell-Pearson's book is an important and very welcome contribution to a neglected area of research: Nietzsche's political thought. Nietzsche is widely regarded as a significant moral philosopher, but his political thinking has often been dismissed as either impossibly individualistic or dangerously totalitarian. *Nietzsche contra Rousseau* takes a serious look at Nietzsche as political thinker and relates his political ideas to the dominant traditions of modern political thought. In particular, the nature of Nietzsche's dialogue with the philosophy of Jean-Jacques Rousseau is examined, in order to demonstrate Rousseau's crucial role in Nietzsche's understanding of modernity and its discontents. Nietzsche and Rousseau share an interest in the degeneration of human civilization, each providing a history of human moral and political development, and a paradoxical critique of liberal political culture. Against this background of similar concerns, Dr Ansell-Pearson contrasts Nietzsche's sovereign and supra-ethical autonomous individual with Rousseau's general will, arguing that Nietzsche's conception of the Dionysian self and the world as will-to-power is a direct response to the challenge of Rousseau's romanticism and historical pessimism. For Ansell-Pearson, it is the problem of history which constitutes the leitmotif of Nietzsche's innermost think on the fate of humanity and the question of civilization. In this study, he shows that a notion of politics is neither peripheral nor incidental to Nietzsche's concerns, but central to his overall philosophical project and emergent from his attempt to effect a 'self-overcoming of morality' which is also an overcoming of history and of metaphysics, of civilization, of tradition.

NIETZSCHE *CONTRA* ROUSSEAU

NIETZSCHE *CONTRA* ROUSSEAU

A study of Nietzsche's moral and political thought

KEITH ANSELL-PEARSON

Lecturer in political theory, Department of Political Studies
Queen Mary and Westfield College, University of London

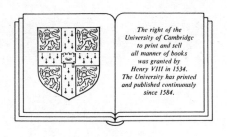

The right of the
University of Cambridge
to print and sell
all manner of books
was granted by
Henry VIII in 1534.
The University has printed
and published continuously
since 1584.

CAMBRIDGE UNIVERSITY PRESS

Cambridge
New York   Port Chester
Melbourne   Sydney

Published by the Press Syndicate of the University of Cambridge
The Pitt Building, Trumpington Street, Cambridge CB2 1RP
40 West 20th Street, New York, NY 10011-4211, USA
10 Stamford Road, Oakleigh, Melbourne 3166, Australia

First published 1991

Printed in Great Britain by the University Press, Cambridge

British Library cataloguing in publication data
Ansell-Pearson, Keith, 1960–
Neitzsche-*contra* Rousseau: Nietsche's moral and
political thought.
1. Politics. Ethics
172.092

Library of Congress cataloguing in publication data
Ansell-Pearson, Keith, 1960–
Nietzsche *contra* Rousseau: Nietzsche's moral and political
thought / Keith Ansell-Pearson.
p.   cm.
Includes bibliographical references and index.
ISBN 0-521-41173-4
1. Nietzsche, Friedrich Wilhelm, 1844–1900 – Contributions in
political science.   2. Nietzsche, Friedrich Wilhelm, 1844–1900 –
Ethics.   3. Rousseau, Jean-Jacques, 1712–1778 – Contributions in
political science.   1. Title.
JC233.N52A58   1991
320′.01 – dc20   91-149 CIP

ISBN 0 521 41173 4 HARDBACK

UP

In memory of my father

For the curious and the courageous

My youth was nothing but a sombre storm,
Shot through from time to time by brilliant sun;
Thunder and rain such havoc did perform
That there remain few fruits vermilion.

Now I have reached the autumn of my mind,
I must with spade and rake turn gardener,
Restore again the inundated ground,
Where water hollows holes like sepulchres.

And who knows if my reverie's new flowers
Will in this soil washed like a sandy shore
Find mystic aliment to make them bloom?

– O sorrow, sorrow! Time eats life away,
The Foe obscure which does our hearts consume
Grows stronger from our blood and our decay!

Baudelaire, 'The Enemy', *The Flowers of Evil* (1857)

Whoever wishes to mediate between two resolute thinkers show
that they are mediocre; they lack eyes for seeing what is unique.
Seeing things as similar and making things the same is the sign
of weak eyes.

F. Nietzsche, *The Gay Science* (1882)

At this moment, when each of us must fit an arrow to his bow
and enter the lists anew, to reconquer, within history and in
spite of it, that which he owns already, the thin yield of his
fields, the brief love of this earth, at this moment when at last
a man is born, it is time to forsake our age and its adolescent
rages. The bow bends; the wood complains. At the moment of
supreme tension, there will leap into flight an unswerving
arrow, a shaft that is inflexible and free.

A. Camus, *The Rebel* (1951)

Contents

Preface

This book is an attempt to examine and explore the nature of Friedrich Nietzsche's (1844–1900) critique of Jean-Jacques Rousseau (1712–78). It aims to show that Rousseau is a crucial figure in Nietzsche's understanding of modernity and its discontents, and that an examination of Nietzsche's exchange with the figure of Rousseau reveals important insights into his ethical and political thought, in particular the way in which the problem of history constitutes the fundamental leitmotif of his innermost thinking on the fate of humanity and the problem of civilization.

The American philosopher Stanley Rosen has recently declared – in a critical vein it should be noted – that today Nietzsche is recognized by many to be the most important philosopher in the Western, non-Marxist world. It is important in debates on the importance of Nietzsche's work, especially in the context of debates over the nature of the transition from modernity to postmodernity, that the effect is not depoliticized. Readers who are interested in how I conceive Nietzsche's role in the context of current debates on the nature of the postmodern turn in Occidental thought are referred to my essay, 'Nietzsche on Autonomy and Morality: the Challenge to Political Theory' (*Political Studies*, June, 1991). This study sets out to make a contribution to the growing body of literature which now exists on the subject of Nietzsche's politics and his political thought. I want to show that, by examining how Nietzsche conceives the problem of history through a confrontation with Rousseau we can appreciate that a notion of politics is neither peripheral nor incidental to Nietzsche's concerns, but is central to his overall philosophical project and emerges consistently and coherently out of his attempt to effect a 'self-overcoming of morality' (which is also, for reasons that will become clear, an overcoming of metaphysics, of civilization, of history, of tradition, etc.). As Tracy Strong pointed out in one of the first attempts to examine Nietzsche seriously as a political thinker in his study of 1975, Nietzsche's thought is not that of an anti-political thinker but of someone who sets out to challenge the conception of the political found in modern thought. In defining what I mean by the term 'political' in this study I will follow the definition offered by Sheldon Wolin in his classic study entitled *Politics and Vision* where the task of political philosophy is defined as 'reflection on matters that concern the community as a whole'. In this study, therefore, I shall use the term 'political' to refer to the 'res publica', the 'commonwealth', and political theory to refer to the examination of the grounds on which a thinker constructs and justifies social order and political rule. As will be seen, both Rousseau and Nietzsche's reflections on the political contain a powerful critique of liberal political culture.

I have not written this study as a disciple of Nietzsche's philosophy. I have, however, intentionally written in a style which endeavours to give the reader a sense of the *experience* which informed Nietzsche's conception of his task (of his 'down-going' or descent) in order to convey something of the spirit and the letter of his thought. Nietzsche is often taken to be the supreme example of a literary philosopher, but this literariness is misunderstood if it is taken in a purely aesthetic sense, for a concern with style is a pedagogical necessity for anyone who proclaims to be a teacher in their task of thinking. The meaning of the key notions of his philosophy (will to power, the overman, eternal return, etc.), and of his texts, are polysemous. This means that, in deciphering and uncovering their meaning, Nietzsche's readers are implicated both in the truth-claims of his key notions and the destinies of his texts. If I am not a disciple, then do I assume the guise of an advocate of Nietzsche? Yes, in the sense in which I understand the task of one becoming what one is: through reading Nietzsche we are to become those that we are. For disciples of Rousseau, chapter six will reveal to them in what sense I am an advocate of Jean-Jacques. This then is my dual descent: I *know* both for I *am* both.

Over the years many people (fellow-travellers along the Way perhaps) have served to encourage and inspire my interest in Nietzsche. I cannot mention every one of them here, but extend my gratitude to them. Many of the arguments in this book have benefited from a number of prolonged discussions with David Owen, and I thank David for the support he has given me over the past two years. Valuable encouragement of my work has come from my colleagues in the Department of Political Studies at Queen Mary and Westfield College, especially James Dunkerley. For financial assistance, I wish to thank the British Academy and the German Academic Exchange Service (DAAD). Funds from both these institutions enabled me to advance my knowledge of Nietzsche's writings by attending a language course in Germany and carrying out a programme of study at the Philosophy Institute of the Free University of Berlin. I am especially grateful to DAAD for awarding me a scholarship in the summer of 1990 to study under the guidance of Wolfgang Müller-Lauter at the Kirchliche Hochschule Berlin.

For their helpful editorial comments on an earlier draft of this study, I would like to thank Professors Ernst Behler, Eckhard Heftrich, Wolfgang Müller-Lauter, and Heinz Wenzel of *Nietzsche Studien*. I also wish to thank Timothy O'Hagan and Stephen Houlgate for reading an earlier version and making a number of helpful suggestions for improving the fluency and accuracy of my argument; the former saved me from making a number of errors in my reading of Rousseau, and the latter supported and encouraged me in my conviction that Rousseau poses as many problems to Nietzsche as Nietzsche does to Rousseau. Richard Schacht has also been a strong advocate of this work and I thank him for lending his support to it. A number of people have been generous in sending me copies of their work. I have learned a great deal about various aspects of Nietzsche's thought from these. In this regard I wish to thank: Daniel Conway, Nicholas Davey, Ian Forbes, Volker Gerhardt, Jacob Golomb, Henry Kerger, Elisabeth Kuhn, Wolfgang Müller-Lauter, Robert Pippin, Renate Reschke, Claus-Artur Scheier, Lars-Henrik Schmidt, Robin Small, Tracy Strong, David Thatcher, and Mark Warren. I am especially indebted to Ian Forbes who was generous enough to send me a copy of his own unpublished work on Rousseau and Nietzsche, as well as a useful translation by Irene Krumins of Herbert Kramer's 1928 dissertation study *Nietzsche und Rousseau*. I offer my sincere thanks to R. J. Hollingdale for his generous assistance with a number of translations from Nietzsche, especially from the *Nachlass* material of *Thus Spoke Zarathustra*, and for answering a number of questions I put to him regarding his translations of certain passages of Nietzsche.

My family, that is my mother, sister, brother and mother-in-law, have been a constant source of emotional support, and I am eternally in their debt. My greatest debt, however, is to my wife Nicky, without whose unflappable love and support it simply would not have been possible to have advanced my studies to their present level. May our child be a new beginning and a sacred Yes.

There are many excellent studies of both Rousseau and Nietzsche available, and I have learned a great deal from them, including those I found myself in fundamental disagreement with on certain points of interpretation regarding the ideas of both thinkers. Full details of my secondary sources, along with my corresponding debts to scholars past and present, can be found in the footnotes which accompany the text and in the bibliography. I gratefully acknowledge the permission granted to me to quote from Baudelaire's *Selected Poems*, translation copyright Joanna Richardson, 1975, reproduced by permission of Curtis Brown Group Ltd., London.

Readers should note that I have adopted the practice of modifying translations for the sake of accuracy and uniformity without explicitly stating so in every instance.

Finally, a note on gender. A major preoccupation of both Rousseau and Nietzsche is the fate of autonomy in the modern world. However, in the writings of both, women are excluded from undergoing the task of authentic self-legislation. For both, women constitute the sex whose role it is to 'obey' and not 'command'. It is important that the history of this exclusion within the tradition of modern political thought is not effaced by contemporary political theorists. In the text I have endeavoured to include women philosophically at all times in my argument, and stylistically where possible. When quoting from Rousseau and Nietzsche and discussing quotations, I have retained their use of the masculine pronoun. Although I do not explicitly deal with the issue here, I explore the relationship between Nietzsche and current feminist thought in the aforementioned essay, 'Nietzsche on Autonomy and Morality'.

Note on the texts and abbreviations

The following abbreviations are used in the notes for texts by Rousseau and Nietzsche. In each case I first provide an abbreviation for the French or German edition which has been used, followed by an abbreviation of the English translation where this is available. The dates given in brackets refer to the publication of each text.

Rousseau

OC   *Ouevres Complètes*, eds. B. Gagnebin and M. Raymond, Paris, Bibliothèque de la Pléiade, Editions Gallimard, 1959–.

DAS   *A Discourse on the Arts and Sciences* (1750–1) in Rousseau, *The Social Contract and Discourses*, tr. G. D. H. Cole; revised and augmented J. H. Brumfitt and J. C. Hall, London, Dent, 1973.

DI   *A Discourse on the Origin of Inequality* (1755) in Cole/ Brumfitt/Hall.

DPE   *A Discourse on Political Economy* (1755) in Cole/Brumfitt/ Hall.

GSHR   *The General Society of the Human Race* (from the Geneva ms. of the *Social Contract*) in Cole/Brumfitt/Hall.

E   *Émile* (1762), tr. Barbara Foxley, London, Dent, 1974.

SC   *The Social Contract* (1762) in Cole/Brumfitt/Hall.

RSW   *Reveries of a Solitary Walker* (composed 1776–8, published posthumously), tr. Peter France, Middlesex, Penguin, 1979.

I have also used the following texts, which are not abbreviated in the notes:

The Confessions, tr. J. M. Cohen, Middlesex, Penguin, 1954.

The First and Second Discourses and Essay on the Origin of Languages, tr. V. Gourevitch, New York, Harper and Row, 1986.

Du Contrat social, edited with an Introduction by Ronald Grimsley, Oxford, Oxford University Press, 1972.

Political Writings, tr. F. Watkins, Nelson, Edinburgh, 1953. J. Hope Mason (ed.), *The Indispensable Rousseau*, London, Quartet Books, 1979.

The Government of Poland, tr. Willmoore Kendall, Indianapolis, Hackett Publishing Co., 1985.

Nietzsche

KSA   *Friedrich Nietzsche. Sämtliche Werke: Kritische Studienausgabe* (fifteen volumes), eds. G. Colli and M. Montinari, Berlin/New York and Munich, Walter de Gruyter and Deutscher Taschenbuch Verlag, 1967–77 and 1988.

GSt   *Der griechische Staat* (*The Greek State*) (1871 – not published by Nietzsche) in *KSA* volume I.

BT   *The Birth of Tragedy* (1872), tr. Walter Kaufmann, New York, Random House, 1967.

UADH   *The Uses and Disadvantages of History for Life* (1874) in *Untimely Meditations*, tr. R. J. Hollingdale, Cambridge, Cambridge University Press, 1983.

SE   *Schopenhauer as Educator* (1874) in Hollingdale 1983.

HAH   *Human, All Too Human* (volume I) (1878) tr. R. J. Hollingdale, Cambridge, Cambridge University Press, 1986.

AOM   *Assorted Opinions and Maxims* (1879) (volume II, first part of *Human, All Too Human*), in Hollingdale, 1986.

WS   *The Wanderer and his Shadow* (1880) (volume II, second part of *Human, All Too Human*), in Hollingdale 1986.

D   *Daybreak. Thoughts on the Prejudices of Morality* (1881), tr. R. J. Hollingdale, Cambridge, Cambridge University Press, 1982.

GS   *The Gay Science* (1882; second edition with book v and an appendix of songs, 1887), tr. Walter Kaufmann, New York, Random House, 1974.

TSZ   *Thus Spoke Zarathustra* (1883–5), tr. R. J. Hollingdale, Middlesex, Penguin, 1969.

BGE   *Beyond Good and Evil* (1886), tr. Walter Kaufmann, Random House, 1966.

OGM   *On the Genealogy of Morals* (1887), tr. Walter Kaufmann, Random House, 1967.

TI   *Twilight of the Idols* (prepared for publication 1888, first edition 1889), tr. R. J. Hollingdale, Penguin, 1968.

AC   *The Anti-Christ* (prepared for publication 1888, first edition 1895), tr. R. J. Holingdale, Penguin, 1968.

EH   *Ecce Homo* (prepared for publication 1888, first edition 1908), tr. Walter Kaufmann, New York, Random House, 1967.

WP*   *The Will to Power* (Notes from Nietzsche's *Nachlass* – posthumously published writings – of the period 1883–88, collected under the title *Der Wille zur Macht* by Nietzsche's sister, Elisabeth Forster-Nietzsche; first edition published 1901, second edition published 1906 containing 1,067 sections), tr. Walter Kaufmann and R. J. Hollingdale, New York, Random House, 1967.

* For a long time now there has been a great deal of dispute amongst scholars of Nietzsche's writings as to the value of this selection of the *Nachlass* material of the 1880s, with Heidegger, for example, claiming that it contains the authentic Nietzsche who never had the chance to consummate his task publicly. I do not wish to enter into the debate here on the use and abuse of this material; suffice it to say that it should be treated with caution and read in conjunction with the material Nietzsche actually published in this period. The serious student of Nietzsche should in the end come to rely on the *complete Nachlass* material available in the Colli and Montinari critical edition of the collected works, and which has been arranged, unlike the Kaufmann edition (which follows the German edition of 1,067 sections), in the order in which Nietzsche composed it, in so far as it was possible to date all the material. On the history of the text known as *Der Wille zur Macht* see Kaufmann's Introduction to his translation with Hollingdale, especially pp. xvii–xx.

Introduction

'My humanity is a constant self-overcoming'.
Nietzsche, *Ecce Homo*, 'Why I am so wise'.

ON THE PROBLEM OF HISTORY AS A PROBLEM OF TIME

To be heirs of the writings of Rousseau and Nietzsche is to be the inheritors of two of the most powerful and disturbing critiques of civilization that the modern period has produced. Indeed, I would go so far as to contend that part of what it means to be a modern man or woman – or even post-modern for that matter – is to take up the task of engaging in some kind of confrontation (*Auseinandersetzung* – denoting 'settlement' and 'exchange') with the paradoxical and ambiguous teachings of both Rousseau and Nietzsche. The questions which Rousseau raised concerning the value of civilization have lost none of their relevance in our ecological age, while Nietzsche's diagnosis of axiological nihilism (a diagnosis resulting from his own deeply felt experience of the death of God) to describe the condition of modern Occidental humanity haunts the events of the twentieth century as a nightmare from which we have yet to wake up. Nietzsche's experience – he once described himself as the first perfect nihilist – has now become our own. Thus, Rousseau and Nietzsche are two thinkers who embody the modern experience and who provide the perfect foil for our own anxieties. Both thinkers' love of paradox accounts for the fact that the key notions of their thinking are still subject to a variety of often conflicting interpretations, and their legacy is deeply ambiguous. Rousseau's spirit of rebellion comes down to us via the bloody excesses and terror of the French Revolution, while Nietzsche's spirit of rebellion comes down to us through the unspeakable evil of the attempted mastery of the earth by Nazism. A settlement with both can only take place by

I

undertaking an analysis of the fundamental problems which animated their intellectual spirit, and by cultivating a sense of the experience which informed their understanding of the spiritual task they set themselves.

In his prize-winning discourse of 1750 on the arts and sciences Rousseau addresses his fellow-men as those 'happy slaves' who are blissfully ignorant of their own miserable, impoverished condition. He looks back to an earlier, more original time when, although human nature was probably not much better than it is now, men at least enjoyed a secure existence and were *transparent* to one another. It was this transparency in human relations which prevented the development of all the vices (excessive pride, vanity, etc.) which corrupt modern humanity. Rousseau laments the 'servile and deceptive conformity' which prevails in modern mores, and he refers to society, in a strangely Nietzschean way, as that 'herd of men'.[1] The discourse on the arts and sciences poses, in a critical, dramatic manner, a number of questions concerning the value of civilization which have now become part of the common experience of modern existence. Is civilization worth having? At what price and through the pursuit of what kind of barbarism? Moreover, are not such kinds of questions riddled with insuperable paradoxes?

At the end of his second untimely meditation on the uses and abuses of the writing and teaching of history (1874), Nietzsche, in what has to be one of his most Rousseauian moments, demands that we moderns think back to our 'real needs' so that we learn that culture means something more than merely a 'decoration of life', more than 'dissimulation and disguise'. In this way, the Greek conception of culture as a new and improved *physis* (nature) will be revealed to us, 'culture as a unanimity of life, thought, appearance and will'.[2] In the prologue to *Thus Spoke Zarathustra*, Rousseau's 'happy slaves' assume the guise of the 'last men', who proudly declare that they have discovered happiness and then blink. The last men are the uniform, characterless mass or herd whose appearance Rousseau finds so distasteful in his first discourse. Nobody grows rich or poor anymore, nobody knows the answer to the question who should rule and who should obey. Such questions are too burdensome, too taxing, to contemplate. Thus, everyone desires the same, everyone is the same. Anyone who thinks differently, Nietzsche has Zarathustra say, goes voluntarily into the madhouse. One of the great political ironies of modern liberal society for both Rousseau and Nietzsche is that it is a social form which seemingly promotes an individualist culture, but which in fact ends up producing social conformity in which there is a complete absence of great human beings and true sovereign individuals.[3]

For Nietzsche, the question mark that constitutes the enigma of Jean-Jacques Rousseau revolves around the pitting of paradox against paradox. If one agrees with Rousseau that there is something pitiable, contemptible even, about modern civilization, then one is faced with the following choice: either one agrees with Rousseau that civilization is to be held responsible for our 'bad morality', or one disagrees with Rousseau and inverts his position in the manner of Nietzsche by locating the problem of civilization, not within civilization itself, but within our so-called 'good morality'; in other words one undertakes a revaluation of values in order to attain a standpoint beyond the opposition of 'good' and 'evil'.[4] Nietzsche's major critique of Rousseau is that it is his moralism – his belief in a natural moral world-order which results in a belief in man's natural goodness, and which, as we shall see, is *not* the same as Nietzsche's standpoint beyond good and evil – that prevents him from finding an adequate solution to the riddle of the problem of civilization that he has posed in such ominous terms. Nietzsche considers Rousseau's question concerning the value of civilization, of whether the human animal has been improved by it, to be an amusing one, since the reverse is the case and it is this which enables one to speak in favour of it.

For Nietzsche, the problem Rousseau has posed concerning the fate of civilization and the condition of modern humanity is really a problem about history and the nature of time. The problem of humanity lies in its failure to establish a genuine relationship to the past. Time, whose essence lies in the moment, is intractable. The human will cannot break the inexorable movement – the becoming – of time, but only watch as an innocent bystander and see itself become a victim of the play of time. This leads the human will to seek revenge on life in a futile effort to break time's spell and logic. We cannot will backwards and thus punish life, ourselves, and others, simply because we cannot undo what has been done. The problem we are faced with as modern human beings constituted by a historical consciousness is that of how to achieve a genuine relationship to the past by becoming authentically historical (even if that means, paradoxically, learning how to become *unhistorical*). For

Nietzsche the human being can only overcome the spirit of revenge
which informs its attitude towards life by learning how to affirm
the very timeliness of time which consists in learning to affirm
the moment (*Augenblick*). To affirm the moment is to affirm the
innocence of becoming, which means that we neither justify the
present in terms of some promised, but ill-defined, future, nor justify
the past in terms of the present by which, from the vantage point of
a post-historical position, we justify all that has been because we
deem that it has necessarily led to our present 'superior' position.
On Nietzsche's reading, the spirit of resentment characterizes the
entire history of Western metaphysics from Plato to Kant. In
constructing a two-world theory in which a world of being (a
beyond) is portrayed as the true world, and a world of becoming (the
here and now) is portrayed as the merely apparent world, Western
metaphysics and religion have devaluated life through a devaluation
of time and transience. For Nietzsche, Rousseau is an important and
integral part of this Christian–moral tradition whose crisis of faith
lies behind the modern experience of nihilism.[5]

This study is an exploration of the theme of history (as a problem
of time) as it is found in Nietzsche's writings, and as it is born out of
Nietzsche's attempt to overcome the attitude of *ressentiment* which for
him informs the politics of the modern epoch. I see the problem of
history, considered as a problem of time, as the fundamental
leitmotif running throughout Nietzsche's work and unifying the two
major works of his 'mature' thought, *Thus Spoke Zarathustra* and *On
the Genealogy of Morals*. However, it is important to appreciate that
a satisfactory resolution of the problem of time (if indeed that is what
it is), is something which Nietzsche arrives at only after a great deal
of intellectual development, struggle, and turmoil. It is certainly not
something which characterizes his thought from its beginnings. On
the contrary, in his early writings, in which Nietzsche is operating
largely under the influence of Kant's dualistic metaphysics and of
Schopenhauer's philosophy with its pessimism and denial of the will,
his thought is notable for the way in which it shares metaphysics'
resentment towards becoming and time. Before we explore this
major facet of Nietzsche's earliest thinking on the problem of history,
it is necessary to say something about Rousseau's importance as the
political philosopher who 'discovers' history to be the central
problem of the modern experience of existence.

The work of Leo Strauss is well known for the way in which it construes the problem of modernity in terms of a crisis of the historical consciousness. In his penetrating short essay on 'The Three Waves of Modernity'. Strauss informs his readers that the crisis of modernity is best understood as a crisis of political philosophy, and he names Machiavelli, Rousseau, and Nietzsche as the three major figures whose work exemplifies the development of this crisis. The crisis of modernity exposes itself in the form of a crippling ethical relativism produced by the historical sense in which modern Western man no longer has an idea what he wants, since he does not know what is good and what is bad, what is right and what is wrong.[6] The crisis of modernity is a crisis of political philosophy because all the problems of modern humanity can be reduced to an inability to answer the traditional question of classical political thought, namely, that concerning the good, or best, order of society.

According to Strauss, Rousseau constitutes an important wave of modernity because of the way in which he conceives of the development of human sociability and rationality in historical terms. In his depiction of the pre-political state of nature, a conception Rousseau takes over from Hobbes and Locke, radicalizing it in the process by showing its historical presuppositions, man is subhuman and even pre-human. But here we encounter the great paradox of Rousseau's thought: man only becomes fully human (because he becomes *moral*) on account of the historical process, and yet the historical process, which is at the centre of his thinking on man, is at the same time held responsible for producing, not a rational and moral humanity, but present-day corrupt and degenerate mankind. What went wrong in this secularized version of the biblical Fall? What is to be done about it?

It is the raising of these urgent questions in such stark, life or death, terms which constitutes the brilliant and terrifying nature of Rousseau's legacy. As one commentator has noted, Rousseau is the prophet of history who despaired of history.[7] Rousseau's relation to historical reality displays a terrible ambiguity. Only in this world, the world that is the product of historical development, can man attain moral freedom, for such freedom requires a sense of rationality and rational self-discipline which is the result of the historical evolution of the social animal. And yet this same process of historical development leads to the destruction of man's simple, transparent, self-sufficient happiness. Rousseau is acutely aware of the dilemma which his thinking on the problem of civilization must face, an

awareness which is accompanied by a profound despair. There can
be no going back to the natural innocence of an earlier, golden age.
Looking into the future he sees only a worsening of the evils of the
present corrupt human condition. It is at this point in his thinking
that Rousseau's discontent with civilization becomes generalized as
time 'appears as the absolute enemy, time which makes it impossible
that any harmony could ever be preserved or any happiness
sustained'.[8] Time is the enemy for Rousseau because time represents
the inexorable process of change and decay. Time thus appears as
something to be transcended. Nothing is permanent, everything is
allowed, we might say, paraphrasing the famous maxim 'nothing is
true, everything is permitted' from Dostoyevsky, which Nietzsche
refers to in the third essay of the *Genealogy of Morals*.[9]

The source and tragedy of Rousseau's despair on the fate of
civilization is that he is the first to look into human history itself for
the totality which humanity had previously sought in transcendental
worlds – in divine providence, in an unchanging world of forms, and
so on – but he cannot find in history only what history can give him,
namely, redemption and the solution to the riddle he has posed.[10]
Rousseau finds himself caught in the trap of time. If there can be no
going back, then our only hope of redemption, our only chance of
realizing true human happiness, justice, equality, and harmony of
social relationships, lies in the future. But, 'the very law of historical
development that showed there was no going back on time also
showed the future to be destructive of human values'.[11] Rousseau
thus confronts us with an antimony, that of nature on the one hand,
and of civil society, morality, reason, and history on the other.[12]

Nietzsche is well aware of the tragic ambiguity which characterizes
Rousseau's meditations on history. Historical existence is necessarily
tragic because there can be no final redemption for humanity in its
rage against time, as it is the law of life that everything will die and
perish. The test for Nietzsche is whether human beings are strong
and brave enough to affirm the tragic character of their existence, or
whether they wish to take flight from it by seeking a beyond or
afterworld, through the worship of idols, and by doing so necessarily
taking revenge on life by denying its essential reality – cruel,
terrifying, seductive, illusory, transitory, changing, 'immoral'.

For Nietzsche, Rousseau is the political philosopher of *ressentiment*
of the modern age *par excellence*. Rousseau, says Nietzsche, is 'the first
modern man',[13] whose portrayal of civilization is designed to inspire
pity for man, and which in turn can only lead us to feeling contempt

and disgust for him. Consider, for example, Rousseau's disquieting end to the exordium of the second discourse on the origins of inequality, where he informs modern men and women that:

Discontented with your present state, for reasons which threaten your unfortunate descendants with still greater discontent, you will perhaps wish it were in your power to go back; and this feeling should be a panegyric on your first ancestors, a criticism of your contemporaries, and a terror to the unfortunates who will come after you.[14]

Towards the end of his life, Rousseau himself underwent the experience of the moment in very similar terms to the way in which Nietzsche poses the challenge of the thought-experiment of eternal return, in his well-known passage in *The Gay Science* (aphorism 341). In this passage Nietzsche presents the thought of eternal return in terms of an existential test. It is the 'greatest weight' which the human being is freely to bear on its shoulders and the means by which it is able to overcome its resentment towards life through a tragic affirmation. Nietzsche invites us to imagine a demon who descends upon us in the hour of our loneliest loneliness (genuine truth and insight being possible only in the moments of our deepest solitude), and tells us that the life we now live, and have lived, we will have to repeat once more, and innumerable times more, all in the same succession and sequence without subtraction or addition. This means that there will be nothing new in this repeatable life; instead, every pain and every joy, everything unutterably small and contingent in our lives, will return to us again and again. How would we respond to such a demon? Would we throw ourselves on the ground and curse it, or would we experience a tremendous revelation when we recognize that the divine – a god of some sort perhaps – is speaking to us? The test of eternal return asks the question of how well-disposed we would have to be to ourselves and towards life to desire nothing more passionately than this ultimate confirmation and seal. Clearly, for Nietzsche, the test of eternal return reveals a great deal about the one who freely undergoes its necessity. Do they suffer from an overfullness of life, a rich, polyvalent abundance springing from a feeling of courage for life and its perpetual self-overcoming? Or do they suffer from a destitution and impoverishment of life, and therefore experience a revulsion towards the thought of the eternal return of the moments of their life, leading to a sense of pity for life and a desire merely for its self-preservation?

In the fifth walk of his *Reveries* Rousseau declares, in a highly

Nietzschean manner, that 'everything is in constant flux on earth'.[15] Owing to the passage of time nothing retains the same shape or form. Our affections recall a past which is always gone and a future which might never be. There is nothing solid that the human heart can attach itself to. As a result, we are reduced to being creatures of the moment who are incapable of experiencing lasting happiness. Is there a single moment, Rousseau asks, of which one could truthfully declare: 'Would that this moment could last for ever!' It would be a moment in which the self attained a moment of complete, sufficient, and perfect happiness because it would have transcended time – both time's regret ('it was') *and* time's anxiety ('it might never be').

It may be an unfair comparison to make between Rousseau and Nietzsche on this point by drawing on a passage which comes from a work that Rousseau wrote in the last years of his life, in which he is experiencing all the torment and indignity which comes from being a social outcast. Nevertheless, the comparison is instructive for its shows clearly the resentment which animates Rousseau's life and genius, and the different spirit towards life that Nietzsche is striving for. For Nietzsche, the bitterness and resentment, which is so apparent in Rousseau's last reflections, is simply the outcome of the moralism which guides all his thinking, from the first attack on civilized humanity in the discourse on the arts and sciences onwards. In *Zarathustra*, Nietzsche has his hero recognize the moment of time, not as a way of escaping from its clutches, but as a way of affirming time's flux and inexorable becoming. The significance of the thought of eternal return for Nietzsche is not so much that it teaches that everything literally returns (a highly dubious teaching if taken as a cosmological doctrine), but rather that through the contemplation of the *possibility* of the eternal return of all the moments in one's life, including the inestimably small and trivial, one is led to appreciate the very nature of time itself and the *innocence* of one's own becoming. If one has the strength and courage to affirm the moment that constitutes the timely quality of time (its passing away and perishing), then one will be able to affirm the nature of time itself, as well as affirming the whole of one's existence as inseparable from the fate that one is. Such an affirmation is based on the recognition that one's life is both a totality and a fatality, that the moment is neither isolated nor self-sufficient from all other moments, for the experience of the moment as eternal reveals all (the totality and fatality) that one is. We must learn how, in Nietzsche's paradoxical formulation, to *become* what we *are*. What we find in Rousseau's reveries is a desire to negate time, through the isolated moment which is *beyond* time and its grasp (hence Rousseau's quest for the moment that is self-sufficient). Where Nietzsche seeks in the moment an affirmation of time and of existence in its totality, Rousseau seeks, as he himself tells us, a 'compensation' for the joys he has not been allowed in society, a compensation 'which neither fortune nor mankind can take away from him'.[16] This experience of 'compensation', however, must be had at a price, that of the annihilation of the temporal (and vulnerable) self, for the desire for a self-sufficient moment is the desire for the oblivion of the self.

Nietzsche, by contrast, presents a teaching which affirms the 'innocence of becoming', and which consists in the belief that no one gives a human being their qualities (God, society, parents, ancestors, etc.), that nobody is accountable for their actions, for being constituted as they are, for living in the circumstances and surroundings in which they find themselves. The fatality of a person's nature cannot be disentangled from the fatality of all that which they have been, and will become. We are thus not to think of human existence as the result of any special design, will, or purpose. Moreover, 'man' is not to be conceived as the subject of an attempt to achieve an ideal of happiness or of morality, for it is we who have invented the concept of purpose; in reality purpose is lacking. 'One is necessary', Nietzsche writes, 'one is a piece of fate, one belongs to the whole, one *is* in the whole – there exists nothing which could judge, measure, compare, condemn the whole... *For nothing exists apart from the whole*!'[17] In a note from the *Nachlass* of Summer 1883 Nietzsche calls for the total emancipation of 'absolute necessity' from any notion of 'ends' (*Zwecken*). Otherwise, he says, 'we should not be allowed the attempt to sacrifice ourselves and let ourselves go. Only the innocence of becoming gives us the *greatest courage* and the *greatest freedom*!'[18]

It is one of the principal ironies of Nietzsche's work that it sets out to debunk the pretensions and deceptions of the modern age by drawing upon the same historical sense which it judges to be one of the main symptoms of its decadent condition. Thus, for example, in one of the opening passages of *Human, All Too Human*, Nietzsche declares that lack of historical sense is the family failing of all philosophers, and he demands a new style of analysis which he

designates as 'historical philosophizing'. Such a mode of philosophizing will show that man is not an '*aeterna veritas*', not something
'that remains constant in the midst of all flux, as a sure measure of
things'. 'Everything', Nietzsche declares, 'has become'. There are,
therefore, no eternal truths and no absolute values.[19]

Nietzsche's whole thought is directed towards the creation of the
new, which can only be brought about by cultivating recognition of
the innocence of becoming. Like Rousseau, he seeks the possibility of
a second innocence. However, unlike Rousseau, Nietzsche's new
'conscious type of innocence' will not be the return of some imagined
original 'natural goodness', but rather the recognition that the
innocence of becoming, of the flux of time, means that human
creativity is genuinely *beyond* good and evil. The precise significance
of this teaching will be explored in detail as the study unfolds. But
it is clear that the task of becoming those who we are is both a
paradoxical and a demanding one, requiring of the creative
individual the ability to preserve the tension between innocence and
experience, ignorance and knowledge, so that he knows when to
remember and when to forget. The task of becoming those who we
are demands a strange combination of blindness and insight. This
explains why, for example, Nietzsche says that in order to become
what one is *one must not have the faintest idea what one is*. For even the
blunders of life have their part to play in making us what we are.[20]
However, to affirm the totality of life, including that of one's own, by
attaining a standpoint beyond good and evil, requires not only a new
conscious form of innocence, but also a higher form of knowledge
which is able to surpass the negative feelings of resentment and
revenge by recognizing that the relationship between good and evil
is one of a creative entwinement.

For Nietzsche, the modern sense of history is a sure sign that
humanity no longer feels at home in the world but experiences a
fundamental homesickness. The present is a burden, the past has
become forgotten or re-written in accordance with the prejudices of
the modern age, and the future will take care of itself. The historical
sense has led to a vapid relativism and a gnawing scepticism
concerning forms of truth and knowledge. Our age is the cynical age.
In the *Genealogy of Morals* Nietzsche describes the modern writing of
history (*Geschichtsschreibung*) as 'nihilistic' since, having rejected
teleology, it no longer desires to 'prove anything', it wishes neither
to affirm nor to deny.[21] What concerns Nietzsche is the way in which

the historical sense of the nineteenth century, which has come in the wake of an 'enchanting and mad *semi-barbarism* into which Europe had been plunged by the democratic mingling of classes and races', results in a kind of chaos constituting the very nature of 'modern souls'.[22] It is this concern with reforming the chaos that we are, and producing a new noble culture out of its deformation and corruption, which constitutes a major theme of Nietzsche's early, untimely meditation on history.

Commentators usually take Nietzsche's second untimely meditation to be what it proclaims to be, namely, a treatise on history. But it is in fact more accurately understood as one of Nietzsche's earliest attempts to grapple with the awesome reality of time. It is a work inspired as much by Emerson as it is by Burckhardt.[23] In this work Nietzsche is as much preoccupied with the nature of the unhistorical as he is with that of the historical, emphasizing the necessity of both in the healthy life of an individual, a people, and a culture. This early meditation on history provides many valuable insights into why the conception of the 'moment' occupies such an important place in Nietzsche's mature thought.

The aim of the meditation is to argue that a people and a culture need history for the sake of life and action, not in order to stultify life and action. We serve history (*Historie*), therefore, to the extent that history serves life. In order to appreciate the extent to which modern man suffers from his historical sense, Nietzsche asks us to consider some grazing cattle who pass us by without knowing the meaning of yesterday or today. Instead, they are fettered to the pleasure or displeasure of the moment. A human being can only look upon them with envy, for, although it thinks of itself as superior to animals, it desires the life they have, a life without boredom and pain, but which as an animal that is also not an animal (on account of its self-consciousness) it cannot have. The human being who reflects upon the grazing cattle will quickly discover that the source of its unhappiness is that it cannot learn how to forget, but clings relentlessly to the past. Nietzsche writes:

...a moment, now here and then gone, nothing before it came, again nothing after it has gone, nonetheless returns as a ghost and disturbs the peace of a later moment. A leaf flutters from the scroll of time, floats away – and suddenly floats back again and falls into the man's lap. Then the man says 'I remember' and envies the animal, who at once forgets and for whom every moment really dies, sinks back into the night and fog and is extinguished for ever. Thus the animal lives *unhistorically*; for it is contained in the present...it does not know how to dissimulate, it conceals nothing and at every instant appears wholly as what it is...[24]

By contrast, man is an animal which, on account of its possession of a memory, is continually oppressed by the pressure of the past, pushing him down and bending him sideways, reminding him of his base origins whenever he strives for greatness. To see the herds grazing only serves to provide him with the vision of a lost paradise, or to remind him of the child who plays in blissful blindness between the hedges of past and future. 'Yet its play', Nietzsche writes, 'will soon be disturbed', as it is drawn out of its state of forgetfulness. 'Then', he says, 'it will learn to understand the phrase "it was"': that password which gives conflict, suffering, and satiety access to man so as to remind him what his existence fundamentally is – an imperfect tense that can never become a perfect one'.[25]

Nietzsche thus invites us to reflect upon the proposition that, not only is the unhistorical sense as necessary as the historical sense to healthy living, but the capacity to feel unhistorically is *more* vital and *more* fundamental, since it constitutes the foundation upon which things truly great and human can grow. A human being who felt historically through and through at every instant would be like someone forcibly deprived of sleep, like an animal condemned to live only by 'ever repeated rumination'. Nietzsche praises the supra-historical individual who sees no redemption in the process of history, but for whom 'the world is complete and reaches its finality at each and every moment. What could ten more years teach that the past ten years were unable to teach!'[26]

Already in this early work we find Nietzsche intimating at his later major doctrines, not only that of the eternal return, but also that of the overman. The highest goal of humanity, Nietzsche informs us, does not lie in its end or *telos*, but only in its highest exemplars. To this end, there is no better aim of living unhistorically than that of perishing – of going-down – 'in pursuit of the great and the impossible'.[27] The great danger of suffering from an excess of history is that the vital life-instincts are cut off prematurely, and the innocence of youthfulness corrupted at an early age by the knowledge of maturity. The reason why Nietzsche is so hostile towards the influence of Hegelianism on the study and writing of history is because he believes it condemns us to living life as if we were mere epigones. Nietzsche thus invites us to learn how to become unhistorical through learning 'the art and power of *forgetting*', of 'enclosing oneself within a bounded *horizon*'.[28] Here is a parable for everyone: we must organize the chaos within ourselves, that which is the result of the accident of our birth and descent, by thinking back to our real needs. We will then rebel against a culture which is no more than convention, and which teaches us only what we already know and imitates only that which already exists.

If history is to be placed in the service of the creative energies of life, then, Nietzsche argues, we need to recognize three principal forms of historical writing and study. These are the monumental, the antiquarian, and the critical. History above all should be about the noble human being who performs great and heroic deeds. Through an appreciation of the lives of great men and women we are able to see the possibility of imposing an eternity upon the flux of becoming. A great work of art and a great deed live on because posterity cannot do without them. In this way greatness overcomes the transitoriness that is the nature of all things. Through the monumentalistic conception of the past, and the engagement with the classic and rare of earlier times, we learn that greatness once existed and may thus be possible once again. However, monumental history is not without its dangers. In order to show that something is worthy of imitation (that it is exemplary) it must deal in approximations and generalities, and make the dissimilar similar and the unique not so unique. However, this process of monumentalizing the past can easily degenerate into a mythical fiction through its reliance on free poetic invention. If the monumental conception of the past rules over the two other modes of historiography, the antiquarian and the critical, whole segments of the past become forgotten, despised, and neglected. In this way monumental history deceives by analogies, 'with seductive similarities it inspires the courageous to foolhardiness and the inspired to fanaticism'. Imagine, Nietzsche says, such a use and abuse of history in the hands, not only of gifted egoists and visionary monsters, but in the hands of the impotent and the indolent.

The second form of history is the type which preserves and reveres. With the aid of a 'we' the individual looks beyond its own transitory existence and feels itself to be part of a greater whole, a race, a town or city, and a nation and culture. With love, loyalty, and piety it gives thanks to its ancestors for its existence. The great danger of this form of historical study is that it loves only that which is past, so that all that is past is taken to be equally worthy of reverence, while everything that is new and changing is rejected and despised.

Antiquarian history thus lacks a discriminating power, the main feature of the third and final mode of historical study Nietzsche discusses, that of critical history. If humanity is to live, it must possess and employ from time to time the strength to break up the past, to subject what has been to the bar of critical judgement. Nietzsche is clear that it is not justice, which sits in judgement here (even less is it mercy), but life itself:

...that dark, driving power that insatiably thirsts for itself. Its sentence is always unmerciful, always unjust, because it has never proceeded out of a pure well of knowledge; but in most cases the sentence would be the same even if it were pronounced by justice itself. 'For all that exists is *worthy* of perishing. So it would be better if nothing existed'. It requires a great deal of strength to be able to live and to forget the extent to which to live and to be unjust is one and the same thing.[29]

To break up and condemn the past in the manner of critical history is always a dangerous process, Nietzsche points out, for as we are the product of earlier generations, so are we the product of their errors, passions, and mistakes; indeed, as Nietzsche says, of their crimes. Thus, in condemning these errors and crimes, are we not condemning ourselves? Condemning ourselves perhaps to repeating the same mistakes and errors? The best that a culture or a people can do, says Nietzsche, is to confront its inherited past and hereditary nature with knowledge of it and, through a new and stern discipline, struggle against its inborn heritage and try to create a new habit and new instinct, a 'second nature'. It is not necessary for there to be fear and anxiety that one is only *second*, for there is the recognition that what is taken to be first was once a second nature, and that a new and victorious second nature will become a first. It is in this way, therefore, that Nietzsche attempts to combat the transformation of historiography into an objective science concerned with hard, empirical 'facts'. He is well aware of the dangers of the uses and abuses of history once its putative scientific pretensions are dispelled. But the recognition of history as fable and narrative does have at least the virtue of honesty, in spite of the fact that history can be placed in the service of a politics of violence.

What is noticeable about Nietzsche's early reflections on the problem of history considered as a problem about the nature of time and our attitude towards it, is the extent to which his thinking is motivated and determined by an antipathy towards becoming, that is, towards precisely that which his later thought sets out to affirm and celebrate. Thus, he says that the human being who does not know how to forget must forever be condemned 'to see everywhere a state of becoming'.[30] Such a human being would lose himself in this stream of becoming, reduced to an insignificant piece of life that is forever being mercilessly swallowed up by time's inexorable flux. In his meditation on history, Nietzsche sees human greatness in terms of an heroic act or deed which creates a moment of eternity in the face of the manifest, remorseless injustice of time. Heroism, Nietzsche says in his third untimely meditation entitled *Schopenhauer as Educator*, consists in ceasing to be the toy which time plays with, for in 'becoming everything is hollow, deceptive, shallow, and worthy of our contempt; the enigma which man is to resolve he can resolve only in being, in being thus and not otherwise, in the imperishable'.[31] Aware of the character of Nietzsche's mature thought with its Dionysian celebration of becoming, it is possible to see from this passage the attitude of resentment that Nietzsche had to overcome within himself, and the magnitude of effort which must have been involved in this task. The contrast between the early and mature Nietzsche is readily apparent when one considers that the thought of eternal return revolves around an affirmation of the moment as an *exemplification* of becoming, of time's essential timeliness. In the meditation on history, however, what we see is an opposition between the moment and becoming, not the affirmation of their interdependence and entwinement. In the thought of eternal return we are taught that the moment cannot be separated from becoming, that is, from all that has been and that has made the moment what it is. Thus, in willing the moment we are also willing all that has led to it. Perhaps the key point to appreciate about this teaching on eternal return, on the unity of the moment and becoming, is that it does *not* mean that one simply accepts, through a kind of trusting, but blind, fatalism, whatever exists because it has existed, because it has a past. Affirmation does not equal uncritical acceptance. As we shall see, the greatest challenge Nietzsche faces in narrating the descent of Zarathustra from his solitude to humanity is that of how to teach redemption through teaching that the will must learn how to will the impossible – time's 'it was'. Nietzsche's teaching of redemption presents us with another paradox. The redemption of the will from time and time's 'it was' is attained by the will learning that to will backwards can only be achieved by willing forwards, that is, the redemption of the past lies in a creative willing of the future. It is only on account of this act of a future creative willing that one is able – that one has the *right* – to will the past and redeem it. Willing the past thus becomes an act of re-willing that is constituted by the act of a new creative willing. Such a willing is to be performed not in terms of a sacrifice of the present for the future – this would be a supreme act of resentment and revenge – but within the innocent moment that always lies ahead of us in the future, guaranteeing the arrival of the new and the unique. Redemption is always possible on account of the coming of the future (as in the birth of a child, for example) in which the new is created out of the old, and out of what is past. It is interesting to note that in his autobiography, *Ecce Homo*, Nietzsche portrays the significance of his life in terms of a dual descent. He is both a decadent – therefore, a product of the past and a modern – and a new beginning, a chaos out of which a new self-discipline and self-overcoming can be born. He understands *his* humanity, therefore, to be that of a constant self-overcoming.[32]

The essential challenge of Nietzsche's thought consists in the way in which it presents history as something which cannot be read as a moral drama – as the unfolding of human freedom, as the march of God on earth, as the realization of a kingdom of ends – without devaluing life, and yet nevertheless as something that can, and must, be affirmed. It is this confrontation with the problem of history, I want to show, which constitutes the nature of Friedrich Nietzsche's fundamental engagement with the figure of Jean-Jacques Rousseau. The decisive question to be posed of Nietzsche's innermost thinking is to what extent it succeeds in overcoming the spirit of revenge, which he holds has haunted the historical sensibility of Occidental humanity.

The argument of the book is structured as follows. In chapter one I offer a general introduction to the image (*Bild*) of Rousseau we find in Nietzsche's writings from the *Birth of Tragedy* to the *Will to Power Nachlass*, not necessarily in strict chronological fashion but around what I hope are a number of illuminating themes. It is shown that Nietzsche had neither a subtle, nor a sophisticated, reading of Rousseau's thought, of its complexities and paradoxes, but that nevertheless his work can be seen to provide a major insight into the impasse which Rousseau's thought reaches on the problem of history and the fate of civilization. In chapters two and three I develop an interpretation of two of Rousseau's principal works, the *Discourse on*

Inequality and *The Social Contract*, around the notions of man's natural goodness and the general will. Rousseau's originality as a political philosopher is shown to lie in the peculiarly modern way in which his thought poses the question of political legitimacy. I argue that the relationship between the two works, which has been a source of constant controversy amongst scholars of Rousseau, is best construed in terms of Rousseau's attempt to confront – and transcend – the problem of history.

In chapter four, through an analysis of the *Genealogy of Morals*, I examine the significance of Nietzsche's attempt to construct an understanding of morality that is neither simply a straightforward history of morals, nor a philosophy of morals. It is argued that, through a genealogy of morals that is at one and the same time an exercise in monumental history and critical history, Nietzsche sets out to show not only how we have become what we are but, more importantly, how we *can become* those that we are by effecting a self-overcoming of morality, of history, of the past, etc. It is shown how Nietzsche dramatizes the problem of civilization and the self-overcoming of morals in terms of what he calls a 'Dionysian drama on the destiny of the soul'. In chapter five I show how in *Thus Spoke Zarathustra* Nietzsche, through the figure of Zarathustra and his teachings of the overman and eternal return, reveals the *way* to the performance of a self-overcoming of morals. In both works I show how Nietzsche suspended Rousseau's question concerning political legitimacy: in the *Genealogy of Morals* in favour of a genealogy of the moral subject, and in *Zarathustra* in favour of a notion of the overman.

In chapter six I turn my attention to the question of Nietzsche's politics in the light of the task of the self-overcoming of morals examined in the previous two chapters, and in the context of an understanding of the problem of the legislator as framed by Rousseau and Nietzsche. I consider the extent to which, through the positing of a world-historical conception of the overman, Nietzsche's conception of a great politics succumbs to the resentment of the spirit of revenge by sacrificing the present for the willed production of some ill-defined future. I argue that there has to be some kind of mediation between the extremes of Zarathustra's exile and the great politics of the philosopher–legislator who divides humanity into two, the strong and the weak, in which Nietzsche leaves us with an informative, but disabling, choice between the eternal return of the

overman and the human herd on the one hand, and self-imposed
solitude on the other. It is argued that if Nietzsche's thought exposes
the inadequacies of Rousseau's moralism, then perhaps Rousseau's
politics are able to reveal the deficiencies of a Nietzschean-inspired
politics, with Rousseau's political vision of a tragic democracy
providing the necessary supplement to Nietzsche's exclusively
aesthetic conception of the tragic and the Dionysian. The possibility
of a Dionysian politics that is both agonistic and democratic?
Perhaps. I conclude with some reflections on the fate of rebellion in
modern times, and on what it means to think through the problem
of history today by conducting an engagement with Rousseau and
Nietzsche in which we become those that we are.

CHAPTER I

Nietzsche contra Rousseau

'What is the occasion?' the people asked.
'We're waiting to see Jean-Jacques', came the reply.
'Who or what is Jean-Jacques?'
'We don't know, but he's going to pass this way'.
    A crowd gathered in the square of the Palais Royal

INTRODUCTION

On a number of occasions Nietzsche described himself as being *'contra* Rousseau'.[1] Rousseau was without doubt a key thinker for Nietzsche, one who played an important adversarial role in his construal of modernity, and whom he had to come to terms with in order to clarify his own status as a philosopher and educator.[2] In a revealing passage in *Assorted Opinions and Maxims*, Nietzsche informs his readers that there are only eight thinkers that he has had to come to terms with, and from whom he will accept judgement. Significantly, Rousseau is one of them.[3] In Nietzsche's account of modernity Rousseau plays the role of the moral fanatic whose writings inspire the slave revolts in morality of the modern era (notably the French Revolution).[4] But, in conceiving his relation to Rousseau in such antagonistic terms, Nietzsche reveals just how important Rousseau is to him. The ambiguous nature of the Rousseau–Nietzsche relationship has been captured well by Karl Löwith:

As a critic of the existing world, Nietzsche was to the nineteenth century what Rousseau had been to the eighteenth century. He is a Rousseau in reverse: a Rousseau, because of his equally penetrating criticism of European civilization, and in reverse, because his critical standards are the exact opposite of Rousseau's ideal of man.[5]

Nietzsche is close to Rousseau because like him he demands a transfiguration of human nature, a transfiguration which for both must take place in the context of a decadent civilization.[6] What separates the two is how they construe the problem of decadence, which can be seen in their opposing conceptions of how the humanity of the future is to be cultivated. Rousseau wishes humanity to realize, albeit in a modified form, its 'natural goodness', while Nietzsche teaches that humanity must learn how to become more 'evil'.

It is evident that Nietzsche did not develop a grasp either of the subtleties, or of the complexities, of Rousseau's thought. Of Rousseau's writings, he was most familiar with *Émile* and the autobiographical pieces such as the *Confessions*.[7] To what extent Nietzsche was familiar with the details of Rousseau's political philosophy is debatable, but, if he was as familiar with Rousseau's *Émile* as the evidence suggests that he was, then he would have had at least a rudimentary knowledge of his political thought, given that the final book of the text closes with a synoptic account of Rousseau's political theory as outlined in detail in the *Du Contrat social* published in the same year. Nietzsche was certainly aware of Rousseau's tremendous impact on German philosophy and culture, such as his profound influence on Kant's Copernican revolution in moral philosophy, for example, and of the mythical status that his writings had accrued in European culture.[8] Rousseau's ideas, in fact, play a key role in Nietzsche's genealogy of modern decadence, which, in his writings of the mid to late 1880s, takes the form of a history of European nihilism where he locates in Rousseau's writings the origins of a distinctly modern sensibility.

What is notable about Rousseau's and Nietzsche's investigations into the origins of social order and into the problem of civilization is that, although they begin from similar premises, chiefly that man is above all a historical being, the two arrive at very different solutions to the problem of humanity's self-overcoming. A major aspect of Nietzsche's critique of Rousseau is that he criticizes his thought for postulating an unmediated opposition between the natural goodness of human nature, on the one hand, and social institutions which corrupt it, on the other, culminating in the delusion that, once corrupt social institutions have been overthrown and reformed, our hidden, repressed natural goodness will emerge and blossom innocent and free. Nietzsche's critique of Rousseau is also a critique of the revolutionary spirit which has inspired the politics of the modern age.

It cannot be denied that Nietzsche misconstrues and simplifies Rousseau's position on a number of fronts. He too readily associates his thought with the French Revolution, failing to appreciate the complexity of Rousseau's argument on man's natural goodness, and neglecting Rousseau's emphasis on political education as the way in which goodness and virtue are brought to expression through careful cultivation. A number of commentators have noted the parallels between Rousseau's and Nietzsche's investigation into the origins of man and society. However, this should not lead us to conceal the important differences which separate the two thinkers.[9] For, although Nietzsche shares Rousseau's quest for authenticity, there exists for him no such thing as a natural morality, such as Rousseau's law of the heart, which is to serve as the inspiration for the creation of a new social order based on the sentiment of pity, and from which one can deduce an objectively valid account of true social and moral man. Whereas for Rousseau the problem lies in the corrupt condition of social institutions that stand in the way of cultivating our true moral nature, for Nietzsche the problem lies with morality itself. It is the slave morality of good and evil which stands in the way of the further advancement and cultivation of the human animal. A necessary precondition of any self-overcoming of morality, therefore, is the cultivation of a mode of thought that recognizes that life is beyond good and evil. It is on the question of morality that Nietzsche inverts Rousseau's position. In contrast to Rousseau, he argues that it is not a question of positing humanity's natural goodness and attributing responsibility for its corrupt nature on the ills of society, but rather of revaluing what we mean by 'good' and 'evil'. Nietzsche's originality lies not simply in the attempt to construct a history of morals (this he shares with Rousseau), but in the attempt to carry out a revaluation of values based on the insights gain from an inquiry into humanity's historical evolution. It is not, therefore, simply a question of performing a 'hypothesis-mongering' on the origins of morality for Nietzsche, but of calling into question the very value of morality.

Both Rousseau and Nietzsche have been subjected to a double reading in the area of their moral and political thought. Both have been described as ethical individualists, and as thinkers whose radically different conceptions of politics prefigure the totalitarian regimes of the twentieth century. It is frequently asked of Rousseau's political thought whether it is based on liberal or totalitarian principles,[10] while the studies of Nietzsche as *politique et moraliste* that have emerged since the Second World War reveal an inexplicable antinomy at the centre of his thinking. On the one hand, it is claimed that Nietzsche eschews any concern with the limits of political responsibility and advocates an amoral individualism, and, on the other hand, his political thought is construed in terms of an authoritarianism which abandons the liberal gains of the modern period such as the doctrine of equal rights.[11] How is it possible to construe Rousseau and Nietzsche in terms of being teachers of both existential liberty and political totalitarianism?

I would contend that both Rousseau's and Nietzsche's thinking on the fate of the political is determined by the antinomical nature of modern political life.[12] One could go so far as to claim that Rousseau is the first thinker to articulate the antinomies of modern political life (between individual and society, man and citizen, autonomy and authority, freedom and necessity, and so on) in their peculiarly and recognizably modern form. Reflection on these antinomies has been of major concern to German philosophy since Kant and it is on the basis of their inheritance in his work, I would argue, that the paradoxes of Nietzsche's political thought can be best appreciated. For it can be shown that, in its concern to trace the evolution of the autonomous individual through a historical labour of social discipline, Nietzsche's project of a genealogy of morals is closely related to the modern tradition of thought inspired by Rousseau's recognition of the antinomical nature of modern political life.

What is original about Rousseau's political thought is that it attempts to answer the ancient question about the nature of justice (about the just or well-ordered polity) posed by classical political theory in such a thoroughly modern way by establishing the legitimacy of the social order on the basis of the primacy of the will of the autonomous individual. Rousseau's political thought is a unique blend of individualism and communitarianism, of classical and modern thinking, which seeks to completely sublate the opposition between individual liberty and social discipline. What Rousseau's political thought sets out to do is to educate the modern individual, which has been emancipated from the constraining hierarchies of traditional social order, that genuine liberty is to be had only as a member of a social community in which one becomes a unique moral person capable of exercising free will, making promises, and cultivating political judgement. Rousseau's attempt to overcome the opposition between the individual and society results in the notion of the general will in which the law that the individual freely imposes upon itself is both individual and social, both 'I' and 'we' for there no longer exists any opposition between these terms.

The significance of Nietzsche's reflections on the political, lies in the way in which they confront the specificity of the modern. He argues that the two dominant theories in modern ethical and political thought, Kantianism and Utilitarianism, simply provide a rationalization of conventional morality, for, despite the differences between them, both attempt to define what is moral by reference to an abstract universal, be it the greatest happiness of the greatest number, or a kingdom of ends. Within Nietzsche's reflections we find a deep recognition that the ethical dilemmas of modern political culture are, to a large extent, determined by the dominance of an abstract individualism. A philosophy of individualism is one which posits the existence of the discrete or isolated individual, with private interests and 'rights', independent of the existence of public life.[13] C. B. MacPherson in his classic study of 'possessive individualism' identifies the rise of this individualist ethic with the early liberalism of Hobbes and Locke. The possessive quality of liberal individualism is to be seen in the way it conceives the individual as the proprietor of its own personhood, with capacities of free will and self-reflection, owing nothing to society for their existence. Freedom becomes associated with possession, and society conceived in terms of a collection of free and equal discrete individuals related to each other as owners of their natural capacities. Society is thought of as no more than a calculated device for the protection of private property, the pursuit of private gain, and the maintenance of orderly relations of exchange.[14] But, like Rousseau, Nietzsche argues that individual capacities and attributes such as free will, conscience, and rationality, cannot be thought of apart from their social and historical formation and their embeddedness in cultural practices. This means that the existence of sovereign individuality must be viewed in terms of a historical formation and deformation.

Nietzsche shares Rousseau's concern with self-mastery through self-legislation. However, unlike Rousseau, who posits the act of autonomous legislation in terms of a universal lawgiving, Nietzsche argues that the achievement of sovereign individuality with the arrival of the individual who has earned the 'right to make promises' reveals an aristocratic mark of distinction. Nietzsche attacks the fundamental ethical claim of Rousseau's notion of the general will, that there has to be an almost absolute identity between every particular will and the universal will. Nietzsche is highly suspicious of any attempt to define morality, and what is moral, by reference to laws which are claimed to be universal in their validity and application, for this is the perfect example of a slave morality which can only arrive at an affirmation of its own identity through a negation of others and of their difference.[15]

Nietzsche's political thought recognizes that self-legislating individuality, in which the individual is compelled to produce its own laws of self-preservation and self-enhancement through submitting only to laws it has created itself, is a peculiarly modern achievement. However, he insists that a new creative ethical and political life is not possible by the individual simply generalizing its own laws as universal. This is how he reads – mistakenly, I shall attempt to show – Rousseau's politics of the general will. Perhaps the most serious problem facing Nietzsche's own thinking on the supra-ethical and autonomous sovereign individual is that of amoral solipsism, for there seems to be no recognition in his thought of the importance of solidarity and community in the achievement of genuine sovereign individuality. 'All community', Nietzsche argues, 'makes common'.[16] Thus, it would appear that Nietzsche's political thought presents us with an informative but debilitating choice between the overman and the herd, in which the strong, independent human being – the overman – assumes the guise of Aristotle's god (or beast), capable of living without, and beyond, the polis. The extent to which Nietzsche offers a coherent and constructive political vision can only be decided upon by examining the tensions which result from the ethical import of his teaching, and the political conclusions he draws from his insights into European nihilism.

In this chapter my concern is with examining the roles that 'Rousseauism' and the Rousseauian man play in Nietzsche's writings. It should be pointed out that an examination of Nietzsche's scattered remarks on Rousseau provides no more than a useful entry point into the meaning and significance of the question of 'Nietzsche *contra* Rousseau'. In order to carry out a more adequate construal of that question, it is necessary to reconstruct Nietzsche's thought in the context of an independent examination of Rousseau's moral and political thought, which will be performed in chapters two and three.

ROUSSEAU AS EDUCATOR

In his early writings we see Nietzsche's conception of Rousseau as the political philosopher of *ressentiment* in its nascent phase. Nietzsche criticizes Rousseau's paean to nature, and his belief in man's natural goodness, which have their basis in romanticism. In the *Birth of Tragedy*, for example, Nietzsche criticizes the romanticism of the modern age for conceiving of the artist in terms of Rousseau's *Émile*. Nietzsche's argument is that Rousseau's portrait of Émile's realization of his fundamental human nature and the achievement of oneness with nature, achieved by withdrawing the child and adolescent from the degenerative effects of corrupt social institutions and allowing his natural goodness to flourish, fails to recognize the dark and terrible forces of nature which must be overcome in order to arrive at a harmonious relationship with nature. In other words, there is no place in Émile's education for recognition of the dark and mysterious Dionysian forces of nature.[17]

The longing for community, so evident in Rousseau's work, is argued by Nietzsche to be attainable only through the medium of aesthetic semblance (*Schein*). In his early work the Dionysian experience symbolizes precisely that oneness with nature yearned for by Rousseau with such longing. The Apollonian, on the other hand, symbolizes the tremendous artistic powers which need to be employed in order to transfigure the horror and absurdity of existence, experienced by the disclosure of the Dionysian underworld. Thus, for example, Nietzsche defines the Dionysian in terms of the overcoming of the subjective, of the '*principium individuationis*'. The experience of Dionysian intoxication brings with it a feeling of 'mystical self-abnegation' (*Selbstentäusserung*).[18] The Dionysian reveals to man that he is not simply an individual but a species-being (*Gattungswesen*):

Under the charm of the Dionysian not only is the union between man and man reaffirmed, but nature which has become alienated, hostile, or subjugated, celebrates once more her reconciliation with her lost son, man. Freely, the earth proffers her gifts, and peacefully the beasts of prey of the rocks and desert approach ... Now the slave is a free man; now all the rigid, hostile barriers that necessity, caprice, or 'impudent convention' have fixed between man and man are broken. Now, with the gospel of world harmony, each one feels himself not only united, reconciled, and fused with his neighbour, but as one with him, as if the veil of *māyā* had been torn aside and were now merely fluttering in tatters before the mysterious primordial unity (*Ur-Einen*). Singing and dancing man expresses himself as a member of a higher community; he has forgotten how to walk and speak and is on the way toward flying into the air, dancing.[19]

In the text the Dionysian is construed as a revolutionary force which destroys the barriers set up by the conventions of the polis and which serve to divide and alienate men from one another. However, it is important to recognize that the attainment of community is only possible for Nietzsche in the medium of tragic art. Nietzsche does not employ the concept of the Dionysian in the argument of the *Birth of Tragedy* in order to advocate political revolution.[20] Indeed, Nietzsche is at pains to disassociate the meaning of his concept of the Dionysian from any 'contemporary socialistic movements' which base their ideology on the belief, *à la* Rousseau, in the natural goodness of primitive man.[21] 'There is nothing more terrible', Nietzsche writes, 'than a class of barbaric slaves who have learned to regard their existence as an injustice, and now prepare to avenge, not only themselves, but all generations'.[22] Nietzsche goes even further, suggesting that one finds 'in every case in which Dionysian excitement gains any significant extent how the Dionysian liberation from the fetters of the individual finds expression first of all in a diminution of, in indifference to, indeed, in hostility to, the political instincts'.[23] The central teaching of Nietzsche's first published book is that, 'it is only as an *aesthetic phenomenon* that existence and the world are eternally *justified*'.[24] This aesthetic understanding of existence is already linked in Nietzsche's thinking with a standpoint 'beyond good and evil'. Thus, if the Dionysian is divorced from any connection with politics in *The Birth of Tragedy*, it is equally divorced from morality.

Nietzsche was quite correct to argue in his self-criticism on the text, written in 1886, that 'art, and *not* morality, is presented as the truly *metaphysical* activity of man'. He adds:

one can call this whole artists' metaphysics arbitrary, idle, fantastic; what matters is that it betrays a spirit who will one day fight at any risk whatever the *moral* interpretation and significance of existence. Here, perhaps for the first time, a pessimism 'beyond good and evil' is suggested.[25]

Thus, we find in Nietzsche's first published work the grounds of his opposition to Rousseau's moralism which characterizes his 'mature' thought. Despite Rousseau shifting the problem of evil from the realm of theology into the realm of ethics and politics, his thinking still adheres to the metaphysical belief that the world is actually structured in accordance with a moral world-order.[26] The crucial lesson of Nietzsche's teaching 'beyond good and evil' is that there are no fixed and immutable qualities of 'good' and 'evil' in the world; or rather, in accordance with Nietzsche's perspectivism and the emphasis on a *typology* of morals, good and evil must be seen to have a certain structural relationship to each other, constituting a particular architectonic (as in the parable of the lamb and eagle in the first essay of the *Genealogy of Morals*) in which the qualities vary, so that just as there is a pessimism of weakness there is a pessimism of strength, a courageous and strong cruelty as well as a cowardly and base one.[27] Moreover, the relationship between good and evil has to be understood in terms of a creative entwinement.

In the third of his *Untimely Meditations*, *Schopenhauer as Educator*, Nietzsche presents a portrait of the 'Rousseauian man' and develops further his reading of Rousseau as the moral revolutionary, whose teaching spurs the masses to an act of social revolution in the belief that happiness for all can be attained on earth. However, Nietzsche's critical distancing of himself from Rousseau conceals a striking resemblance between the two in their thinking on nature and in their scathing attacks on the moral bankruptcy of modern society. Both believe in man's capacity for self-overcoming, that is, his potential for transfiguring his own nature and which distinguishes him from the animals. Where Rousseau speaks of man's 'perfectibility', Nietzsche speaks of culture in terms of an 'improved *physis*'.[28]

Reflecting on his life's work in *Ecce Homo* Nietzsche poses the fundamental question of culture: What is the goal of culture? Nietzsche's answer reveals the aristocratic basis of his thought. The question, we are told, is:

...how can your life, the individual life, receive the highest value, the deepest significance? How can it be least squandered? Only by your living for the good of the rarest and most valuable exemplars, and not for the good of the majority... the goal of culture is to promote the production of true *human beings*.[29]

Culture for Nietzsche is the domain of man's transfigured *physis*, the manner in which he achieves unity and wholeness, what Nietzsche calls the 'unanimity of life, thought, appearance, and will'.[30] In these early meditations of culture as *physis* we find present a

Rousseauian desire for immediacy and authenticity of experience. Nietzsche's critique of the degenerative effects of modern culture is remarkably similar in tone and substance to that evinced by Rousseau in his prize-winning essay on the corrupting influence of the arts and sciences.

In defending and promoting the cause of culture, the text contains a scathing attack on the egoism of modern society. Nietzsche sees an important link in German politics between the build up of military power and the emergent capitalist economic order. Nietzsche's criticism of the political effects of the rise of militarism and economism has much in common with that of de Tocqueville, whose main ideas Nietzsche would have been familiar with from his reading of John Stuart Mill.[31] What is common to the two thinkers is a comparison between the French Revolution and the Christian religion. Both see the Revolution as ushering in a new historical period of religion without God (the modern, bureaucratic State as the new idol).[32] Nietzsche locates one of the main causes of modern man's spiritual crisis in the 'reaction of declining Christianity'. Part of our experience of discontent with civilization stems from the fact that we oscillate between an 'imitated or hypocritical Christian morality' and a 'despondent and timid revival of antiquity'. Modern humanity seeks a new simplicity and honesty in thought and deed but experiences only unhappiness with its Christian inheritance, and deep discontent at the futility of a return to the naturalness of antiquity.[33]

At one point the text anticipates the major argument on the fundamental antagonism between 'Culture' (*Cultur*) and the 'State' (*Staat*) to be found in *Twilight of the Idols*.[34] Nietzsche challenges the political philosophy of German Idealism, derived from Rousseau, which holds that the moral–collective body embodied in the State represents the highest goal of mankind, and that man has no higher duty than that of serving the State.[35] He argues that, 'Every philosophy which believes that the problem of existence is touched on, not to say solved, by a political event is a joke – and pseudo-philosophy ... How should a political innovation suffice to turn men once and for all into contented inhabitants of the earth?'[36] In seeking to promote the idea of culture as the production of 'true human beings', Nietzsche feels obliged to draw attention to a species of 'misemployed and appropriated culture'. In particular, he refers to the 'greed of the money-makers' and the 'greed of the State', both of which seek to disseminate and universalize culture for their own self-interest. 'However loudly the State may proclaim its service to culture', Nietzsche tells us, 'it furthers culture in order to further itself and cannot conceive of a goal higher than its own welfare and continued existence'[37] State patronage of art can only lead to its corruption. For Nietzsche, great art must be uncompromising and untimely. Only in this way can it fulfil its role of challenging all political authority and accepted wisdom and convention, and producing great and noble images of humanity. Nietzsche challenges the modern view, which asserts that there is a necessary connection between 'intelligence and property', and between 'wealth and culture'. Here lies 'a hatred of any kind of education that makes one a solitary'.[38] Education in the modern State has become degraded, restricted to the task of breeding money-makers. Nietzsche thus calls for a 'revolution of education' as being the only way of stemming the tide of barbarism which is swamping genuine culture in the modern age.

For Nietzsche, therefore, the modern age is characterized above all by an 'atomistic chaos' in which the forces of society are in danger of disintegrating and tearing it asunder. The question Nietzsche raises in response to this social disintegration is whether genius, 'the highest fruit of life ', can justify life:

the glorious, creative human being is now to answer the question: 'Do you affirm this existence in the depths of your heart? Is it sufficient for you? Would you be its advocate and redeemer? For you only have to pronounce a single, heartfelt Yes! – and life, though it faces such heavy accusations, shall go free'.[39]

It is in the context of an approaching social revolution that Nietzsche introduces his idea of the three images of man, which modern souls can employ as a way of inspiring themselves to transfigure their lives and to educate themselves *against* the prejudices of their age in order to achieve untimeliness. They are the man of Rousseau, the man of Goethe, and the man of Schopenhauer.

The man of Rousseau is the man of social revolution. From him 'there has proceeded a force which has promoted violent revolutions... in every socialist earthquake and upheaval it has always been the man of Rousseau who, like Typhon under Etna, is the cause of the commotion'. Nietzsche recognizes, however, that, in the Rousseauian cry for a return to natural goodness, the man of Rousseau can be seen to despise himself and thus longs to 'go beyond himself'.[40] Such an attitude prepares the soul for fearful decisions

and calls up from the depths what is noblest and rarest in it. The
man of Goethe, on the other hand, is the anti-revolutionary whose
nature is invulnerable to the emotional excitations which stir the
heart of the Rousseauian man. Nietzsche writes: 'The man of
Goethe is... the contemplative man in the grand style... The
Goethean man is a preservative and conciliatory power'.[41] Finally,
there is the Schopenhauerean image of man who teaches man to live
a heroic life in the midst of a world full of suffering. The
Schopenhauerean man is the man of courage who is prepared to
sacrifice his own life for the sake of cultural greatness.

Nietzsche's estimation of Rousseau was not to undergo any major
change in his later work; his estimation of Goethe underwent a
slight, but significant, modification in response to Nietzsche's revised
conception of the Dionysian; and his estimation of his mentor
Schopenhauer was to undergo a dramatic transformation. In
contrast to the philosophies of life inspired by Rousseau and
Schopenhauer, Nietzsche came, in his later writings, to exalt Goethe
as the embodiment of the Dionysian human being. Nietzsche's
depiction of the Dionysian Goethe recalls his earlier definition of
culture as *physis*, in which the *telos* of life consists in achieving a
unanimity of thinking, feeling, and willing. Thus, for example, in
Twilight of the Idols we find that Nietzsche speaks of Goethe's
attainment of 'totality' in terms of a synthesis of 'reason, sensuality,
feeling, and will'.[42] But how, we need to ask, does Goethe's
naturalness and his return to nature differ from that which is found
in Rousseau? Immediately preceding Nietzsche's paean to Goethe,
we find the kind of harsh critical reflection on Rousseau so typical of
Nietzsche's later assessment of his ideas and their baneful influence:

I too speak of a 'return to nature', although it is not really a going-back
(*Zurückgehen*) but a *going-up* (*Hinaufkommen*) – up into a high free, even
frightful nature and naturalness, such as plays with great tasks, is *permitted*
to play with them... But Rousseau – where did *he* really want to return to?
Rousseau, this first modern man, idealist and *canaille* in *one* person; who
needed moral 'dignity' in order to endure his own aspect; sick with
unbridled vanity and unbridled self-contempt... where, to ask it again, did
Rousseau want to return to? – I hate Rousseau even *in* the Revolution: it
is the world-historical expression of this duplicity of idealist and *canaille*.
The bloody farce enacted by this Revolution, its 'immorality,' does not
concern me much: what I hate is its Rousseauesque *morality* – the so-called
'truths' of the Revolution through which it is still an active force and
persuades everything shallow and mediocre over to its side.[43]

The kind of 'return to nature' Nietzsche favours, and finds in Goethe, is a Dionysian one in which the fundamentally amoral character of existence is recognized and affirmed and which depends on adopting an attitude towards life that is beyond good and evil. As Walter Kaufmann pointed out, Goethe came to symbolize for Nietzsche the triumph over romanticism which he sought in his own life, namely the triumph of artistic nobility and strength over weakness and resentment.[44]

What is most notable about Nietzsche's early writings is that, although the image he constructs of Rousseau is consistently, if not a hostile one, then certainly an oppositional one, his scathing criticism of modern society is remarkably similar to Rousseau's. In both we find an appeal to simplicity and honesty in human relationships, along with a demand for genuine culture as opposed to mere adornment. Nietzsche's elevation of artistic sensibility and genius in the face of the philistinism of modern culture can even find its prefiguration in Rousseau's first discourse. Although this work contains a vitriolic attack on the degenerative effects of the arts, what Rousseau is condemning is the effects of superfluous art, that is, the kind which is no more than the luxury of the idle rich (Nietzsche's 'greedy money-makers'). Rousseau's attack on the arts does not at all mean that he is unable to sing the praises of true genius. On the contrary, it is precisely a cultivation of genius that Rousseau desires in order to combat the conformity of modern art. As we shall have occasion to see, time and time again Nietzsche creates an enemy of Rousseau when he ought to see him as an ally in his relentless criticism of the barbarism and philistinism of modern culture.

ROUSSEAU AND THE FRENCH REVOLUTION: A POLITICS OF 'RESSENTIMENT'

Within Nietzsche's writings we find both a subtle, and not-so subtle, reading of the relationship between Rousseau and the French Revolution. The aphorism in *Human, All Too Human*, entitled 'A delusion in the theory of revolution', in which Nietzsche criticizes the revolutionary implications of the central motif running through Rousseau's work, that man is naturally good but has been made evil by corrupt social institutions, is an example of a subtle reading. The passage also prefigures a problem which was to preoccupy Nietzsche in the *Nachlass* of the late 1880s, the problem of civilization and the intellectual battle between Voltaire and Rousseau around 1760 on the fate of man. Here Nietzsche criticizes those 'political and social visionaries':

who with fiery eloquence demand a revolutionary overthrow of all social orders in the belief that the proudest temple of fair humanity will then at once rise up as though of its own accord. In these perilous dreams there is still an echo of Rousseau's superstition, which believes in a miraculous primeval but as it were *buried* goodness of human nature and ascribes all the blame for this burying to the institutions of culture in the form of society, state and education. The experiences of history have taught us, unfortunately, that every such revolution brings about with it the resurrection of the most savage energies in the shape of the long-buried dreadfulness and excesses of the most distant ages: that a revolution can thus be a source of energy in a mankind grown feeble but never a regulator, architect, artist, perfector of human nature. It is not *Voltaire's* moderate nature, inclined as it was to ordering, purifying, and reconstructing, but *Rousseau's* passionate follies and half-lies that called forth the optimistic spirit of the Revolution against which I cry: '*Ecrasez l'infâme!*' It is this spirit that has for a long time banished *the spirit of the Enlightenment and of progressive evolution*: let us see – each of us within himself – whether it is possible to call it back![45]

The critical point of this passage is that any teaching like Rousseau's, which posits an undialectical opposition between the innocence of man and the corruptness of society, only serves to inspire revolutions based on the delusion that once corrupt social institutions have been removed, natural man will suddenly emerge innocent and in-corruptible. Although this is undoubtedly a simplification of Rousseau's position, it cannot be denied that it contains a potent critique of the *naïvetés* which have animated the revolutionary spirit of the modern period. Once again, Nietzsche criticizes the revolutionary spirit from the standpoint of an anti-political understanding of the Dionysian. His argument is that revolution exposes not the innocence of natural man, but rather the dangerous frenzy of wild, prowling man.[46]

A characteristic feature of Nietzsche's reading of Rousseau, therefore, is that it links Rousseau's teaching indissolubly with the 'optimistic spirit' of the French Revolution. In particular, he associates Rousseau with what he calls the 'morality' of the Revolution, meaning the doctrine of equality.[47] In fact, Nietzsche's critique of what he regards as Rousseau's pernicious influence is highly reminiscent of the nineteenth-century response to the

Revolution amongst French men of letters, to be found, for example, in the writings of liberals such as Hippolyte Taine and Benjamin Constant. The manner in which these writers framed the question of Jean-Jacques in terms of a choice between egalitarianism and individuality, conformity and creativity, mediocrity and mass culture versus excellence and cultural greatness is remarkably close to how Nietzsche came to understand the significance of Rousseau and his influence.[48] Nietzsche was certainly influenced by Taine in adopting a psychological approach to the study of the revolutionary mentality. For Taine the Revolution may have been justified in the limited area of fiscal reform, but the result was a greater centralization of power, the destruction of authority, and social atomization.[49]

As one commentator has noted, Nietzsche's view of the Revolution as a spectacle which seduces the spectator stands in sharp contrast to 'Kant's "moralistic perspective", in which history appears in terms of an instructive and edifying drama'.[50] Nietzsche is sharply critical of what he calls, in a *Nachlass* fragment from the beginning of 1888, the 'praxis of revolutionary reason' and the 'revolution of "practical reason"', which reveals a hatred against nature and becoming, and which believes that a new society can come into being that will be in conformity with man's true nature.[51] In Kant, for example, history represents the stage of man's moral evolution as an end-in-itself. The philosophy of history concerns not a history of morals, Kant tell us, but rather man's realization of his moral essence as a rational being (man becomes moral through the exercise of his rational will). Thus, interpreting the significance of Rousseau's tracing of the transition from the reign of instinct in the state of nature, to that of moral liberty in civil society, Kant says that the question whether man has won or lost in this process – which is the question of Rousseau's framing of the problem of civilization – is no longer an open one 'if one considers the destiny of the species'.[52] In this moral reading of history, history is the stage of conflict between nature and morality, it is the means by which man reaches his end as a moral being in a kingdom of ends. It is 'culture', for Kant, which represents the reconciliation of the antagonism between nature and morality depicted so poignantly and dramatically by Rousseau in his second discourse on the origins of inequality.[53] For Kant, the history of nature begins with 'good' as it is the work of God, while the history of freedom begins with 'wickedness' for it is the work of man. But, Kant consoles us by teaching that man becomes 'evil' only in order to become 'good'. There should be, therefore, no desire to 'go back' to any imagined place of simplicity and innocence. Instead, we must accept the burden of history by patiently taking up the toil of our moral labour. That Nietzsche finds the sophistry behind Kant's philosophy of history loathsome is evident from the following passage: 'Kant believed in morality, not because nature and history demonstrate it, but in spite of the fact that nature and history continually contradict it'.[54] What if, Nietzsche wonders, our *faith* in history is unfounded, is no longer believed in...what if God is dead?

For Nietzsche, nihilism is the ever-present possibility of a moral and teleological reading of history, and explains why for him the French Revolution is one of the 'causes' of modern nihilism in its moral and political manifestations (the 'rights of man' are discovered to be as illusory as the existence of God). Nietzsche in fact understands the modern ideology of revolution not in terms of something fundamentally new and innovative, but as a mere episode in the history of Christian–moral culture. For him the principles of the French Revolution – equality and liberty – are to be read as secularizations of Christian teachings: the former of the notion of the equality of all souls before God, and the latter of the Christian–metaphysical teaching of freedom of the will.[55] Thus, Nietzsche interprets the 'text' of the French Revolution to a large extent through his reading of the moral philosophies of Rousseau and Kant. It is debatable to what extent Nietzsche buries the text of the Revolution under the weight of his interpretation, thus never engaging with the legitimacy of the Revolution, but dismissing its principles *tout court* by engaging in psychological and historical reductionism. One of the major weaknesses of Nietzsche's political reflections is that they only view the question of social cohesion and unity on the basis of an aristocratic model of social order, a model which sees society organized along the lines of a rigid hierarchy, or what Nietzsche calls an order of rank. Nietzsche's reading of Rousseau stands in marked contrast to that of Hegel for whom it is really Rousseau, as opposed to Machiavelli or Hobbes, who merits the title of the first modern political theorist, establishing the autonomous will of the individual as the sole basis of legitimate political power, and placing at the very centre of politics the whole question of political legitimacy.[56] And while it may be true that Hegel wishes ultimately to sublate the individualism of Rousseau's grounding of the modern polity on the free will of the individual, it cannot be denied that such a grounding also constitutes the starting-point of his own dialectical inquiry into the principles of political right.

In grounding politics on such a basis Rousseau's thought has, quite literally, enormous revolutionary implications, for it raises the whole question of political legitimacy. It has to be said that nowhere in Nietzsche's writings do we ever find an adequate response to the question which was of such central concern to Rousseau in his effort to examine and overcome the corruptness and decadence of modern society. As to the reasons behind this neglect in Nietzsche, we could point to the disdain for politics and for a political solution to the ills of civilization which runs throughout his intellectual career. Nietzsche always saw the social problem in terms of a problem of an aesthetic education. The demand for the transfiguration of humanity is never motivated in his work by a concern for social justice, but always in terms of the enhancement of the type 'man' (as in his early teaching that the goal of humanity cannot lie in its end but only in its highest exemplars). This is why, for example, Nietzsche holds that the only justification of the French Revolution that can ever be put forward is that it produced Napoleon, that inspiring combination of the inhuman and superhuman.[57] Nietzsche is prepared even to sacrifice humanity for the sake of a higher human type, a type that is beyond ('over') man.

One of Nietzsche's great fears, a fear which informs his criticism of the major social movements of the modern period such as socialism, is that any political revolution will serve merely to unleash a destructive spirit of revenge and resentment on mankind, since, in order to win support amongst the disgruntled masses, it must appeal to the basest human instincts. The notion of *ressentiment* plays a key role in Nietzsche's political reflections. Indeed, as will be examined in detail in a later chapter, the central teaching of Zarathustra – the teacher of the meaning of beyond good and evil and of the self-overcoming of morality in Nietzsche's writings – is that of the eternal return by which human beings may be liberated from the bonds of revenge and resentment. For Nietzsche the attitude of resentment is born out of suffering. Indeed, he attributes *his* freedom from, and enlightenment about, the phenomenon of resentment to his own protracted bouts of sickness.[58] Resentment expresses itself when action is denied to a person and they compensate themselves with an imaginary revenge. Such an attitude is typical of a slave con-sciousness which, instead of affirming itself and its existence in the manner of the noble soul, defines itself in terms of a negative morality, declaring, first of all, the other ('masters', 'society', etc.) to be 'evil' and, second, declaring itself to be, in contrast, pure and 'good'.

Nietzsche locates the nature of Rousseau's *ressentiment* in the way in which Rousseau gives his own personal life and suffering the status of a universal meaning. Unable to find the source of his suffering, Rousseau places blame and responsibility for it on society:

Men like Rousseau know how to employ their weakness, deficiencies, and vices as it were as manure for their talents. If he bewails the depravity and degeneration of society as the deplorable consequence of culture, he does so on the basis of a personal experience; it is the bitterness deriving from this that gives to his general condemnation the sharpness of its edge and poisons the arrows with which he shoots; he unburdens himself first of all as an individual and thinks to seek a cure that, operating directly upon society, will indirectly and through society also be of benefit to him himself.[59]

Nietzsche's portrait of Rousseau here finds confirmation in Jean Starobinski's psychological study around the theme of 'transparency and obstruction' in Rousseau. Rousseau meditates in solitude on the fate of man's collective nature. But, Starobinski points out, Rousseau's meditation is far from being disinterested since it allows him 'to blame history and society for the defects in his personal life. He will prove that he is right to be so unusual and to live alone.'[60] As a 'beautiful soul' – a soul defined by Hegel in terms of someone who dreads damaging the *inner* purity of their heart by contact with the external world, but chooses instead to persist in their self-willed impotence and the 'transparent purity of their moments'[61] – Rousseau's life can be seen in terms of a yearning for a state of 'universal Sameness'. As such, the problem of the relationship of self to the other is crucial to understanding the psychological underpinnings of his writings. By seeking an absolute identity between the self and the other, Rousseau obliterates otherness altogether. Rousseau does not see the world, says Starobinski, but only himself. Thus, in his writings, the self assumes the form of the ontological absolute, and the individual appears as the alienated victim of a corrupt 'other' – society.

In the *Reveries of a Solitary Walker* Rousseau consoles himself as a social outcast by believing that one day everything will find its proper place in a moral world-order and that his time will come. In the third walk he confesses, 'in the corresponding moral order which my researches have brought to light, I find the support I need to be able to endure the miseries of my life'.[62] Rousseau owes his faith in eternal truth to the voice of his conscience, that moral instinct which has never deceived him. Nowhere is the tension between the competing desires for community and individuality given better expression than in Rousseau. So long as he acts freely and alone, Rousseau says, he does nothing but good, but as soon as he experiences the yoke of human society he becomes rebellious.[63] What he desires is a state of perfect self-sufficient happiness: self-mastery is only possible through solitude. Rousseau confesses that when he is alone he is his own master; as soon as he engages in social intercourse he becomes the plaything of everyone around him. He imagines a state in which he could happily converse with his fellow human beings as a social being, a state which is only attractive to him so long as he could interact with the features of his face completely unknown to men.

It is this dialectical interplay between solitude and gregariousness, between the private and the communal self, which Rousseau captures so well for we moderns. It is also a major theme running through Zarathustra's experience of going-down (*untergehen*) to men after ten years of solitude. It is unfortunate that Nietzsche did not cultivate a more sensitive appreciation of Rousseau's paradoxical nature. If he had, then perhaps he might have appreciated the real nature of the pathos of distance which stood between his own life as a philosopher–artist and that of Rousseau's life as a philosopher–saint. It is a fundamental paradox of both Rousseau and Nietzsche that their untimeliness condemns them to solitude, to a kind of Stoic fate writing for an audience ('modern men') who do not wish to hear, but prefer instead to find repose in their dogmatic slumbers and to blink in their happiness. Starobinski locates in Rousseau what he believes is a radical contradiction between the withdrawal into solitude and the appeal to the universal. But this is a necessary paradox common to both Rousseau and Nietzsche, for both come to mankind 'too early', their time is 'not yet', and thus the question of the universal status of their teaching has to remain open, which explains why Nietzsche, for example, explicitly addresses his teaching in *Thus Spoke Zarathustra* to all and none.[64]

Nietzsche does not believe that resentment can ever be effaced from human experience, but what he seeks is a triumph over its destructive nature, both to the self and to others. One of his models

of what he means to have succeeded in overcoming the malignant
spirit of resentment is, interestingly enough, a man of the very
Revolution he holds in such contempt, the celebrated French
revolutionary Comte de Mirabeau. The overcoming of *ressentiment*
Nietzsche finds in a figure like Mirabeau is achieved by not taking
one's enemies and misfortunes seriously for a long time; instead, a
strong and full nature will have the power to recuperate and to
forgive by learning to forget.[65] In opposition to a politics of
ressentiment – a politics in which man's worst instincts, such as his
thirst for revenge and desire for punishment, are allowed to express
themselves and flourish – Nietzsche offers a teaching which celebrates 'the innocence of becoming'.

Nietzsche's philosophy embraces a tragic understanding of life.
Indeed, in *Ecce Homo* Nietzsche, with characteristic boldness and
exaggeration, described himself as being the first tragic philosopher.
The tragic philosopher accepts life in its totality and says 'yes' to its
variegated nature: to opposition and war, to passing away and
destruction, to becoming and suffering, 'Saying Yes to life even in its
strangest and hardest problems; the will to life rejoicing over its own
inexhaustibility even in the very sacrifice of its highest types – that is
what I called Dionysian'.[66] This tragic understanding of man's
existence rests on what Nietzsche calls a 'pessimism of strength',
which he defines in terms of 'an intellectual predilection for the
hard, gruesome, evil, problematic aspect of existence, prompted by
well-being, by overflowing health, by the *fullness* of existence'.[67]
With this notion of the pessimism of strength Nietzsche understands
himself as the antipodes of Rousseau for whom the existence of evil
had to be eradicated. Nietzsche regards morality as 'the danger of
dangers' because it does not affirm life, but *resents* it.[68]

NIETZSCHE ON THE MACHIAVELIANISM OF POWER

In the history of Western thought, 'Machiavellianism' has come to
signify the principle of *Realpolitik*, that expediency is always
preferable to morality in statecraft.[69] As Machiavelli exhorted his
Prince in the treatise of the same name, a leader should not deviate
from what is good if possible, but he should know how to do evil if
that is necessary.[70] Irrespective of whether or not Machiavelli
deserves his reputation as a teacher of evil, his thought does rest on
a profoundly anti-Christian understanding of social life which had a
powerful influence on Nietzsche's philosophy of beyond good and

evil.[71] Nietzsche derives two important conceptions from Machiavelli. Firstly, he accepts what he calls 'the Machiavellianism of power (*Macht*)',[72] that is, the view that morality can always be seen to have been built on 'immoral' foundations; in other words Nietzsche accepts Machiavelli's relativization of the notions of good and evil, and of moral and immoral. Secondly, in his thinking on morality Nietzsche is tremendously influenced by Machiavelli's notion of *virtù*, a notion which he constantly counterposes to the Christian understanding of virtuous action. It will be worthwhile to examine briefly the nature of Machiavelli's influence on Nietzsche, for it is largely a Machiavellian conception of existence which lies at the basis of his critique of Rousseau's construal of the problem of civilization.

As Sheldon Wolin points out, the modernity of Machiavelli consists in his rejection of natural law as a moral standard for judging political life, and in the construction of a pragmatic method in focusing on questions of power.[73] Machiavelli's notion of politics is predominantly an aesthetic one in which the prince experiences the aesthetic exhilaration of stamping reality with his own personality. Machiavelli promulgates a new kind of political knowledge in that he recognizes that evil is implicated in the possibilities for creative political action. Contrary to Plato's positing of a world of forms, Machiavelli grasps that reality is movement. Because humanity finds it difficult to live in a world of becoming, it creates an illusory transcendental world, treating it as a real basis for action. In Machiavelli the emphasis is not so much on the moral basis of political legitimacy, as on achieving political stability and order through a proper understanding of the mechanics of power, 'the ability to exert mastery by controlling an unstable complex of moving forces'.[74] That the application of violence is regarded as abnormal represents, Wolin argues, a significant achievement of the Western political tradition. He argues that Machiavelli's economy of violence aims at the 'pure' use of power undefiled by pride, ambition, or motives of petty revenge. In his writings we do not find any child-like delight in the contemplation of the barbarous and savage destructive potentialities of power. Concerning Machiavelli's reputation as an immoralist, Wolin's perception that his conception of politics amounts to the view that politics is not to be conducted without ethical criteria, but that the criteria are not to be imported from outside, still remains one of the most apposite in my opinion. Machiavelli rejects the idea of any literal translation of ethical acts into ethical situations, and replaces it with a notion of political irony by introducing an appreciation of the alchemy of the political in which good is transmuted into evil, and evil into good.

Nietzsche is clearly a descendant of Machiavelli's aesthetic appreciation of power and of politics. Nietzsche is concerned, however, not so much with mastery as with art, not manipulation but architectonic, political sculpture rather than political mastery in which there is a fusion of the human actor with his materials. Nietzsche was in fact a great admirer of Machiavelli's *Il Principe*.[75] On a number of occasions he refers to 'the grand politics of virtue' in terms highly reminiscent of Machiavelli's fundamental insight that legitimacy has its roots in illegitimacy, that civil society has its roots not in justice but in injustice, and that all social orders have been established with the aid of morally questionable means. Nietzsche writes, for example: '*By which means does a virtue come to power?* By exactly the same means as a political party: the slandering, inculpation, undermining of virtues that oppose it and are already in power, by rebaptizing them, by systematic persecution and mockery. Therefore: through sheer "immorality"'.[76] The victory of a moral ideal is achieved by the same 'immoral' means as every victory, namely, force, lies slander, injustice.[77] Indeed, Nietzsche intended to write his own treatise on politics under the title 'The Grand Politics of Virtue':

This treatise deals with the grand *politics* of virtue (*Politik der Tugend*). It is intended for the use of those whose interest must lie in learning, not how one *becomes* virtuous, but how one *makes* virtuous – how virtue is made to dominate. I even intend to prove that to desire the one – the domination of virtue – one absolutely must *not* desire the other; one automatically becomes virtuous oneself...

This treatise, as already stated, deals with the politics of virtue: it posits an ideal of these politics, it describes them as they would have to be, if anything on earth could be perfect. Now, no philosopher will be in any doubt as to the type of perfection in politics; that is Machiavellianism. But Machiavellianism *pur, sans mélange, cru, vert, dans toute sa force, dans toute son âpreté* [Pure, without admixture, crude, fresh, with all its force, with all its pungency], is superhuman, divine, transcendental, it will never be achieved by man, at most approximated.[78]

There are a number of similarities between Machiavelli's notion of 'virtù' and Nietzsche's notion of 'will to power'. Both notions refer to creative public action that is beyond the opposition of 'good' and 'evil'. There is no satisfactory equivalent in English of 'virtù' as the word 'virtue' has too many moral overtones to be acceptable. The term has been translated in a variety of ways as prowess, ability, strength of character, and talent. The word comes from the Roman *vir* (man) and *virtus* (what is proper to man). As one commentator has noted the word has nothing to do with Christian notions of virtue and virtuousness; rather, 'Courage, fortitude, audacity, skill and civil sprit – a whole classical and renaissance theory of man and culture underlies the word'.[79] Whatever translation is used, one must appreciate the creativity the notion attributes to human action. It is this aspect of the notion which so appealed to Nietzsche, for creative and courageous action implies that a person may find it necessary to defy established convention (including conventions of good and evil). Thus, Nietzsche's use of the notion removes it from its overtly political context (denoting primarily 'civic' or public-spirited action, that is, action for the common good) and provides it with an aesthetic meaning denoting any kind of action which is based on the creative entwinement of good and evil. Thus, for example, Nietzsche argues that:

For every strong and natural species of man, love and hate, gratitude and revenge, good nature and anger, affirmative acts and negative acts, belong together. One is good on condition one also knows how to be evil; one is evil because otherwise one would not understand how to be good.[80]

In several places in the *Nachlass* of the mid to late-1880s Nietzsche criticizes Rousseau's ideal of nature because of what he regards as its similarity to Christianity, and contrasts it with the Renaissance notion of virtù. Thus, for example, he writes: 'My struggle against *romanticism*, in which Christian ideals and the ideals of Rousseau unite, but compounded with a nostalgia for the old days of priestly–aristocratic culture, for *virtù*, for the "strong human being"'.[81] Nietzsche interprets the nineteenth-century picture of man as a triumph over the sentimental portrait of man in the eighteenth century which he finds in Rousseau. What Nietzsche seeks to undermine is the notion that the ideal man is always the one who is 'good':

In place of the 'natural man' (*Naturmenschen*) of Rousseau, the nineteenth century has discovered a *truer image of* 'man'... On the whole, the Christian concept 'man' has thus been reinstated. What one has *not* had the courage for is to call *this* 'man in himself' good and to see in him the guarantee of the future. Neither has one dared to grasp that an increase in the terribleness of man is an accompaniment of every increase in culture; in this one is still subject to the Christian ideal and takes *its* side against paganism, also against the Renaissance concept of *virtù*. But the key to culture is not to be found in this way and *in praxi* one retains the falsification of history in favour of the 'good man' (as if he alone constituted the progress of man) and the socialist ideal (i.e., the residue of Christianity and of Rousseau in the de-Christianized world).[82]

Rousseau was also a great admirer of Machiavelli, and regarded his masterpiece *The Prince* as a satirical work in which Machiavelli, for certain practical reasons (namely, seeking a job from the Medici), concealed his real political morality, which for Rousseau was one of patriotism and republicanism.[83] There is no doubt that Machiavelli's realism served to temper the idealism of Rousseau's political philosophy. In the first chapter of book three of *The Social Contract*, for example, Rousseau acknowledges that there is no single unique and absolute form of government that can be regarded as valid for all communities at all times. Rousseau agrees with Machiavelli that Christianity has done great damage to political life. His statement that 'true Christians are made to be slaves' echoes Machiavelli's claim that whereas paganism praised greatness of soul – magnanimity, physical vigour, and everything that serves to make individuals bold and courageous – Christianity preaches humility, abjection, contempt for human things, and glorifies humble and contemplative human beings, not human beings of action and great deeds.[84]

But how genuine is Rousseau's appreciation of Machiavelli? One commentator has argued that Rousseau's approval of Machiavelli in the *Social Contract* (a work also, one could argue, addressed to princes), serves to conceal his divergence from a Machiavellian-inspired politics of *virtù*.[85] In Rousseau, for example, the lawgiver is to respond to public opinion, not establish it. Perhaps the major source of their disagreement from which the rest spring, is Machiavelli's view that whoever founds a State and gives a people laws must assume that human nature is intrinsically weak and wicked, a view which clearly clashes with Rousseau's belief in humanity's natural goodness.[86] Thus, the main difference between Rousseau and Nietzsche in their appropriation of Machievelli is that whereas Nietzsche is prepared to accept Machiavelli's radical concessions to immorality in the reform of political life, Rousseau is not. One commentator has recently argued that Rousseau never seriously confronts the tragic dimension of politics which is so central to Machiavelli's concerns.[87] Informing such a tragic conception of politics is the view – shared by Nietzsche – that power can never ultimately be justified but only creatively used and abused. In an early, unpublished essay on the Greek State, for example, Nietzsche puts forward the view that 'power (*die Gewalt*) gives the first law (*Recht*), and there is no law which is not in its fundamental presumption a usurpation of this act of power'.[88]

Nietzsche's critique of modernity is informed by an appreciation of the Renaissance. If ages are to be assessed according to their positive forces, then, Nietzsche says, the age of the Renaissance appears as the last great age. 'We moderns', he writes, 'with our anxious care for ourselves and love of our neighbour, with our virtues of work, of unpretentiousness, of fair play, of scientificality – acquisitive, economic, machine-minded – appear as a *weak* age'. The modern age is lacking in 'stern and frightful customs'. The cult of equality and demand for equal rights is a sign of decline and exhaustion, for 'the chasm between man and man, class and class, the multiplicity of types, the will to be oneself, to stand out – that which I call the *pathos of distance* – characterizes every *strong* age'.[89] For Nietzsche, the Renaissance represented the revaluation of Christian values in order to bring about the triumph of the opposing values, 'noble values': 'I behold a spectacle at once so meaningful and so strangely paradoxical', Nietzsche tells us, that 'it would have given all the gods of Olympus an opportunity for an immortal roar of laughter – *Cesare Borgia as Pope*...Am I understood?'[90]

For Nietzsche the eighteenth century of Rousseau represents the emergence of a sentimentalism, of a cult of pity, which undermines the strong virtues of the Renaissance culminating in the modern experience of nihilism and decadence. It is to an examination of the role Rousseau plays in Nietzsche's delineation of a history of European nihilism that I now turn.

THE PROBLEM OF CIVILIZATION: ROUSSEAU AND EUROPEAN NIHILISM

In a startling inversion of Rousseau's construal of the problem of civilization in a passage from *Daybreak* Nietzsche argues '*contra* Rousseau':

If it is true that our civilization has something pitiable (*etwas Erbärmliches*) about it, you have the choice of concluding with Rousseau that 'this pitiable civilization is to blame for our *bad* morality' or against Rousseau that 'our *good* morality is to blame for this pitiableness of our civilization. Our weak, unmanly, social concepts of good and evil and their tremendous ascendancy over body and soul have finally weakened all bodies and souls and snapped the self-reliant, independent, unprejudiced men, the pillars of a *strong* civilization: where one still encounters *bad* morality one beholds the last ruins of these pillars'. Thus paradox stands against paradox! The truth cannot possibly be on both sides: and is it on either of them? Test them and see.[91]

It is precisely this inversion of Rousseau that Nietzsche takes up in the *Nachlass* of the mid- to late-1880s in the context of an examination of the struggle between Voltaire and Rousseau on 'the problem of civilization'.[92] In order to fully understand how Nietzsche construes this problem, and the struggle between Voltaire and Rousseau around it, it is necessary to situate it in the wider context of his delineation of a history of European nihilism.

Nihilism for Nietzsche is very much to be conceived as a historical condition and not as a universal state of mind. It is a deeply ambiguous condition which can be interpreted in either of two ways: it can be taken either as a sign of the increased power of the spirit (what Nietzsche calls 'active nihilism') or as decline and recession of the power of spirit (of what Nietzsche called 'passive nihilism').[93] As Nietzsche puts it: '*Overall insight: the ambiguous* character of our *modern world* – the very same symptoms could point to *decline* and to *strength*'.[94] Nietzsche construes the advent of nihilism as providing the occasion for a supreme act of self-examination on the part of humanity, namely, a revaluation of all values, including a revaluation of the value of civilization.

The advent of nihilism for Nietzsche is the result of a general decline in faith (the death of God), in particular of a withering away of faith in morality, in the belief in absolute and universal values. 'Radical nihilism', the conviction that existence is worthless when it comes to the highest values one recognizes, is a consequence of the cultivation of man's will to truth, which itself, is a consequence of faith in morality. Nietzsche expands:

Among the forces cultivated by morality was *truthfulness*: this eventually turned against morality, discovered its teleology, its partial perspective ... Now we discover in ourselves needs implanted by centuries of moral interpretation – needs that now appear to us as needs for untruth; on the other hand, the value for which we endure life seems to hinge on these needs. This antagonism – *not* to esteem what we know, and not to be *allowed* any longer to esteem the lies we should like to tell ourselves – results in a process of dissolution.[95]

Nietzsche adds: 'This is the *antinomy*: Insofar as we believe in morality we pass sentence on existence'.[96] Morality for Nietzsche is a system of thought which attempts to impose an absolute standard of right and wrong, of good and evil, upon existence, thus cutting off the full experience of life's rich, abundant forces. Morality is an attempt to deny existence. He offers the following '*Definition of morality*: Morality – the idiosyncrasy of decadents, with the ulterior motive of revenging oneself against life'.[97] Morality is an attempt to deny the will to power, man's basic instinct for growth and development. Viewed historically, however, it has been morality, Nietzsche writes, that:

protected life against despair and the leap into nihilism, among men and classes who were violated and oppressed by *men*: for it is the experience of being powerless against men, not against nature, that gives rise to the most desperate embitterment against existence. Morality treated the violent despots, the doers of violence, the 'masters' in general, as the enemies against whom the common man must be protected…Morality conse- quently taught men to hate and despise most profoundly what is the basic character trait of those who rule: their will to power. To abolish, deny, and dissolve this morality – that would mean looking at the best-hated drive with an opposite feeling and valuation.[98]

Nietzsche's argument is that in rebelling against the masters the weak and the oppressed have denied their own nature, their own will to power, and have thus internalized it. This is an illustration of what Nietzsche means when he speaks of 'the Machiavellianism of Power': that the will to power is as much a drive of the weak and the oppressed as it is of the strong.

For Nietzsche, Rousseau's construal of the problem of civilization, his critique of society and glorification of altruistic values, constitute, along with Christianity, the Reformation, and the French Rev- olution, an essential part of the history by which the slave revolt in morality has implanted in humanity a particular form of the will to power. The French Revolution is the continuation of Christianity with Rousseau portrayed as 'the seducer' who

again unfettered woman who is henceforth represented in an ever more interesting manner – as suffering. Then the slaves and Mrs. Beecher-Stowe.

Then the poor and the workers...next comes the curse of voluptuous-
ness...the most decided conviction that the lust to rule is the greatest vice;
the perfect certainty that morality and disinterestedness are identical
concepts and that the 'happiness of all' is a goal worth striving for...We are
well along the way: the kingdom of heaven of the poor in spirit has begun.
– Intermediary stages: the bourgeois (a *parvenu* on account of money) and
the worker (on account of the machine).[99]

In his 'critique of modern man' Nietzsche constructs an image of the
modern period in terms of the spirit which animates the three
centuries. The seventeenth century is the century of 'aristocratism'
(Descartes), consisting in the 'rule of reason' and the 'testimony of
the sovereignty of the will'. The aristocratic seventeenth century
'looks down haughtily upon the animalic', it is severe against the
heart, without sentimentality and un-German. It is the century of
strong will and strong passion. The eighteenth century is the century
of 'feminism' (Rousseau), it is the rule of feeling and 'testimony of
the sovereignty of the senses'. It is the age of enthusiasm in which the
human spirit is placed in the service of the heart, 'libertine in the
enjoyment of what is most spiritual', it undermines all authorities.
The nineteenth century is the century of 'animalism' (Schopenhauer), submissive before every kind of reality, it is the age of honesty
and realism, but also weak in will, 'full of dark cravings', and
'fatalistic'.[100]

Rousseau inspires the age of romanticism, which establishes 'the
sovereign right of passion' and the cult of naturalness, leading to a
fascination with madness and 'the absurd vanity of the weak man,
the rancour of the mob as judge'.[101] In opposition to Rousseau,
Nietzsche does not call for a return to nature, for 'there has never
been a natural humanity...man reaches nature only after a long
struggle – he never "returns" – Nature: i.e., daring to be immoral
like nature'. 'More natural', Nietzsche says, is the first society of the
rich, the leisure class in which 'love between the sexes is a kind of
sport in which marriage furnishes an obstacle and a provocation'.
'More natural' is the attitude to morality which recognizes that
morality is founded on instinct. 'More natural' is the attitude
towards politics which sees 'problems of power' in terms of 'one
quantum of power against another...we feel all rights to be
conquests'. 'More natural' is the estimation of great human beings
in which passion is considered a privilege, in which 'all being-great'
consists in 'placing-oneself-outside as far as morality is concerned'.

'More natural' is the attitude towards nature which no longer loves it on account of its supposed innocence, but recognizes it as devilish and dumb. Instead of despising it on this account, we need to learn to feel at home in it. 'In summa', Nietzsche writes:

there are signs that the European of the nineteenth century is less ashamed of his instincts; he has taken a step toward admitting to himself his unconditional naturalness, i.e., his immorality, *without becoming embittered*...
This sounds to some ears as if corruption had progressed – and it is certain that man has not come close to the '*nature*' of which *Rousseau* speaks but has progressed another step in civilization, which Rousseau *abhorred*.[102]

A major part of Nietzsche's overcoming of the age of Rousseau consists in inverting Rousseau's construal of the problem of civilization. Nietzsche writes:

Contra Rousseau: Unfortunately, man is no longer evil enough; Rousseau's opponents who say 'man is a beast of prey' are unfortunately wrong. Not the corruption of man but the extent to which he has become tender and moralized is his curse.[103]

This passage is a good example of Nietzsche's revaluation of the problem of civilization, as it shows that this rests on an overturning of the conventional understanding that civilization represents the story of a progress in which man becomes tamed and domesticated. Nietzsche does not refute the argument that civilization has corrupted man, but instead laments the fact that it has not corrupted him sufficiently.[104] It needs to be appreciated that for Nietzsche decadence – consisting of 'waste, decay, elimination' – is not to be condemned, for it represents a necessary feature of life and its growth. 'The phenomenon of decadence is as necessary as any increase and advance of life', he writes, 'one is in no position to abolish it. Reason demands, on the contrary, that we do justice to it.'[105] Nihilism is not to be construed as the cause of decadence but as its logical result: 'Every fruitful and powerful movement of humanity has also created at the same time a nihilistic movement.'[106] It is in this context that we can appreciate Nietzsche's insight that the high points of culture do not coincide with those of civilization. From a moral point of view the great moments of culture are always times of corruption and decadence; similarly, the periods when the taming of the human animal is required and enforced are times when the boldest and most spiritual natures are not tolerated.[107]

In thinking through the problem of civilization Nietzsche does not simply side with Voltaire against Rousseau. As Nietzsche informs us, he intends to embark on a 'critique of both points of view in regard to the *value of civilization*'.[108] As Peter Heller has noted, in a penetrating essay on Nietzsche's relation to Voltaire and Rousseau, Voltaire anticipates one of Nietzsche's most cherished ideals, that of the synthesis of aristocratic civilization and spiritual freedom.[109]

Nietzsche dedicated *Human, All Too Human* to Voltaire as 'one of the greatest liberators of the human spirit'. He praises him for his moderation, for his tolerance, for his unbelief, for his enlightenment, for being a '*Missionary of culture*, aristocrat, representative of the victorious, ruling classes and their valuations'. By contrast, Rousseau 'remained a *plebeian*... his impudent contempt for all that was not he himself'. Whereas Voltaire 'still comprehended *umanita* and *virtù* in the Renaissance sense', Rousseau established feeling and sentiment as the rule, 'nature as the source of justice'.[110] Against Rousseau, Voltaire argues that the state of nature is terrible, that 'our civilization represents a tremendous triumph over this beast-of-prey nature'.[111] Thus, for Nietzsche, where Voltaire defends culture and civilization as a triumph over the state of nature and man's bestiality, Rousseau moralizes nature and, through the fiction of an innocent and uncorrupted state of nature, gives expression to his fundamental *ressentiment*.

Nietzsche desires that man *become* more natural – his aim is to 'translate man back into nature' – not in Rousseau's sense of an inherent natural goodness, but by becoming sceptical, self-reliant, and amoral like nature itself.[112] In response to the Stoic ethic that one must learn how to live according to the nature, Nietzsche argues that one should not make a principle of what one is and must be, namely, a piece of nature and life itself. Nietzsche invites us to imagine a being like nature. It will be wasteful and indifferent beyond measure, 'without purposes and consideration, without mercy and justice, fertile, desolate, and uncertain at the same time'. If indifference itself is power, Nietzsche asks, how could one live according to this indifference? While the Stoic pretends rapturously to read the canon of its law in nature, what it really seeks, argues Nietzsche, is something quite different and opposite, namely, its pride wishes to impose its morality and its ideal on nature, for the demand to live according to the indifference of nature proves too hard and cruel for it.[113] Nietzsche's criticism of the Stoic doctrine is part of his attempt to de-deify nature, to '"*naturalize*" humanity in terms of a pure, newly discovered, newly redeemed nature'.[114]

Nietzsche's synthesis of vitality and nobility is often presented by commentators in terms of his image of a Julius Caesar with the soul of Jesus Christ.[115] But perhaps a better model is that of Napoleon and Goethe, which represents a synthesis of the courage and power of the soldier and the transfigured nature and accumulated humanity of the poet and artist.[116] Whatever image of Nietzsche's model of the overman one ends up accepting, the point to be grasped is that for Nietzsche it is necessary to maintain and deepen the tension between man's enfeeblement and his ennoblement in order that both the descending and the ascending aspects of life can ultimately accrue to the benefit of humanity by producing an enrichment of man's potential for self-overcoming. As Peter Heller has noted: 'A movement of reaction is to be turned into a movement of progress – not by the victory of the destructively regressive tendencies but by way of a process in which the regressive forces are assimilated, suspended, and overcome'.[117] If Heller is right on this point, and I believe he is, this must mean that, in the end, Nietzsche's critique ends up with a justification of Rousseau and the modern slave revolt in morals – justification in the sense that it must lead to something higher and greater than itself by accepting the necessity of its own perishing and transfiguration in an act of self-overcoming.

CONCLUSION

In describing himself as 'contra Rousseau' it is clear that Nietzsche is compelled to exaggerate and distort certain aspects of Rousseau's moral and political thought in order to highlight, in a rhetorical manner, his challenge to the Christian–moral tradition and its secular successors. Nietzsche constructs an image of the Rousseauian man and ends up depicting a caricature of Rousseau: Rousseau as the utopian and visionary, as the social revolutionary whose attitude of *ressentiment* towards life finds expression in a political ideology of radical egalitarianism, a secular successor to the Christian teaching of the equality of all souls before God, and an ethics of the herd which served to inspire the major political movements of the nineteenth century such as socialism.

In truth, Rousseau was far from advocating a levelling form of equality. His political philosophy makes an important distinction between government (the corporate or executive will) and sovereignty (the general or legislative will). He holds that there never has been, and never will be, a real democracy since 'it is against the natural order for the many to govern and the few to be governed'.[118] His model of government is that of an elective aristocracy, which implicitly accepts a degree of social and economic inequality as an ineliminable feature of social life. Together with the importance he attaches to the notion of the legislator, Rousseau is in fact quite close to Nietzsche's politics of an 'aristocratic radicalism' in that both recognize that great politics requires great leadership.

Nietzsche's portrait, however, is too simplistic in that it too readily associates Rousseau with the French Revolution – in particular its bloody excesses – and fails to take into account Rousseau's argument that the reform of social institutions must be based on a prior reform of our inner moral sensibilities.[119] Rousseau is careful to acknowledge that any programme of political reform must take into account the importance of what has been engraved in the hearts of citizens by their mores and customs[120] Nietzsche's appeal to each one of us to find and cultivate the spirit of enlightenment within ourselves, and to strike down the revolutionary impulse whenever it threatens to overwhelm us, accurately captures the spirit of Rousseau's own teaching.[121] Rousseau certainly had a vision of a revolution to come, but did not himself advocate revolution as the solution to the problem of civilization.

Nietzsche caricatures Rousseau's position on man's natural goodness by attributing to him a naive yearning for a return to an innocent state of nature which he never seriously entertained. To this extent Nietzsche's major critique of Rousseau, that he posits a dangerous and naive unmediated opposition between the innocence of human nature on the one hand, and the corruptness of social institutions on the other, is misplaced. As one commentator has recently noted, the fear of an uncontrollable violence waiting to be unleashed by the overthrow of all recognized authority, constitutes an essential component of Rousseau's political thought.[122] What Nietzsche's critique of Rousseau on this point neglects is that the emphasis in his work is on education as the way in which the individual is to be brought to a realization of its real moral nature.

Furthermore, Rousseau criticizes Christianity for preaching withdrawal from the world and for its emasculation of political life. His model of political discipline was that of the sacrifices endured by the ancient Spartans – hardly the choice of the kind of sentimental windbag we find depicted in Nietzsche's portrait.[123] Rousseau specifically intended his model of political virtue as being applicable only to small republics, not large nations. In many ways, therefore, Nietzsche's understanding of Rousseau as the philosopher who celebrated a sentimental view of life and whose political philosophy heralds the age of modern egalitarian politics represents a simplistic and one-sided portrait. Nietzsche's reading of Rousseau was undoubtedly coloured to a large extent by his acceptance of Voltaire's view, shared by *les philosophes*, that Rousseau's critique of civilization was motivated by nothing more than misanthropy and represents the exaggerated critique of a sentimental madman.

Nietzsche's critique of the central motif running through Rousseau's work, the belief in man's natural goodness, is remarkably consistent throughout his writings, from *The Birth of Tragedy* in 1872 to the writings and *Nachlass* of the 1880s. Throughout his writings Nietzsche opposes the kind of political reading of the notion of the Dionysian he detects in Rousseau's political philosophy, which rests on the belief (Nietzsche calls it a delusion) that man is naturally good and that a social and political revolution will bring about the realization of this natural goodness by creating a social order free of corruption and exploitation. This non-political reading of the Dionysian would seem to lend support to those commentators who argue that Nietzsche is a profoundly anti-political philosopher. Walter Kaufmann, for example, in his major rehabilitation of Nietzsche's thought after the Second World War argued that the fundamental leitmotif of Nietzsche's work was 'the theme of the antipolitical individual who seeks self-perfection far from the modern world'.[124]

However, it would be misleading to present the question of Nietzsche's relationship to Rousseau in terms of an opposition between a thinker who advocated the primacy of politics and political revolution, and a thinker who advocated an anti-political response to the problem of social transformation and cultural change. Those commentators who construe Rousseau's thought in terms of the primacy of politics ignore the fact that he produced two books in 1762 as a response to the problem of civilization, *The Social Contract* and *Émile*. Those commentators who construe Nietzsche's thought in terms of an anti-politics neglect the fact that in his later writings Nietzsche speaks of the need for a Platonic conjunction of philosophical legislation and great politics in order to transform humanity. It is a transformation which will necessarily require a fundamental change in the political structures of modern society. These points suggest that we need to adopt a 'double reading' of Rousseau's and Nietzsche's thinking on the fate of civilization, in that it is possible to identify in both thinkers an overtly political solution to the problem of civilization, which focuses on the need for great political leadership, and a more subtle, pedagogic solution to the problem which focuses on the need for self-enlightenment and individual reform. The paradoxes which run through the writings of both Rousseau and Nietzsche stem from a tension between the ethical and the political aspects of their teaching.

CHAPTER 2

Civilization and its discontents: Rousseau on man's natural goodness

'Your goodness must have some edge to it, – else it is none.'
R. W. Emerson, 'Self-Reliance' (1841)

INTRODUCTION TO ROUSSEAU'S POLITICAL THOUGHT

Rousseau's political philosophy attempts a novel solution to the antinomies of modern political life – the oppositions of man and citizen, desire and reason, freedom and necessity, individuality and community – and was to have a tremendous impact on modern German thought, notably Kant, Hegel, Schiller, and Marx.[1] Rousseau's political philosophy is frequently presented in terms of either a liberal, or a totalitarian, response to modern political life. He is seen, on the one hand, to extol the primacy of individual liberty, while, on the other, to sacrifice the liberty of the individual to the authority of the State. Thus, several commentators have argued that there is a contradiction within Rousseau's thinking on the individual and society. It has been suggested, for example, that whereas the *Discourse on the Origin of Inequality* (1755) offers an eloquent account of the rights of the individual, the *Social Contract* (1762) proposes the total subordination of those rights to the demands of the State.[2]

However, this construal of Rousseau's political thought fails to recognize its unique nature, which lies in the fact that, although it begins with the same individualistic premises as the liberal tradition of modern political thought (namely, Hobbes and Locke), it sees the goal of the *res publica*, or commonwealth, not merely in prudential terms but, rather, in moral ones. For Rousseau the social contract, by which the individual elects to join society and obey its rules through an act of free choice, is premised not merely on an exchange basis where the individual agrees to become a member of society and consents to obey its laws in return for peace and security; rather the social contract is the means whereby isolated individuals come together through a creative political act and transform themselves into moral beings by becoming self-legislating citizens. Thus, Rousseau argues that society exists not only to provide individuals with peace and happiness, though this is one of its aims, but also to educate them into moral beings. With Rousseau politics has become education. In contrast to Hobbes and Locke, the transition from the pre-political state of nature to civil society is construed by Rousseau in terms of a process by which human beings forsake their natural liberty in exchange for a higher moral or ethical liberty. In other words, Rousseau's argument is that we only become truly free and independent when we become moral beings united in society. This is a fundamentally different account of political obligation to the one we find in the early liberal tradition of political theory.[3] Rousseau is closest to Hobbes in holding that human beings become moral through political education; but he departs from Hobbes in holding that sovereignty cannot be alienated.

Of course, Rousseau's political thought faces a crucial paradox on this point when it is recognized that its argument is circular: If individuals are to transform themselves into moral beings who no longer act in accordance with the maxims of self-interest, but with those of the general will, must they not *already be* moral beings? Rousseau's response to this paradox, as we shall see in detail in the next chapter, is to be found in his argument on the need for a great and wise legislator. On Nietzsche's reading of politics, it is at this point that Rousseau's vision of a morally educated mankind must accept the necessity of a politics of force and an economy of violence.

In this chapter I shall carry out an examination of the second discourse by focusing on Rousseau's historicization of human rationality and his ambiguous relation to the tradition of natural law, and conclude by suggesting that his inquiry into humanity's origins results in a historical impasse. It is in the context of this problem of history that we can best appreciate Rousseau's attempt to square the circle with the notion of the general will.

THE STATE OF NATURE: ROUSSEAU 'CONTRA' HOBBES

In the preface to his prize-winning first discourse on the arts and sciences Rousseau says that the audience of any published work can be divided into two, the public and a few wise men. He speaks of the volatility of public opinion, of the fact that men are tied to the opinions and prejudices of their century. The freethinker, therefore, must necessarily address his writing to a future audience if he wants to live beyond his century: he is *condemned* to untimeliness.[4] Although the second discourse was also occasioned by a competition set by the Academy of Dijon, Rousseau this time felt free to give full vent to his feelings and did not feel the need to flatter the prejudices of his contemporaries. It is a discourse not addressed to the 'academicians' but to the 'human race'. It is a work which explicitly rejects divine revelation as a source for the authority of truth. It is Rousseau's 'testimony' whose truthfulness can only be judged by whether it speaks to the hearts of men, that is, to our 'true selves'. Again, Rousseau's thought faces a crucial paradox: if we have been corrupted, if we are decadents, then how is it possible for us to re-discover our real selves? Rousseau will address himself to both the common man and to the philosopher. He will relate the history of the human species as it should be read, not in the books of one's fellowmen who are all liars, but in the 'book of nature' itself which, we are told, 'never lies'. Rousseau's intention is to replace the written thought of men with nature as the true standard of human existence, a move which is only possible because man's degeneration is not yet complete.[5]

The *Discourse on the Origin and Foundation of the Inequality of Mankind*, a work which continues to haunt the Occidental imagination in the way in which it shows that the cultural achievements and wealth of civilization rest on barbarism, poverty, and injustice, was published in 1755 as a response to the question set by the Academy concerning the origin of inequality among men, and whether or not it is sanctioned by natural law. For Rousseau the problem of civilization reduces itself to the task of determining what is original and what is artificial in the nature of man. However, an investigation into this problem is compounded, Rousseau tells us, by the problem of reflecting on a state of nature 'which no longer exists, perhaps never did exist, and probably never will exist', but of which it is necessary to have an idea in order to form a judgement of our present state.[6] In reflecting on this problem Rousseau makes the point that the more the human race advances the more difficult it becomes to know the 'true nature' of man, and thus we are faced with the paradox that, 'it is, in one sense, by our very study of man, that the knowledge of him is put beyond our grasp'.[7] Rousseau's point is later echoed in the preface of the *Genealogy of Morals*, where Nietzsche says that, as disciples of knowledge, we moderns are furthest from ourselves and hence strangers to what we 'really are'.

Because of the simplistic manner in which philosophers have dealt with this issue, Rousseau argues that the term 'natural law' is mystifying. They have attempted to define natural law by considering what rules are expedient for human beings to agree on for their common interest. The attempt to inquire into the philosophical foundations of society rests on the idea of a state of nature, but, as Rousseau points out, the fact that so many conflicting accounts have been given of this state, shows that there exists no universally agreed upon definition of natural law. He makes the crucial point that, in conceiving of man in the state of nature, philosophers have attributed to natural man qualities which could only have been acquired in a social state. The focus of Rousseau's critique is Hobbes's depiction of the state of nature in terms of a war of all against all. Rousseau concentrates a great deal of attention on Hobbes's argument because of his depiction of human behaviour in the state of nature as one of natural wickedness. Such an account of man's natural condition clearly poses a major challenge to Rousseau's belief in man's natural goodness.[8]

The idea of the state of nature plays a double role in Rousseau's political thought. On the one hand, it is conceived in philosophical terms as a legal fiction, best conceived as a Kantian regulative Idea which tells us that we must think *as if* such a state existed in order to understand the nature of social man, and, on the other hand, it is understood to be an actual historical condition which preceded the emergence of political man.[9] Thus, for example, Rousseau argues that in answering the question set by the Academy we must begin 'by laying all facts aside, as they do not affect the question'. Furthermore, 'the investigations we may enter into, in treating this subject, must not be considered as historical truths, but only as mere conditional and hypothetical reasonings, calculated to explain the nature of things, than to ascertain their real origin'[10] – an impossible task, according to Nietzsche's understanding of a genealogy of morals, since only that which has no history can be defined.[11] Thus, a thing's nature cannot be understood apart from its origins and development in a play of forces, which is an evolution to be understood not in terms of a logical progression towards a telos or final goal, but in terms of the appropriation and interpretation of a will to power.

Rousseau's major argument with his predecessors is that they attribute to human beings in a state of nature qualities which could only be acquired via a process of socialization. The idea of man's natural goodness is a rebuttal of Hobbes's argument that human beings are inherently aggressive and possess an innate desire for dominion over others. Instead, Rousseau aims to show that the desire for power over others is a result of a certain historical development in which the rise of inequalities in social and political power have given birth to certain qualities such as vanity and pride. This is why, for example, Rousseau tells us that the precise subject of his investigation into the origins of inequality is to mark 'the moment at which right took the place of violence and nature became subject to law, and to explain by what sequence of miracles the strong came to submit to serve the weak, and the people to purchase imaginary repose at the expense of real felicity'.[12] Here we encounter a major problem of Rousseau-interpretation to which we shall return: the question whether Rousseau provides a materialist, or an idealist, account of the transformation from innocent 'primitive' man to corrupt social man.

Although Rousseau actually begins from very similar premises to Hobbes – the belief, for example, that man is not naturally sociable, and that the major motive of human action is a desire for self-preservation – he draws from them radically different conclusions. While in Rousseau the precise historical status of the idea of the state of nature is ambiguous, there is no such ambiguity in Hobbes. Where in Rousseau the account of the state of nature is given a historical form and placed in the remote past, with the evolution of man as a social animal described in terms of evolutionary stages, in Hobbes the state of nature has no historical pretensions whatsoever. For Hobbes the state of nature is not a condition which lies in the remote past, but is rather a condition we are constantly liable to fall into.[13] On this account the state of nature provides us with a picture of what life would be like in the absence of political authority: 'Hereby it is manifest, that during the time men live without a common Power to keep them all in awe, they are in that condition which is called Warre; and such a warre, as is of every man, against every man.'[14] In such a state there are no notions of right and wrong, of justice and injustice; because there is no common power, and where there is no law there can be no injustice (a view shared by both Rousseau and Nietzsche). The only law of life under such conditions is that of self-preservation.

In Hobbes the origins of society and of political obligation are to be accounted for through the exercise of human rationality by which individuals learn to recognize that the pursuit of power in the state of nature is self-defeating, and that their desire for self-preservation and fundamental fear of death would be best served by them coming together and creating a sovereign power, a commonwealth, which would guarantee them peace and security – in fact, an end to the grim and terrible war of all against all – in exchange for their near-unconditional obedience. Individuals can achieve this, Hobbes argues, through recognizing the 'laws of nature'. Although Hobbes is following traditional usage in calling these laws of nature 'laws', his use of the term is merely metaphorical; they are best understood as prudential maxims of what is conducive to self-preservation, what Hobbes calls 'dictates of right reason'. All the laws of nature and all political obligations are derived from the individual's right to self-preservation. Thus, Hobbes distinguishes between 'the right of nature' and 'the law of nature'. The right of nature (*Jus Naturale*) is defined as the liberty each man has to use his own power as he himself wills for the preservation of his own nature. By contrast, a law of nature is defined as a precept or a general rule, discovered by reason, which forbids a human being to do anything which would be destructive of its existence.[15] So long as human beings possess their natural right to everything, which is necessary for their self-preservation in a state of nature, the state of war will persist in determining their fate.

From this argument on the state of nature Hobbes derives his first two fundamental laws of nature. The first one stipulates that where possible human beings should exercise their reason in order to seek peace and follow it when they find it; the second law of nature stipulates that each person ought to be willing to divest itself of its right to all things when others are also willing, and that it ought to be satisfied with just as much liberty against others as it allows others against itself. This mutual renunciation of natural rights is accomplished by the social contract wherein each one of a multitude of people oblige themselves, by contract with each of the rest, not to resist the commands of the human being or the body they have recognized as their sovereign, a sovereign that is granted absolute power.

It is clear that in Hobbes's account of the foundations of civil society self-interest constitutes the basis of morality. Perhaps the most notable feature of his account lies in his formulation of the laws of nature. It is evident from his deduction of these laws that, although posited as laws of 'nature', they are in fact laws of 'reason'. The laws of nature are the means by which human beings overcome their irrational pursuit of self-preservation in the warlike state of nature, and act in accordance with rational maxims of action. The laws of nature are a set of rules according to which any rational being would pursue its own advantage if it were perfectly conscious of the circumstances in which it was acting, and had overcome the irrationality of its impulses. Moreover, the laws of nature are the postulates according to which a rational construction of society is to take place. As one commentator has noted, the laws of nature 'are at once the principles of perfect prudence and of social morality, and therefore they make possible the step from the psychological motives of individual action to the precepts and values of civilized law and morality'.[16] In construing rationality in such terms, Hobbes anticipates both Rousseau's notion of the general will and Kant's notion of the categorical imperative in that the idea of the universalization of reason constitutes the basis of his account of political obligation. Of course, Kant's understanding of morality differs fundamentally from Hobbes's in that it allows no room for self-interest. Indeed, the sole moral worth of human action, according to Kant, lies in whether it has been performed out of the motive of duty and not out of any heteronomous maxims of self-interest.[17] In this respect, Rousseau is closer to Hobbes, for his notion of the formation of the moral–collective body appeals directly to the self-interest of the individual. Indeed, the novelty of Rousseau's deduction of the social contract lies in the fact that it seeks to educate the isolated individual as to the real basis of its self-interest, that is, that it is best served by acting in concert with others through the general will. Both Hobbes and Rousseau justify the social contract by arguing that if individuals are left to define good and evil, justice and injustice on their own as private individuals, then society becomes impossible. The difference between them lies in their accounts of sovereignty. For Hobbes, sovereignty must reside in an absolute power on account of the untrustworthiness of human nature, but for Rousseau sovereignty is inalienable and must reside with each individual considered as a participant in the general will, that is, as a citizen.[18]

In Hobbes the state of nature does not mark the literal origins of political society, but denotes a relapse, a reversal of time.[19] It is a fall from civilized society without any sacral overtones and without sin. Its condition is ahistorical in the sense that it is a condition which exists outside of history. Political society represents the triumph of man over nature. Since nature has no history in the human sense, the birth of society marks man's creation of history. The establishment of social order fundamentally changes man's experience of time, since it brings about an end to the fear and anxiety of a state of nature and the uncertainty over the future.

Rousseau's relationship to natural law is an ambiguous one which has been the source of much disagreement amongst scholars of his work. The debate is between those commentators who believe that Rousseau fundamentally breaks with the concept of natural law, and those who argue that he reformulates it.[20] Put simply, the question can be asked, can there be a 'law' prior to a reflective, moral state? If the natural law is merely metaphorical, how can it obligate us? Is the law of nature simply a synonym for a shared sense of what is just and unjust which develops over time, or is it something which exists prior to social development, but which is dependent on the cultivation of reason in order for its binding nature to be recognized?

In his work Rousseau makes a distinction between a primitive natural law which exists prior to reason, and a fully realized rational natural law which can only be cultivated in a civil state. Thus, in the transition from a state of nature to civil society, natural law undergoes a similar transformation to that undergone by humanity. It is clear that Rousseau believes in a moral order based on innate principles and recognized by all human beings independent of human conventions and customs. Indeed, it is only on such a basis that he is able to launch such a powerful attack on modern civilization whose mores and morals are criticized for not being in accordance with our true nature of goodness.

The role the concept of natural law plays in Rousseau's thought is, however, paradoxical, for in the state of nature it is present, but not known, while in civil society it is understood, but corrupted. In the just polity its function as a rule of conduct is replaced by the will of the legitimate sovereign and by civil law. Rousseau thus does not deny the validity of natural law, but only its effectiveness, in that he does not regard it as sufficient for the establishment of social order. However, it is important to recognize that, if the function of natural law is replaced by political education in Rousseau's thought, then this education must not violate the voice of nature, but develop in accordance with it, in spite of its impotence to generate itself.

In the second discourse Rousseau suggests that Hobbes had seen all the previous defects of the modern definitions of natural right which consists in assuming that man is by nature fully capable of using his reason. But if natural law is the subject of a historical development, this does not mean that it does not have its roots in principles anterior to this development. Rousseau, however, detects a fundamental inconsistency at the heart of Hobbes's thinking on the state of nature. He agrees with the premises of Hobbes's deduction of political obligation that natural law must be rooted in passions that are anterior to reason, the most important of which is self-preservation. However, he argues that Hobbes is guilty of gross inconsistency for, although he denies man's natural sociability, he nevertheless establishes the character of natural man by referring to experiences which can only be those of social man. Rousseau's major argument *contra* Hobbes here is that even human rationality has to be explained in terms of a process of socialization.[21] In a 'true', pre-political and pre-civil state of nature there would be no need for obligations in the absence of social relationships; on the level of an instinctual, pre-reflective mode of existence there would not even be a consciousness and an anxiety about death. Thus, for Rousseau our notions of property (of 'mine' and 'thine'), of obligations and rights, of exploitation and domination even, only become meaningful in the context of a moral and social development of the human animal.

In contrast to Hobbes, Rousseau argues that in a state of nature man is characterized by a natural goodness. His argument is that the qualities of intentional action which Hobbes attributed to humanity in the state of nature are qualities which are only acquired through extensive and fairly sophisticated social relationships. Rousseau agrees with Hobbes that life in the state of nature would be solitary and non-social. However, in contrast to Hobbes, and because he has a fundamentally different understanding of human nature, Rousseau does not deduce from this insight the claim that human beings would seek out of necessity the acquisition of more and more power. According to Rousseau there are only two natural pre-political sentiments: self-preservation – what he calls *amour de soi* (literally love of self) – and compassion (*pitié*). Rousseau argues that in the state of nature men will only injure each other if it is absolutely necessary to their self-preservation. They will not act to take delight or joy in hurting others or by seeking glory. Indeed, passions like vanity or pride are completely alien to man in the state of nature according to Rousseau. We can go so far as to say that, for Rousseau, natural man is premoral and subhuman.

In referring to man's natural goodness Rousseau is drawing our attention to the fact that man in a state of nature is beyond good and evil: he is neither good nor evil, neither virtuous nor vicious, but rather his actions are completely and fundamentally innocent.[22] In Rousseau, as Leo Strauss has put it, 'man is by nature good because he is by nature that subhuman being which is capable of becoming either good or bad. There is no natural constitution of man to speak of: everything specifically human is acquired or ultimately depends on artifice or convention. Man is by nature almost infinitely perfectible'.[23] Rousseau recognizes that the term 'goodness' can only be a retrospective ascription applied from the vantage point of sociality. His point seems to be that man has the potential to develop a moral consciousness. The ambiguity arises when we try to determine how man acquires this consciousness and begins to understand his actions morally. Far from advocating a return to the state of nature, it is Rousseau's intention to draw our attention to the radical difference between natural man and social man, to show us that what we call humanity is the product of a historical process. In this respect, therefore, it can be said that Nietzsche fundamentally misunderstood, or chose to misrepresent, the intentions behind Rousseau's argument on man's natural goodness. It is only possible to answer the problem of civilization for Rousseau by developing a history of the human species in which it is shown that human beings are not, *contra* Hobbes, naturally aggressive and wicked.

The aim of Rousseau's political philosophy is not to advocate a return to the state of nature, but rather to show in what way it is possible to legitimize the social bond. However, it is still the case that Rousseau's depiction rests on a privileging of certain sentiments over others, and that this privileging is the result of Rousseau confusing what is 'original' with what is 'natural' in mankind. In the next section I wish to illustrate this point by examining the role the notions of *amour de soi*, *amour-propre*, and *pitié* play in Rousseau's thought.

'AMOUR DE SOI', 'AMOUR PROPRE', AND 'PITIÉ'

Rousseau introduces the notions of *amour de soi*, *amour-propre*, and *pitié* in the context of his discussion of the way in which various thinkers have arrived at a definition of natural law from an account of human nature. He argues that philosophers have made the mistake of inquiring into the rules necessary which men must agree on for their common interest, and have then proceeded to ascribe the name of natural law to these rules without any real knowledge of human nature. He argues that so long as we are ignorant of natural man it is in vain for us to attempt to determine either the law originally prescribed to him, or that which is best adapted to his constitution. All we can know with any certainty is that, if it is to be a law, then not only the wills of those it obliges must be capable of submitting to it, but also, if it is to be natural, it must come directly from the voice of nature.[24] If we throw aside all 'scientific books' which teach us only to see human beings such as they have made of themselves, and contemplate the first and most simple operations of the human soul, we will perceive in it two principles prior to reason, one of them deeply interesting us in our own welfare and preservation, and the other exciting a natural repugnance at seeing any other sentient being, and particularly any of our own species, suffer pain or death. 'It is', says Rousseau, 'from the agreement and combination which the understanding is in a position to establish between these two principles, without it being necessary to introduce the idea of sociability, that all the rules of natural right appear to me to be derived – rules which our own reason is afterwards obliged to establish on other foundations, when by its successive developments it has been led to suppress nature itself'.[25]

Although Rousseau agrees with Hobbes that natural man possesses an innate desire for his own welfare and preservation, he disagrees fundamentally with the argument that natural man also has an innate desire for glory. For Rousseau the latter is only possible in an advanced social condition. The life of natural man, being solitary and unsociable, has no place in it for such comparative passions. In an important footnote in the discourse on inequality Rousseau elaborates on this crucial point of difference between himself and philosophers who attribute a natural wickedness to man:

L'Amour propre must not be confused with *l'Amour de soi-même* (love of self); for they differ both in their nature and in their effects. *L'Amour de soi-même* is a natural feeling which leads every animal to look to its own preservation, and which, guided in man by reason and modified by compassion (*la pitié*), creates humanity and virtue. *Amour-propre* is a purely relative and factitious feeling, which arises in society, and leads each individual to make more of himself than any other, causes all the mutual damage men inflict on one another, and is the real source of the sense of honour. This being so, I maintain that, in our primitive condition, in the true state of nature, *l'Amour propre* did not exist.[26]

Amour-propre represents a desire for recognition and the need for self-esteem which can only be found in the evaluation of oneself by others. It is necessary to make a distinction between vanity and pride, for in his work Rousseau does not simply adopt a critical tone towards *amour-propre*, but towards its excessive or inflamed manifestations. Where pride involves seeking recognition in the possession of qualities of intrinsic worth, and is suitable to the creation of a community since these are qualities which are recognized when they are placed in the service of others, vanity consists in the individual attaching itself to objects of no intrinsic value.[27]

In the state of nature each human being is the judge of their own actions simply because they are the only observer of them. In other words, each person is not dependent on any other for their self-estimation. In the state of nature there are no comparative assessments of value between human beings. For this reason, Rousseau argues, natural man knows neither hatred nor the desire for revenge, as these are passions which depend on a sense of injury. Rousseau's argument which follows from this point is remarkably similar to Nietzsche's – that, in considering the moral worth of human actions, the last thing that was considered in the life of early man (what Nietzsche calls the pre-moral period of human existence), were the *intentions* behind human action.[28] Rousseau argues that as it is the intention to hurt, and not the harm done, which constitutes the injury, human beings who neither valued nor compared themselves could do one another much violence when it suited them without experiencing a sense of injury. 'In a word', says Rousseau, 'each man, regarding his fellows almost as he regarded animals of different species, might seize the prey of a weaker or yield up his own to a stronger, and yet consider these acts of violence as mere natural occurrences, without the slightest emotion of insolence or despite, or any other feeling than the joy or grief of success or failure'.[29] Thus, both Rousseau and Nietzsche share the belief that to attribute intentions of wickedness or wrongdoing to human action presupposes the development of a moral sense, a sense which, according to both thinkers, can only be the result of a long process of social development.

We have seen that the basis of Rousseau's disagreement with the philosophers of the natural law school is that they deduce a notion of natural law by attributing to natural man sentiments and passions (such as *amour-propre*) which human beings can only acquire through a process of socialization. However, one wonders how it is possible for Rousseau to arrive at a more convincing definition of natural right. What is to say that his account of the state of nature in terms of man's historical evolution is any more authentic? As we have seen, Rousseau is ambivalent on the precise status of his depiction of the state of nature, informing us that it has the status merely of a legal fiction, but then proceeding to offer us a historical account of human nature as a basis for understanding, if not man's real 'origins', then at least his real 'nature'. The problem can be illuminated by considering Rousseau's understanding of the sentiment of pity.

In the *Discourse* Rousseau speaks of compassion as the pure emotion of nature that is prior to all reflection and from which flows all the later virtues which make social relationships possible. He argues that 'compassion (*la pitié*) is a natural sentiment which, by moderating the activity of *l'amour de soi même* in each individual, contributes to the preservation of the whole species'.[30] It is compassion which in the state of nature takes the place of laws, morals, and virtues, and

which will always prevent a sturdy savage from robbing a weak child or a feeble old man of the sustenance they may have with pain and difficulty acquired, if he sees a possibility of providing for himself by other means: it is this which, instead of inculcating that sublime maxim of rational justice, *Do to others as you would have them do unto you*, inspires all men with that other maxim of natural goodness; *Do good to yourself with as little evil as possible to others*. In a word, it is rather in this natural sentiment than in any subtle arguments that we must look for the cause of that repugnance, which every man would experience in doing evil, even independently of the maxims of education.[31]

As we see from this passage, Rousseau posits *la pitié* in terms of a natural law of the heart, a 'law' which is present in man prior to his reason and his socialization. But is there not a contradiction in Rousseau's account? If man in a state of nature possesses a natural goodness which means he is neither virtuous nor vicious, how is it possible for him to have this natural sentiment of pity which teaches him to pursue his self-preservation in such a way that he will do as little evil to others as possible? How, in the state of nature, will natural man know what 'evil' is?

As we have seen, Rousseau argues that natural man leads a solitary and unsociable existence. Furthermore, he does not act out of any sense of *amour-propre*. Rather, such a sense of the self which arises out of comparison with others, is only present in a state where there exists advanced social relationships. Given these points, it would then seem that there is a fundamental contradiction at the heart of Rousseau's understanding of the notion of pity as a natural sentiment. If, for example, natural man has no sense of himself in relation to others, how is it possible for Rousseau to attribute to natural man a natural repugnance at seeing another sentient being suffer pain or death? Surely such an understanding of pity presupposes the kind of identification between human beings which Rousseau has denied as being present in the life of natural man. In order to be consistent surely it is necessary for Rousseau to argue, not only that man is not naturally wicked, but equally that he is also not naturally compassionate, as both presuppose an identification between human beings which on his own account must be lacking in the state of nature. There would thus appear to be the same kind of illegitimate deduction of natural law at the centre of his political philosophy that he detects in other philosophers. Rousseau has not only argued *contra* Hobbes that man is naturally good, meaning that he is neither good nor evil, but also that he possesses a natural sentiment of pity which provides him with a knowledge, however primitive it may be, of 'evil'.

In order to resolve the contradiction in Rousseau's account it is necessary to recognize a distinction between natural pity and social pity. The crucial difference between the two can be seen in the context in which pity operates and is drawn into play. In a natural state, for example, an individual's sense of itself as a creature of compassion does not arise out of a comparison with others, but out of a spontaneous self-affirmation (like Nietzsche's master type of morality), while in society the individual's disposition to experiencing pity at the sight of pain and suffering is susceptible to corruption at the hands of a perverted *amour-propre*. Here its original goodness is lost, for it only affirms itself by negating the other (as in Nietzsche's type of slave morality).[32] The pity of natural man is 'good' because innocent. It does not arise from a comparison with others, but is a purely physical sensation accompanied by a spontaneous feeling of compassion.

In the account given in *Émile* it is clear that Rousseau's notion of pity rests on the presupposition that individuals' identities are formed in such a way that they have a sense of their own self-identity only through the mediation of another. For Rousseau the relation of the self to the other is able to take place largely on account of the natural sentiment of pity. He thus describes pity in the following terms:

We are drawn towards our fellow-creatures less by our feeling for their joys than for their sorrows; for in them we discern more plainly a nature like our own, and a pledge of their affection for us. If our common needs create a bond of interest our common sufferings create a bond of affection... Imagination puts us more readily in the place of the miserable man than of the happy man... Pity is sweet because, when we put ourselves in the place of one who suffers, we are aware, nevertheless, of the pleasure of not suffering like him.[33]

In *Émile* Rousseau recognizes that in order to experience the sentiment of pity one must have a sense that there exists a form of life which is beyond one's own, that is, the life of the other, and which we can share because of our common sufferings. In this way pity is born, 'the first relative sentiment which touches the human heart according to the order of nature'. To become sensitive and pitiful the child must know that it has fellow-creatures who suffer as it suffers and who can feel the pains it has felt. For this to happen the imagination must be aroused so that the child can be carried outside itself.[34]

However, the role the sentiment of pity plays in Rousseau's thought is both ironic and, like that of natural law, paradoxical. Pity is a comparative sentiment or passion which involves imagining the sentiments felt by another by placing oneself in their shoes. The way to prevent envy and excessive *amour-propre* is, ironically, though the cultivation of pity by which we experience a feeling of superiority in relation to one who suffers. The sensation of pity is 'sweet' because when we use our imagination to identify with the suffering of another we realize that it could quite easily be us. Pity is thus the only moral sentiment which partakes of the characteristics of love of oneself and *amour-propre* simultaneously. Roger Masters argues that pity is prevented from degenerating into *amour-propre*, however, as it depends on an imaginative transportation of the self into the shoes of a less fortunate being. However, Nietzsche is astute in showing how the sentiment of pity is far from being an innocent sentiment, how expressing pity is often equal to expressing contempt towards the independence of another, and how the seemingly altruistic sentiment of pity can be used to conceal the resentment of the weak individual. The paradoxical role of pity in Rousseau's thought is to be found in the fact that although the sentiment plays a crucial role in his critique of philosophers such as Hobbes, its effectiveness must be doubted on account of it being a buried sentiment in civilized humanity. In the natural savage, pity is a sentiment which arises spontaneously from a physical sensation, but its presence is both 'vivid' and 'obscure' (vivid on account of it being the result of an immediate physical sensation, and obscure because to be fully realizable it requires an act of imagination that is lacking in primitive man), while in civilized man it requires an act of imagination that is completely absent owing to the reign of vanity in public life.[35] Thus, in the domain of nature, pity is spontaneous but ineffective, for it is without a sense of justice which would add reflection to it, while in the realm of society it can be cultivated but is easily corrupted.[36]

Reflection on the use and abuse of pity plays an important role in Rousseau's thinking on the problem of civilization. It is the sentiment which accounts for our capacity for social relationships and which serves to account for Rousseau's belief in the possibility of establishing a harmonious society in which the particular and the universal are united in a general will. For the cultivation of the general will is dependent on an act of imaginative identification between the self and others which, like pity, transports the self outside of itself. My argument assumes that a reading of the *Social Contract* in terms of a historical problematic is possible, that is, that the book represents Rousseau's response to the fundamental problematic of the second discourse of how a new social ethic of solidarity and community is possible in the wake of the ruinous subjectivism and individualism of civil society which has brought about the rule of inequality based on pride and vanity. Although it is a reading which many would dispute, I would wish to maintain that such a reading is an apposite one when viewed in the context of Rousseau's attempt to establish human sociality on the basis of the sentiment of pity viewed in terms of a natural law of the heart. However, it is important to appreciate that, although pity is recognized by Rousseau to be an important emotive force in establishing an identity between human beings who have become alienated from each other, it is not sufficient in itself for the establishment of a new social order based on moral or ethical foundations. Pity is too precarious a sentiment to play this role; instead, the only way in which social harmony and order can be brought about is through the rule of justice.

MORALITY

In the first part of the *Discourse on the Origin of Inequality* Rousseau claims to have established that in his natural state man possesses four intrinsic qualities or properties: a concern for self-preservation, a sentiment of pity, a capacity for perfectibility, and the capacity for free agency. In the second part of the essay Rousseau turns his attention to the process of man's socialization. His major argument is that man only becomes fully moral through a process of socialization which takes place in terms of historical development. Thus, in contrast to a philosopher like Locke, for example, Rousseau argues that in the state of nature man cannot be regarded as a moral being.[37] Rather, natural man is only *potentially* moral; his faculties of language, reason, and perhaps even his conscience, are superfluous in the state of nature, and can only be activated and awakened when he enters a social state. For Rousseau it is the capacity for free agency which distinguishes man from the rest of the animal kingdom. The ability to will, and not to will, has to be considered as one of the first operations of the human soul in its 'primitive' state. Through its possession of a free will the human creature is able to learn from experience and to modify its behaviour. By not being simply a creature of instinct the human animal is able to defer and train its impulses. In addition to this faculty of choosing, man possesses a faculty of self-improvement which is deemed to be inherent in the species and in the individual and by which, along with the aid of circumstances, the human animal develops the rest of its faculties and raises itself above its animal nature. By the term 'morality' Rousseau simply means the way in which human action is conceived in terms of social interaction, that is, the manner in which human beings arrive at an understanding of the moral value and significance of their actions through the mediation of social relations.

The main stages of Rousseau's argument can be summarized as follows:[33]

(a) In the state of nature man lives in isolation and has only a few elementary and easily satisfied needs. Human beings begin to associate and create a provisional order when they discover the utility of labour.

(b) As a result of technical progress a first revolution comes about as human beings begin to build shelters and families begin to stay together in groups. Humanity enters a patriarchal period.

(c) The use of language and reason develops from the consolidation of the first social relations. By an unhappy chance, human beings discover the division of labour which enables them to make the transition from a primitive subsistence economy to an economy of productive development. The second revolution in man's evolution is thus a result of material development, the appearance of metallurgy and agriculture: 'It was iron and corn', Rousseau informs us, 'which first civilized men and ruined humanity'.[39] Now that human beings have reached the stage of economic development whereby they can produce more than they actually need, they vie for the surplus, as they want not only to use things, but desire to possess and own them. In other words, they are no longer concerned with merely satisfying their present needs, but now have a sense of their future wants and desires. They have reached a state of conflicting interests in which competition and rivalry reign.

(d) We thereby reach the unstable stage in man's evolution which necessitates the creation of civil society and social order, and which had been described by Hobbes in terms of a war of all against all. Rousseau's argument *contra* Hobbes is that this warlike condition is not the condition of abstract individuals but rather that of individuals who have undergone a particular process of socialization. The social contract is set up by the strong in order to bring peace and order to the unstable state they are in, to the threatening anarchy, and who succeed in persuading the weak and disadvantaged that such a contract is as much to their advantage as it is to that of the strong. The 'rich man', urged by necessity,

conceived at length the profoundest plan that ever entered the mind of man: this was to employ in his favour the forces of those who attacked him, to make allies of his adversaries, to inspire them with different maxims, and to give them other institutions as favourable to himself as the law of nature was unfavourable... after having represented to his neighbours the horror of a situation which armed every man against the rest, and made their possessions as burdensome to them as their wants, and in which no safety could be expected either in riches or in poverty he readily devised plausible arguments to make them close with his design, 'Let us join', he said, 'to guard the weak from oppression, to restrain the ambitious, and to secure to every man the possession of what belongs to him: let us institute rules of justice and peace, to which all without exception may be obliged to conform; rules that may in some measure make amends for the caprices of fortune, by subjecting equally the powerful and the weak to the observance of reciprocal obligations. Let us, in a word, instead of turning our forces against ourselves, collect them in a supreme power which may govern by wise laws, protect and defend all the members of the association...and maintain eternal harmony among us'...Such was, or may well have been, the origin of society and law, which bound new fetters on the poor, and gave new powers to the rich; which irretrievably destroyed natural liberty, eternally fixed the law of property and inequality, converted clever usurpation into irrevocable right, and, for the advantage of a few ambitious individuals, subjected all mankind to perpetual labour, slavery, and wretchedness.[40]

Rousseau disputes the argument that the origin of political society can be explained by the conquest of the powerful, or by the association of the weak. For both of these accounts fail to explain how society gains a *legitimate* basis. If the right of conquest is used to account for the birth of society, then it is necessary to explain how such a state differs from a war of all against all. If one adopts the second account, one is faced with the difficulty of defining the terms 'strong' and 'weak', where one should really employ the terms 'rich' and 'poor'. Rousseau argues that the poor would have no good reason to form their own association as they have nothing to exchange except their freedom, and it would have been absurd for them to give up their only good.[41] What we have with the arrival of modern civil society, however, is only the *appearance* of legitimacy.

After tracing the passage from the state of nature to civil society, Rousseau asks us to consider the vast distance which separates the two states. He suggests that, in tracing this slow succession, we will find the solution to a number of problems in politics and ethics. Above all, he argues, we will discover that human beings are different in different ages. We will learn that,

the passions of men insensibly change their very nature; why our wants and pleasures in the end seek new objects; and why, the original man having vanished by degrees, society offers to us only an assembly of artificial men and factitious passions, which are the work of all these new relations, and without any real foundation in nature.[42]

Rousseau's fundamental point is that, whereas original man finds his source of pleasure only within himself, artificial, or so-called civilized, man is totally dependent on the opinion of others for his identity. Rousseau's concluding point is that man's desire for power and reputation – what Hobbes called 'glory' – is not at all 'natural', but is rather the product of a certain process of socialization.

A major point of contention in Rousseau-interpretation is whether Rousseau provides a materialist or an idealist account of man's social degeneration in the second discourse. It has been argued by one commentator that Rousseau's argument on the changes which take place as men become transformed from natural beings into artificial ones rests on a belief that, while based in material conditions, man's corruptness is fundamentally the result of his entering into social relations with others. If man is naturally good in a state of nature this can only be on account of his independence from social relationships. In other words, the root cause of the problem is not the material interdependence and inequality brought about by man's economic development, but rather the phenomenon Rousseau describes as *amour-propre*.[43] This would seem to suggest that, for Rousseau, the social bond can never be made legitimate, and that a return to nature is the only possible course of action open to man if he is to once again become 'good'.

Rousseau's discussion of morality would seem to lend support to this interpretation. In the *Discourse*, for example, commenting on the gradual rise of social interaction through the establishment of families and permanent settlements, it is argued that:

As ideas and feelings succeeded one another, and heart and head were brought into play, men continued to lay aside their original wildness...They accustomed themselves to assemble before their huts round a large tree; singing and dancing, the true offspring of love and leisure, became the amusement, or rather the occupation, of men and women with nothing else to do. Each one began to consider the rest, and to wish to be considered in turn; and thus a value came to be attached to public esteem. Whoever sang or danced best, whoever was the handsomest, the strongest, the most dexterous, the most eloquent, came to be of most consideration; and this was the first step towards inequality and at the same time towards vice. From these first distinctions arose on the one side vanity and contempt and on the other shame and envy: and the fermentation caused by these new leavens ended by producing the combinations fatal to innocence and happiness. As soon as men began to value one another, and the idea of consideration gained a foothold in the mind, every one put a claim in for it...hence arose the first obligations of civility even among savages; and every intended injury became an affront...Thus, as every man punished the contempt shown him by others, in proportion to his own opinion of himself, revenge became terrible, and men bloody and cruel.[44]

The human being described in this passage stands in marked contrast to the natural man who is confined by instinct and reason to the sole care of his own preservation, and whose actions towards others are restrained by a natural compassion from doing any intentional injury to them. As soon as human beings form together in such a way that social relations become prominent in their interaction, we witness the birth of morality. Morality for Rousseau is the domain of human interaction and social relationships. As he writes in *Émile*:

Man cannot always live alone, and it will be hard therefore to remain good; and this difficulty will increase of necessity as his relations with others are extended. For this reason, above all, the dangers of social life demand that the necessary skill and care shall be devoted to guarding the human heart against the depravity which springs from fresh needs.[45]

These passages would seem to confirm the argument that Rousseau explains man's corrupt state as being a result of his entry into social relationships. However, given, as we shall see in our examination of the *Social Contract*, that Rousseau holds that man only becomes fully human when he becomes a member of society, this argument lacks plausibility. It is necessary, I believe, to recognize a distinction in Rousseau's thought between those social relations which enable man to become 'good' (virtuous), and those which serve to disable his social abilities and therefore imperil his potential goodness. The fundamental aim of Rousseau's political philosophy is not to advocate a return to nature, but to show in what way the social bond can be made legitimate. For Rousseau this entails society being established on the basis of moral relations in which mutual reciprocity and recognition predominate in social interaction.[46]

This argument finds support in the *Discourse* when Rousseau tells us unequivocally that, as far as his investigation into social development is concerned, what he calls 'the evils' of rivalry and competition, together with the desire to profit at the expense of others, are the 'first effects of property, and the inseparable attendants of growing inequality'.[47] Moreover, Rousseau concludes the second and final part of the discourse by informing us that it is sufficient that he has shown that corruption is not by any means the original state of nature, but rather the result of the inequality which society produces, transforming and altering 'all our natural inclinations'.[48] Thus, Rousseau concludes his investigation into man's historical development as a social and moral being by arguing that the social contract which has been set up between the strong and the weak is an illegitimate one because it rests on the basis of unequal social relationships and, consequently, unjust moral

obligations. Rousseau believes he is able to show beyond doubt that
the social contract is illegitimate because it is not in accordance with
man's true nature. In one of the most powerful statements ever
addressed to modern humanity, and that it has had to bear witness
to, he writes:

It follows from this exposition that, as there is hardly any inequality in the
state of nature, all the inequality which now prevails owes its force and
growth to the development of our faculties and the progress of the human
mind, and becomes at last permanent and legitimate by the establishment
of property and laws. Secondly, it follows that moral inequality, authorized
by positive right alone, clashes with natural right, whenever it is not
proportionate to physical inequality...it is plainly contrary to the law of
nature, however defined, that children should command old men, fools wise
men, and that the privileged few should gorge themselves with superfluities,
while the starving multitude are in need of the basic necessities of life.[49]

There would appear to be only one solution to the problem of
civilization as Rousseau has defined it: not to return to nature,
which is impossible – the possibility of returning to the forests to live
among bears is explicitly ruled out by Rousseau[50] – but to outline a
society in which the values of equality and liberty rule in such a way
that individuals interact with one another in terms of free and equal
social relationships. In other words, what is needed according to
Rousseau is a *political* solution.

It has to be admitted, however, that there exists within Rousseau's
writings a fundamental ambiguity over the nature of man's corrupt
state. It cannot be denied that there are passages in his work where
it would seem that he is questioning the very authenticity of all, and
any, social relationships. This is clearly apparent, as we have seen,
in Rousseau's admission in his *Reveries*, that he would only be happy
in a social environment if he could be rendered invisible. I do not
think it is wise for any interpreter of Rousseau to resolve once and for
all the ambiguity which lies at the heart of his thinking on the
problem of the social domain; instead, I believe that it is better to
preserve the richness of his thought with all its paradoxes and
tensions, for they capture and illuminate the paradoxes and tensions
which define our experience of what it means to exist as 'modern'.

CONCLUSION

Rousseau was not to develop a 'solution' (if that is how it can be described) to the problem of civilization, which he had posed in such brilliantly ominous terms in the second discourse, until eight years later, providing an account of both the moral education of man in *Émile* and the political education of the citizen in the *Social Contract*. Rousseau's critique of civilization demands a twofold reform, that of society in the individual and of the individual in society.[51] In the second discourse no satisfactory resolution of the problem is offered, although the idea of a return to nature is firmly ruled out. In *Émile* Rousseau makes it clear that the choice between man and citizen is not between nature and society, but that society itself is the source of the conflict. The best social institutions are those which know how to denature the individual so as to replace its absolute existence with a relative one, transforming the 'me' into a 'we', that is, from a private person into a citizen. Émile is someone who lives *in* civil society, but is not *of* civil society.[52] He is what a human being would become 'were it historically possible to impose only that degeneration necessary for a human and cultural existence'.[53] In order to create a natural man (someone who leads a simple and honest life), it is not a question of producing a savage deep within the depths of the forest, but rather of creating a social being whose sense of self is not determined by the passions and opinions of others. In other words, it is a question of producing a sovereign individual that is both autonomous *and* moral – or rather, moral on account of being autonomous.

Rousseau's distinction between goodness and virtue is important in this context. In a state of nature man is good, not virtuous. The citizen in a civil state is not merely good but virtuous. It is as a citizen that man is able to become a moral being capable of virtue, not merely goodness. Goodness is innocence, simply consisting in not harming others, and exists in an isolated, asocial state where there is an absence of wickedness. Virtue on the other hand, is dependent upon education for its cultivation, denoting mastery over the passions, and can only exist in a social state where it is dependent on recognition by others who live uncorrupted in a community not dominated by the rule of vanity.[54] The good man living in society is freer than the natural man, since he lives as a self-legislating being. But here we encounter another paradox at the centre of Rousseau's thought: to be fully natural man must be capable of being a citizen.

He is to be educated for society, but not by it. The education of Émile thus reveals the full extent of Rousseau's profound ambivalence towards society. The task of education is internally contradictory for its aim is to educate the individual *for* society by preserving it *from* all social influence.

Nietzsche was quite mistaken in attributing to Rousseau a naive and ahistorical desire to return to nature. Instead, it is important to appreciate that in Rousseau it is education, both ethical and political, which is assigned the task of transforming human nature and overcoming corruption.[55] Before turning to examine how the notion of the general will operates in Rousseau's thought, however, I wish to conclude this chapter by considering the view that the importance of the second discourse lies in Rousseau's placing of the problem of history at the centre of political theory.

This view has been most persuasively argued for in recent years by Asher Horowitz in his important study on the concepts of nature and history in Rousseau.[56] 'For Rousseau', Horowitz writes, 'the problem of politics must be grasped in the context of the contradictory unfolding of human nature as a historical process'.[57] Horowitz argues that Rousseau moves away from the Enlightenment and from the theory of natural law which is based on the idea of a static and transcendent human nature. The consequence of this, it is argued, is that Rousseau is led to abandon an abstract opposition between nature and artifice, replacing it with a historical and dialectical theory of human nature: 'A historical existence is one in which the spontaneity and immediacy of the instinctual impulses of the savage man give way increasingly to the fetters, constraints, and compulsions of the artifice governing not only modern European culture but culture itself'.[58]

To a large extent Horowitz's reading is a revision of the debate on the whole question of the status of natural law in Rousseau. But while it is the case that Rousseau is a deeply historical thinker who radicalizes the notion of natural law, it would be mistaken to infer from his historicization of human nature that he simply abandons a notion of natural law. On the contrary, Rousseau requires such a notion in order to mount his potent attack on the excessive degeneration and corruption of modern civilization. As he makes clear in the preface to the second discourse, unless we have an understanding and knowledge of natural man (which is only possible through a study of man's natural faculties and their 'successive development'), then it is impossible for us to pass judgement on our present corrupt state. Rousseau requires the concept of history, not simply in order to abandon the notion of natural law, but in order to challenge the political theory put forward by thinkers such as Hobbes. By showing that the human species has a history and that what we take to be 'natural' is in fact 'social', Rousseau is able to challenge Hobbes' construal of the state of nature as a war of all against all. The force of Rousseau's critique of Hobbes stems largely from his picture of original man in possession of pity and natural goodness.

In the end, therefore, Rousseau's construal of the problem of civilization is both puzzling and disturbing. For if the state of nature is, strictly speaking, pre-human, sub-human even, it seems not only absurd to wish to go back to such a state but equally strange to use it as a norm for judging humanity. Man's humanity is the result of a historical process, but the product of this process fills Rousseau with both revulsion and despair. Rousseau may have written the second discourse in order to arouse modern men out of their complacency and stir them to action; but equally, the effect of its reading and teaching could be to fill men with loathing and contempt for humanity, leading them to engage in a bloody politics of revenge and resentment.

Implicit in Rousseau's reading of the problem of civilization is a moral interpretation of the meaning of history and historical development. History is only meaningful to the extent that it leads to a moral end: namely, man as an ethical, self-legislating and autonomous agent. But if one loses one's faith in history, as Rousseau did, then one's construal of the problem of civilization must culminate either in a paralysis of the will, or in an attempt to transcend the problem of history altogether. Both of these positions can be found in Rousseau; the former, for example, in the autobiographical works like the *Reveries*, the latter in a work such as the *Social Contract*. To what extent, we need to ask, is Rousseau's response to the problem of history, which I have identified as the principal theme of the second discourse, in the form of the notion of the general will an attempt to construct a will which is so abstract and so pure that it can never be subjected to the vicissitudes and vagaries of social and historical life?

CHAPTER 3

Squaring the circle: Rousseau on the General Will

Putting law over men is a problem in politics comparable to
that of squaring the circle in geometry.

Rousseau, *The Government of Poland* (1771–2)

ON THE 'SOCIAL CONTRACT'

The opening lines of the first chapter of Rousseau's *Du Contrat
social* can fairly be described as the motto which has inspired most
the modern revolutionary spirit. 'Man is born free', Rousseau
writes, 'and everywhere he is in chains'.[1] In this work Rousseau is
less concerned with the origins of man's social slavery, than with how
the social bond can be made legitimate. The idea that the famous
opening sentence of the first chapter of the book advocates a return
to nature is part of Rousseauian mythology. In fact, it is Rousseau's
aim to show in what way the social bond can lay claim to a
legitimate hold on men's hearts. The work is an inquiry into the
principles of *political* right.[2] In other words, Rousseau's concern is
not so much with studying existing governments and social practices,
but more importantly with examining the foundations of legitimate
government and showing the legitimate basis of political obligation.
Rousseau's investigation into the principles of political right is one
which leads him to ask what form of government, and what type of
society, would bring about not the rule of corruption, but that of
virtue. The work is premised, therefore, on Rousseau's belief in
man's natural goodness; without this belief such an inquiry would
neither be possible nor worthwhile.

It has to be appreciated, however, that Rousseau's inquiry into
political right is also premised on the claim that the social order,
although a sacred right, is a right which does not come from nature
and must, therefore, be founded on conventions. This explains why

the work is presented in terms of an inquiry into the principles of 'political' right, and not into principles of 'natural' right. Thus, in the opening chapters of the work Rousseau dismisses the claim that legitimate authority – political right – can be founded on notions such as the right of the strongest and slavery: 'Since no man has a natural authority over his follows', Rousseau writes, 'and force creates no right, we must conclude that conventions form the basis of all legitimate authority among men'.[3] Against Hobbes, however, he argues that the social contract cannot be based on a renunciation of man's liberty to the authority of the State. To renounce liberty in this way is to renounce one's status as a human being, since it is one's capacity for free agency which gives a person their humanity. Moreover, such an alienation of one's liberty involves removing all morality from man's actions. He thus rejects Hobbes's solution to the problem of sovereignty which presents us with a stark choice between absolute authority on the one side and unlimited obedience on the other. In a condition in which a natural right of conquest or slavery lies at the foundation of political authority, Rousseau says, one sees no more than a master–slave relationship, not a people and its ruler, but an aggregation instead of an association of human beings. From this argument Rousseau informs us that he will move on to examine that act by which a people becomes an association, for this is the only true foundation of society. In attempting to overcome Hobbes's stark choice between absolutism and anarchism with the notion of the conventional general will, however, Rousseau constructs a model of legitimate political authority which reveals both absolutist and anarchist tendencies.[4]

In introducing a notion of the social compact, Rousseau supposes that individuals 'have reached the point at which the obstacles in the way of their preservation in the state of nature show their power of resistance to be greater than the resources at the disposal of each individual for his maintenance in that state'.[5] In other words, Rousseau premises his argument on the belief that the individual can no longer subsist on its own in the state of nature and must out of necessity join with others to form a community. However, having made this point, Rousseau is immediately faced with a huge difficulty. If such a compact is to be formed, how can it be created in such a way that the individual finds in it not the sacrifice of its natural liberty, but its fulfilment? In other words, what moral reasons can be given to the pre-political individual for leaving the state of nature and joining a society in which he will be brought into relationships resting on interdependence with others? Rousseau states his difficulty in a well-known passage in which he writes that:

'The problem is to find a form of association which will defend and protect with the whole common force the person and goods of each associate, and in which each, while uniting himself with all, may still obey himself alone, and remain as free as before'. This is the fundamental problem of which the social contract provides the solution.[6]

Rousseau is attempting nothing less than the resolution of the fundamental antinomies of modern political thought: liberty and authority, the individual and society (man and citizen), freedom and necessity, desire and reason. Through the social contract man is to elevate himself into a moral being. Rousseau's argument presupposes that through this creative act of political formation there will no longer be any split between the interests of the individual and those of the community, but that they will now be identical. On account of this it is stated that, in constituting such a political form, the social contract should demand the, 'total alienation of each associate, together with all his rights, to the whole community; for in the first place, as each gives himself absolutely, the conditions are the same for all; and, this being the case, no one has any interest in making them burdensome to others'.[7] In other words, the individual of the state of nature will not simply lose the independence he enjoyed in this state, but will gain another form of independence, the independence that is gained through dependence, through being a member of a moral community based on free and equal social relationships. With this account of the social contract Rousseau's inversion of Hobbes is complete.

   Rousseau accomplishes this inversion of Hobbes by attributing to the 'moral–collective body', that has been set up through the act of association, the status of a sovereign power. He employs the term 'general will' to describe this form of sovereignty in which there exists a complete identity between the individual and the moral–collective body. Instead of the individual will being renounced, as in Hobbes's account of sovereignty, it is claimed to be realized in Rousseau's account. In Hobbes, the problem of the existence of a plurality of wills is resolved by the creation of one particular will which is vested with absolute power. By contrast, Rousseau seeks a solution in which the plurality of particular wills create a community in which there exists an identity between the individual and the universal in a general will. In fact, as a number of commentators have noted, Rousseau's employment of the term 'social contract' is misleading in this respect, since the association that is to be created through it does not depend for its existence, for its 'will', on a contractual relationship between 'rulers' on the one hand and 'ruled' on the other. On Rousseau's understanding of the social contract there is no such distinction. In obeying the general will, for example, the individuals of Rousseau's social contract are merely obeying themselves; in other words, they are not obeying at all but commanding, they are not enchained but free. The community that is created through the act of association is not itself party to the contract, as there is no exchange of power in this act of sovereignty between community and individuals.[8] If this is the case, then why does Rousseau appeal to a notion of contract? The answer lies in the original solution he provides to the antinomical nature of modern political life, chiefly that of the relation between the individual and society.

Rousseau requires the notion of a social contract in order to account for the formation of the general will in the first place. The most striking aspect of Rousseau's formulation of the problem of the social contract, however, is not that it advocates the subjugation of the particular will by the general will, or that it rests on an abstract and purely formal unification of particular wills – both common criticisms – but rather that it appeals directly to the isolated, autonomous self of civil society depicted by Hobbes and Locke as a way of constituting a new ethico-political community in which the particular and the universal are united in a common identity. One of the most interesting pieces in Rousseau's writings in this regard is a piece which originally formed chapter two of the first version of the *Social Contract*, known as the 'Geneva Manuscript', but which was discarded by Rousseau in the final published version. The piece is entitled 'The General Society of the Human Race'.[9] Here Rousseau addresses himself to the pre-political individual who is strong and independent, and who thinks he has no need of a community. It is not a question of teaching this independent being what *justice is*, but rather of showing him what interest he has in *being just*. 'Where is the man', Rousseau asks 'who can separate himself from himself? If self-preservation is the first precept of nature, can he be forced to consider in this way, the human race in general and to impose on himself duties whose relation with his own individual constitution he cannot see?...Do we not need to show how his personal interest demands that he submit himself to the general will?'[10] By what kind of reasoning could the independent being achieve this? How can he overcome the conflict between his inclinations and his obeying of the law? How can he override his own inner voice and conscience? Rousseau's response is to imagine a society which provides the independent human being with the kind of moral education that is absent in the state of nature.

The transition from the state of nature to a civil state emancipates the individual from the tyranny of his desires and gives him the freedom of reason: 'Instead of a stupid and unimaginative animal', Rousseau informs us, society now provides us with 'an intelligent being and a man'.[11] Rousseau explains the terms of the social contract by saying that, while individuals lose through it their natural liberty and unlimited right to things, they gain by it civil liberty and the ownership of all they possess. In other words, it is only by participating in the making of a social contract based on the principles of liberty and equality that human beings can gain all the advantages which a thinker like Locke construes as already in existence in the state of nature. For Rousseau a human being's entrance into the social state entails a profound transformation in their nature. The most important thing he gains by undergoing this transformation, according to Rousseau, is the acquisition of moral liberty, which alone makes a person master of him- or herself. It is at this point in his argument that Rousseau offers his definition of moral liberty in terms of self-mastery: 'the mere impulse of our appetites is slavery, while obedience to a law we have prescribed to ourselves is liberty'.[12]

The opening sentence of Rousseau's inquiry into the principles of political right shows that his prime concern is with justice. Rousseau's intention is to inquire whether if 'in the civil order, there can be any sure and legitimate rule of administration, men being taken as they are and laws as they might be'. The aim is to unite 'right' and 'interest' so that justice and utility coincide, so that what the individual wills and achieves by self-mastery is both just *and* useful to its self-interest.[13] In the 'Geneva Manuscript' Rousseau had referred to the constitution of the body politic, not to its 'administration'. But as Maurizio Viroli points out, by 'administration' Rousseau does not mean the management of private or public business, but the order of the State, namely the political or constitutional laws which spell out the relations between governors and governed. Thus, the task is to identify the rule which will provide the backbone of a just constitution.[14] A just constitution is one which does not rest on force to support its rules and laws, but which satisfies the needs and desires of the members of society, and which is something more than a mere collection of individuals who have simply come together to place their pursuit of private gain and self-interest on a more secure footing. The tension in Rousseau's model of the just polity stems from his attempt to arrive at a conception of the well-ordered society from individualistic premises, for it is a society in which the pursuit of virtue in public or civic affairs is not only recognized to be the highest good, but which requires the individual to constantly sacrifice their self-interest. It is thus the task of an education in citizenship and in civic virtues to persuade the strong, independent human being who believes he can attain freedom in his lofty isolation, that true liberty is attained when one becomes a moral agent, a citizen acting in society in accordance with the reign of virtue. Rousseau in fact is faced with the same problem which faces Socrates in the *Republic*, that of convincing the individual of the nobleness and rightness of the moral way of life. Natural law is completely ineffective simply because human beings do not naturally follow the precepts of justice, since they find it more profitable to do wrong than to lead a moral life.[15]

In order for the unity of justice and utility to be achieved, several conditions have to be established, such as, for example, building into the system of justice a principle of reciprocity (of rights and duties) which ensures that all citizens enjoy juridical equality and a symmetrical relation with the deliberations of the sovereign body. Thus, in seeking his own interest, the individual can only do so by pursuing the common interest, for they are one and the same. It is in the interest of everyone to be governed by universal laws, for only in this way can justice and equality be secured and guaranteed.[16]

Viroli wishes to defend Rousseau against Hegel's critique that he has failed to resolve the antinomies of modern political life. Hegel's argument *contra* Rousseau is that the notion of the general will, in which the opposition between the particular and the universal has supposedly been overcome, is not a rational universal will, but little more than the sum of individual wills. Clearly this is a distortion of Rousseau's position which separates the idea of the 'will of all'

(which would be a mere aggregate of particular wills) from that of
the general will properly understood. Viroli argues that Rousseau's
politics are based on the principle of the sovereignty of law, and
hence of the *rational* will, and not as Hegel supposes merely of the
individual will.[17] However, this vigorous and insightful defence of
Rousseau presupposes that there can be the identity between the
particular and the universal required for the existence of a general
will, not simply from Lockean premises of an abstract individualism,
but from Rousseau's own premises of the autonomous individual
who is in possession of free will and conscience. It is here that we can
see the relevance and pertinence of Nietzsche's argument on the
mutual exclusivity of autonomy and morality, because it shows that
autonomy is always excessive, and that genuine independence
demands that the individual does not conform to an abstract general
will, but proudly accepts responsibility for its deed and for who it
is and is to become.

SOVEREIGNTY: THE 'GENERAL WILL'

The notion of the general will is without doubt the most complex
and controversial aspect of Rousseau's moral and political thought
– comparable in this regard, one might suggest, with Nietzsche's
doctrine of the will to power. To a certain extent it is fair to say that
the role the notion of the general will plays in Rousseau's political
philosophy is the same as that which the notion of natural law plays
in the political thought of Hobbes and Locke. For Rousseau it is the
source of law and of sovereignty; indeed, it is, on his account, the
basis of political right. The most controversial aspect of the notion of
general will stems from Rousseau's argument, in the first book of the
Social Contract, that whoever refuses to obey the general will shall be
'forced to be free'.[18] For many such a statement proves that the
doctrine of the general will is a tyrannical one which prefigures the
totalitarian regimes of the modern age, including that of the French
Revolution during the reign of Terror.[19] In this discussion I want to
consider to what extent the complexities and tensions of the notion
stem from Rousseau's attempt to ground morality on the basis of the
individual will *universalizing* its interest. There are important
differences, as well as important similarities, between Rousseau and
Kant in their formulations of morality, and these must be recognized
when considering to what extent it is possible to locate in Nietzsche's
argument against Kant the basis of his critique of Rousseau. I shall

argue that it is possible to defend Rousseau's principle of the general will as an attempt at a novel politicization of ethics, but that in his formulation of it the necessity of a complete identity between the particular and the universal obliterates the ethical principle of autonomy informing the political ideal of the general will.

The general will seeks to establish society on the basis of common interest. If the clashing of particular wills makes the establishment of societies necessary, it is the agreement of these wills which makes it actually possible. It is the common element in these different interests of particular wills which constitutes the social tie or bond, and without which society could not exist. It is this idea of a general will as the will of the common interest which Rousseau develops into a theory of sovereignty. 'I hold then', he writes:

> that Sovereignty, being nothing less than the exercise of the general will, can never be alienated, and that the Sovereign, who is no less than a collective being, cannot be represented except by himself: the power (*le pouvoir*) may be transmitted but not the will.[20]

Society on Rousseau's account is the product of the free rational will. This implies that the origins and foundations of society lie in a convention; in other words, society is a human artifact. However, this argument was not original to Rousseau, but is equally present in the deduction of civil society found in Hobbes and Locke. The originality of Rousseau's political philosophy lies in his argument *contra* Hobbes and Locke, that sovereignty is inalienable.

Rousseau's theory of sovereignty shows the importance he places on the problem of power in political theory.[21] The notion of sovereignty refers to the ultimate source of political authority and power; it is the *summa potestas* (supreme power). As soon as society comes into existence as a moral–collective body, the question of power assumes paramount importance. It is from the establishment of this common force that society derives its stability and strength. The nature and source of sovereignty are determined by the kind of association which is created at the moment of the social contract. The freedom of each individual can only be guaranteed by the power of the whole community understood as a common force. Sovereignty is essentially the power to make law. As laws are the conditions of civil association, the people who are subject to them must at the same time be their author. Sovereignty must lie with the whole body of citizens, and its interest must always be general. Rousseau clarifies his argument in the following manner:

What then, strictly speaking, is an act of Sovereignty? It is not a convention between a superior and an inferior, but a convention between the body and each one of its members. It is legitimate because based on the social contract, and it is equitable, because it is common to all; useful because it can have no other object than the general good, and stable, because guaranteed by the public force and the supreme power (*le pouvoir suprême*). So long as subjects have to submit only to conventions of this kind, they obey no one but their own will.[22]

When viewed in this light, Rousseau argues, it will be seen that there is no real renunciation in the social contract on the part of individuals, that the condition these individuals now find themselves in is far preferable to that found in the state of nature: 'Instead of a renunciation, they have made an advantageous exchange'.[23] The exchange consists in gaining a secure existence in place of the old precarious way of living in the pre-political state; in place of natural independence there is now moral liberty.

If sovereignty is inalienable it is equally indivisible, for either the will is general or it is not, that is, it is either the will of the whole body or only of part of it: 'In the first case', Rousseau writes, 'the will, when declared, is an act of Sovereignty and constitutes law: in the second, it is merely a particular will, or an act of magistracy, and at the most of decree'. Sovereignty, therefore, resides in the unity of force and will, that is, of legislative power and executive power (*puissance*).[24] Were sovereignty to be either alienated or divided, the association or community which has been set up would, in effect, be dissolved and human beings would return to the state of nature. Rousseau's notion of the general will would seem to present us not with the stark choice between Hobbesian absolutism and anarchism, but between the absolute sovereign power of the general will and the amoral state of nature. Does this not show that the general will is indeed absolutist?[25]

In his *A Discourse on Political Economy* Rousseau defines virtue as the conformity of particular wills with the general will.[26] In the *Social Contract*, however, the general will is no longer simply construed in terms of the sum of all individual wills, for it is recognized that there is 'a great deal of difference between the will of all and the general will'.[27] The difference between the will of all and the general will is that whereas the former takes private interest into account the latter aims at the common interest of the whole community. This must mean, therefore, that the general will cannot be taken to mean merely the sum of particular wills – 'the will of all' that Rousseau speaks of – but must be something over and above this. In order for the general will to be truly general, that is independent of any particular will, it must have its own independent existence. But does this not mean that it merely assumes the identity of a very large particular will? According to Rousseau it does not, since the aim of the general will is to pursue the common good – however defined – and this is a good which must be in the interests of all the members of the community, even if it is neither identical with their own particular wills nor reducible to the sum of their particular wills. The generality of the general will refers, therefore, to the common interest which is common to all the particular wills of the members of the community. In other words, the general will does not obliterate different interests but rather presupposes their existence.[28] On this point of the generality of the general will, Rousseau writes:

To be really general the general will must be so in its object as well as in its essence; that it must come from all and apply to all; and that it loses its natural rectitude when it is directed to some particular and determinate object, because in such a case we are judging of something foreign to us, and have no true principle of equity to guide us… Thus, just as a particular will cannot stand for the general will, the general will, in turn, changes its nature, when its object is particular, and, as general, cannot pronounce on a man or a fact.[29]

What makes the will general as such is, according to Rousseau, not so much the number of people who are constituted by it, but the common interest uniting them. Its fundamental principle must necessarily be that of equality:

From whatever side we approach our principle, we reach the same conclusion, that the social compact sets up among the citizens an equality of such a kind, that they all bind themselves to observe the same conditions and should therefore all enjoy the same rights. Thus, from the very nature of the compact, every act of Sovereignty, that is, every authentic act of the general will, binds or favours all the citizens equally.[30]

As a number of commentators have pointed out, the inequality Rousseau attacks is the type founded on accident and caprice, not merit and virtue. As Judith Shklar has shown, the societies Rousseau most admired, such as Sparta and Rome, were aristocracies based on a clear distinction between rulers and ruled, in which the striving for distinction formed an integral part of the public-spirited nature of their polities. Thus, it is not distinctions which Rousseau attacks as such, but those based solely on wealth. 'The will against inequality', she argues, 'is a will against wealth and privilege, not against political rulership'.[31] A recent commentator argues that the equality which Rousseau thinks necessary to a just society is not arithmetical, ascribing the same to everyone, but proportional or geometric. Thus, for example, public honour and esteem should be commensurate with the degree of individual merit. A major problem, however, facing Rousseau's thought, is that of how to make equal degrees of liberty compatible with a principle of hierarchy in which different degrees of honour and worth are recognized.[32]

The significance of the doctrine in the general will lies in the novel way it attempts to deduce and justify the social bond from the basis of the individual rational will attaining the universal, not simply through positing an identity between particular wills, but through participation and self-education in the political arena. The key question to be asked of the notion is that of how the individual is to be educated to the level of the general will. For, if the general will is not to be defined merely in terms of the sum of particular wills, then the question of universalization becomes crucial. Is it, for example, merely arrived at by the individual rational will universalizing its particular interest as the general interest? A number of Rousseau's remarks indicate that this is decidedly not the case. His argument, as we have seen, is that the general will presupposes that different interests exist and that without their existence the general will would never come into being, for it can only be a 'general' will in opposition to the wills of individuals which have their own 'particular' interests. The general will is the rational will of the community, not that of particular individuals.

It is in this context that we can best understand the controversial notion that whoever refuses to obey the general will 'shall be forced to be free'.[33] When speaking of forcing the individual to be free, Rousseau is making the point that the individual must be trained not to confuse or mistake the interest of its particular will with that of the general will (this is what leads to tyranny). The problem Rousseau faces is that of how the sovereign can ensure itself of the fidelity of its subjects. Moreover, the emphasis in Rousseau's notorious statement – 'forcer d'être libre' – is as much on empowerment as it is on force. Rousseau was no doubt carried away by his love of paradox, but his message is clear and sound: namely, that political participation in a self-legislating democratic agon requires a political education of the will.

The general will makes individuals free Rousseau claims ironically, because it protects them from being subjected to the whim of another's individual or particular will. Although an individual may have a particular will, it must never be allowed to stand as the general will. Thus, the aim of his thinking is to preserve and create freedom, not to cancel and destroy it. What the notion clearly reveals is that there is nothing at all natural about the existence of the general will, or even indeed about Rousseau's belief in man's capacity for free agency on account of his possession of a free will. The entire argument of the *Social Contract* is built on the conviction that the individual needs to undergo an educative process in order to become a moral agent.

Nietzsche in fact, would not have a great deal to quarrel with here, for a major aspect of his thinking is that all morality represents a tyranny against nature, that is, a long compulsion by which the human animal is disciplined and trained to control its instincts. However, the point on which Nietzsche would criticize Rousseau's argument on the general will would be to argue that it simply remains at the level of what he calls 'the morality of custom' (*die Sittlichkeit der Sitte*) and has not attained the level of genuine liberation, which for Nietzsche means that one is 'supra-ethical'.[34] The importance of morality for Nietzsche, when viewed historically in terms of a political cultivation of the human animal, is that it constitutes a long compulsion which breeds in the human animal a sense of responsibility and of political obligation. But where Rousseau sees the apotheosis of man's moral evolution in terms of a notion of the general will, Nietzsche views the apotheosis of the same evolution in terms of a notion of the sovereign individual who has transcended the morality of custom and who is like only to *itself*.[35] It would be a mistake to read Nietzsche's argument on the cultivation of the sovereign individual as implying an individual who has transcended the need for society altogether – that Nietzsche's sovereign individual must be either a beast or a god. It is clear that, for Nietzsche, the attainment of sovereign individuality is only possible in a social setting (it presupposes the morality of custom as its basis), and, therefore, that a notion such as that of 'rights' is only meaningful in such a socio-cultural context. One must have one's equals and one's peers to recognize one's self as a sovereign individual.

Nietzsche's attack on modern notions of morality and ethical life rests on a critique of an idea which he believes lies at the basis of Rousseau and Kant's formulation of morality, namely that it is possible to arrive at a notion of the universal by the individual universalizing his own interest in terms of a rational will. However, it is not clear that Nietzsche has made such a radical break with the tradition as he thinks he has. In section 11 of the *Anti-Christ*, for example, he argues, '*contra* Kant', that every person must create their own virtue and their own categorical imperative, failing to realize that this is not to contradict Kant's ethical teaching but to affirm it. In Kant, as in Rousseau before him, the emphasis is on the self constructing its maxims of action, which means that it does not accept them as given but instead freely assumes the creative labour of self-legislation. However, the notion of willing a unique and incomparable categorical imperative, of the kind which Nietzsche seems to be demanding in section 11 of the *Anti-Christ*, is a contradiction in terms, for the maxims of action that are created through the willing of a categorical imperative must be capable of being universalized to all rational beings in order to be described in imperative terms. Nietzsche's point against Kant (and by implication Rousseau) would appear to amount to the claim that creative action cannot be constrained by established moral norms, but must always exceed their boundaries and create new values and norms. Thus, when we create our maxims of action we have no way of knowing whether they will be universalizable or not, and such a criterion should not act to constrain or guide their original creation.

Both Rousseau and Kant reveal their modernity in the attempt to arrive at a notion of community from a basis in the individual, an individual who is conceived as free and autonomous. As we have seen, Rousseau defines liberty in terms of the individual freely prescribing laws to itself. This liberty is defined as 'moral' because the laws which the individual prescribes must be universal and rational. The definition of self-mastery is of someone who can transcend obedience to 'the mere impulse of appetite', and act politically in terms of voluntary obedience to a collective rational autonomy.[36] The act of universalization, however, should not be confused, as it is in Nietzsche's reading of Kant, for example, with that of the individual simply universalizing its particular perspective. Rather, what it needs to do is to *transcend* its particularity and attain a viewpoint which enables it to consider action from the standpoint of the universal.

There are, however, a number of important differences between Rousseau and Kant in their accounts of a moral autonomy. A key difference between them is that whereas Rousseau bases morality on heteronomy, that is, on appeal to enlightened self-interest in which the individual is educated to realize that its self-interest is best served by acting in accordance with the general will, Kant makes no appeal to heteronomy in his deduction of the autonomous nature of human action. On the contrary, Kant rules out self-interest as a basis for morality. A moral action can only be defined as one which is performed out of the motive of duty, where duty makes no appeal to any gains or ends one may hope to achieve by performing the action. Another important difference concerns the emphasis each place on the element of universalization in human action. Although morality is a matter of generalization for both Rousseau and Kant, in the former it is only the proposed course of action that is generalized (in order to decide which rules of behaviour society needs to be constituted upon, for example), while in the latter it is a necessary characteristic of the moral quality of an action that the agent must generalize its own point of view. One commentator has expressed Kant's position well by suggesting that the rational human agent must consider his proposed course of action not from his own viewpoint, but from that of all rational beings considered as equally rational. In Rousseau's account of the general will, on the other hand, only that which is of common interest to all is to be willed on a universal basis.[37] This is important for understanding just how novel Rousseau's account of a free, rational will is.

This will is not simply free in an ethical sense, but also in a political one: moral liberty is a precondition of civil or political liberty. It must not be supposed that Rousseau envisages the formation of the general will in terms of universalizable acts of particular wills, for this would simply be the universalization of selfishness. Rather, through the social compact the individual is to become a citizen who is both an active member of the sovereign body, and a subject of its will who must obey its commands (an act which is neither simple obeying, nor simple commanding, since this distinction has really been overcome). The citizen is a political actor who performs in the public arena in order to promote the common good, not simply the good of its own particular will. A significant transformation takes place in Rousseau's thinking from the time of the *Geneva Manuscript* to the writing of the *Social Contract*. In the conception of the general will found in the former, the individual must strive through its own strenuous efforts to pursue the universal, which is little more than an impossible act of social imagination; in the latter, however, the general will exists as the legitimate sovereign authority, and the citizens assemble as the sovereign body in terms of a collective rational autonomy in which any opposition between the individual and the collective has been sublated. This is not to say that the individual has totally abandoned its particular will and any concern with its self-interest, but that it sees the fate of the 'I' as dependent on that of the 'we'. Thus, when the politically cultivated sovereign individual acts in the political arena, it is not concern with promoting its own particular will which guides its thoughts and deeds. The real self, for Rousseau, is not the noumenal self of Kant, which exists behind the veil of the phenomenal self; rather, it is the political self who acts in concert with others for the advantage of the common good. This may be a difficult freedom – for Rousseau it is certainly one which requires of the individual great courage and fortitude – but it is not necessarily or intrinsically a tyrannical one. The general will is within us, not 'out there'. The problem is how it is to be articulated ethically and socially.

The precise meaning and significance of Rousseau's notion of the general will has been interpreted in different ways by different commentators. It would be foolish, in my opinion, to arrive either at a complete acceptance of Rousseau's doctrine, or a complete and outright rejection. Instead, it is necessary to appreciate both its promise, and its danger, by recognizing that the general will represents Rousseau's novel attempt to overcome the antinomies of modern political thought which insists on portraying the relationship between the individual and society in oppositional terms. If the general will, for example, is guilty of being a purely formal notion (a charge frequently brought against Kant's categorical imperative), then this may simply reflect the appositeness of Rousseau's response to the ethical and political dilemmas of modernity in which the standards and norms of social and communal life are no longer given, or ready made, but have to be created and constituted anew. Thus, what is taken to be a fatal weakness in Rousseau's account could turn out to be the source of its strength. It must not be forgotten that Rousseau's political thought is directed towards finding a satisfactory solution to the peculiarly modern problem of political legitimacy. Rousseau's concern with the question of legitimacy is founded on his insight into the recession of the regulative role of custom in modern political life, and its replacement by the supremacy of law.[38] Thus, instead of interpreting the general will simply in terms of a mere regulatory, authoritarian power,[39] it is possible to read the notion as denoting an active, dynamic political will. In order to do the notion 'justice', therefore, it would be necessary to make a distinction between a static conception and a dynamic one. A static general will would be one in which the rules and conventions animating public life become rigidified and ossified, but cannot be challenged without either the will dissolving itself into anarchy, or without the will assuming a tyrannical, despotic form. A dynamic will, on the other hand, would be one in which political rule provides the space for, and encourages its members to, freely challenge social rules and norms.[40] Thus one commentator, for example, has argued that the notion of a general will must incorporate political discussion and debate within its definition. He thus reads Rousseau's notion of the general will as one which envisages political life in terms of an '*agon*' operating within an '*agora*'.[41]

Of course the great danger of the notion of the general will is that instead of producing genuine independence by fostering identity in difference, it produces tyrannical uniformity by obliterating difference altogether. Thus, the main difficulty which faces Rousseau concerns how the general will is actually formed. Nietzsche for one reads Rousseau's political thought as pointing in the direction of a simple tyranny of the majority. The general will thus leads to the rule of the herd. Once formed the general will is discovered in a decision of the majority. In the fourth book of the *Social Contract* Rousseau says that the individual who stands alone and apart from the voice of the majority is simply in error, and what he thought was the general will has proved not to be.[42] But, in sacrificing the general will be to a majoritarian principle, Rousseau destroys the agonal basis of social life by failing to recognize the tragic nature of politics, that is, that political life is conflictual. Any harmony must be fought for to be genuine, and consensus must be reached through struggle and combat, not simply artificially created by being imposed from outside. For Nietzsche the tendency of the general will to degenerate into either mob-rule, or into despotic rule, is a result of Rousseau's account of moral autonomy. For in asking whether its actions and beliefs conform to the precepts of the general will, the individual is being encouraged to abdicate itself of responsibility for its actions and beliefs. The mark of the genuinely independent human being, according to Nietzsche, is that at all times one has the courage of one's convictions and is proud to accept responsibility for what one is, and what one does. Freedom is 'the will to self-responsibility'.[43] Thus, to deduce autonomy in terms of objective, universalizable laws is to conceive of the individual will as 'blind, petty, and frugal', since it betrays the fact that it has not yet created itself and its own laws.[44] The abuse of authority which many commentators interpret as being built into the notion of the general will is, on Nietzsche's reading, a consequence of the definition of moral autonomy which informs it.

The debate between Rousseau and Nietzsche on autonomy reveals a difference in their understanding of law. For Rousseau law guarantees justice only through its universality. Law is the public deliberation of the legitimate sovereign body which applies equally to all individuals, 'always judging the actions of citizens in an abstract way', the law 'cannot "judge a man or deed as if they were unique"'.[45] But for Nietzsche this conception and justification of law only serves to reveal its fundamental injustice and its prejudice against 'the new, the unique, and the incomparable'. Thus, a notion such as the general will serves to impose a spurious equality and universality on human action.

The great strength of Rousseau's notion of the general will is that it shows that an adequate response to the modern problem of legitimacy must lie in a theory of democratic participation. Its great weakness, however, especially when seen in the wider context of Rousseau's argument in the *Social Contract*, is that it is a notion which is forced to rely on conformity and uniformity, forced to obliterate conflict and dissent, in order to retain its purity. It is not difficult to sympathize with a recent commentator's judgement that the way in which a politics based on a notion of the general will protects its purity is by presiding over a society in which it is seldom needed to call this will into play.[46] It is one of the great paradoxes of Rousseau's political thought that, although it sets out to establish politics on the ethical principle of the free autonomous will, it is forced to fall back on notions of coercion and constraint in order to save its argument on the moral transfiguration of humanity from total collapse.

LAW AND THE LEGISLATOR

The general will can be defined as the desire which each member of the moral–collective body has to promote what is in the common interest of all the members of the community. Therefore, if one wants to give content to the general will, it is first necessary to determine what the common interest is. By ascribing a general will to the notion of a common interest Rousseau wishes to stress the point that it is an interest which needs to be *willed* by all. It is in the context of this understanding of the common interest as the general will that Rousseau introduces his notion of law. For Rousseau it is to law, and law alone, that men owe their justice and liberty: 'It is this salutary organ of the will of all which establishes, in civil right, the natural equality between men. It is this celestial voice which dictates to each citizen the precepts of public reason.'[47] It is through law that the individual is able to educate itself to the level of citizenship and leave the state of nature for civil society. 'Make men, therefore, if you would command men', argues Rousseau, for, 'if you would have them obedient to the laws, make them love the laws, and then they will need only to know what is their duty to do it'.[48] But what is law?

In the argument of the *Social Contract* the notion of law is discussed in terms of its role of providing the social compact by which a community has come into existence with movement and will. It is not enough to ask citizens to be good, says Rousseau, rather they must be trained to be so: 'Conventions and laws are therefore needed to join rights to duties and to refer justice to its object'.[49] In considering the nature of law in a civil state it is no good relying on metaphysics, Rousseau argues, since it is impossible to arrive at a definition of law through reflecting on natural law. For Rousseau, the source of law lies not in nature, but in the will of man. A law is defined as an act of the general will by which the whole people decrees for the whole people. The aim of law is to unite universality of will with universality of object. Properly speaking, therefore, Rousseau says, laws are nothing more than the conditions of civil association: 'The people, being subject to the laws, ought to be their author: the conditions of the society ought to be regulated solely by those who come together to form it'.[50] This passage reveals a crucial point about Rousseau's political thought: namely, that he does not simply posit the rule of law as a precondition of liberty and equality in the just polity, but stresses that law cannot be abstracted from the wider social relationships of which it is a part. Thus, it is not law that is supreme for Rousseau, but the legislative will.

It is at this point in his argument that Rousseau discusses what we have referred to as one of the main paradoxes of his political thought. The paradox can be enumerated as follows: If law provides the means by which the individual elevates itself to the level of the general will – and by which it becomes *moral* – how is it possible for the will of every member to be brought into conformity with the general will? Would individuals not have *to be* moral before they *become* moral? Rousseau formulates the problem facing his argument as follows:

> How can a blind multitude, which often does not know what it wants, because it rarely knows what is good for it, carry out for itself so great and difficult an enterprise as a system of legislation? Of itself the people wills always the good, but of itself it by no means always sees it. The general will is always upright, but the judgement which guides it is not always enlightened.[51]

What is needed, Rousseau argues, is a legislator who will bring the particular wills of individuals into conformity with their reason and teach the public will – that is, the general will – to *know* what it wills.

The legislator plays a key role in Rousseau's political theory, and serves to show that his attempt to resolve the fundamental antinomies of modern political thought, especially the relation between autonomy and authority, is not possible without the intervention of an external power. The legislator is a man of superior intelligence who possesses almost god-like qualities in his powers of perception.[52] The concern of the legislator is not with legislation in the narrow sense of decrees promulgated by a constitutional government, but rather with the general and fundamental laws which constitute the conditions of civil association. Although the lawgiver is not to possess political power as in Machiavelli, the goal of both is the same, that of the creation and pursuit of the common good. But where Machiavelli's prince is 'prudent', Rousseau's 'lawgiver' is wise.[63] As Rousseau writes:

> He who dares to undertake the making of a people's institutions ought to feel himself capable of changing human nature, of transforming each individual, who is by himself a complete and solitary whole, into part of a greater whole from which he in a manner receives his life and being; of altering man's constitution for the purpose of strengthening it; and of substituting a partial and moral existence for the physical and independent

existence nature has conferred on us all. He must, in a word, take away from man his own resources and give him instead new ones alien to him which are incapable of being made use of without the help of others. The more completely these natural resources are annihilated, the greater and more lasting are those which he acquires, and the more stable and perfect the new institutions; so that if each citizen is nothing and can do nothing without the rest, and the resources acquired by the whole are equal or superior to the sum of the natural resources of all the individuals, it may be said that legislation is at the highest possible point of perfection.[54]

The legislator, therefore, has the task, of transforming human nature in such a way that the community which is formed is built on the basis of the mutual dependence of individuals on one another. Individuals relinquish the natural independence they enjoy in the state of nature, and are provided with a higher moral independence in the civil state, an independence which is gained by making the individual dependent on the general will.

The great paradox at the heart of Rousseau's political theory is a result of the fact that, in the original contractual situation in which individuals find themselves, the motives they require in order to raise themselves above the self-interest of their particular will and embrace a general will cannot in any way be seen to exist at the moment the compact is made, since one of Rousseau's major arguments is that individuals only *become* moral through the process of socialization they undergo once they have become members of society. In a statement which echoes the manner in which Nietzsche has Zarathustra express his teaching of redemption and learn that when the creator speaks to 'all' he is speaking to 'none', Rousseau writes: 'Wise men, if they try to speak their language to the common herd (*au vulgaire*) instead of its own, cannot possibly make themselves understood.'[55] The individual in the state of nature is simply incapable of recognizing any laws other than those which are not concerned with its own self-preservation, especially laws which demand that it forego its self-interest and attain the level of a general will. Rousseau expresses the paradox which lies at the heart of his argument as follows:

For a young people to be able to relish sound principles of political theory and follow the fundamental rules of statecraft, the effect would have to become the cause; the social spirit, which should be created by these institutions, would have to preside over their very foundation; and men would have to be before law what they should become by means of law.[56]

Rousseau recognizes that the notion of the legislator is not original to him, and that it sits uncomfortably in his political theory. He mentions Machiavelli's remark that every wise legislator in history has had to have recourse to God in order to persuade the people of the divine nature of his teaching, and without which the laws would never have met with acceptance.[57] In other words, politics employs religion as its instrument. Does this mean, therefore, that Rousseau does indeed accept what Nietzsche calls the 'Machiavellianism' necessary to the establishment of power? He certainly speaks of the legislator in highly favourable terms, and even argues that, while some may see in him no more than an imposter, the true political theorist admires in the institutions he sets up a great and powerful genius. However, Rousseau would not accept the cynicism which informs Nietzsche's understanding of the so-called 'improvers of mankind', that is, his recognition that not only does immorality lie behind the establishment of a moral system, but that political power is often maintained through the exercise of force and the deployment of the noble lie.[58] Rousseau accepts the necessity of the legislator, and the apparent contradictory nature of his role, only at the inception of moral life. Rousseau acknowledges that the idea of a legislator may appear to be incompatible with the principles on which he has attempted to establish the general will, chiefly the principle of autonomy. However, he argues that the legislator has no actual power within the State once it has been constituted and that, consequently, he must be seen in terms of an authority that has no authority. The legislator must persuade without convincing and constrain without force. I shall return to how Nietzsche construes the problem of the lawgiver bequeathed by Rousseau in a later chapter devoted to examining the figure of Zarathustra.

The ingenuity of Rousseau's deployment of the notion of the legislator in the argument of the *Social Contract* cannot be doubted. However, one cannot fail to recognize the tensions which result from his attempt to unite the requirements of voluntarism – establishing the political on the basis of the rational will of man – with those of socialization. Although Rousseau recognizes that the legislator is called upon to perform what can only be regarded as an almost impossible task, his argument looks even less plausible without it. Nietzsche would not quarrel with Rousseau's argument on the necessity of social discipline and constraint, but only with the attempt to dress it up in the language of morality and 'virtue'.[59] The

chapter on civil religion which closes the *Social Contract* is evidence
that Rousseau's ethical teaching on autonomy and self-legislation is
dependent on external forces and on political coercion in order for
it to be actualized.

CONCLUSION

The argument of the *Social Contract* is not set in a definite time, but
simply assumes that individuals have reached the point in their social
evolution where they must leave the uncertainties and inadequacies
of the state of nature and come together to form a moral–collective
body. The concept of the social contract, therefore, refers not simply
to a historical act which supposedly takes place at the foundation of
every society, but to the question of 'right'. This explains why
Rousseau is able to concede that, although political rule may have
been, historically speaking, established through force, this does not
touch on the question of the legitimate basis of 'right'.

Nevertheless, in recognizing that the work addresses itself
primarily to the question of right, it is important not to ignore or
disregard the historical problematic which informs Rousseau's
inquiry into the principles of political right. Jean Starobinski, for
example, has argued that the *Social Contract* does not provide an ideal
model by which the corrupt condition of modern societies can be
judged, and that it is a mistake to read the work in terms of a
programme for revolution. According to Starobinski's argument,
Rousseau simply sidesteps the problem of the transition from an
unjust society to a just one; instead, it is argued, Rousseau moves
straight from the state of nature to the decision which establishes the
primacy of the general will, a decision that is inaugural and not
revolutionary in character. It is significant, Starobinski argues, that
in the discussion on the legislator the figure is not given any location
in a specific point in history. Thus, the legitimate social contract
belongs to a purely normative dimension which is situated outside
historical time.[60]

But such a reading merely confirms my claim that at the heart of
Rousseau's thinking on social change and the fate of civilization
there lies the problem of history. According to one commentator, for
example, the *Social Contract* needs to be read as an attempt to provide
a solution to the problem of the Lockean State criticized in the
second part of the discourse on the origins of inequality.[61] Thus, the
social contract Rousseau portrays for us is not simply a prescriptive

ideal, but a response to the concrete and specific historical problematic of bourgeois society. Horowitz offers an interesting and important interpretation of the difficulties which ensue from Rousseau's attempt to solve 'the problem of bourgeois society'. He argues that the sovereignty of the general will is derived from principles inherent in modern social life, and represents the best polity realizable in a society modelled upon market relations such as predominate in the bourgeois social form. But, as he points out, 'since in that society the ideal remains unattainable, life under the sovereignty of the general will amounts to the alienation of communal life in the state'.[62] Rousseau's solution is thus an ambivalent one, for 'it announces the project of human mastery over a previously reified history, but under conditions in which that project must, in perpetually failing, reproduce reification'. Thus, the 'solution' is in need of a solution itself; in other words, we require 'educators who are themselves educated' – a position, it is interesting to note, that we find in *both* Marx and Nietzsche.[63]

But if commentators are agreed that Rousseau's political thought culminates in a theoretical impasse, they disagree as to the causes underlying it. Is the impasse the result of Rousseau being caught in a period of history when it would have been simply impossible for him to imagine any practical transcendence of the alienation of the individual living in an atomized society?[64] Or is it the result of Rousseau's own personal psychological make-up, of his experience of being torn between the desire for social transparency and a need of personal anonymity?[65] For Nietzsche, however, the impasse Rousseau reaches on the problem of civilization considered as a problem of history is the result of his moralism – a moralism which conceals an aversion and resentment towards time, change, and becoming.

In conclusion, therefore, we can say that it is important to appreciate that the *Social Contract* constitutes Rousseau's response to a historical predicament. It is a work whose failure is instructive in revealing the problem of history which underlies modern thinking on social change and political transfiguration. If man is naturally 'good' but has been made 'evil' by corrupt social institutions, then how is it possible to reform human nature in accordance with its natural goodness? Despite Rousseau's immense achievement in showing the problem of human nature to be a historical problem, the importance of a standard of nature to his argument cannot be denied (as Horowitz's argument seems to, for example). The significance of the relationship between the discourse on the origins of inequality and the inquiry into the principles of political right, for example, is that the latter represents Rousseau's attempt at a solution to the problem of the former, that of discovering a political order which is in accordance with humanity's natural goodness.[66]

Although Nietzsche's thinking on the problem of civilization departs radically from Rousseau's construal of the problem, it nevertheless partakes of the fundamental problem of history which animates Rousseau's life-work. If human nature is, like life itself (which is will to power), beyond good and evil, but has been made 'good' through a historical development involving the taming and discipline of the human animal, then how can a new humanity be created that can overcome morality and attain a standpoint which is also beyond good and evil, immoral like nature itself? Moreover, what paradoxes result from Nietzsche's attempt to think through the problem of the self-overcoming of morality? In order to overcome the problem of civilization and the impasse of nihilism that has been reached in the historical evolution of humanity, does Nietzsche simply advocate a return to a pagan aristocracy of blond beasts, to the 'evil' nature of wild, free, prowling early man that is the very opposite of Rousseau's depiction of natural goodness? To what extent does Nietzsche's political thought overcome the politics of resentment in thinking through the problem of history? It is to an examination of such key questions that I now turn.

CHAPTER 4

Nietzsche's Dionysian drama on the destiny of the soul: on the 'Genealogy of Morals'

> He who has grown wise concerning old origins, behold, he will
> at last seek new springs of the future and new origins.
> 'Of Old and New Law-Tables', *Thus Spoke Zarathustra*

THE SELF-OVERCOMING OF MORALITY

Both Rousseau and Nietzsche offer a teaching on how to live one's life which is in accordance with nature. But where nature is conceived as moral by Rousseau, it is understood as decidedly immoral by Nietzsche. In Rousseau the notion of pity is used to support the claim that man is naturally good. Similarly, in Nietzsche the notion of will to power is employed to support a philosophy which seeks to be beyond good and evil. Does this mean, therefore, that with the notion of will to power Nietzsche offers us a new natural law to take the place of the old ones which, once supported by metaphysical and moral arguments for the existence of God, are now no longer tenable in the age of the death of God? Interestingly, Nietzsche does speak of 'self-overcoming' (*Selbstüberwindung*) in terms of being a 'law of life' (*Gesetz des Lebens*).[1] But Nietzsche's teaching is that there is neither a fixed and immutable human nature for the individual to live in accordance with, nor an eternal moral order on which one could base a deduction of the social and political. Rather, it is the law of *life* that everything must overcome itself again and again without final goal or ultimate purpose.

Nietzsche's conception of the task of the self-overcoming of morality represents an attempt to bypass the question of obligation and suspend the question of legitimacy. Through willing the self-overcoming of morality we are to become those that we are. The task of self-overcoming thus becomes a fate that transcends the opposition of freedom and necessity. The only way in which the burden of the past can be overcome is through a creative future willing. As one commentator has noted, the concept of self-overcoming does serve to denote in Nietzsche's thinking a perspective of human perfectibility in spite of his rejection of good and evil as values embedded in nature. But it means that ethics cannot be based on either extra-natural norms, or on transcendental percepts. Neither can it posit a moral world-order which has to be copied so as to provide a guide for moral obligation.[2]

In Nietzsche self-overcoming presupposes a new conception of life which he names 'will to power', and which is designed to allow life to re-shape and sublimate itself, not simply in the sense of conscious mastery and control but, more importantly, in the sense of letting go and letting be. However, in Nietzsche's thinking on political life this conception of will to power is transformed into a principle which supports a politics, if not of domination, then of hierarchy and supremacy. In contrast to Rousseau's attempt to replace a discourse on 'force' with one on 'right' through the deduction of the legitimate social contract, Nietzsche offers a teaching on sovereignty in which the nature of self-legislation is shown to lie in the commanding and obeying of a will to power. The notion of will to power is intended to show that all willing involves elements of commanding and obeying, and thus designed to overcome the opposition between autonomy and heteronomy, and between freedom and necessity by showing us the unity of 'will' and 'power'. It is in this context of Nietzsche's attempt to articulate a notion of will to power that we can appreciate the nature of his 'failure' to develop a philosophy of right. For Nietzsche a discourse on the principles of political right is untenable, since it rests on the assumption that power is something which can be rationally established and legitimated on a moral basis. For Nietzsche the justification of the political must lie beyond the State in the realm of culture and genius, which means that society must be structured and designed in a way which leads to the production of a higher type of human being. This argument informs Nietzsche's conception of the political from the early unpublished essay on the *Greek State* to *Beyond Good and Evil*. For Nietzsche the political is the domain of force or coercion. Since morality concerns compulsion there can be no objective, neutral justification of legitimate political power. In terms of understanding the nature of Nietzsche's politics, this elision on his part of the problem of legitimacy is important, for it shows that where Hobbes offers a stark choice between absolutist rule or anarchism, a similar stark choice can be seen to inform Nietzsche's political thinking, a choice between the war of all against all on the one hand, and the aristocratic rule of masters and slaves on the other. For Nietzsche the justification of social order does not lie in any ethical ends, but in its existence as a site on which the production of a 'choice type of human being', as he puts it, can take place.[3]

In his writings, Nietzsche sets out to subject the privileging of morality in Western metaphysics to critical scrutiny by showing that underlying its will to truth is a particular form of the will to power. In contrast to any attempt to demonstrate man's natural goodness, Nietzsche sets out to subvert our understanding of good and evil by undertaking a history of morality in the form of a genealogy of morals, in which the decisive turning point in human evolution is shown to lie in a slave revolt in morals. If morality is shown to have a history then it will automatically lose much of its mythical status as something natural and given. Nietzsche's originality lies in his attempt to demonstrate the necessity of a revaluation of the value of morality by showing that it is the result of a particular historical labour of culture, and hence is shown to be neither universal nor natural. He writes:

Hitherto, the subject reflected on least adequately has been good and evil: it was too dangerous a subject. Conscience, reputation, Hell, sometimes the police have permitted and continue to permit no impartiality; in the presence of morality, as in the face of any authority, one is not *allowed* to think, far less to express an opinion: here one has to – *obey*! As long as the world has existed no authority has yet been willing to let itself become the object of criticism; to criticise morality itself, to regard morality as a problem, as problematic: what? has that not been – *is* that not – immoral?[4]

In calling for 'the self-overcoming of morality' Nietzsche's argument is that we moderns should regard our present form of morality as a *critique* of morality.[5] However, in demanding that we perform a critique of morality as our present form of morality, Nietzsche is not asking that we carry out a simple outright condemnation of morality. On the contrary, he demands that we recognize the historical importance of morality:

Morality as an illusion of the species, designed to motivate the individual to sacrifice himself to the future: apparently allowing him an infinite value, so that by means of this self-consciousness he should tyrannize over and keep down other sides of his nature and find it hard to be content with himself.

Profoundest gratitude for that which morality has achieved hitherto: but now it is only a burden which may become a fatality! Morality itself, in the form of honesty, compels us to deny morality.[6]

An outright condemnation of morality would be insufficient for Nietzsche's purposes, since it would be based on the same kind of abstract, unjustified moralism which he holds has characterized metaphysics from Plato to Kant. Thus, the importance of the notion of the self-overcoming of morality is that it draws our attention to what is essential in Nietzsche's critique of morality: that is, that it calls not for the suppression of morality but rather for its transfiguration. Morality must learn how to overcome itself. The great significance of the figure of Zarathustra in Nietzsche's writings is that it is he who is assigned the task of teaching humanity the meaning of the labour involved in 'the self-overcoming of morality (*die Selbstüberwindung der Moral*)'.[7]

Even if we recognize that morality has grown out of fear, error, and superstition, this does not begin to touch on the problem of its value.[8] Instead, we need to cultivate an understanding of morality as a creative act. One of the best accounts that Nietzsche gives of his understanding of the notions of good and evil is in the following passage from *Human, All Too Human*:

The complete unaccountability of man for his actions and his nature is the bitterest draught the man of knowledge has to swallow if he has been accustomed to seeing in accountability and duty the patent of his humanity. All his evaluations, all his feelings of respect and antipathy have thereby become disvalued and false: his profoundest sentiment, which he accorded to the sufferer, the hero, rested on an error; he may no longer praise, no longer censure, for it is absurd to praise and censure nature and necessity. As he loves a fine work of art but does not praise it since it can do nothing for itself, as he stands before the plants, so must he stand before the actions of men and before his own ... all these motives, whatever exalted names we choose to give them, have grown up out of the same roots as those we believe evilly poisoned; between good and evil actions there is no difference in kind, but at the most one of degree. Good actions are sublimated evil ones; evil actions are coarsened, brutalized good ones ... every society, every individual always has present an order of rank of things considered good according to which one determines one's own actions and those of others. But this standard is continually changing.[9]

Nietzsche poses the decisive question whether humanity has the strength and the courage to transform itself '*from a moral to a knowing mankind*'. With this knowledge beyond good and evil, Nietzsche looks forward to the time – he is thinking in terms of thousands of years

– when mankind will have the power to bring into existence 'the wise, innocent (conscious of innocence) man as regularly as it now brings forth – *not his antithesis but necessary preliminary* – the unwise, unjust, guilt-conscious man'.[10] Nietzsche argues that humanity can attain this victory of knowledge over evil by recognizing that it is neither fundamentally evil and corrupt nor is it the opposite.[11]

At the base of Nietzsche's philosophy beyond good and evil is a new conception of life: life thought as will to power. 'Will to power' is the principle Nietzsche deploys in order to perform the task of revaluing all previous values. Concerning the matter of the value of values it asks the question whether they are signs of ascending life or signs that life is exhausted and degenerating, We misconstrue life if we take it to be an end-in-itself; rather, we should view it as 'only a *means* to something; it is the expression of forms of growth of power'.[12] Fundamental to this conception of life is the idea that life is constant movement and change, it is 'becoming', not 'being'. To think life as becoming is to think of it without the need for a moral interpretation of its meaning and significance. In a note from the *Nachlass* of 1887–8 Nietzsche says that he seeks a conception of life that takes into account the fact that existence does not aim at a final state:

Becoming must be explained without recourse to final intentions; becoming must appear justified at every moment (or incapable of being evaluated; which amounts to the same thing); the present must absolutely not be justified by reference to a future, nor the past by reference to the present. 'Necessity' not in the shape of an overreaching, dominating total force, or that of a prime mover; even less as a necessary condition for something valuable. To this end it is necessary to deny a total consciousness of becoming, a 'God', to avoid bringing all events under the aegis of a being who feels and knows but does not *will*: 'God' is useless if he does not want anything...[13]

Nietzsche puts forward three fundamental propositions concerning life conceived as becoming. Firstly, that 'becoming' does not aim at a final state, which means that it does not become 'being'; secondly, that 'becoming' is not merely an apparent state – rather the world of being may be only apparent; thirdly, and perhaps most important, 'becoming' is of equivalent value *every moment*: 'the sum of its values always remains the same'. In other words, becoming has no value at all for nothing exists against which it can be measured and evaluated. Thus Nietzsche reaches the startling and bewildering conclusion that the word 'value' has no meaning in a world conceived as pure becoming: '*The total value of the world cannot be evaluated*; consequently philosophical pessimism belongs among comical things.'[14]

If this is the case, if the value of becoming cannot be evaluated, then how is it possible for Nietzsche to reconcile his commitment to life conceived as becoming – which means that life must appear justified at every moment (in other words, it is beyond justification) – with his demand that in order to overcome nihilism it is necessary to perform a revaluation of values? Would not such a project be a supreme example of the attitude of resentment towards life conceived as becoming? The act of judgement, as Nietzsche constantly points out in his work, is always an attempt to make life more regular and calculable by imposing uniformity and standards of measurement on it. Judgements serve to rationalize the past, or to make the uncertainty of the future less fearful and unknown by making it calculable. The problem of passing judgement on the past is nowhere more apparent than in the case of a revaluation of values which asks the question whether the values of past humanity (and which have made us what we are) reflect a strong, abundant will to power or a weak, impoverished will to power. However, the coherence of this task based on the principle of will to power must be seriously questioned. An example will illustrate why. In the *Genealogy of Morals* Nietzsche demands that we need to carry out something which hitherto has been forbidden, namely, a critique of moral values. But can the will to power serve the role of principle in this critique, when, for example, Nietzsche discovers in the first essay of his genealogy that the slave revolt in morals which reflects a degenerating life shows itself, when viewed historically and in the wider context of culture, to have played an important role in the cultivation and discipline of the human animal and has even served to deepen it? Is it not the case that such a distinction between ascending life and descending life – what we may call Nietzsche's discrimination of will to power – stands in contradiction to a standpoint which strives to be beyond good and evil? Does not such a standpoint affirm life in its totality, as a movement of becoming which is beyond judgement, for it recognizes that good and evil, ascending and descending life are both necessary to life and its perpetual self-overcoming? Of course, I am aware that Nietzsche is a thinker who is celebrated for his love of contradiction; however, a contradiction of this nature would be fatal to the coherence of Nietzsche's entire philosophical project and to our reception of it.

However, it is possible to rescue Nietzsche's thinking from internal collapse by recognizing the specific manner in which he articulates the task of revaluation and the principle of will to power in terms of a countermovement to nihilism. Nietzsche's fundamental thinking is an attempt to educate human beings on how to overcome the condition of nihilism by cultivating an appreciation of life in terms of the innocence of becoming. However, the problem of the past remains in spite of all attempts to establish a new mode of thinking and doing. Thus, as will be shown in detail in an examination of the *Genealogy* and *Zarathustra*, the past is in need, not only of some kind of reconciliation, but of an *affirmation*. The only way in which this can be done is through a creative future willing which redeems even all that is past. How can the will achieve this redemption? By engaging in the task of becoming what it 'is' – where 'is' does not denote a final state or end-goal, but rather refers to the process of self-overcoming where life is conceived as will to power (that is, as continual growth, decay, rebirth, regeneration, etc.). Underlying Nietzsche's conception of life as will to power is a notion of justice, and it is such a notion that serves to give the concept of will to power a wider ambit that takes it beyond the role of simple judgement.

The notion of justice is a crucial aspect of Nietzsche's thought in its role as the advocate of life and the circle (Dionysus as a judge?). Justice denotes a particular type of thinking: '*Justice* as constructive exclusive annihilating way of thinking, out of evaluation: *highest representative of life itself*', Nietzsche writes in a *Nachlass* note from the beginning of 1884.[15] Justice is the perspective of life viewed as self-overcoming, and is the opposite of the attitude which sees life merely in terms of self-preservation and which requires fixed moral categories. To practise 'justice' in Nietzsche's sense demands of a person that they are able to value life beyond the opposition of 'good' and 'evil'. The human being who is both wise and just would be the one who is the wealthiest in contradictions, capable of making harmony out of the discordant elements of its existence, of creating a new order of values out of the disarray of the conflicting forces within itself 'extremely multifarious, yet firm and hard. Supple'.[16] Justice is the 'function of a panoramic power (*Macht*) which looks beyond the narrow perspectives of good and evil... the intention to preserve something that is more than this or that person'.[17]

Like Rousseau before him then, Nietzsche attempts, in his guise as the advocate of life conceived as will to power, to speak the 'voice of nature' – but nature conceived as immoral and as beyond good and evil. Nietzsche's notion of justice is important in enabling us to clarify some of the apparent inconsistencies and contradictions (and some of them are more than merely apparent) of his thinking, for it shows us that he construes valuation, not simply as a denial of becoming, but as a necessary aspect of life. But in conceiving justice in terms of a mode of valuative thinking that proclaims itself to be 'the highest representative of life', he offers us a choice between resentment and justice, that is between a way of thinking and being which values life from a moral standpoint of 'good and evil', and one which seeks to go beyond the moral judgement of 'good and evil'. Thus, it can be argued that Nietzsche's innermost thinking is not incoherent, provided it is recognized that the task of revaluation by which the self-overcoming of morality is to be effected does not denote a 'moral' task. It is, nevertheless, one which claims to have justice on its side. However, the validity of Nietzsche's argument rests on our recognizing the justice of his claim that life *is* will to power, and that his thought succeeds in speaking the voice of (immoral) nature.

The will to power plays a similar role in Nietzsche's thinking to that played by self-preservation and *amour de soi* in the thought of Hobbes and Rousseau.[18] But instead of bifurcating our passions and sentiments in terms of a distinction between the natural and the artificial in the manner of Rousseau, in which certain ones are deemed to be good (pity) and others deemed to be bad (vanity or pride), the notion of will to power defines them all as deriving from an elemental pathos or affective disposition.[19] In fact it could be argued that Rousseau's attack on Hobbes is more appropriately aimed at the kind of thinking on power we find in Nietzsche than in Hobbes. Hobbes does not posit a blind and irrational desire for power in the manner in which Rousseau sometimes portrays. Rather, it is only possible to fully appreciate Hobbe's conception of power if one takes into account the form he argues power must take in the insecure conditions of the state of nature. It is on account of the insecurity of this condition and the absence of any common standards of right, rather than on account of any natural lust for power, that Hobbes argues we must explain the striving for power. Nevertheless, a lust for power and domination is clearly a threatening force to social order for Hobbes, to the extent that he is led to embrace a justification of political absolutism. Nietzsche, on the other hand, does posit a drive for power as an essential part of our original human nature. Indeed, it is possible to construe his articulation of a basic drive for power, which necessarily entails, for Nietzsche, that the will to power assumes under cert cumstances a desire for supremacy over others, in terms of an explicit critique of those thinkers like Rousseau who attempt to senti- mentalize human nature by imposing altruistic values on it. In the *Genealogy of Morals*, for example, Nietzsche defines the will to power in terms of a historical method that is designed to show that in all events a will to power is operating. By will to power Nietzsche makes it clear that an important element of this will is a desire for supremacy (*Herrschaft*):

> I emphasize this major point of historical method all the more because it is in fundamental opposition to the now prevalent instinct and taste which would rather be reconciled even to the absolute fortuitousness, even the mechanistic senselessness of all events than to the theory that in all events a power-drive (*Macht-Willens*) is operating. The democratic idiosyncrasy which opposes everything that dominates and wants to dominate, the modern *misarchism* [hatred of rule or government]...has permeated the realm of the spirit and disguised itself in the most spiritual forms to such a degree that today it has forced its way, has acquired the *right* to force its way into the strictest, apparently most objective sciences; indeed, it seems to me to have already taken charge of all physiology and teaching about life – to the detriment of life... since it has robbed it of a fundamental concept, that of *activity*...Thus the essence of life, its *will to power* (*Wille zur Macht*) is ignored and one overlooks the essential priority of the spontaneous, aggressive, expansive, form-giving forces that give new interpretations and directions.[20]

In this passage Nietzsche is arguing that life cannot be understood without positing the motive force of a *will* to power. It understands this will in terms of a form-giving force which provides life with new directions and new interpretations, without which it would become stagnant and inert. One of the ways in which this will to power exerts itself for Nietzsche is through a drive for supremacy.

Nietzsche argues that the phenomenon of willing can only be understood within the realm of 'morals': 'morals (*Moral*) being understood as the doctrine of the relations of supremacy under which the phenomenon of "life" arises'.[21] Nietzsche's argument here is admittedly somewhat elliptical, but what I take him to be arguing is that it is not possible to speak of willing in abstraction from the actual social and historical relations of power which constitute the will, whereby the will is given an essentialist content (such as 'good' or 'evil') independently of its expression and embodiment within these relations. By attempting to formulate questions of freedom ('will') and action ('power') in a way which shows their inseparability, Nietzsche is subverting traditional construals of the relationship between the subject (the 'free' will) and power in political theory. Thus, instead of conceiving of a subject which exists *prior* to its social and historical formation by relations of power, Nietzsche speaks of power relations in terms of their being *constitutive* of the human subject. Thus, he arrives at the following definition of willing: 'In all willing it is absolutely a question commanding and obeying, on the basis, as already pointed out, of a social structure composed of many "souls"'.[22] Although Rousseau conceives of man's development as a moral and social being in historical terms, he nevertheless holds to the belief that the subject itself is given on account of its possession of conscience and a free will. Nietzsche, however, even views the capacity of a free will in terms of a historical invention and social construction. Free will does not develop on account of mans 'perfectibility', but through cruel, stupid and tyrannical methods of social discipline.

It cannot be denied that Nietzsche posits the drive of the will to power, not in neutral terms, but in terms of it having a bias in favour of the aggressive and expansive aspects of life. Has Nietzsche not, therefore, committed the same error as the one Rousseau attributes to Hobbes's philosophy of power, namely of ascribing to natural man attributes – such as an instinct for aggression, domination, and cruelty – which properly speaking only belong to social man? Here we encounter a fundamental difference in the thought of Rousseau and Nietzsche. Whereas Rousseau conceives of life in terms of a natural moral world-order governed by the sentiment of pity, Nietzsche argues that life only becomes perceived in moral terms (where pity is conceived as good and egoism in the form of pride is conceived as bad) with the advent of a particular form of morality which he defines in terms of a 'slave revolt in morals'. In other words, Nietzsche's fundamental argument against Rousseau is that man's drive for supremacy and for power only becomes conceived in moral terms through a slave revaluation of noble values. This is the moment of history for Nietzsche in that man now becomes a reflective animal in possession of a 'soul'.

At the heart of Nietzsche's quarrel with Rousseau on the problem of civilization is a fundamental disagreement over the value of certain values. For Nietzsche the unegoistic values prized by Rousseau, such as pity for example, only serve to preserve degenerating and weak forms of life. In this sense pity is not a creative sentiment since it merely preserves what might be ripe for destruction and self-overcoming. This explains why *contra* Rousseau Nietzsche argues that it is not the pitiable state of civilization which is to blame for our 'bad morality' but rather our 'good morality' (one of pity) which is the problem. For Nietzsche, Rousseau's attempt to establish a new social order on the basis of the sentiment of pity reflects a slave type of morality in which the strength and courage of the independent human being is made to feel guilty and weaken itself by feeling pity for the weak and lowly. Nietzsche's quest for knowledge of evil, and for a standpoint beyond good and evil, seeks to invert Rousseau's whole argument on natural goodness and his critique of *amour-propre*. For, in calling for a new conscious type of innocence, he challenges Rousseau's entire construal of the problem of civilization. His argument is that if phenomena such as egoism and vanity are as necessary to the production of the human type as are the altruistic sentiments such as compassion and self-sacrifice – just as error is necessary to the production of truth and knowledge – then it is absurd to denigrate the means which led to the goal, or end, of self-enlightenment, self-redemption, and self-overcoming.[23] Like Rousseau, however, Nietzsche regards the social contract of civil society to be a fraud: not of the strong over the weak, but of the weak over the strong. For Nietzsche, it is the slave, not the master, who has been victorious in modern history. Thus, what is needed in order for morality to be overcome is a new nobility that must be both inhuman and superhuman.

INTRODUCTION TO THE ARGUMENT OF THE 'GENEALOGY OF MORALS'

The title of Nietzsche's book *Zur Genealogie der Moral* is ambiguous in that the prefix '*Zur*' could serve to indicate that the work represents a contribution to an approach to the study of morals that already exists (as in '*on* the Genealogy of Morals'), or it could mean that Nietzsche believes that a genealogy of morals represents a completely new approach to the study of morals and that the book is written as a work in progress designed to inaugurate a whole new approach to the problem of morality (as in '*towards* a Genealogy of Morals').[24] If one carefully examines the book evidence can be found to support both translations, thus indicating that Nietzsche's title is intentionally playful and ironic: the work is intended as a contribution to a subject which already exists, but equally it is intended to show how a *proper* genealogy of morals should be conducted. It is important to note that the work is subtitled 'A Polemic' (*Eine Streitschrift*), indicating that Nietzsche understands his project in terms of an engagement with an existing genealogy of morals. In the opening section of the first essay Nietzsche refers to the 'English psychologists' as the only group of thinkers who have so far attempted a 'history of the origin of morality' (*Entstehungsgeschichte der Moral*).[25] But in the following section of the first book he argues that in truth the thinking of these psychologists and philosophers is far from being historical, and that the way in which they have 'bungled their moral genealogy' comes to light when one carries out an investigation into the descent (*Herkunft*) of the concept 'good'. The same argument is repeated in section four of the second inquiry of the book where Nietzsche refers to the attempt to construct a 'history of morals' (*Geschichte der Moral*) by tracing the descent (*Herkunft*) of the concept 'guilt' (*Schuld*)).

Evidence to support the view that 'towards' would be a better translation of Nietzsche's title can be found in the note which Nietzsche places at the end of the first inquiry.[26] Here Nietzsche invites a faculty of philosophy to take up his challenge of a historical study of morality through the promotion of a series of academic prize-essays, and adds 'perhaps this present book will serve to provide a powerful impetus in this direction'. But, like Rousseau's second discourse, the *Genealogy of Morals* is a book on the fate of civilization which is addressed not only to academicians, but to humanity. Like any book which embraces the paradoxes of adopting the guise of the teacher it can only offer itself out of a sense of honesty as a book for all and none. Nietzsche suggests the following question for the first prize-essay: 'What light does linguistics, especially the study of etymology, throw on the historical development of moral concepts?' The interest of physiologists and doctors will have to be solicited, as well as that of academic philosophers, in order to approach the study of morals from many diverse perspectives and in order to properly answer the question of value. In raising the critical question of the value of values, Nietzsche says, we open up a distinction between the 'well-being of the majority' and that of 'the few'. Thus, the very project of revaluation to which the *Genealogy* is a contribution, represents Nietzsche's concern to invert from an explicitly aristocratic perspective the democratic prejudices of the modern age which serves to level humanity. This concern with the question of value shows the extent to which Nietzsche's thinking on morals is not simply an attempt at a 'hypothesis-mongering' on the origins of morality, but rather an attempt to call into question the very value of morality: 'From now on', Nietzsche concludes the note attached to the end of the first essay of the book, 'all the sciences have to prepare the way for the future task of the philosopher: this task understood as the attempt to solve the *problem of value*, of the determination of the *order of rank among values*'.[27]

The question whether Nietzsche intends 'on' or 'towards' in his title cannot be settled either way and it is best that the attentive reader bears in mind the ambiguity of Nietzsche's polemical contribution when reading it. What is clear, however, is that the *Genealogy of Morals*, in raising the question about the value of morality, is an example of the task of philosophical legislation which Nietzsche describes in section 211 of *Beyond Good and Evil*, where it asserted that genuine philosophers are commanders and legislators who say 'thus it shall be!' In determining the 'whither' and the 'for what' of man, they have to hand the preliminary labours of philosophical labouring which has 'overcome the past': 'With a creative hand they reach out to the future, and all that is and has been becomes a means for them, an instrument, a hammer'. Thus, their 'knowing' is transformed into a 'creating', their creating a 'legislation', and their 'will to truth' a 'will to power'. The retrieval and remembrance of old origins is not an exercise in antiquarian studies, but an attempt to become what one is in order to create *new origins*. This means, therefore, that it is possible to read the inquiry of the *Genealogy of Morals* as an exemplification of how Nietzsche wishes 'us' (I shall attend to the question of the 'we' that the book addresses shortly) to understand the project and task of the self-overcoming of morality: the past is to be remembered and overcome through a creative willing of the future(– and then forgotten?).

In his autobiography, *Ecce Homo*, Nietzsche divides his life's task into two periods, a Yea-saying period, which includes the writings up to *Beyond Good and Evil*, and a Nay-saying one, which includes the writings from *Beyond Good and Evil* onwards. The Nay-saying part refers to the project of revaluation which Nietzsche describes as a 'day of decision', and a preparation for 'the great war'. From the time of *Beyond Good and Evil* – a book which, Nietzsche says, constitutes 'in all essentials a *critique of modernity*' – he informs his readers, all his works are designed as 'fish-hooks'.[28] How are we to interpret the significance of this characterization by Nietzsche of his life-work? Of course, to a large extent it has to be read as a clever piece of rationalization on Nietzsche's part which allows him to attribute some kind of intelligent, controlled design (a fate which one becomes) to the course his writings took. But a neat division of his work into an unequivocal Yea-saying part and an unequivocal Nay-saying part is far too simplistic a characterization of his work.[29] As Nietzsche himself points out in the preface to the *Genealogy*, his inquiry into the origin of humanity's moral prejudices received their first, provisional exploration in *Human, All Too Human*, a book which marks the beginnings of what is commonly referred to as Nietzsche's positivist phase (1878–82), of his break with his two great teachers, Schopenhauer and Wagner, and which clearly belongs to the 'Yea-saying' period. In section two of the preface of the *Genealogy* Nietzsche reveals that the ideas of this youthful work were already in essentials the same ideas which he takes up in the present treatise, but that they have now become 'riper, clearer, stronger, more perfect'. The fact, however, that these ideas on the origins of morals still appeal to him, he says, show that they are not isolated or sporadic but grow out of a common root, from 'a fundamental will to knowledge'. 'This alone', says Nietzsche, 'is fitting for a philosopher':

We have no right to *isolated* acts of any kind: we may not hit upon isolated errors or upon isolated truths. Rather do our ideas, our values, our yeas and nays, our ifs and buts, grow out of us with the necessity with which a tree bears fruit…evidence of *one* will, *one* health, *one* soil, *one* sun.[30]

It is fitting that, in a book devoted to making a polemical contribution to a genealogy of morals, Nietzsche should devote the preface to outlining his own genealogy as a philosopher and seeker after knowledge, situating his work in the context of his own previous work, that of his life's-concerns, and that of the tradition of moral philosophy. In section three of the preface, for example, Nietzsche gives us a quick portrait of the *young* Nietzsche at the age of thirteen reflecting on the great question of the origin of evil, and learning at an early age the necessity of separating theological prejudice from moral prejudice, thus ceasing to look for the origin of evil 'behind' the world.

The *Genealogy*, therefore, represents a continuity with Nietzsche's fundamental concerns. It sets out to both clarify a number of ideas first presented in *Beyond Good and Evil* (notably the creation of a typology of morals into master and slave moralities), and to develop further the 'art of interpretation' (*Auslegung*) required in order to effect a self-overcoming of morals, which is first presented in its educative form in *Thus Spoke Zarathustra*. But the relationship between affirmation and negation in Nietzsche's innermost thinking is a complex one. In reading the *Genealogy* (1887) before *Zarathustra* (1883–5) I have been influenced by a remark of Nietzsche's in *Ecce Homo*, which I take to be crucial, when he says that 'negating and *destroying* are conditions of saying-Yes'.[31] This is a crucial remark because it shows us that the Nay-saying part of Nietzsche's work is not merely secondary to his Yea-saying nature and task, is not less authentic than the Yea-saying period, but, on the contrary, it is only through carrying out the critical and destructive task of revaluation (of saying No) that Nietzsche is led to a proper understanding of his own genealogy and what it means to say Yes. The Yes can only be born from the No, for there can be no simple return to pure innocence, but only the discipline of a new form of conscious innocence. In order to become what one is, we might say somewhat teasingly, it is necessary that one must first remember in order to forget. Or, in other words, it is necessary to be unjust (to say No) in order to be just (to say Yes), and in order to be moral it is necessary to be immoral.

Nietzsche in fact begins the work by drawing attention to the paradox that although there is in the modern age a greater flourishing of forms of knowledge than ever before, never has man been more unknown to himself. We are strangers to ourselves to the extent that we cannot answer the question 'who are *we*?' The project of genealogy, Nietzsche tells us, is to 'traverse with novel questions, as though with new eyes the enormous, distant, and so well hidden land of morality' so as to '*discover* this land for the first time'.[32] But the great paradox of Nietzsche's attempt to show us how we may become what we are through a genealogy of morals, is that, although it is about the ignorance of 'modern men' (their lack of knowledge, their inability to live up to the task set by the Delphic oracle), it cannot on account of this ignorance be addressed to them but only to a possible future audience, that is the humanity which is constituted *over*-man. In the closing section of the preface, for example, Nietzsche says that it may be some time before his writings are readable since modern man does not know how to practise the art of interpretation – that is, that art which liberates us from enslavement to a moral world-order and affords us the opportunity of creating the world anew. Only through the practice of an art of interpretation can one achieve a foothold beyond morality, beyond good and evil.[33]

The problem of morality is to be taken seriously, Nietzsche argues in section seven of the preface, for such seriousness brings with it the reward of cheerfulness (the death of God leads to new seas). On the day that humanity can say to itself 'Onwards! our old morality is part of *the comedy*!', *it* will have discovered, Nietzsche says, a new possibility for 'the Dionysian drama of "The Destiny of the Soul"'.[34] Here Nietzsche alerts our attention to the way in which his polemic of genealogy of morals dramatizes human history in terms of a Dionysian tragi-comedy on the fate of the human soul. Each of the three essays which make up the book, for example, concludes on a dramatic note: the first essay, on the origin of 'good and bad' and 'good and evil', closes with Nietzsche reflecting on the significance of the 'fearful struggle' waged on earth for thousands of years between these two great movements ('Rome against Judea', 'Judea against Rome') and demanding a higher nature that has learned how to become 'beyond good and evil'; the second essay, on guilt and the bad conscience, points in the direction of a dramatic redemption of reality from the reign of 'good and evil', and ends with the vision of the one (namely, Zarathustra) 'who must come one day'; the third essay, on the meaning of ascetic ideals, closes with Nietzsche suggesting ironically that the meaning of the ascetic ideal is that humanity no longer knows why it suffers (its ascetic existence has become *meaning-less*). Both the essay and the book conclude with the recognition that 'man would rather will nothingness than not will at all'.[35]

The book presents two accounts of humanity's evolution as a moral species. In the first essay Nietzsche examines the difference between master and slave moralities, and argues that the formation of the human animal undergoes a significant transformation through a slave rebellion in morals. In the second essay of the work, he traces humanity's moral evolution in terms of the development of a *bad* conscience which, it is argued, was bound to develop once man became enclosed within the confines of society and peace. Nietzsche regards humanity's development into a moral being as both a dangerous, and a hopeful, spectacle, because it is full of promise and could move in either a negative or a positive direction. Central to Nietzsche's argument is the conviction that the social and political structures of modern society rest on moral values and judgements whose origins and development are unknown, either because they have been deliberately forgotten, or because there exists a deep-seated prejudice that one know what morality is. Today, Nietzsche argues, we know in Europe what Socrates proclaimed he did not know, namely, what is 'good' and what is 'evil'.[36] By revealing the historical status of morality Nietzsche hopes that doubt will be cast on its universalistic claims. Philosophers have not recognized morality as a problem, but instead have preferred to supply the common faith in morality with a rational foundation. What has not been carried out, Nietzsche argues, is anything like 'an examination, analysis, questioning, and vivisection of this very faith'.[37]

A genealogy of morals represents a double questioning. Firstly, its aim is to pose the question concerning the *origins* of morality: under what conditions and circumstances did morality arise (we shall presently attend to the question of what Nietzsche precisely intends by reflecting on man's 'origins')? Genealogy will consider morality as 'consequence, as symptom, as mask, as tartufferie, as illness; but also morality as cause, as remedy, as stimulant, as restraint, as poison'.[38] In this respect genealogy represents a kind of knowledge that has never previously existed, or even been desired, since the existence of morality has been taken for granted. Secondly, genealogy poses the question concerning a critique of morality. It is with this second demand that the originality of a genealogy of morals can be located, for the aim is not simply to perform a 'hypothesis-mongering' on the origins of morality, which has only a limited value, but rather to call into question the value of moral values, in other words, to perform a *revaluation* of moral values.[39] For Nietzsche this primarily means a revaluation of the unegoistic values such as pity and self-sacrifice. In these values Nietzsche locates a will turning against life and towards nihilism. What is at stake is the *value* of morality. The question which concerns Nietzsche most in carrying out this project of genealogy of morals, is how a specifically *moral* view of the world comes to dominate humanity's existence and the interpretation of its will to power. However, the two aspects of genealogy are closely related in that a critique of the value of morality is only possible on the basis of a knowledge of its historical conditions of existence. The decisive question is posed:

Under what conditions did man devise these value judgements good and evil? *and what value do they themselves possess?* Have they hitherto hindered or furthered human prosperity? Are they a sign of distress, of impoverishment, of the degeneration of life? Or is there revealed in them, on the contrary, the plenitude, force, and will of life, its courage, certainty, and future?[40]

Through a genealogy of morals Nietzsche responds to Rousseau's construal of the 'problem of civilization' by questioning to what extent it is the 'good man', as opposed to the 'evil one', who represents the future prosperity and advancement of humanity. Nietzsche's fundamental aim is to revalue moral values in such a way that our attitude towards actions decried as egoistic will be deprived of its bad conscience. For Nietzsche, 'This is a very significant result! When man no longer regards himself as evil he ceases to be so!'[41]

In its concern to trace the evolution of the human animal into a moral being, the *Genealogy of Morals* bears a striking resemblance to Rousseau's second discourse. Fundamental to both works is the conviction that man is not naturally a political animal, and that the transition from the state of nature to civil society produces a profound and ambiguous transformation in human nature. Nietzsche's argument on the origins of morality, however, differs significantly from Rousseau's in that it does not posit an original natural goodness which is corrupted and made evil by a process of socialization, but, on the contrary, argues that the 'value' of civilization lies in the fact that it deepens humanity by providing it with a knowledge of evil. Nietzsche completely inverts Rousseau's argument. Moreover, unlike Rousseau, Nietzsche's concern is not with deducing the nature of a legitimate social contract, of replacing 'force' with 'right', but with the self-overcoming of morality and the creation of the over-man, that is, the humanity whose will to power is beyond the opposition of good and evil.

GENEALOGY AND HISTORY: NIETZSCHE AND 'URSPRUNG'

The *Genealogy* has been interpreted as a conservative text in its attitude towards history by Jürgen Habermas, and as a radical text in its attitude by Michael Foucault. For Habermass the project of genealogy is fundamentally ahistorical in that it seeks a return to aristocratic origins. Poststructuralist critics and commentators, on the other hand, celebrate it as a new kind of history which eschews the teleological (and theological) pretensions of a philosophy of history. Genealogical narrative, it is argued, shows the futility of any attempt to locate meaning in history. Gilles Deleuze, for example, goes so far as to posit nihilism as 'the *a priori* of universal history'.[42]

Habermas's critique of genealogy depends on the sustainability of his major claim that genealogy is an exercise in conservative history because it equates questions about ancestry and origin with questions about validity. In reducing objective claims to truth to elements of subjective taste and power, it is Nietzsche's aim, Habermas argues, to express his own preference for noble morality as opposed to slave morality. Genealogy, Habermas contends, asserts that which is more original in time is 'better'; in this way 'ancestry and origin serve simultaneously as the criteria of rank in the social, as well as in the logical, sense. It is in this sense that Nietzsche bases his critique of morality on genealogy'.[43] The *Genealogy of Morals* can be read as offering an inverted image of Rousseau's innocent state of nature in which the wild, prowling blond beasts have yet to be corrupted by the poison of morality.

Habermas's argument can only be maintained if it can be shown that Nietzsche is arguing for an ahistorical return to some form of pagan aristocracy. In fact, it could be argued that Habermas's critique is much better directed at Rousseau than it is at Nietzsche, for it is Rousseau's second discourse that represents a search for origins which will validate the 'original' in history as being more authentic because it is, in some fundamental sense, more 'natural'. Nietzsche, by contrast, is radical in that he undermines the tenability of Rousseau's crucial distinction between what is natural and what is artificial in human nature.

According to Foucault, Nietzsche's project of genealogy does not conceive of history as a search for origins. The *Genealogy of Morals* is not only a polemic against the values of the modern period, but also against a certain way of construing the origins, meaning, and ancestry of those values. The search for origins represents a deluded quest for knowledge about ourselves. Instead, genealogy undermines the distinction between truth and illusion by showing that all knowledge rests on injustice. Genealogy does not aim to discover the roots of human identity, but rather seeks to establish the various modes by which the human being has been created as a subject. Where the search for origins presupposes essences and fixed identities, genealogy records the singularity of historical events in all their contingency and lack of finality: 'What is found at the historical beginning of things', Foucault writes, 'is not the inviolable identity of their origin; it is the dissension of other things. It is disparity'.[44]

Perhaps the central notion Nietzsche employs in carrying out a genealogical history is that of will to power. With this notion Nietzsche attempts to combat the view that historical reality manifests only a fortuitousness and mechanistic senselessness. Central to his argument is the necessity of making a distinction between 'origin' and 'purpose'. He argues that no matter how well the historian has understood the utility of something (whether a social custom or a legal institution for example) this will reveal nothing about its origins because purposes and utilities are only 'signs' that a *will to power*, a will to subdue and master, is operating.[45] Nietzsche's genealogical critique is based on this major principle of 'historical method'. What this means is that there is no meaning independent of interpretation, that 'there are no moral facts, but only a moral interpretation of these so-called facts'. For Foucault interpretation is not to be conceived in terms of a gradual uncovering of hidden meanings, but as the violent and surreptitious appropriation of a system of rules and codes which in itself has no meaning, in order to subject it to new forces and a new will to power. But although no meaning is possible without interpretation, Nietzsche does seek to uncover some 'sense' of history from his genealogical inquiry into the origins and evolution of morality. As one commentator has pointed out, Nietzsche's conception of the will to power as a principle of historical method does have the appearance of a metaphysical principle which sets out to cut through deceptive appearances to uncover the hidden, underlying structure of reality in order to reveal things 'as they really are'.[46] Foucault's reading of the role of will to power in the project of genealogy is much too anarchic for Nietzsche's taste. However, in assessing the role the notion of will to power plays in Nietzsche's thinking, much depends on how we interpret in what sense genealogy is occupied with questions of origins and ancestry.

There is another important aspect to Nietzsche's conception of genealogy which concerns the relation between genealogy and critique. Nietzsche is aware that to subject morality to historical investigation is to undermine its transcendental claims. However, he is also aware that this in no way constitutes a sufficient basis on which to mount a critique of morality – a confusion which, I would argue, informs Foucault's reading of genealogy. Showing that morality is a species of immorality, or that justice is a product of injustice is not equivalent to a critique. As Nietzsche informs us:

> The inquiry into the *origin of our evaluations* and tables of the good is in no way identical to a critique of them, as is so often believed: even though the insight into some *pudenda origo* [shameful origin] may bring with it a feeling of diminution in the value of the thing that originated and thus prepare the way for a critical attitude.[47]

However, I think it can be fairly argued that nowhere does Nietzsche ever satisfactorily resolve this problem of critique in his writings. His criterion of 'ascending and descending life' is deeply problematic in that it seeks to impose a judgement on life in terms of an abstract metaphysical dualism of the kind that the rest of his thought seeks to overcome. The values which inform our judgement of whether a form of life represents an ascending mode, or a descending one, may be totally arbitrary and little more than the reflections of a purely subjective will to power.[48]

If Nietzsche wishes to separate the question of 'purposes' from the question of 'origins', in what sense is he concerned with 'origins'? Foucault sees the originality of his reading of Nietzsche – and in this he has been copied by numerous commentators – in that it shows that Nietzsche employs several terms to denote the word 'origin', and that genealogy is above all a critique of the deluded search for origin (*Ursprung*), where 'origin' denotes an *archē*, a basic and fundamental principle from which all else derives; instead, Foucault argues, genealogy is an attempt to construct an ancestry and descent (*Herkunft*) which abandons any concern with finding original and essential identities. For Foucault, Nietzsche is the anti-*Ursprung* thinker *par excellence*, and for whom a preoccupation with *Ursprung* represents the supreme metaphysical delusion that one can retrieve one's identity by recollecting one's origins. But historical identity resides not in *Ursprung* but in *Entstehung* (emergence, rise), which does not denote a single, privileged point of origin giving rise to an uninterrupted continuity, but rather the locus where historical forces of domination meet and struggle.

Against Foucault, not only can it be shown that Nietzsche's

expression of a 'fundamental will to knowledge' is ironic, but that he has completely misread the intentions behind Nietzsche's deployment of the related terms of *Ursprung*, *Herkunft*, and *Entstehung*. In the German tradition which derives from Herder, for example, *Ursprung* denotes dialectical tension and confrontation, and *Entstehung* denotes unbroken continuity (in the *Birth of Tragedy*, for example, the origin – *Ursprung* – of tragedy lies in the conflict and tension between Apollo and Dionysus).[49] It is thus neither *Herkunft* nor *Entstehung*, but *Ursprung* which identifies the site where competing values come into conflict and give rise to human institutions. *Ursprung* should not be taken to denote an undifferentiated unity, but understood as the site of a primal division, as in Nietzsche's tracing of morals in the first essay to the competition between master morality and slave morality.[50] In the crucial section on method in the second essay of the *Genealogy*, for example, Nietzsche argues that genealogists are guilty not of conflating 'origin' and 'purpose' in the sense of *Ursprung*, but in that of *Entstehung*. The so-called genealogists of morals, the English psychologists of the utilitarian school who Nietzsche criticizes, are the ones who practise *Entstehungsgeschichte*.[51]

For Nietzsche, therefore, it is *Ursprung* which is to provide the foundation for a genealogy of morals. Thus, as the way in which we are to become what we are, genealogy shows us that our origins reveal to us not an unbroken continuity, but the conflict and struggle of will(s) to power. What this shows is that, considered as an exercise in monumental history which sets out to uncover a forgotten noble past, genealogy is at the same time an exercise in critical history, in that the particular sense which Nietzsche imputes to *Ursprung* is designed to break up the past by breaking up our supposed univocal identities. Perhaps here is an appropriate place to consider an important objection to genealogy raised by one commentator who has argued that there has to be a connection between origins and outcome in history, for either genealogy remains a variant of teleological history, or it is irrelevant by its own standards of relevance. If origins are not constitutive then they are irrelevant; if they are constitutive then they imply a *telos*.[52]

This critique of genealogy, although a pertinent one, can be answered by arguing that it separates the project of a genealogy of morals from the task of becoming what one is. For such a task does not at all rest on a passive recollection of origins, but on an active construction of the past which prepares the ground for a creative future willing (a willing which, as we will see, takes place through the cultivating thought of eternal return). Genealogy rejects 'contemplative, sentimental history' by placing into question the passive standpoint of the historian and the historian's readers, as well as any supposed 'innocent aestheticism' of the past.[53] As an attempt to 'solve' the problem of history, Nietzsche's *Genealogy of Morals* affirms the historicity of the human condition by aiming to effect a non-teleological self-overcoming of 'morals'. If we recognize self-overcoming as the 'law of life', then this means that all laws must eventually be transgressed since all great things bring about their own destruction on account of the fundamental law of life; it means that to create is to destroy, but that this act of simultaneous creation and destruction must take place free of the spirit of resentment so that one does not create a new future by taking revenge on the past – but innocently.

The *Genealogy of Morals* is best read in terms of an exercise in self-mastery. In looking back on our origins and formation we will inevitably experience great pain for we remember the sufferings and injustices of the past. But it is only pain, Nietzsche informs his readers, that compels us to descend into the depths and to put trust, good-naturedness, and everything which would interpose a veil, aside. Such pain may not make us 'better', but it may make us 'more profound':

Whether we learn to pit our pride, our scorn, our will to power against it, like the American Indian who, however tortured, repays his torturer with the malice of his tongue, or whether we withdraw from pain into that Oriental Nothing called Nirvana into mute, rigid, deaf resignation, self-forgetting, self-extinction: out of such long and dangerous exercises of self-mastery one emerges a different person, with a few more question marks – above all with the *will* henceforth to question further, more deeply, severely, harshly, evilly and quietly than one had questioned before. The trust in life is gone: life itself has become a *problem*.[54]

The attraction of the problematic should not, however, lead to paralysis of the will, but to a more spiritualized delight in the mysteriousness and profundity of human existence. We should return from such abysses and sicknesses of suspicion and questioning as 'newborn'; having shed our skin we now have a more delicate taste for joy, 'with a second dangerous innocence in joy, more childlike and yet a hundred times more subtle than one has ever been before'.[55] However, our will to truth that is a will to power should not be mistaken for a desire to know and expose everything, for we 'no longer believe that truth remains when the veils are withdrawn; we have lived too much to believe this'. Instead, we should have respect for the bashfulness with which nature hides itself behind riddles and iridescent uncertainties. Perhaps in seeking truth we learn that truth is a woman 'who has reasons for not letting us see her reasons'? Is truth perhaps a woman who goes by the Greek name of Baubo?[56]

In order to substantiate these points, and in order to show how Nietzsche understands the *Genealogy* as a complex exercise in the monumental, critical, and innocent task of becoming those that we are, it is necessary to analyse the key arguments of the book in some detail.

MASTER MORALITY AND SLAVE MORALITY: ON THE ORIGINS OF 'GOOD AND EVIL', 'GOOD AND BAD'

If Nietzsche's *Genealogy* does not represent a straightfoward history of morals, then neither does it represent a philosophy of morals, for such a philosophy is only possible if one believes that the meaning of moral terms is static and universal. For Nietzsche, however, the extra-moral task of becoming what one is is inseparable from the unique life-experience of the 'one'. If for Nietzsche there cannot be a moral philosophy, then there can also neither be a 'philosophy of morals'. In accordance with Nietzsche's demand for an 'art of interpretation', morals must be read as 'signs' in need of a 'symptomatology'. The process of reification in language is nowhere more apparent than in the language of morals. In the *Genealogy* Nietzsche challenges the distinction between 'natural' and 'artificial' by breaking down the distinction between literal and figurative language. Just as notions of literal meaning reflect the tendency of language to harden into fixed form, so moral values conceal their material basis and take on a 'natural' character. In both the first and second essays of the *Genealogy* Nietzsche traces the process whereby certain notions are subjected to moralization, and the original material context in which these notions originated becomes forgotten and buried over. In section six of the first essay, for example, Nietzsche argues that all the concepts of ancient humanity were at first 'incredibly uncouth, coarse, external, narrow, straightforward, and altogether *unsymbolical* in meaning to a degree that we can scarcely conceive'. Nietzsche gives the example of the 'pure one'. The original meaning of purity precedes the distinction between the figurative and the literal in that no distinction is recognized by 'primitive' man between the spiritual and the material.

As an exercise in etymology genealogy traces the process whereby material terms (such as being in debt) develop into moral ones (such as the experience of guilt). Meaning, therefore, cannot be understood in terms of stable categories, whether literal or figurative, but needs to be grasped as something radically historical.[57] All meaning is a making meaningful (hence *Wille zur 'Macht'*); and there can be no meaning apart from interpretation. If meaning is historical, there can be no natural hierarchy of meanings; rather, all meaning must ultimately by poetic and the result of human making (*machen*). For Nietzsche humanity's will to power conceived as a will to making and creating is best understood in terms of a process of culture by which the human animal is trained and disciplined into becoming an animal with a sense of responsibility and with the capacity to make promises – in other words, the cultivation of a *political* animal.

In carrying out an inquiry into the historical origins of morality what is it, Nietzsche asks in the opening section of the first essay, that we really want? Do we wish to belittle man? Are we disappointed idealists who have grown gloomy and spiteful? Are we the victims of a 'petty subterranean hostility and rancour toward Christianity' that has not yet become fully conscious? Or do we have a 'lascivious taste for the grotesque, the painfully paradoxical, the questionable and the absurd in existence'? Perhaps, Nietzsche reflects, we are determined a little by all of these motives. Whatever motivates our search for origins, we should at all times be, in our guise as 'microscopists of the soul', 'brave, proud, and magnanimous' spirits who know how to keep our sufferings in bounds so that we are able to sacrifice everything to truth, to 'every plain, harsh, ugly, repellent unchristian immoral truth. – For such truths do exist'.[58] Nietzsche's inquiry into morals is informed by respect for the 'intellectual conscience' – that is, the need to stand joyfully in the centre of the marvellous uncertainty and rich ambiguity of existence but still question – which he considers absolutely fundamental to the human task of becoming what one is.[59]

The *Genealogy* begins with Nietzsche castigating moral philosophers for the lack of historical spirit (*historische Geist*) they have displayed in approaching questions of morality. The way in which morality has been misunderstood is apparent when one examines the way in which moral philosophers have tried to investigate the descent (*Herkunft*) of the judgement 'good'. It has been the prevailing argument of moral philosophers that the origin of the concept 'good' is to be sought by considering the point of view to whom actions are useful. In other words, the concept of 'good', when applied to human actions, rests on an essentially utilitarian foundation. However, Nietzsche argues that this account of the origin of 'good' ignores the fact that altruism contradicts its own criterion of what is moral in that action is praised or blamed in accordance with whether or not it brings advantages to the self. In opposition to this altruistic account of the origin of 'good', Nietzsche puts forward the arguments that the judgement 'good', concerning human actions, did not originate with those to whom goodness was shown, but rather with the 'good' themselves, that is those noble and powerful individuals who felt and established themselves and their actions as good, independent of any altruistic concerns, and in contradistinction to all they considered low, common and plebeian. It was out of this 'pathos of distance' that the 'right' (*Recht*) to create values was first seized. Having criticized the utilitarian bent of the English psychologists in tracing the descent of the judgement 'good' in altruism, Nietzsche goes on to locate the real 'origin' (*Ursprung*) of the antithesis 'good and bad' in the pathos of nobility, that is in the feeling a ruling class has in relation to a lower one. Nietzsche even goes so far as to suggest that the very origin (*Ursprung*) of language might be conceived in terms of an expression of the power felt by the ruling classes.[60]

In section four Nietzsche informs us that his own insights into the origin of 'good' were made possible by reflecting on the etymological significance of the designation of the concept 'good' coined in various languages. He discovers that in all places the concept 'good' derives from a social basis in noble and aristocratic cultures. In respect of a 'moral genealogy' Nietzsche argues this to be 'a *fundamental* insight'.[61] The fact that it has not been recognized until now is the result of the democratic prejudices of the modern age towards questions about the descent (*Herkunft*) of morals. A democratic age pre-judges the question of origins by reading back into history the equalizing and levelling tendencies of its own morality. Nietzsche argues, however, that is only with the decline of aristocratic value judgements that the opposition of egoistic and unegoistic actions comes to the fore.

The way in which Nietzsche clarifies his argument on the origin of the judgement 'good' is through introducing the notions of master and slave moralities. This distinction between types of moralities is crucial for Nietzsche, and it is first introduced by him in section 260 of *Beyond Good and Evil*. Indeed, in section 186 of that work Nietzsche criticizes moral philosophers for merely carrying out rationalizations of existing moralities and argues that in order to carry out a critique of morality what is needed is to construct a 'typology of morals' (*Typenlehre der Moral*). It should be noted that, although Nietzsche conceives a close correlation between concepts denoting political superiority and those denoting superiority of soul, he does not employ the designations of master and slave moralities in terms of biological essences, but more in the manner of ideal types. Thus, for example, Nietzsche writes that although human beings of higher social rank designate themselves by their superiority in power (as in 'the masters', 'the commanders') or by their superiority in riches (as in 'the possessors'), they also designate themselves by 'typical character traits'. It is this aspect of the noble and aristocratic classes which interests Nietzsche, not simply the power they gain from their political superiority.[62]

It is with this typology of a master and a slave morality that Nietzsche attempts to locate the origin of the distinction between 'good and bad' on the one hand and between 'good and evil' on the other. His main argument is that whereas a master morality – a morality of strength, courage, and independence – defines itself by self-affirmation and is unconcerned with how its actions are perceived and judged by others, a slave morality, by contrast – a morality of weakness and dependence – can only define itself by negating others and declaring that everyone is equal and the same. Thus, whereas, the noble and strong declare themselves first as 'good', independent of any unegoistic concerns, and only define others as 'bad' after they have defined and affirmed themselves, the plebeian and weak define their identity by first defining others as 'evil', and only after this designation of the other do they then define themselves as 'good'. In conscious opposition to an innocent noble self-affirmation, for example, the Jews – the priestly people *par excellence* for Nietzsche[63] – perform a radical revaluation of aristocratic values through an act of supreme spiritual revenge. The aristocratic value-equation of good = noble = powerful = beautiful, etc. is transformed and inverted by the hatred of impotence into 'the wretched alone are the good; the poor, impotent, lowly alone are the good; the suffering, deprived, sick, ugly alone are pious and blessed by God', while the powerful and the noble are, on the contrary 'the evil, the cruel, the lustful, insatiable, the godless to all eternity'.[64] Only through this slave revolt in morals do actions become subject to a moral interpretation and described as 'evil', 'cruel' and 'wicked'.

The defining feature of this slave morality is the phenomenon of *ressentiment*. A slave morality can only exist by negating what it is not, what exists outside of it, and what is different to it. Unlike the master morality, the slave morality is totally dependent on a hostile external world for its identity. It is with the rise of this attitude of *ressentiment* towards all forms of otherness that Nietzsche locates the slave revolt in morals which begins:

when *ressentiment* itself becomes creative and gives birth to values: the *ressentiment* of natures that are denied the true reaction, that of deeds, and compensate themselves with an imaginary revenge. While every noble morality develops from a triumphant affirmation of itself, slave morality from the outset says No to what is 'outside', what is 'different', what is 'not itself'; and *this* No is its creative deed. This inversion of the value-positing eye – this *need* to direct one's view outward instead of back to oneself – is of the essence of *ressentiment*: in order to exist, slave morality first needs a hostile external world... its action is fundamentally reaction.[65]

Nietzsche contrasts the ethic of the noble and the strong with this negative and destructive morality of *ressentiment*, pointing out that while the slave morality can only exist through its opposite, the noble morality seeks its opposite only so as to affirm even more its independence and difference. The strong and noble do not have to establish their happiness and pleasure with existence artificially by examining their enemies and by deceiving themselves that they are indeed what they proclaim themselves to be, happy and good. If resentment should make its appearance in the noble self, it immediately consummates and exhausts itself in reaction and does not remain to poision him. 'To be incapable of taking one's enemies, one's accidents, even one's misdeeds seriously for very long', Nietzsche says, 'is the sign of strong, full natures in whom there exists an excess of the power to form, to mold, to recuperate, and to forget'.[66] An example of this nobility in modern times is the Comte de Mirabeau who, says Nietzsche, had no memory for insults and injuries done to him. The noble man honours and respects others, including his enemies, as his mark of distinction and not as a need for identification. By contrast, the weak man of resentment creates a picture of his enemy as 'the evil one' as his basic concept from which he then arrives at a definition of himself as the 'good one'.[67] Nietzsche draws our attention to the difference between the notions of 'bad' and 'evil', even though both are conceived in opposition to the notion of 'good'.[68] The 'evil' in the morality of 'good and evil' refers to the 'good man' of the noble morality. It is the vengefulness of the impotent which results in the first significant revaluation of values to take place in man's historical evolution. With this fundamental inversion of noble morality, morality now comes to designate altruistic or unegoistic values. Nietzsche imagines a modern 'free spirit', an honest animal and a democrat by definition of being modern, who confesses that today everything has become 'Judaized, Christianized, mob-ized'. The morality of the mob and of the common man has won against everything rare, noble, and privileged. Given this triumph of the slave revolt, the free-spirited democrat asks whether the church today still has any necessary role to play, for it seems to hinder rather than hasten this progress, it alienates and no longer seduces. Would 'we' still be free spirits if the church did not exist? For 'it is the church, and not its poison' which repels us – 'apart from the church, we, too, love the poison'.[69]

Nietzsche's main insight into the moral evolution of humanity at this stage of his argument is that moral designations first apply to human beings and only later to human actions. In other words, the noble human being honours himself as one who is powerful and has power over himself. The noble and courageous human being is actually proud of the fact 'that he is *not* made for pity'.[70] By contrast, slave morality defines itself in terms of a negation of what is different to it, and is, therefore, a morality born out of weakness which results in a pessimistic view of existence in which the only values to be esteemed are those which serve to preserve the weak and make their existence endurable. The most important value esteemed by slave morality, says Nietzsche, is pity. It is possible, therefore, to define Nietzsche's typology of master and slave moralities in accordance with types of will to power. Nietzsche writes, for example, that: 'The longing for *freedom*, the instinct for happiness...belong just as necessarily to slave morality and morals as artful and enthusiastic reverence and devotion are the regular symptom of an aristocratic way of thinking and evaluating'.[71]

By inventing the notion of free will the slave morality is able to hold the strong accountable for their actions, to assign evil intentions to them, and to make them feel culpable for being strong and powerful. He writes:

To demand of strength that it should *not* express itself as strength, that it should *not* be willing to overcome, a desire to throw down, a willing to become master, a thirst for enemies and resistance and triumphs, is just as absurd as to demand of weakness that it should express itself as strength. A quantum of force (*Kraft*) is equivalent to a quantum of drive, will, effect – more, it is nothing other than precisely this very driving, willing, effecting, and only owing to the seduction of language (and of the fundamental errors of reason that are petrified in it) which conceives and misconceives all effects as conditioned by something that causes effects, by a 'subject', can it appear otherwise. For just as the popular mind separates the lightning from its flash and takes the latter for an *action*, for the operation of a subject called lightning, so popular morality also separates strength from expressions of strength, as if there existed a neutral substratum behind the strong man, which was *free* to express strength or not to do so. But there is no such substratum; there is no 'being' behind doing, effecting, becoming; the 'doer' is merely a fiction added to the deed – the deed is everything…no wonder if the submerged, darkly glowering emotions of vengefulness and hatred exploit this belief for their own ends and in fact maintain no belief more ardently than the belief that *the strong man is free* to be weak and the bird of prey to be a lamb – for thus they gain the right to make the bird *accountable* for being a bird of prey.[72]

Nietzsche's argument is that the manner in which we have learned to view moral action in terms of a distinction between the *subject* of action and the action itself (a distinction between doer and the deed) is the product of a slave revolt in morals by which the weak attempt to undermine the noble's sense of strength and power through holding them accountable for being what they are. Through the self-deception of impotence the weak convince themselves that all human action is the product of a free will; moreover, they convince themselves that what they regard as 'evil' actions is the result of an intentional desire on the part of the strong to make them feel degraded and worthless. The weak needed to believe in a neutral, independent subject for their own self-preservation:

The subject (or, to use a more popular expression, the *soul*) has perhaps been believed in hitherto more firmly than anything else on earth because it makes possible to the majority of mortals, the weak and oppressed of every kind, the sublime self-deception that interprets weakness as freedom, and their being thus-and-thus as a *merit*.[73]

On the one hand, Nietzsche's distinction between master and slave types of morality can be seen to correspond to Rousseau's distinction between *amour de soi* and *amour-propre*; in both cases the former term denotes a pure, spontaneous and innocent self-affirmation, while the latter term denotes the masked, deceitful actions of the impotent who are totally dependent on others for their sense of self-worth. On the other hand, however, the typology of master and slave moralities can be seen to pose a major challenge to Rousseau's account of morality. What Nietzsche does with his analysis of the origins of 'good and bad', and 'good and evil', is to provide what Rousseau regards as 'evil' actions with a good conscience. Thus, Nietzsche argues that so-called 'evil' or cruel actions also belong in their primitive, pre-moral mode to a self-preserving, self-enhancing, and self-overcoming will to power. Thus, it is with the notion of a slave revolt in morals that Nietzsche attempts to give historical specificity to Rousseau's understanding of social degeneration. On Nietzsche's account, Rousseau would have to be included amongst those moral philosophers who lack a genuine historical sense.

It would be mistaken, as well as misleading, to infer from Nietzsche's construction of a typology of morals that he is simply *for* master morality and *against* slave morality. Such an assessment would fail to appreciate the historical basis of Nietzsche's attempt to trace the evolution of humanity as a moral species. Although he holds the slave revolt in morals responsible for instituting what he calls a 'grand politics of revenge' (*grossen Politik der Rache*) into human existence[74] – a politics which was last repeated in human history with the French Revolution[75] – Nietzsche acknowledges at the same time that 'history would be altogether too stupid a thing without the spirit that the impotent have introduced into it'.[76] It is only on the soil of a priestly form of existence, which comes to the aid of the weak and the oppressed, that man first becomes '*an interesting animal*... only here did the human soul in a higher sense acquire *depth* and become evil'.[77] The transition from a warrior–aristocratic culture to a priestly–aristocratic culture brings with it the moralization of man's existence, as everything in life, from revenge and love, to virtue and disease, is endowed with a metaphysical meaning and significance. This transition brings with it both great danger and great promise. It is not simply a case, therefore, of Nietzsche simply glorifying master morality over slave morality. On the contrary, the slave for Nietzsche is considered to have more depth to its nature because the reality of its oppressed condition means that it is compelled to internalize its action and thereby develop a 'soul'. As Nietzsche points out, 'while the noble man lives in trust and openness with himself, the man of *ressentiment* is neither upright nor naive nor honest with himself... A race of such men of *ressentiment* is bound to become *cleverer* than any noble race'.[78] What Nietzsche admires about the master morality is that it reveals a mastery of itself that is positive and affirmatory, although it is totally instinctive and pre-reflective.

Nietzsche is far from advocating a return to the pagan aristocracy of the blond beast referred to in section 11 of the first essay. Nietzsche is not arguing for the restoration of a pre-Christian morality for the simple reason that he believes that the changes brought about to the human soul by the slave revolt in morals have *deepened* it. As he informs us:

Supposing that what is at any rate believed to be the 'truth' really is true, and the *meaning of all culture (Kultur)* is the reduction of the beast of prey 'man' to a tame and civilised animal, a *domestic animal*, then one would undoubtedly have to regard all those instincts of reaction and *ressentiment* through whose aid the noble races and their ideals were finally confounded and overthrown as the actual *instruments of culture*; which is not to say that the *bearers* of these instincts represent culture.[79]

What Nietzsche demands is that humanity overcome itself once again by incorporating and transfiguring all that has been necessary and educative in human development so far in order to reach a higher state of nobility founded on a conscious 'second innocence' of joy and self-affirmation. Such a synthesis of master morality and slave morality into something higher is no easy task, but then Nietzsche does not pretend otherwise. In order to carry out this task adequately man must learn to know what it means to be beyond 'good and evil', which does not mean beyond 'good and bad'.[80]

Nietzsche's historical understanding of the moral evolution of humanity rests on a notion of 'culture' conceived as 'discipline' (*Zucht*). By defining culture in this way Nietzsche is showing that this process of moral evolution must be understood in educative terms. But in contrast to Rousseau, Nietzsche argues that there is no such thing as a 'natural' morality since every morality represents a form of tyranny against nature. Thus, the most important thing about any form of morality is that it constitutes:

a long compulsion (*Zwang*) ... this tyranny, this caprice, this rigorous and grandiose stupidity has *educated* the spirit. Slavery is ... the indispensable means of spiritual discipline (*Zucht*) and cultivation (*Züchtung*) too ... 'You shall obey someone and for a long time, otherwise you will perish and lose respect for yourself' – this appears to me to be the moral imperative of nature which, to be sure, is neither 'categorical' as the old Kant would have it nor addressed to the individual, but to peoples, races, ages, and classes, – but above all to the whole human animal, to *man*.[81]

It is this understanding of morality in terms of discipline and cultivation that lies at the basis of Nietzsche's argument in the second essay on the problem of breeding an animal which can make promises, and on the origins of the bad conscience, to which I now turn my attention.

THE SOVEREIGN INDIVIDUAL

In the second essay on 'guilt, bad conscience, and the like' Nietzsche develops further his argument on the imperative of culture. He offers two accounts of the formation of man as a moral and political animal, one in terms of what he calls the 'morality of custom' (*Sittlichkeit der Sitte*) and the other in terms of the bad conscience (*schlectes Gewissen*). It is in this inquiry that Nietzsche can be seen to provide a response to some of the paradoxes of Rousseau's political thought. The paradox which lies at the heart of Rousseau's thinking on the politicization of ethics concerns how individuals are to become moral (virtuous citizens) prior to their actually being moral. How can human beings become social and moral creatures, Rousseau asks, prior to their formation as political animals? In his investigation into the nature of the bad conscience Nietzsche shows that it is a mere piece of sentimentalism to attempt to establish a legitimate political order on the basis of a social contract, since this contract presupposes precisely what needs to be accounted for, namely the development of free will, rationality and conscience. What Nietzsche does is to suspend the question of political legitimacy and replace it with what Foucault has called 'a political technology of the human subject'.[82] What concerns Nietzsche is the way in which the process of compulsion leads not only to the production of the individual who is sovereign over its warring fractions – the individual who has a sense of responsibility and the ability to make promises – but also to the internalization and repression of the instinct of will to power in the form of a bad conscience. The significance of this process for considering the question of political legitimacy and political obligation is that, for Nietzsche, it is pointless to posit the 'will' as the ground of 'right', since this will itself has been constituted by social forces and through political compulsion. A discourse on the principles of political right must give way to a genealogy of morals in which the formation and deformation of the human subject conceived as a will to power is traced in terms of an ambiguous moral education.

It is only in recent years that research has been carried out into the sources which most influenced Nietzsche's thinking on ethics and politics in the *Genealogy of Morals*.[83] One of the most important influences on the second essay was that of Rudolf von Ihering's (1818–92) *Der Zweck im Recht*, the first volume of which appeared in 1877, the second in 1883.[84] Nietzsche made notes from this work, although not much remains. In a note written in the summer of 1883 he jots down Ihering's views on justice, evil action, punishment, guilt responsibility, etc.[85] Von Ihering's work influenced Nietzsche's thinking on a number of crucial notions.

Ihering was an important critic of the natural law tradition in that he argued that it artificially separated the individual from its historical connection with society. The formation of the human will has to be understood in terms of a social process: 'There is no greater miracle in the world', Ihering writes, 'than the disciplining and training of the human will, whose actual realization we embrace in its widest scope in the word society. The sum of impulses and powers which accomplish this work I call social mechanics'.[86] Ihering, while praising the natural law theorists for raising the question about the origin of law, criticizes the school of natural law for conceiving the origin of the 'historical State' in terms of a social contract: 'This is a pure construction without regard to actual history'.[87] Instead, the origins of the State lie in coercion. He makes a distinction between social coercion which brings about the realization of morality, and political coercion, which brings about the realization of law. The strong decide to set a limit to force by establishing norms and conventions of right and wrong, etc., and which becomes 'law'. 'Force', Ihering writes, 'produces law out of itself as a measure for itself'. What we must realize is that it is the 'despots and inhuman tyrants' who have done 'just as much for educating mankind in law as the wise lawgivers.'[88] Prior to the establishment of law we find much cruelty in human interaction, but we need to appreciate that 'the ethical standard with which we quite unhistorically equip them, was quite foreign to them'.[89] In abandoning the 'ground of history', and attempting to answer the question 'from the nature of the subjective will abstracted from society and history', the natural law theorists deprived themselves of any solution to the problem of the origins and nature of law and right.[90] The 'purpose' of law, Ihering argues, resides solely in its practical function. 'Society' represents the bearer of the 'regulated and disciplined coercive force'. The principle by which it functions as a dicipline of coercion is what we call 'law'. The end of the State, as well as that of law, is 'the establishment and security of the conditions of social life. Law exists for the sake of society, not society for the sake of law.'[91] Ihering's political theory is an interesting one in that, although it adopts a kind of sociological positivism in thinking about the origins of the State and law, it culminates in a Rousseauian-inspired politics in which the individual is completely subordinated to the 'State', to the extent that it may force the individual to be free: 'The State compels you to do that which, if you had time and insight, you would do of your own accord'.[92]

Although it cannot be claimed that Nietzsche ever came to hold a political theory similar to that of Ihering – Ihering's theory smacks too much of that modern worship of the State (the 'new idol') Nietzsche castigates in *Zarathustra* – his demand that the relationship between individual and society be conceived in terms of a historical problematic of the disciplining of the human will, can be seen to have had an important impact on Nietzsche's thinking on the whole problem which preoccupies him in the second essay and with which it begins:

To breed an animal *with the right to make promises* – is not this the paradoxical task that nature has set itself in the case of man? Is this not the real problem regarding man?[93]

It is in this context of the diciplining of the human will that Nietzsche argues that human memory is first developed. It is a development which takes place through the most rigorous and cruel of societal procedures. If the task of breeding the human animal so that it can make promises is to be successful, the force which needs to be overcome is the active and positive faculty of forgetfulness. This overcoming takes place through the cultivation of memory in man. Memory, Nietzsche argues, is not to be regarded merely as a passive inability to dispose of impressions, but rather as an active desire for the continuation of experience, which presupposes that one has a memory of the will, so that between one's original command of 'I will', and the actual discharge of the will in action, an entire world of strange and new things and circumstances can be interpreted by the self without breaking the chain of the will. This facility of the will, however, presupposes a great deal. It presupposes, for instance, that the self can ordain the future in advance by distinguishing necessary events from chance ones. In order for humanity to have knowledge and consciousness of its existence, in terms of a temporality directed towards the future, it must first of all have become regular and calculable.

For Nietzsche this process of making man regular and calculable is best described in terms of the long history of the descent (*Herkunft*) of responsibility. The task of breeding an animal which has the 'right to make promises' presupposes a preparatory task which first makes human beings uniform, necessary, and regular. Here Nietzsche understands social evolution in terms of the morality of custom. It is with this type of morality that the cultivation of man as a political animal takes place:

The tremendous labour of that which I have called 'morality of custom'... the labour performed by man upon himself during the greater part of the existence of the human race, his entire *prehistoric* labour, finds in this its meaning, its great justification, notwithstanding the severity, tyranny, and idiocy involved in it: with the aid of the morality of custom and the social straitjacket man was actually *made* calculable.[94]

Nietzsche's appreciation of the role that the morality of custom has played in the formation of the animal-man as a moral being, leads him to argue that the autonomous individual – the individual in possession of a free will and a conscience (the moral sense of right and wrong) – is a late fruit and the product of cultural forces which lie at the beginning of our prehistoric existence.[95] Central to Nietzsche's understanding of conscience and the memory of a will is the argument that the methods employed to solve this 'primeval problem' were not at all gentle, but rather involved methods of cruelty and asceticism that today we find difficult to contemplate.[96] It is on account of the cultivation of his memory by the use of such methods that the human being learns the significance of its obligations to society. These obligations to perform social duties are made in the form of the individual making promises in return for which society offers it protection and security. It is in the context of this exchange between the individual and society that Nietzsche locates man's power of reasoning and capacity for rational thought. He argues that man's capacity for reflection rests on the methods of cruelty that have been used to cultivate him as a rational and political animal. He thus understands conscience, not in terms of the voice of God in man, but in terms of an instinct of cruelty that turns back after it can no longer discharge itself externally.

Nietzsche's formulation of the development of man's reason, free will, and conscience, in terms of a historical labour of culture, is of tremendous importance for how we are to understand his relation to the tradition of modern political thought. For what that tradition, including Rousseau, takes for granted – free will, conscience, and other so-called innate 'moral' capacities – are shown to be the product of a historical process of socialization. Nietzsche's formulation of this problem of socialization is more radical than the one Rousseau provides in the *Discourse*, because it shows that even the most apparent natural attributes and capacities of the human animal depend on a historical labour for their existence. Nietzsche constantly emphasizes that there existed a period in history in which morality as we conceive it today did not exist. He thus speaks of 'the pre-moral period of man', describing it as the decisive phase that has 'determined the character of mankind'.[97] In the pre-moral period man is not concerned with locating the 'moral' source of his actions in intentions, but only with their success or failure. It is only with the cultivation of self-knowledge that man becomes a reflective being concerned with the moral origins of actions, that is, with a free will and with identifying the conscious intentions which supposedly lie behind all human action.

With this understanding of the moral evolution of humanity Nietzsche asks us to consider the possibility of entering into an extra-moral period of history. One way of achieving a self-overcoming of morality is to recognize that our sense of morality has evolved, and that consequently it cannot be claimed that there exists one particular natural morality, such as the view that the essence of a 'moral' action lies in the intentions behind it. The intention, Nietzsche says, is merely a sign, and a sign that requires an interpretation. It can be seen, therefore, that Nietzsche understands the evolution of what we consider to be morality in a specific way. In a passage in *Daybreak* for example, he distinguishes between various terms that can denote morality in German:

In comparison with the mode of life of millenia of mankind we live in a very unethical (*unsittlich*) age: the power of custom (*Sitte*) is astonishingly enfeebled and the ethical sense (*Gefühl der Sittlichkeit*) so rarified and lofty that it may be described as having more or less evaporated. This is why the fundamental insights into morality (*Moral*) are so difficult for us latecomers, and even when we have acquired them we find it impossible to enunciate them, because they sound so uncouth or because they seem to slander morality... This is, for example, already the case with the chief proposition: morality (*Sittlichkeit*) is nothing other than obedience to customs (*Sitten*)... customs, however, are the *traditional* way of behaving and evaluating. In things which no tradition commands there is no morality (*Sittlichkeit*)... What is tradition? A higher authority which one obeys, not because it commands what is *useful* to us, but because it *commands*... Originally all education and health care, marriage, cure of sickness, agriculture, war, speech and silence, traffic with one another and with the gods belonged within the domain of ethical life (*Sittlichkeit*): they demanded one observe prescriptions *without thinking of oneself* as an individual.[98]

The essence of the morality of custom is that the human being is trained to think of itself not as an individual, but as part of a community in which originality and individuality of any, and every, kind are forced to acquire a bad conscience.

Clearly the widespread conception of Nietzsche as an extreme individualist has to be revised in the light of this construal of his political thought, for it shows that the individual is not an assumption of his thinking, but rather that he conceives the individual as the historical product of certain social forces of evolution. In section 335 of the *Gay Science* Nietzsche writes that as sovereign individuals, '*we want to become those who we are* – the ones who are new, unique, incomparable, who give themselves laws, who create themselves'.[99] However, he recognizes that autonomy, the capacity for self-legislation and self-determination, is not the original fact of history but rather its product:

During the longest and most remote periods of the human past, the sting of conscience was not at all what it is nowadays. Today one feels responsible only for one's will and actions, and one finds one's pride in oneself. All our teachers of law start from this sense of self and pleasure in the single individual (*Einzelnen*), as if this had always been the source of law. But during the longest period of the human past nothing was more terrible than to feel that one stood by oneself. To be alone, to experience things by oneself, neither to obey or to rule, to be an individual (*Individuum*) – that was not a pleasure but a punishment: one was sentenced to 'individuality'... To be a self and to esteem oneself according to one's weight and measure – that offended taste in those days... There is no point on which we have learned to think and feel more differently.[100]

For Nietzsche, therefore, the autonomous individual equipped with free will and conscience has to be viewed not as the presupposition, but as the product, of history. What is notable about the description of the autonomous individual in the *Genealogy of Morals* is that Nietzsche describes its arrival not as a 'moral' or 'ethical' event but rather as 'supra-ethical' (*übersittlich*). For Nietzsche the arrival of the autonomous individual should not be regarded as an occasion for establishing a communal ethic on a rational foundation, but rather for producing aristocratic sovereign individuals who are unique, and who bear a will to self-responsibility. He writes:

> If we place ourselves at the end of this tremendous process where the tree at last brings forth fruit, where society and the morality of custom at last reveal *what* they have simply been the means to, then we discover that the ripest fruit is the *sovereign individual*, like only to himself, liberated again from the morality of custom, the autonomous and supra-ethical individual (*das autonome übersittliche Individuum*) (for 'autonomous' and 'ethical' are mutually exclusive), in short the man who has his own independent, protracted will and the right to make promises.[101]

Nietzsche defines the sovereign individual in terms of an emancipated individual who has become master of a free will that gives it mastery over itself, over nature, and over all those who have not achieved a condition of sovereignty. The sovereign human being is 'aware of its superiority over all those who lack the right to make promises and stand as their own guarantors'.[102] It possesses its own protracted free will as a 'measure of value' and 'mark of distinction', which enables it to consider itself in relation to others either in terms of honouring peers who also have earned the right to make promises, the strong and the reliable, or despising those distrustful and mendacious weak souls who make promises without the right to do so. 'Conscience' is simply the name we give to the instinct of power and consciousness the individual has over itself and fate, and which has become dominant in the sovereign individual.

Clearly an account of political obligation is to be found in this argument. However, it is a very different one from the deduction we find in Rousseau. For Nietzsche the exchange relationship between the individual and society is not explained in terms of a voluntarism by which the pre-moral and pre-social self is to be educated about its 'higher' moral self, and which comes from the recognition that the moral liberty to be gained by entering into a social contract with others is of a higher order than the natural liberty one enjoys in a natural state; rather, political obligation is to be understood as a prehistoric development which *precedes* conscious volition and individual choice. On Nietzsche's account the individual is compelled and constrained to obey society by the methods of cruelty employed in the morality of custom, which discipline and cultivate its 'moral' faculties and provide it with the capacity for rational deliberation concerning the future.

If the sovereign individual is the product of a historical labour of culture, and not simply a presupposition of social and political life, this means for Nietzsche that sovereignty is not a question of the individual transferring its power, either to a sovereign monarch (Hobbes) or to a sovereign moral–collective body such as the general will (Rousseau), but rather of the individual retaining its power in proud awareness of the discipline it has attained over its warring factions, and, being 'supra-ethical', by making its own decisions and choices and accepting responsibility for them. The sovereign individual displays courage and independence, for it enters into social relationships with others on the basis of a proud awareness of its sovereignty over itself, and of its distinction from others. *Contra* Rousseau, Nietzsche argues that to pose the question of the nature of political life in terms of a will which either defines its own maxims of action as universal ones, or which must always conform to universal maxims, is not to establish politics on the basis of an ethics of generosity, but rather on an ethics of selfishness and cowardice. Only the weak will, that is, the will which does not have the courage to stand alone and proudly declare '*I* willed it!' in response to an action, desires a common or general will. This explains why Nietzsche argues that pity is the most agreeable sentiment amongst those who have little pride and few prospects for great conquests in life.[103] In considering the question of 'Nietzsche *contra* Rousseau' as a question about the political, the important point concerns the value-basis on which individuals are to establish social relationships, namely on the basis of pity for the preservation of life, or on the basis of courage for its perpetual self-overcoming? As we shall see in the next chapter on Zarathustra, for Nietzsche the current position of humanity can be instructively described in terms of the metaphor of a bridge: the politics of modern man stands on a bridge between pity for the *last* man and a will to power for the *over*-man.

BAD CONSCIENCE

Nietzsche's account of the long history of the origins of responsibility is not simply the story of the production of sovereign individuality, and attainment of self-mastery through free will and conscience. It is also the history of how a *bad* conscience developed, and of how a deformation takes place in the social evolution of the will to power of the human animal. According to Nietzsche's account in the second essay there are two significant developments which account for this deformation. Firstly, the moralization (*Vermoralisierung*) of concepts which initially develops in the material sphere of legal obligations, and secondly, the internalization (*Verinnerlichung*) of man. Before offering his hypothesis – and it is no more than a hypothesis, offered somewhat in the manner of modern political thought's account of the state of nature – on the origins of the bad conscience, Nietzsche explores the origins of what he calls 'the moral–conceptual world', including notions such as guilt, punishment, duty, justice, etc., as a way of illuminating the process by which existence becomes increasingly subjected to a moral interpretation.

Nietzsche's major argument is that it is in the sphere of legal obligations (*Obligationen-Rechte*) that the moral–conceptual world has its origin (*Enstehungsheerd*). Thus, for example, he argues that the major moral concept of guilt (*Shuld*) has its descent (*Herkunft*) in the material sphere of debts (*Schulden*). It was in this sphere of civil law (*privatrechtlich*) that promises were made, and that a memory had to be created. It is on the basis of contractual relations between creditors and debtors, that is, between legal subjects, that the origins of our present moral world order of justice and punishment are to be understood.[104] Originally justice is nothing other than the good will among groups possessing roughly equal power to come together for the purposes of reaching an understanding 'by means of a settlement'. Punishment, on the other hand, evolves independently of any belief in the freedom, or non-freedom, of the will, since it requires a long period of cultural evolution before the animal 'man' is able to make subtle distinctions between intentional actions and accidental ones. The idea that punishment is imposed on a criminal who deserves it because the criminal was free to act otherwise is, Nietzsche argues, an extremely late and subtle form of human judgement which cannot be simply transposed back into the psychology of primitive mankind.[105] Throughout the greater part of human history, punishment is not imposed because the wrongdoer is held responsible for its actions, but in accordance with the legal relation between creditors and debtors, which is based on the notion that every injury has its equivalent. The origins of the institution of justice have equally been misunderstood. Justice does not arise out of an instinct for revenge, but from an attempt on the part of a master morality to struggle against the reactive feelings such as *ressentiment*. It is in this sphere of contractual–legal obligations that we find a great deal of the cruelty associated with the morality of custom. It is here that the human being learns how to make promises and how to create a will so that it can be held accountable for its actions. An intrinsic part of this process for Nietzsche is the spiritualization and deification of cruelty which rests on deriving pleasure and enjoyment from seeing others suffer: 'To see others suffer does one good, to make others suffer even more'.[106] Without cruelty, Nietzsche informs us, there are no festivals in human affairs, and it is through the festival that the human will has been disciplined and trained.[107]

The origin (*Ursprung*) of the sense of personal obligation (guilt), therefore, lies in the sphere of the oldest and most primitive personal obligations, those between buyer and seller, creditor and debtor. It is here, Nietzsche says,

that one person first encountered another person, that one person first *measured himself* against another…Setting prices, determining values, contriving equivalences, exchanging, these preoccupied the earliest thinking of man to so great an extent that in a certain sense they constitute thinking *as such*: here it was that the oldest kind of astuteness developed; here likewise, we may suppose, did human pride, the feeling of superiority in relation to other animals, have its first beginnings. Perhaps our word 'man' (*manas*) still express something of precisely *this* feeling of self-satisfaction: man designated himself as the creature that measures values, evaluates and measures, as the 'valuating animal as such'.[108]

It is in the context of these primitive relationships of buying and selling which bring men together that Nietzsche locates the beginnings of social forms of organization, and the establishment of legal rights through contracts, obligations, settlements, etc. It is here that individuals first become aware of their power and adopt the custom of 'comparing, measuring, and calculating power against power (*Macht*)'.[109] Justice develops as an institution representing the

interest of equal powers to reach a settlement. 'Law' (*Recht*) is
invented by the active and the strong so as to prevent the destructive
emotions of revenge and resentment from gaining control of the
institution of justice.[118] It is not unthinkable, Nietzsche argues, that
a society could attain such a consciousness of its power that it could
give itself the noble 'luxury' of letting those who offend it go
unpunished: 'This self-overcoming (*Selbstaufhebung*) of justice: one
knows the beautiful name it has given itself – *mercy*'. Mercy is the
privilege of the 'most powerful man', it is his 'beyond the law
(*Jenseits des Rechts*)'.[111]

'The darkening of the sky above mankind has deepened',
Nietzsche writes, 'in step with the increase of man's feeling of shame
at man', that is, with man's fundamental instincts (for pleasure, for
pain and suffering, for 'freedom', etc.).[112] What Nietzsche is
referring to is the process by which the human animal comes to
perceive itself as a *moral* being which feels *guilt* towards its actions:
man develops a *bad* conscience. It is in section 16 of the second essay
of the *Genealogy* that Nietzsche offers his hypothesis on the origin of
the bad conscience. His hypothesis is worth citing at length:

> I regard the bad conscience as the serious illness that man was bound to
> contract under the stress of the most fundamental of all changes he ever
> experienced – that change which occurred when he found himself enclosed
> within the walls of society and peace. The situation that faced sea animals
> when they were compelled to become land animals or perish was the same
> as that which faced these semi-animals, well adapted to the wilderness, war,
> to prowling, to adventure: suddenly all their instincts were devalued and
> 'suspended'. From now on they had to walk on their feet and 'bear
> themselves' where as hitherto they had been borne by the water: a dreadful
> heaviness now lay upon them. They felt unable to cope with the simplest
> undertakings; in this new world they no longer possessed their former
> guides, their regulating, unconscious, and infallible drives: they were
> reduced to thinking, inferring, reckoning, co-ordinating cause and
> effect... they were reduced to their 'consciousness', their weakest and most
> fallible organ! I believe there has never been such a feeling of misery on
> earth, such a leaden discomfort – and the same time the old instincts had
> not suddenly ceased to make their usual demands! Only it was hardly and
> rarely possible to humour them: as a rule they had to seek new and, as it
> were, subterranean gratifications.[113]

With this highly arresting imagery of primitive, natural man
undergoing the incredible and terrifying experience of acquiring
consciousness, Nietzsche offers what he understands to be a 'strange
hypothesis' on the origin (*Ursprung*) of the bad conscience. Perhaps

the most important presupposition of his account of the origin of the bad conscience is that the transformation takes place without man's conscious volition. The change from beast to man was neither gradual nor voluntary, but needs to be understood as a leap, a compulsion, and an ineluctable event which precluded all struggle and even all resentment.[114] The specific origin of the bad conscience is to be explained in terms of the internalization of man's instincts. Through this internalization man develops what is called his 'soul'. Once man becomes domesticated by the experience of living in society and conditions of peace, his natural aggressive instincts are subjected to the discipline of custom. Out of this experience man first encounters the possibility of developing not simply a conscience but a bad conscience. Nietzsche writes:

Those fearful bulwarks with which the State organization protected itself against the old instincts of freedom – punishments belong among these bulwarks – brought about that all those instincts of wild, free, prowling man turned backward *against man himself*. Hostility, cruelty, joy in persecuting, in attacking, in change, in destruction – all this turned against the possessors of such instincts: *that* is the origin (*Ursprung*) of the 'bad conscience'.[115]

It is important to appreciate that for Nietzsche the transition from the state of nature to society is neither something to be lamented nor something to be celebrated since it proceeds on unconscious, pre-reflective lines. Although Nietzsche never describes his depiction of pre-social man in terms of a state of nature, it is clear that his account shares many similar features to the descriptions found in political theorists like Hobbes. Nietzsche also conceives the origins of society along conventional Hobbesian lines as arising largely out of fear and insecurity.

Having offered his hypothesis on the origin of the bad conscience, Nietzsche goes on to define it. In its beginnings the bad conscience is the turning inwards and repression of the human animal's instinct of freedom – of its will to power.[116] The bad conscience does not develop in the warrior master race, Nietzsche informs us, but at the same time it would not have developed without them. In other words, the bad conscience – the internalization of man's will to power – would not have developed in the violent way it did if man's instinct for freedom had not been so aggressive in its original form. The blond beasts themselves had no knowledge of responsibility or guilt in their understanding of action, which was purely instinctual and pre-reflective. The origin of the moral values of unegoistic actions, however, are to be explained solely in terms of the bad conscience.

For Nietzsche the arrival of the bad conscience is neither simply good nor bad; rather, it is an illness, but only in the sense that pregnancy is an illness. On account of the bad conscience, man is now pregnant with a future that is both promising and dangerous.[117] It is promising because it shows that 'man' is only a bridge and a goal: if man has developed in the way of the bad conscience, why can he not develop and advance again, but this time in a different and higher way? It is dangerous because it could happen that the internalization of man develops so far that he is unable ever to discharge his actions externally. For Nietzsche this is precisely what has happened in the process of social evolution with the rise of Christianity as a world-dominant religion. It is here that the dangerous moralization of the concepts of guilt and duty takes place. But the aim of this process of moralization is to preclude the possibility of a final discharge. It is in the context of Nietzsche's examination of this moralization of man by Christianity that one can best appreciate the nature and full impact of his teaching on the death of God. The relationship of creditor–debtor which is argued to be at the basis of man's social relations, is interpreted by the priestly culture in terms of a relationship between God, the creditor, and man, the debtor. This relationship culminates with the concepts of guilt, punishment, and duty being turned back against, first of all, the debtor (man), in whom the bad conscience is firmly rooted, and then, secondly, they are turned back against the creditor too (God) as God himself sacrifices himself for the guilt of humanity: 'God himself makes payment to himself, God as the only being who can redeem man from what has become unredeemable for man himself – the creditor sacrifices himself for his debtor out of love for his debtor!'[118]

We have yet to consider an important aspect of the second essay: Nietzsche's theory on the origins of the State. The State is to be understood as the institution which gives shape, form, and order to humanity considered as a 'formless mass of animal–men'. The oldest State appears as a dreadful and fearful tyranny. Nietzsche calls it 'an oppressive and remorseless machine' which deploys tremendous degrees of violence and cruelty in order to mould man. In other words, Nietzsche is rejecting the idea that the origins of the State are to be found in a social contract. Instead he revives the old idea of conquest to explain the State's origins. He speaks of a pack of blond beasts, a master race (*Herren-Rasse*), which was organized for war, and which possessed the ability to organize and conquer a populace which had greater numbers but which was formless and nomad. He dismisses the 'sentimentalism' behind the notion of social contract to explain the origins of the State by saying: 'He who can command, he who is by nature "master"... what has he to do with contracts (*Verträgen*)!'[119]

Nietzsche's dismissal of the notion of a social contract might seem misdirected if applied as a criticism of a thinker like Rousseau, in that the idea is used by him not simply in order to trace the *origin* of the State, but rather to deduce its *legitimacy*. Rousseau's major concern is to show that society can only be established on a legitimate foundation through 'right', and not through 'force'. Rousseau and Nietzsche would seem to have different aims in carrying out an account of the State. Where Rousseau is concerned with the philosophical question of legitimacy, Nietzsche appears to be only concerned with the historical question of origin. However, the matter is not so straightforward. Nietzsche's argument would seem to be that one cannot raise the question about the legitimacy of the State without first tracing its origins. His intention is to reveal the bloody, cruel, and violent origins of the State that have been, he believes, concealed by the slave revolt in morals, in an effort to establish the social bond on the basis of the values of pity and reciprocity. However, could it not be argued that Rousseau is also concerned with both the origin *and* the legitimacy of the State, indeed, that it is a concern with both which provides the link between the *Discourse* and the *Social Contract*? After tracing an illegitimate historical social contract in the first work, Rousseau then attempts to deduce a legitimate social contract in the second. However, the link between the two is problematic as we have seen. For, although Rousseau intends to offer an account of the legitimate foundations of the State, not simply an account of its origins in the *Social Contract*, he is forced to recognize the major problem which his thinking arrives at: If men have been formed and made 'evil' by corrupt social institutions, then how can they be *reformed* and made 'good' by social institutions which inculcate moral virtue? A similar problem can be seen to lie at the heart of the paradoxes of Nietzsche's political thought: If individuals have been taught to be 'good' through a process of moralization, how can they now be taught to be 'beyond good and evil'? Both Rousseau and Nietzsche respond to this problem by seeking to cultivate an appreciation of the politics of the legislator. Precisely in what sense Nietzsche construes the role of the legislator, and in what way his construal departs from that of Rousseau, will be examined in the final chapter. Nowhere in his writings does Nietzsche ever entertain the idea of establishing the legitimacy of the political on the basis of a social contract, not only because he regards the notion of a social contract as an untenable transhistorical standard of right, but more importantly because his political vision of the reign of the overman entails the sacrifice of this question of legitimacy. The aim of the politics of the overman is not to unite people, but to divide them into the strong and the weak. Nietzsche's politics of division and discrimination cannot rely on a basis of consent, but instead must have recourse to the Platonic noble lie and to a Machiavellian appreciation of controlled political violence.

In contemplating the evolving sickness of man, of his growing shame at his instincts and descent into the madness of guilt, we are liable to fall into despair. At the very end of the second essay of the *Genealogy*, in sections 24 and 25, Nietzsche ends with a number of question marks all of which point in the direction of the teaching of Zarathustra the godless and immoralist. 'We modern men', he writes, are the heirs of the conscience-vivisection and self-torture of millenia'. For too long man has had 'an evil eye for his natural inclinations', to the extent that they are now inseparable from the bad conscience. Is an attempt at a reversal of this situation possible? Against those who seek to go beyond man stand not only the 'good' men, but also 'the comfortable, the reconciled, the vain, the sentimental, and the weary'. Do we realize, Nietzsche asks, 'how much the erection of *every* ideal has cost on earth' in terms of blood, sacrifices, and lies? We must recognize the law which teaches: 'If a temple is to be erected, then a temple must be destroyed'.[120]

Nietzsche closes the second essay with a prefiguration of the redeeming man of 'great love and contempt', a 'creative spirit whose compelling strength will not let him repose in any aloofness or any beyond', and 'whose isolation is misunderstood by the people as a flight *from* reality'. This 'man of the future' will redeem humanity not only from the 'hitherto reigning ideal' but also from that which may grow from it – the will to nothingness, in a word, 'nihilism'.

Who is this man that must descend to mankind one day? There can be only one answer, that of the name of 'Zarathustra' – the 'Anti-Christ and antinihilist... this victor over God and nothingness'.[121]

CONCLUSION

In the third essay of the book Nietzsche examines the possibilities which exist at present for the enhancement of man by inquiring into the meanings of the ascetic ideal. In carrying out a genealogy of morals the psychologist in us will realize that humanity has become mistrustful of itself and stands on the threshold of the 'great nausea' and a 'European Buddhism'. The fatality of European civilization is that not only has the fear of man been lost, but also the love and reverence for him. Standing on the threshold of weariness the great danger facing humanity is that it will experience contempt for itself and end up by pitying itself, thus lacking the courage to overcome itself and to affirm the will to power. In spite of the 'monstrous and calamitous effects' of the ascetic ideal, the question must still be posed concerning its meaning: What is the meaning of its power? 'Why has it been allowed to flourish to this extent? Why has it not been resisted?' If the ascetic ideal expresses a will, where is the opposing will and the opposing 'ideal'? In the final sections of the book Nietzsche considers and rejects a number of candidates for this role of counter-ideal: modern science, historiography, the free spirits, and atheism, for what we take to be something new and different turns out to be one more expression of the power and reign of the ascetic ideal. Our problem is that we still believe in the unconditional and absolute value of truth, that we do not recognize our will to truth as a will to power. Thus, for example, modern historiography stands before reality as before a number of 'petty facts' refusing to evaluate, either to affirm or to negate. The ascetic ideal has dominated all previous philosophy because it posited 'God as the highest court of appeal' in which truth was not permitted to be a problem. Atheism, on the other hand, is not simply the reversal of the ascetic ideal, but rather 'only one of the latest phases of its evolution, one of its terminal forms and inner consequences'. Atheism is 'the awe-inspiring *catastrophe* of two thousand years of training in truthfulness that finally forbids itself the *lie involved in belief in God*'.[122]

Nietzsche thus makes a new demand upon humanity – that it

embarks on a critique of the will to truth, which means that it experimentally calls the value of this will into question. What has really 'conquered' the Christian God, Nietzsche argues, is Christianity itself: the 'confessional subtlety of the Christian conscience translated and sublimated into scientific conscience, into intellectual cleanliness at any price'. Nietzsche explains:

> To view nature as if it were a proof of the goodness and providence of a God; to interpret history to the glory of a divine reason, as the perpetual witness to a moral world order and moral intentions; to interpret one's experiences...as if everything were preordained, everything a sign, everything sent for the salvation of the soul – that now belongs to the *past*, that has the conscience *against* it, that seems to every more sensitive conscience indecent, dishonest, mendacious, feminism, weakness, cowardice.[123]

It is the rigour with which we pursue this logic of the 'self-overcoming' of Christianity which makes us, Nietzsche argues, 'good Europeans' and 'the heirs of Europe's longest and bravest self-overcoming'.

It is through this process of Christianity's self-overcoming that the will to truth is compelled to call itself into question. The self-overcoming of the will to truth is at the same time the self-overcoming of 'morals', for our drive for truth, being, and redemption has been built on moral foundations and has been inspired by moral needs.[124] Thus, Nietzsche can write, for example, that as 'the will to truth now gains self-consciousness... morality will perish (*die Moral zu Grunde*)'. Here is the

> great spectacle reserved in a hundred acts for the next two centuries in Europe – the most terrible, most questionable, and perhaps also the most hopeful of all spectacles.[125]

The origin (*Ursprung*) and descent (*Herkunft*) of our moral values have been revealed to us in a way which is designed to be not only terrifying but instructive. For Nietzsche there can be no going back – such an attitude would be the perfect expression of contempt towards humanity which we must do all we can to overcome – but only a going forward. We must learn to will the over-man. In the very final section of the *Genealogy* Nietzsche informs us that the meaning of the ascetic ideal is that mankind has had *no meaning apart from this ideal*. The ascetic ideal 'means' that 'something was *lacking*, that man was surrounded by a fearful *void* – he did not know how to justify...to affirm himself'. Man could find no answer to the great question of life: 'why do I suffer?'[126] It is the meaninglessness of suffering, not suffering itself, which accounts for the 'curse' which has lain over mankind and its history. Christianity placed suffering under the perspective of guilt and, in this way, served to deepen it by making it 'more inward, more poisonous, more life-destructive.' The will that is concealed in the ascetic ideal hides a hatred of the senses, of happiness, of beauty; it is a 'longing to get away from all appearance, change, becoming, death, wishing, from longing itself'. However, the importance of Christianity viewed in the context of the historical formation and deformation of the human will to power, is that it at least saved the will from a suicidal nihilism. In spite of it being a 'rebellion against the most fundamental presuppositions of life' the will of the asectic ideal nevertheless was a will, albeit a paradoxical and perverted one. But now, however, with the advent of the death of God, mankind is once more plunged into the possibility of a crippling nihilism. It is in need of a new teaching of redemption which will teach it how to 'will its own will' as an abundant, fecund will to power that is beyond good and evil – a will to eternal change and destruction, without a final goal and without ultimate justification.

It is at this juncture in Nietzsche's thought on Europe's brave self-overcoming that we can fully appreciate the role the figure Zarathustra plays in Nietzsche's thought. As we have seen, there are a number of places in the *Genealogy* where the figure of Zarathustra is anticipated, notably the two closing sections of the second essay. In *Ecce Homo* Nietzsche argues that 'until Zarathustra' a counter-ideal to the asectic ideal was lacking. It is in the story of Zarathustra's 'down-going' (*Untergang*) to humanity that Nietzsche provides his most dramatic and educative answer to the problem of the ascetic ideal (of human suffering), and it is to an examination of the nature of this fascinating and perplexing work to which I now turn in the next chapter.[127]

CHAPTER 5

Zarathustra's descent: on a teaching of redemption

All history is sacred ... the universe is represented in a moment of time.

Emerson, 'The Over-Soul' (1841)

The Tao which can be spoken is not eternal Tao.

Tao Te Ching

INTRODUCTION

It cannot be without significance that the climatic points of several of Nietzsche's major works culminate in a prefiguration of Zarathustra. In *Twilight of the Idols* Zarathustra appears at the end of Nietzsche's terse history of Western metaphysics which results in the abolition of any distinction between a true world and an apparent world. It is the moment at which man experiences the end of the longest error and the zenith of mankind. At the end of the second inquiry of the *Genealogy of Morals*, in sections 24 and 25, Zarathustra is referred to as 'the redeeming man' who may bring home the redemption of man the sick animal; he is the man of the future who will redeem humanity from nihilism by teaching the liberation of the will; he is the victor over God and nothingness. The justification for reading *Thus Spoke Zarathustra* (1883–85) after the *Genealogy of Morals* (1887) stems from the key role that Nietzsche assigns to Zarathustra as a teacher of redemption who appears at a certain juncture in man's evolution to deliver a teaching of redemption. It is a teaching about the nature of time and history designed to show how nihilism can be overcome and a Dionysian affirmation and celebration of life attained.

Perhaps the most significant reference to Zarathustra's *Untergang* occurs in section 342 in *The Gay Science*. In a passage entitled 'Incipit tragoedia' Nietzsche invokes the figure of Zarathustra as one who has gathered too much wisdom and is like a bee that has gathered too much honey who needs to impart and distribute it to others: he wills to go under and become who he is, the teacher of eternal return.[1] The position of this passage is particularly significant, for not only does it close the original version of the *Gay Science*, appearing as the last aphorism of book four (book five was added by Nietzsche in a new edition published in 1887), but is preceded by Nietzsche's first published announcement of the doctrine of eternal return. A few passages before both, in section 337, Nietzsche speaks of the 'historical sense' as the 'distinctive virtue and disease' of present-day humanity. This section contains a reflection on the problem of history which is absolutely crucial for understanding how Nietzsche conceives the task of self-overcoming. His reflection is worth citing at length:

Anyone who manages to experience the history of humanity as a whole as *his own history* will feel in an enormously generalized way all the grief of an invalid who thinks of health, of an old man who contemplates the dreams of his youth, of a lover deprived of his beloved, of the martyr whose ideal is perishing, of the hero on the evening after a battle that has decided nothing but brought him wounds and the loss of a friend. But if one endured, if one *could* endure this immense sum of grief of all kinds while yet being the hero who, as the second day of battle breaks, welcomes the dawn and his fortune, being a person whose horizon encompasses thousands of years past and future, being the heir of all the nobility of all past spirit – an heir with a sense of obligation, the most aristocratic of old nobles and at the same time the first of a new nobility – the like of which no age has yet seen or dreamed of; if one could burden one's soul with all of this – the oldest, the newest, losses, hopes, conquests, and the victories of humanity; if one could finally contain all this in one soul and crowd it into a single feeling – this would surely have to result in a happiness that humanity has not known so far: the happiness of a god full of power and love, full of tears and laughter, a happiness that, like the sun in the evening, continually bestows its inexhaustible riches, pouring them into the sea, feeling richest, as the sun does, only when even the poorest fisherman is still rowing with golden oars! This godlike feeling would then be called – humaneness (*Menschlichkeit*)![2]

This passage compels the reader to ask a number of questions: Is Nietzsche, the teacher of cruelty and hardness, of will to power and aristocratic rule, also to be understood as the philosopher of 'humaneness'?! Who is the god 'full of power and love' that must come one day? What is clear is that for Nietzsche the way of descent is also a way of ascent. In order to go over it is necessary that first one perishes by going under, that one must do evil to become good, that one must die in order to be born anew.

It is in *Ecce Homo* that Nietzsche reveals why the name of Zarathustra has been chosen to signify the redeeming man of the future. He informs us that the figure of Zarathustra has been chosen because he was the Persian god who was the first to commit the 'error' of morality and so it is he who must be the first one to repudiate it. The figure of Zarathustra embodies the meaning of the teaching of the self-overcoming of morality within himself:

I have not been asked, as I should have been asked, what the name Zarathustra means in my mouth, the mouth of the first immoralist; for what constitutes the tremendous historical uniqueness of that Persian is just the opposite of this. Zarathustra was the first to consider the fight of good and evil the very wheel in the machinery of things: the translation of the moral into the metaphysical... is *his* work. But the question itself is at bottom its own answer. Zarathustra created this most calamitous error, morality; consequently he must also be the first to recognize it.[3]

In the *Nachlass* from the Autumn of 1881 Zarathustra is portrayed by Nietzsche as one of the great lawgivers and aristocrats in human history, whose descent, or lineage, includes figures such as Moses, Mohammed, Jesus, Plato, Buddha, Brutus, Spinoza, and Mirabeau.[4] In his autobiography, *Ecce Homo*, however, Nietzsche is adamant that Zarathustra should not be thought of as a prophet or founder of a religion or cult. Moreover, 'It is no fanatic that speaks here; this is not "preaching"; no *faith* is demanded here'; Zarathustra is no 'world-redeemer'.[5]

From these passages it is evident that Nietzsche wishes to give the story of Zarathustra's *Untergang* a lightness of touch, even a childlike playfulness and innocence, perhaps in order to undermine the sombre, serious, heavy feelings which we expect to accompany the arrival of a teacher and lawgiver whose teaching aims to move mountains and penetrate the fleshly hearts of men. As we have seen in the analysis of the *Genealogy*, the task of the self-overcoming of humanity hitherto demands both tragedy and comedy. Thus, for example, it cannot be without significance that Nietzsche begins the *Gay Science* with a reflection on the 'comedy of existence' in which Nietzsche construes a gay type of science resulting from a fusion of laughter and wisdom, and closes with a reflection on tragedy in which '*great seriousness* really begins, that the real question mark is posed for the first time' – now the 'hand moves forward' and the 'destiny of the soul changes'.[6] In Nietzsche's thought Zarathustra represents a new type of being. In this type 'all opposites are blended into a new unity'; it is Dionysian in that it is a spirit which 'says No' and 'does No' to an hitherto unheard-of degree, and is nevertheless the opposite of a Nay-saying spirit. The type which bears the heaviest burden and the 'fatality of a task' is also the 'lightest and most transcendent' spirit, for it recognizes that the abysmal nature of existence is no objection to it, but rather constitutes one more reason for declaring 'the eternal Yes to all things' – to the extent of 'justifying, redeeming even all of the past'.[7] The 'physiological presupposition' of this new type is 'great health' which is 'tougher, more audacious, and gayer than any previous health'.

The gay type is playful and serious at one and the same time; it plays naively – that is, 'not deliberately but from overflowing power and abundance' – with everything that hitherto has been called good and holy, but it plays seriously for it also recognizes that it represents a new phase in the 'destiny of the soul'. It will, therefore, appear to be both superhuman and inhuman: superhuman in its strength, courage, and benevolence in relation to the cowardice and weakness of present-day humanity, and inhuman in its parodic treatment of all earthly solemnity and seriousness so far.[8] The type that Zarathustra embodies not only conceives reality as it is because it is strong enough to do so, but 'is reality itself' who 'exemplifies all that is terrible and questionable in it'. And yet, the type is only 'superhuman' (*übermenschlich*) in relation to the 'good and the just' who call the 'overman' (*Übermensch*) 'devil'.[9]

It is important to appreciate that the manner in which Zarathustra relates his teaching to man is as important as its message. Zarathustra is clearly assigned the role of educator and teacher in that his task is to descend to human beings in order to teach them how to overcome themselves. However, it is not enough that Zarathustra teaches and humanity learns, since this kind of relationship will simply repeat the teacher–disciple relationship of Christianity and lead to the establishment of a new God to be worshipped (the Overman) that Nietzsche refuses. Zarathustra wants neither to create disciples, nor to establish a new God or religion. But how can he offer his teaching that God is dead and that man is impotent without attributing special and divine significance to his teaching? Throughout the book Nietzsche relates Zarathustra's teaching in such a way that it is constantly called into question to the extent that the identity of *who* and *what* Zarathustra is and is to become, is left open. One example will serve to illustrate this point: in the discourse in book three entitled 'Of the Spirit of Gravity' Zarathustra informs us that he came to 'his truth' about the nature of existence by diverse paths and in diverse ways. He tells us that it is to *his* taste to live life by constantly questioning and learning how to answer such a questioning. It is not a good taste, nor is it a bad taste, but it is at least *his taste*. He then challenges us: '"This is *my* Way: where is yours?" Thus I answered those who asked me "the Way". For *the* Way – does not exist!'[10] The aim of Zarathustra's *Untergang* is to discover the nature of good and evil. What he learns by discovering *his* truth and by refining his taste is that 'good for all, evil for all' do not exist.[11] Moreover, what lies at the end of 'the Way', the affirmation of the moment in the thought-experiment of the eternal return, and the central teaching of Nietzsche's entire thought in which everything culminates and from which everything emanates, cannot be taught but only experienced – only *undergone*.

The problem which faces Zarathustra in trying to get his message across is, in fact, the same one which Rousseau had located in his recognition of the problem of legislator. As Zarathustra begins to learn the meaning of his *Untergang* he learns what Rousseau had identified as the chief problem of all lawgivers (the political genius who must also be a great artist or architect): that in trying to teach individuals through speaking the language of the over-human it is impossible that they will make themselves either heard or understood. But to speak the language of the human, all too human is to speak a language which has only served to cripple and constrain them. Zarathustra will learn the meaning of this insight when he realizes that when he was speaking to 'all' he was actually speaking to 'none'. But this dilemma facing Zarathustra, of finding and addressing an audience, reveals to us the tragic consequences of the lawgiver – namely, that his teaching compels him either to withdraw into solitude (into a kind of self-imposed exile from humanity)[12] or to inspire a bloody politics of resentment and revenge. Of course, it is the aim and ambition of Nietzsche, in the form of Zarathustra's teaching of redemption, to show humanity how it can overcome the spirit of revenge that has haunted its historical sensibility and imagination. In order to achieve this it is necessary for Zarathustra to show us how we can will the beyond of humanity (the over-man) without experiencing any negative feelings of pity, contempt and disgust at past and present-day crippled humanity, but only the deep joy of eternity. Rather, our experiences of disgust and contempt should transmute themselves into an innocent new creation, so that any entrapment in the past, and bondage to the past, is overcome. However, the great danger facing Zarathustra's demand that the overman shall live and now be the meaning of the earth, is that should this vision of a future nobler humanity not materialize, then his thought condemns humanity to the great nausea and disgust, possibly leading to the unleashing of the terrible spirit of revenge. This is the crucial and critical question which needs to be posed concerning Nietzsche's deepest thinking on the problem of history and the fate of humanity, and which I will consider in the next chapter: to what extent does the vision of the overman – the vision which emerges from the riddle of the eternal return – constitute Nietzsche's revenge on humanity?

PROLOGUE: THE OVERMAN

The prologue reveals several important aspects of Zarathustra's teaching. It begins with a declaration of Zarathustra's need to return to human beings after ten years of solitude. He had departed from humanity at the age of thirty years. He is a man of knowledge, and the analogy is drawn between his need to impart the wisdom he has accumulated and stored in his solitude and the sun's need to shine for those who benefit from its light. Zarathustra is a bringer of enlightenment. On his way down from the mountain where he has been leading his solitary existence, Zarathustra comes across an old man who recognizes him, but remarks how much he has changed since he last saw him. The old man remarks that Zarathustra has become like a child again, an 'awakened one' (like the Buddha), but asks what he wants with the 'sleepers' below who are happy in their ignorance and content with their impotence. Zarathustra replies by saying that he loves mankind. The old man, however, reveals that he reserves his love not for man but for God; man is too imperfect a creature to be loved. At the end of this encounter when Zarathustra is alone again he speaks to his heart: 'Could it be possible! This old saint has not yet heard in this forest that *God is dead!*'[13]

The prologue reveals that Zarathustra is a special kind of wandering figure. He is not one who has turned his back on man for

God, but rather one who has experienced the death of God and now returns to bring the news of this death to man. In other words, his teaching is without meaning unless it can be identified with a historical community. It is the search for such a community (not one of believers or disciples) that engages Zarathustra throughout the story of his *Untergang*. In section three of the prologue Zarathustra arrives at the market square that is first depicted in section 125 of the *Gay Science*, where a madman had announced the death of God (the madman is none other than Zarathustra).[14] Zarathustra speaks to the people gathered there: 'I teach you the *Übermensch*. Man is something that should be overcome (*überwinden*). What have you done to overcome him?' We are entreated to remain 'true to the earth' in willing the *Übermensch* for it is nothing superterrestrial. We are thus presented with a direct challenge: are we prepared to awake from our dogmatic slumbers in which we might wake up only to find ourselves confronted with a great nausea, and begin the task of revaluing all values by embarking on a labour (and play) of self-overcoming? The greatest thing we can experience, Zarathustra tells us, is the 'hour of the great contempt' in which our happiness, justice, reason, and virtue grow loathsome to us. It is at this hour that we are ready to confront the possibility – and the desirability – of going under.

What is exactly meant by the term '*Übermensch*'?[15] Is it the type of being in possession of superhuman powers, the superman of Nietzsche legend? Or is it the symbol of the 'man of the future' who has overcome present-day crippled humanity? The translation of *Übermensch* as 'superman' is misleading in that it suggests an ideal which stands above man, as something beyond the reach of mere mortals. As Walter Kaufmann pointed out, Nietzsche's conception depends on the associations of the word *über*.[16] In *Ecce Homo* Nietzsche repudiates any Darwinian reading of this notion and informs us that the overman is not in any way to be conceived as a transcendental ideal of man.[17] When Nietzsche refers to man as a rope tied between animal and overman, he is referring our attention to the historical possibilities of man's evolution, to the dialectic of nihilism, to man's present ambiguous condition of danger and promise: 'Man is a rope over an abyss', Zarathustra says, 'a dangerous going-across, a dangerous wayfaring, a dangerous looking-back'.[18] What is great about man is that he is a bridge and not a goal (*Zweck*); man can be loved because he is a going-across

(*Übergang*) and a going-down (*Untergang*): 'I love him who justifies the men of the future and redeems the men of the past: for he wants to perish by the men of the present.'[19] He teaches that men should learn to accept their down-going and go across the bridge to the overman by creatively willing their own destiny. Of course, to the last men gathered in the market-place who are content with mere happiness, the one who strives for something higher and nobler will always appear as superhuman. Thus, we see that Nietzsche is playing with the connotations of the word *über*, and that the term *Übermensch* does not possess the one single meaning but, like many of Nietzsche's key notions, is polysemous.

The term only makes sense within the context of Nietzsche's reflections on the drama of the destiny of the soul. If one removes the vision from this context it quickly degenerates into some ridiculous, wild caricature, or a monstrous ideal of social engineering.[20] The term 'ideal' to describe the *Übermensch* is misplaced because the overman simply represents a potential future humanity in which we have become what we *are*. As Michel Haar has pointed out, the overman unfolds a philosophy of the future which is something quite different from a philosophy of progress.[21] Moreover, as Robert Pippin has astutely noted, the *Übermensch* is a radically contingent 'ideal' which can only answer the specific needs of 'late bourgeois culture'.[22] Similarly, Laurence Lampert interprets the significance of the *Übermensch* in terms of a critique of the last man construed as a 'Lockean ideal' of self-contentment in which the social contract serves only to guarantee the production of uniform and universal behaviour and beliefs.[23]

The overman is not to be conceived as a beyond (*über*) of humanity, in the sense of a stepping over and turning our back on it, in which we blindly aim for the unattainable and unknowable. By overcoming himself man comes to know himself as 'man' too. Does this not mean that the overman is the fulfilment or teleological realization of the essence of man? The answer is no, because the overman is a contingent ideal whose willing only makes sense in the context of nihilism and the death of God. As we shall see, the overman cannot properly be thought of apart from the doctrine of eternal return. The overman is the one who stands in the joy of eternity and experiences the unity of all things. In experiencing the moment of eternity the overman breaks the spell of the past and redeems time itself in the affirmation of the innocent moment: the overman thus emerges (literally) from the experience of eternal return. The attitude of *Übermenschlichkeit* (super/overhumaness or super/overhumaneness) is attained when one undergoes the experience of eternal return and is prepared to love life to the point of desiring and willing its eternal return.[24] Of course, many commentators have argued that the two 'ideals' are fundamentally incompatible for, if everything returns, how is the 'new, the unique, and the incomparable' that constitutes the overman possible? However, as we shall see in a discussion of thought of eternal return, it is not a question of the thought of eternal return cancelling out or contradicting that of the overman, but of *reforming* and reformulating it. A careful analysis of the Zarathustra *Nachlass* reveals that Nietzsche put a great deal of thought into how he should present the book's fundamental teachings and conceptions. As Heidegger has noted, Nietzsche had to abandon any thoughts of beginning the book with the doctrine of eternal return, since he recognized that Zarathustra and his audience had first to be prepared for its experience – this preparation takes place through the call to create the *Übermensch* in which we learn to sacrifice ourselves in order to go down and go under. Thus, it needs to be appreciated that the two thoughts are inextricable.[25] I shall return to this crucial point on the precise relationship between the book's two main teachings when I examine the import and significance of part three of *Zarathustra*.

Zarathustra, it is important to note, is not the overman himself, but rather the teacher of the meaning of this notion who must himself go down and learn how to become who he is. Nietzsche in fact says that there has never yet been an overman, for man has not yet learned to go down.[26] The overman is to become the symbol of the meaning of the earth, and of a redeemed humanity which no longer exists enslaved to a moral world-order. The conception of the overman represents Nietzsche's concern with the further discipline of man once the Christian–moral interpretation of the world has lost its power and ascendancy. With this notion he advocates neither an ahistorical return to the wild, prowling man of the blond beast, nor an equally ahistorical and simplistic side-stepping of man to some ideal model of man. Rather, the emphasis is on the notion of *über* that denotes a creative, playful labour of self-overcoming, by which man is able to transfigure all that has made him what he is so far, in order to attain a standpoint beyond good and evil and become what he is. However, we already see the dangers of the notion in Nietzsche's emphasis on 'sacrifice', in particular that present-day humanity must accept the necessity of sacrificing the present by perishing for the sake of the future kingdom of the overman. But is this demand not a perfect example of the malevolent spirit of revenge?

The difficulties facing Zarathustra in communicating his teaching are already apparent to him in the prologue, where he has descended to the human from his solitude. He acknowledges that he is mocked and laughed at the way a madman is mocked and laughed at. He quickly learns that he must approach human beings with caution. To them he appears as a cross between a fool and a corpse. 'I am not the mouth for these ears', he says, 'they have something of which they are proud. What is it that makes them proud? They call it culture (*Bildung*) – it distinguishes them from the goatherds... They do not understand me.'[27] He is advised by a buffoon to depart from the town to which he has descended and to be man again, for the good and the just men despise him and regard him as the evil one. By the end of the prologue Zarathustra no longer speaks of men but only of 'companions' (*Gefahrten*): 'A light has dawned for me: Zarathustra shall not speak to the people but to companions! Zarathustra shall not be herdsman to the herd!'[28] Instead, he declares that he has come to lure men away from the herd. He has come as a law-breaker and law-creator who seeks neither herds nor believers, but only friendship. The creator seeks fellow-creators, those 'who invent new values on new tables'.[29] He recognizes that the creators of new values are always the first ones to be despised and labelled as destroyers of good and evil, when in reality they are the harvesters and rejoicers of new seeds. By the end of the prologue Zarathustra has resolved not to speak to '*alle*', but instead to seek out fellow-travellers who are traversing the bridge to the overman with a creative will.

Nietzsche's portrayal of Zarathustra as a creator of new values is remarkably similar to his historical understanding of the meaning and significance of the teaching (*Torah*) of Jesus. Nietzsche understands Jesus to be a holy anarchist who represented the revolt against the Jewish Church and the social hierarchy of Israel, whose aim was not to bring peace to men, but rather a sword.[30] The significance of Jesus' teaching lies in his practice: 'he died as he *lived*, as he *taught*', Nietzsche tells us, 'not to "redeem mankind"' but to demonstrate how one ought to live. What he bequeathed to mankind was his *practice*.[31] Jesus' practice includes his bearing on

162 *Nietzsche contra Rousseau*

the Cross and his triumph over *ressentiment*. As Zarathustra's story progresses it becomes clear that he has descended not to establish a new religion, but that the significance of his teaching is that it too lies in his *practice*.

PART I: THE WAY OF THE CREATOR

The first discourse of the book is entitled 'Of the Three Meta-morphoses' (*Verwandlungen*) which refer to the camel, the lion, and the child. Man must learn each one in turn in order to become historical and go across the bridge to the overman. The discourse contains a prefiguration of the development (the 'progress') Zarathustra is to undergo in the story of his innocent becoming of what he is. The camel symbolizes the weightiness of man's spirit who kneels down in obedience (the camel is the civilizing, humanizing process represented by the morality of custom). The 'weight-bearing spirit' carries with it the heaviest things and hurries into the desert, like a camel, where the metamorphosis takes place from a camel to a lion. Here the spirit confronts its enemy who responds to the command 'thou shalt!' with a declaration of freedom, 'I will!' The lion symbolizes the process whereby freedom is produced for a new creation in an act of defiant independence (it is the supra-ethical sovereign individual). The lion does not create new values but is needed to create freedom for itself and to say no to duty. The lion seizes the right to those new values which constitutes the most terrible burden for the weight-bearing spirit. The child, in the third and final metamorphosis, symbolizes a new beginning and a play, for it represents the innocence and forgetfulness that signifies a new yes to life; it is a 'self-propelling wheel, a first motion, a sacred Yes'. With the new beginning attained through the child 'the spirit now wills *its own* will' (it is the conscious innocence of becoming).

In 'Of the Despisers of the Body' Zarathustra teaches that the self *is* the body, and that recognition of the unity of body and soul (that the soul is a word for something in the body) is what constitutes the 'awakening'. In 'Of Joys and Passions' we are told that once humanity had passions which it deemed to be evil, but now it has only virtues which grow out of the passions: 'Henceforward', Zarathustra says, 'nothing evil shall come out of you, except it be the evil that comes from the conflict of your virtues'. If we have a virtue, we must recognize it not as a common virtue but as *our* virtue. Our virtue should be too exalted for the familiarity of names (that which renders it common); 'unutterable and nameless' it should be no 'law of God' or 'human statute'. In the discourse entitled 'Of the Tree on the Mountainside' Zarathustra tells us that what separates the noble man from the good man is that the former wants to create new things and a new virtue, while the latter wants only to preserve the old things. In 'Of the Preachers of Death' Zarathustra warns against those who teach pity for humanity, for such pity only hides their contempt for humanity and for themselves. In 'Of War and Warriors' he teaches the value of the spirit of rebellion: 'To rebel – that shows nobility in a slave. Let your nobility show itself in obeying! Let even your commanding be an obeying!'

In 'Of the New Idol' the meaning of the overman is illuminated in the context of a critique of the modern State. The State, Zarathustra teaches, is to be held in suspicion, for its claim to speak for all can only be maintained by its concealing its origins in the act of creation:

Where a people still exists, there the people do not understand the State and detest it as the evil eye and sin against custom and law.

I offer you this sign: every people speaks its own language of good and evil: its neighbour does not understand this language. It invented this language for itself in custom and law.

But the State lies in all languages of good and evil; and whatever it says, it lies – and whatever it has, it has stolen.

The State is depicted as the 'cold monster' which promises everything to the individual in return for worship of it. It is the 'new idol' which sets out to make the unique and the incomparable superfluous. Only where the State ceases, Zarathustra teaches, does the reign of the unique (*einmalig*) and the irreplaceable (*unersetzlich*) begin. In 'Of the Flies of the Marketplace', however, Zarathustra warns against the actor. The people, those gathered like a herd in the market-place, have little appreciation of greatness and creativeness, they have only a taste for good actors: 'The world revolves around the inventor of new values: imperceptibly it revolves', Zarathustra says. 'But the people and the glory revolve around the actor: that is "the way of the world"'. Faced with this challenge of the good actor the only option we nobles have would appear to be that of fleeing into solitude.

In 'Of the Thousand and One Goals' Zarathustra declares that he has seen many lands and many peoples but he has found no greater power (*Macht*) on earth than that of good and evil: 'A table of values hangs over every people', we are told, 'behold, it is the table of its overcomings (*Überwindungen*); behold it is the voice of its will to power'. What a people finds hard it calls praiseworthy, and what it considers its greatest need it celebrates as holy. In language reminiscent of Rousseau's figure of the lawgiver, Zarathustra declares that if we knew a people's 'need and land and sky and neighbour' we would be able to 'divine the law of its overcomings'. From his wanderings Zarathustra has discovered that it was man who first implanted meaning and value into things. Man is the evaluator (*der Schätzende*); it is only through evaluation that values are first brought into being. Evaluation is creation and 'he who has to be a creator always has to be a destroyer'. At first peoples were the creators of values and the individual was considered an insignificant affair. Originally the good conscience was called the herd and the bad conscience the I. Here Nietzsche is relating the history of morals which he will later trace in the *Genealogy* in terms of the transition from the morality of custom to the sovereign individual. 'Hitherto', Zarathustra declares, 'there have been a thousand goals for a thousand peoples', but 'the one goal is still lacking'. But if a goal for humanity is lacking, then is there not lacking 'humanity itself'? In 'Of Love of One's Neighbour' Zarathustra teaches that we should not love our neighbours but that which is most distant, for in our neighbour we only wish to see either a reflection of ourselves or to lose ourselves. Instead, we should seek the friend who may be 'a foretaste of the overman', and in whom 'the evolution of good' takes place through evil 'as the evolution of design through chance'.

In an important discourse 'Of the Way of the Creator' (*Vom Wege des Schaffenden*) Zarathustra develops a teaching on self-mastery and self-legislation. Do we wish to seek 'the Way' to ourselves? If we do, first we must learn that if we wish to find ourselves we may have to first lose ourselves 'on the Way'. We must also learn that the crowd hate those who wish to be apart and go alone. Then we must learn that great courage is needed in order to become 'a new strength and a new right', to become a first motion and a self-propelling wheel. If we declare ourselves free then we should cry out our ruling idea and not simply escape from a yoke: not 'free from what' but 'free *for* what?' 'Can you furnish yourself with your own good and evil', Zarathustra asks, 'and hang up your own will above yourself and as a law? Can you be judge and avenger of yourself and avenger of your law?' Autonomy demands solitude, for 'it is terrible to be alone with the judge and avenger of one's own law'. Both the legislation (the 'will') and the execution ('power') of action come together in Nietzsche's teaching of a creative willing. In advancing a teaching of autonomy Nietzsche discloses to us the intimate relationship between law and morals. Those who create new values must also be prepared to take on the task of law-breaking and law-creating, that is, the task of legislation. Moreover, the autonomous one must recognize that by going into himself he will become his own enemy and demon, and he must be ready to burn himself in his own flame for how could he 'become new' if he had not first 'become ashes'? In 'Of the Adder's Bite' Zarathustra finally encounters the good and the just who call him 'the destroyer of morals' and declare his story to be 'immoral'.

Part one of the story of Zarathustra's *Untergang* closes with a discourse on the 'gift-giving virtue' (*schenkenden Tugend*), which is later revealed in a discourse on the 'Three Evil Things', in part three, to be the name which Zarathustra gives to the 'unnameable' (the will to power). In teaching a new virtue as that which bestows meaning and significance on the earth, Zarathustra teaches a new good and evil: 'It is power, this virtue; it is a ruling idea, and around it a subtle soul: a golden sun, and around it the serpent of knowledge.' Zarathustra has departed from the town called 'The Pied Cow' to which he had become attached, and is escorted by his disciples. He leaves and narrates a story about the nature of the 'uncommon and the useless'. This how Zarathustra describes the 'gift-giving virtue' – useless and uncommon like gold. But this virtue can either be the treasures and riches of the noble soul, or it can be the hungry selfishness of the impoverished soul. It is from the latter soul which *craves* for power that 'sickness' and 'degeneration' speak. But, in the soul of the one overflowing with life, the gift-giving virtue represents the source of a new good and evil, 'a new roaring in the depths' (the lion) and 'a new fountain' (the child). When we are 'the willers of a single will', and when we recognize this will as our essential necessity, that is the moment when we discover the 'origin (*Ursprung*) of our virtue'.

Zarathustra speaks lovingly to his disciples before rejecting them and returning to his solitude. He entreats them to stay loyal to the earth with the power of their new virtue, and declares that mankind is still fighting with the giant 'Chance', the 'senseless' and the 'meaningless'. He tells them that both the madness and reason of millenia break out in them, and for this reason it is dangerous to be an heir of history. He informs his fellow-travellers that the solitaries of today, those who have seceded from society, shall some day constitute a people. From this chosen people there will spring the overman, and the earth shall become a place of healing. The first part ends with Zarathustra speaking cautiously to his followers, pausing like one who has not yet said his last word, but who now adopts a different tone to the one he adopted when he first descended to human beings. He instructs his disciples to guard themselves against Zarathustra, even to be ashamed of him, for he may have deceived them. In this way Zarathustra calls into question the status of what he has taught so far – the death of God, the overman, the virtue of that which cannot be named (power) – and succeeds in keeping his teaching open in a way which prevents it from degenerating into a dogma that is valid for everyone. It is not believers he seeks and it is not belief he wants from his disciples. He speaks to them thus: 'You had not sought yourselves when you found me. Thus do all believers; therefore all belief is of so little account. Now I bid you lose me and find yourselves and only when you have denied me will I return to you'.[32]

Part one closes with the expectation of a great noontide, when man will stand at the middle of his journey between animal and overman and celebrate his standing as his highest hope, for it is a journey to a new beginning.[33] Going under man will bless himself for he is going under in order to go over to the overman, and he thus accepts the necessity of his own perishing. He will be able to proudly declare: 'All gods are dead now: we want (*wollen*) the overman to live'.[34] By the end of the first book Zarathustra has not only imparted the content of his teaching, but also drawn attention to its difficult nature and status. The educative aspect of Zarathustra's *Untergang* is, however, far from complete at this point. He has yet to experience the terrifying nature of his teaching, and his relationship with his disciples and followers has still to undergo new and significant developments.

PART II: REDEMPTION

Part two develops further the two major aspects of Zarathustra's teaching disclosed so far, the doctrine of will to power and the problematic status of the teaching. Two important aspects of the doctrine of life as will to power are now introduced. These are the teaching of the will to power as a doctrine of self-overcoming (*Selbst-Überwindung*) and as a teaching of redemption (*Erlösung*).[35] The section on redemption which appears almost at the end of part two can be seen to be the pivotal point in the book, culminating in Zarathustra experiencing his 'stillest hour' (the conjoining of time and stillness, of movement and moment).

Part two begins with Zarathustra returning to the mountains and his solitude, 'waiting like a sower who has scattered his seed' ('The Child with the Mirror'). Awaking from a dream he is presented with a mirror by a child and learns that his teaching is in peril for his enemies have grown powerful in his absence. He needs to go down once again to his friends – and to his enemies. In the discourse entitled 'On the Blissful Islands' Nietzsche closely identifies the teaching of the overman with that of the will to power. God is a supposition, Zarathustra says, but we should only will what lies in the realm of the possible. 'Could you *create* a god?' Zarathustra inquires, 'So be silent about all gods! But you could surely create the overman'. If we could not create the overman then we can be forefathers and ancestors of the overman. God is a supposition, and our teaching on 'the one and the perfect and the unmoved and the sufficient and the intransitory' reveals a revengeful spirit. But the best images, Zarathustra teaches, should tell 'of time and becoming: they should be a eulogy and a justification of all transitoriness'. 'Creation' is the 'great redemption from suffering', but in order for the creator to exist there must exist 'suffering and much trans-formation'. If we wish to be the child again, if we wish to be 'advocates of transitoriness', we must also be prepared to be the mother of that child, to undergo birth-pangs and experience the mother's pain. The self must be in the action as the mother is in the child: this should be the maxim of our action ('Of the Virtuous'). But can the will say to itself: but 'my creative will, my destiny, wants it thus'? 'Willing liberates', Zarathustra teaches, 'that is the true doctrine of will and freedom'. It is thus his will which drives Zarathustra away from gods and to mankind, 'it drives the hammer to the stone' ('On the Blissful Islands').

All creators, however, he teaches, are hard. It is in the context of the teaching of a creative, 'hard' will that Zarathustra revalues the unegoistic values such as pity. In 'Of the Compassionate' (*Von den Mitleidigen*) Zarathustra teaches that great love for oneself and for humanity must even overcome forgiveness and pity. Has anything in the world, he asks, caused more suffering than the follies of the compassionate? Did not God die of his pity for man? If he is to be compassionate, the noble man does not wish to be called compassionate and will only practice it from a distance. When he saw the sufferer suffer, Zarathustra tells us that he felt ashamed on account of the sufferer's shame, and when he helped the sufferer he injured the sufferer's pride: 'Great obligations do not make a man grateful, they make him resentful'. The noble man, therefore, resolves not to make others feel ashamed but rather to feel shame before all sufferers.

The discourse entitled 'Of the Priests' reveals some important aspects of Zarathustra's teaching of redemption. He reveals that his blood is related to that of the priests, from those who have suffered from life but wish to see others suffer too. He informs us that he pities the priests for he who they call their redeemer has cast them into bondage. 'Into the bondage of false values and false scriptures! Ah, that someone would redeem them from their Redeemer!' If we are to find 'the way to freedom' then we must be redeemed by men greater than any redeemer has ever been. It is at this point that Zarathustra declares that 'there has never yet been an overman', that is, a new humanity which is not only its own redeemer but which can deliver itself from its need of redemption. In the discourse on 'Of the Rabble' Zarathustra expresses his disgust with both rulers and ruled who are engaged in a struggle of petty power politics. Zarathustra, however, must learn to transcend his disgust, for disgust does not breed creation but only revenge. In 'Of the Tarantulas' he discloses a conception of politics beyond the spirit of revenge. In a tremendously revealing passage he says: 'My friends, I do not want to be confused with others or taken for what I am not. There are those who preach my doctrine of life: yet are at the same time preachers of equality, and tarantulas.' He tells us that his highest hope is that man may be delivered from the bonds of revenge: that is the bridge to the 'highest hopes and a rainbow after protracted storms'. He speaks against the preachers of equality who conceal a hidden vengefulness in their soul and who would like to see the world become full of the revenge that calls itself 'justice'. Zarathustra teaches that the doctrine of equality is a doctrine by which the weak and the impotent seek to take revenge on the noble and the powerful. He teaches that all is a creative unity which must constantly overcome itself: 'Good and evil, rich and poor, noble and base, and all the names of the virtues: they should be weapons and ringing symbols that life must overcome itself again and again!'

It is mid-way through the second book that the doctrine of self-overcoming is introduced. Zarathustra begins by offering a challenge to the will to truth – both his own and man's: 'What urges you on and arouses your ardour, you wisest of men, do you call it "will to truth"?' ('Of Self-Overcoming') But the will to truth is a will to power – 'the unexhaustible, procreating life-will' – he declares, even in the assessment of values, of good and evil. In order that his teaching of good and evil can be better understood. Zarathustra relates his teaching about life and the nature of all living things:

> I have followed the living creature, I have followed the greatest and smallest paths, so that I might understand its nature.
>
> ...wherever I found living creatures, there too I heard the language of obedience. All living creatures are obeying creatures... he who cannot obey himself will be commanded. That is the nature of all living creatures.
>
> But this is the third thing I heard: that commanding is more difficult than obeying. And not only because the commander bears the burden of all who obey, and that this burden can easily crush him.
>
> In all commanding there appeared to me an experiment and a risk: and the living creature always risks himself when he commands.
>
> Yes, even when he commands himself: then also must he make amends for his commanding. He must become judge and avenger and victim of his own law.
>
> How has this come about? thus I asked myself. What persuades the living creature to obey and to command and to practise obedience in commanding?
>
> Listen now to my teaching, you wisest men! Test in earnest whether I have crept into the heart of the life and down to the root of its heart!
>
> Where I found a living creature, there I found will to power; and even in the will of the servant I found the will to be master.
>
> The will of the weaker persuades it to serve the stronger; its will wants to be master over those weaker still...

All the goals of life – evolution, procreation, overcoming – come together in the one goal of power. Considered as will to power, as will to grow and develop, life reveals itself as that which must overcome itself again and again. Whatever we create and love we must eventually oppose it in order to overcome ourselves and create anew.

> He who shot the doctrine of 'will to existence' at truth certainly did not hit the truth: this will – does not exist!
>
> For what does not exist cannot will; but that which is in existence, how could it still want to come into existence?

With this disclosure of the nature of life, Zarathustra claims to have
solved the riddle of existence, for he has shown that: 'Unchanging
good and evil do not exist. From out of themselves they must
overcome themselves again and again'. He attempts to awaken
individuals to their will to power by teaching that they exert power
with their values and tables of good and evil. Moreover, the
individual who wants to be a creator of values must at the same time
be a destroyer of values because, 'the greatest evil belongs with the
greatest good: this, however, is the creative good'. Clearly, it is the
doctrine of self-overcoming which underlies Nietzsche's deepest
thinking on life.

Zarathustra does not yet at this stage offer and develop his
teaching of redemption. Instead, in a series of discourses he clarifies
the nature of his teaching and who he is. In 'Of the Sublime Men'
he tells us that 'all life is a dispute over taste and tasting'. All living
creatures must have a table of values and scales with which to weigh
the relative merits of what they esteem. In this discourse Zarathustra
reveals that the overman is not simply a sublime man, for those who
are sublime are still ugly, for they have not yet learned of laughter
and beauty. They may have tamed monsters and solved riddles, but
they need to redeem their own monsters and riddles. The knowledge
of the sublime person is not without jealousy, but the generosity of
the truly magnanimous man ought to include 'gracefulness...Beauty
is unattainable to all violent wills'. 'Beauty' comes into being when
the power becomes gracious and 'descends into the visible'. Only the
'man of power' is capable of beauty. 'May your goodness be your
ultimate self-overpowering', Zarathustra teaches: 'I believe you
capable of any evil: therefore I desire of you the good'. In 'Of the
Land of Culture' (*Bildung*) Zarathustra reveals that nowhere has he
found a home; the 'men of the present', to whom his heart once
drove him, are a mockery. Now, he declares, he shall love only his
'children's land' where he will make amends to his children for
being the children of his fathers: 'and to all the future – for *this*
present!' In 'Of Poets' Zarathustra teaches that the poets always lie
too much, and reveals that he too is a poet. If Zarathustra is a liar
then why do his disciples believe in him? 'Belief', he declares, 'does
not make me blessed'. Zarathustra grows weary of the poets and
declares that, although he is of today and of what has been, there is
also something of him that is of tomorrow and of what shall be. In
'Of Great Events' we are told that the greatest happenings are not

the loudest ones, but those in which we experience our stillest hour:
'The world revolves, not around the inventors of new noises, but
around the inventors of new values; it revolves *inaudibly*.' In the
discourse entitled 'The Prophet', immediately preceding the
climatic one on redemption, we learn that mankind has suffered
from the prophet who teaches that 'everything is past,' therefore
'all is in vain'. If everyone grows weary of their works, if everything
perishes and nothing is permanent, if all harvests eventually turn
rotten, that what is the point and the purpose? Zarathustra too
grows weary and sad listening to the prophet of gloom and doom,
and undergoes a dream from which he emerges as 'the advocate of
life'. The ground has now been prepared for the teaching of
redemption to be related.

In the discourse on 'Of Redemption', the teaching of will to
power, conceived as a teaching on the nature of life as self-
overcoming, takes on a new aspect as Zarathustra attempts to
awaken us to that which lies at the ground of our existence and
which can liberate it from the spirit of revenge. In this discourse the
fundamental question is posed: do we recognize and acknowledge
the will to power as our *creative will*? The discourse begins with
Zarathustra crossing the great bridge to the overman surrounded by
beggars and cripples. A hunchback declares that although the
people have learned from Zarathustra and acquired belief in his
teaching, he has yet to convince the cripples. Zarathustra responds
to the hunchback by uttering a teaching from the people, which
holds that if one takes the hump away from the hunchback one takes
away his spirit, and if one gives eyes to the blind one only allows him
to see the misery of life. In other words, redemption is not to be had.
But men have become 'inverse cripples', Zarathustra declares, who
are one thing only (a big ear, a big eye). He thus resolves not to listen
to the people when they speak on the subject of human beings and
what makes them great. Now, speaking to his disciples, he declares
that he walks among human beings as if walking among fragments
and limbs. He describes himself as a willer and a creator, as a bridge
to the future, but also as a cripple on the bridge; Zarathustra is all
of this. He would despair and declare the past and the present to be
his most intolerable burden if he were not also 'a seer of that which
must come'. He now reveals a crucially important facet of his
teaching of redemption in that it is, in some way not yet specified, to
teach individuals how to redeem all that was past and mere dreadful

chance into something to which the will can say, 'yes, I willed it thus!' We are being prepared for the 'moment'.

It is at this crucial stage in his descent that Zarathustra explicitly questions his own identity. He asks his disciples if they have ever asked themselves who Zarathustra is. Is he a promiser, or a fulfiller? A conqueror or an inheritor? Is he a harvest or a ploughshare? A physician or a convalescent? A liberator or a seducer? A good man or an evil man? Zarathustra understands himself to be a wanderer who wanders among human beings who are only fragments of beings. It is his aim to compose into one, and bring together, the fragmentary and contingent nature of man's existence. It is in this discourse of the work that Zarathustra begins to accept his destiny, to become what and who he is. The decisive question is that of how the will can be taught liberation from the spirit of revenge. He is clearly looking for a doctrine which will teach the will how to liberate itself by acknowledging its willing as a creating.

Zarathustra invites human beings to reflect on good and evil so that they come to know and will that which has formed them, instead of accepting it as a blind fate and a dreadful chance over which they have no control. They must be taught to overcome even that which they feel most impotent in the face of, and which they can only rage in anger and frustration against: the past.

> To redeem the past and to transform every 'It was' into an 'I willed it thus!' – that alone do I call redemption!
> Will – that is what the liberator and bringer of joy is called: thus I have taught you, my friends! But now learn this as well: The will itself is still a prisoner.
> Willing liberates: but what is it that fastens in fetters even the liberator?
> 'It was': that is what the will's teeth-gnashing and most lonely affliction is called. Powerless against that which has been done, the will is an angry spectator of all things past.
> The will cannot will backwards; that it cannot break time and time's desire – that is the will's most lonely affliction.

The will finds that it cannot roll back the die of time, and so out of wrath it takes revenge. The will as a liberator becomes a malefactor. Revenge consists in this experience of impotence towards time and time's 'It was'. Zarathustra thus declares:

> The *spirit of revenge*: my friends, that, up to now, has been mankind's chief concern; and where there was suffering, there was always supposed to be punishment.

'Punishment' is what revenge calls itself: it feigns a good conscience for itself with a lie.

And because there is suffering in the willer himself, since he cannot will backwards – therefore willing itself and all life was supposed to be – punishment!

The experience of the time's passing, and of its solidification into the factitious 'it was' (*es war*) gives rise to the will seeking revenge on the past. But the act of revenge in Nietzsche's eyes is futile, since new acts do not negate past ones even though they stand in a relation of opposition to the contents of certain past events and deeds. As one commentator has noted, the 'problem of "It was" is not a problem about the content of the past, but about pastness itself'.[36] The spirit of revenge fails to solve this problem of the pastness of time since, instead of overcoming the burden of the past through a creative labour of self-overcoming, resulting in the birth of the new and the innocent, it is possessed by the insults and injuries of the past to the extent that it wishes to preserve them. But this attempt to impose guilt and punishment on the past leads to a vicious circle from which there can be no escape, for as soon as an act of punishment has been carried out in response to some past crime or offence, it too becomes 'past' and part of the vengeful spirit's fixation on pastness. It is a paradox of the eternal return of the same that it teaches that a new beginning should be made with each event or deed that is to return, for it recognizes that forgetting constitutes the essential condition of any new action that is to be motivated by bravery and innocence.[37] The repeatability of the past that is found in the experience of the spirit of revenge, on the other hand, prevents the innocence of the new from being born. This point on the eternal return can only be appreciated if it is recognized that what is willed in the experience of return is not the literal contents of the moment but the very momentariness of the moment, that is, time's desire and time's perishing. The notion of the 'same' in the thought of eternal return provides the criterion for judging whether one's actions are motivated by innocence and forgetfulness or by guilt and revenge. As a thought-experiment the eternal return asks us how well-disposed towards life we would have to feel in order to desire nothing more passionately and intensely than its eternal confirmation and seal. I shall expand on these points shortly.

To return to the discourse on redemption. Zarathustra challenges several views which the will adopts in order to explain away time's

'It was', views which reflect a moral view of the world. There is the view which teaches that everything that exists in the world is ordered morally in accordance with eternal laws of justice and punishment, with laws of good and evil. There is also the view of Nietzsche's former teacher on the will, Schopenhauer, which teaches that the will can only succeed in redeeming itself by learning how not to will. In opposition to these various teachings of redemption, which only serve to enslave the will to a moral world-order, Zarathustra offers a teaching that liberates the will from its self-imposed tutelage. He asks:

> Has the will become its own redeemer and bringer of joy? Has it unlearned the spirit of revenge and all teeth-gnashing?
> And who has taught it to be reconciled with time, and higher things than reconciliation?
> The will that is the will to power must will something higher than any reconciliation – but how shall that happen? Who has taught it to will backwards, too?

It is at this point that Zarathustra's discourse on the will and time breaks off, without the question of how the will can learn to will backwards receiving an answer. Zarathustra is in search of a doctrine which will enable him to communicate his teaching of the overman and of the will to power in such a way that the will can be educated to will its own formation and deformation, that is, he is looking for a teaching which shows that freedom lies in willing necessity, in creatively becoming what one is.

  In the discourse on 'Manly Prudence', which follows the dramatic teaching on redemption, Zarathustra confesses that it is not the height, but the abyss, that is terrible. He thus reveals that he possesses a twofold will in that his will clings to mankind because his other will draws him up to the overman. He sits at the 'gateway' and asks who wishes to deceive him? His doubt and secret laughter is that his vision of the overman will be declared to be a vision of the devil. At the end of part two Zarathustra has become defiant and refuses to speak: he is experiencing his 'stillest hour'. A voice cries out to him in the stillest hour saying that he is one who knows but he does not speak. The voice persists in battering him with questions so that he may learn to accept the destiny contained in his *Untergang*:

> Of what consequence are you, Zarathustra? Speak your teaching and break!
> And I answered: 'ah, is it *my* teaching? Who am *I*? I await one who is more worthy; I am not worthy even to break it...'

Then again something said to me voicelessly: 'O Zarathustra, he who has to move mountains moves valleys and lowlands too.'

And I answered: 'My words have as yet moved no mountains and what I have spoken has not yet reached men. Indeed, I went to men, but I have not yet attained them'.

The most unforgiveable thing about Zarathustra, says the voice, is that he has the power, but will not rule, he has learned how to obey, but he will not command. Zarathustra, however, knows that he lacks the lion's right to command and rule, and that he needs to become a child without shame if he is to command with courage and overcome pity and disgust. The book ends with Zarathustra's fruits ripe, but with Zarathustra unripe for his fruits. He needs to go down once more.

At this stage of Zarathustra's *Untergang* the teaching of redemption is not yet completed or fulfilled, for it is in need of a doctrine which will show how the will can will the impossible – backwards. On one level the redemption Zarathustra offers would appear to amount to little more than a desperate heroism, a kind of heroic bad faith, which must result in a humiliating defeat with the will raging against itself in a fury of impotence. However, what needs to be grasped is that in the teaching of redemption Nietzsche is not simply concerned with willing the past – an act which is clearly impossible – but with our attitude towards time itself. Clearly to will the past would be impossible and to believe otherwise would be madness. This shows us that the teaching is directed towards liberating the will from its enslavement to the ordinary conception of time which posits a seriality of past, present, and future events, through an awakening to the moment and its eternity. Through the experience of the moment we learn not only to declare, 'Yes, I *willed* it!', but also 'Yes, I *do* will it, and I *shall* will it!' For the significance of the moment is that it reveals the innocence of time as becoming, including the innocence of the past from which the will suffers and which inspires in it the spirit of revenge. As Pierre Klossowski has pointed out, re-willing what has already been willed becomes creative in the experience of eternal return when we realize that it was forgetfulness and innocence which enabled us to carry out our original acts.[38] But redemption means more than this, for it means that we must become what we are (forgetfulness and innocence) by turning the accident and chance of the past into a fate and destiny. And this is the birth of conscious innocence, of the child that is a self-propelling wheel and a sacred Yes.

PART III: THE VISION AND THE RIDDLE

The central teaching, not only of part three, not only of the book, but of Nietzsche's entire thought, is unquestionably that of the eternal recurrence of the same (*die ewige Wiederkunft des Gleichen*).[39] It is with this doctrine that Zarathustra is able to communicate his teaching on redemption, and it is out of its experience that the overman will emerge as the one who embodies the creative and innocent will to power. The thought and test of eternal return serves to bring together Nietzsche's main doctrines. The significance of the idea of eternal return in the context of Zarathustra's *Untergang* lies in that, through the experience of the thought of return, Zarathustra himself goes under and experiences the redemption he has taught in part two. Zarathustra is on the way to the overman; he must show 'we' his readers how to go under and over to it by overcoming the spirit of revenge and *ressentiment* that has dominated man's formation and deformation so far. Through the experience of the abysmal and terrifying thought of eternal return Zarathustra finally becomes what he is, for he has learned to accept his destiny, that is, who he is: the teacher of eternal return.

In the examination of the doctrine of eternal return which follows I shall focus attention on the role it plays in Nietzsche's teaching on redemption beyond the politics of revenge, and on its significance as providing a solution to the problem of history (the problem of the past which proves to be a problem about the nature of time). I am thus not concerned with the cosmological aspect of the teaching, and the pseudo-scientific status Nietzsche claimed for it in his unpublished writings of the 1880s.[40] I take the most important aspect of the doctrine to lie in its educative aspect. This aspect of the doctrine is most evident in Nietzsche's first presentation of the idea in section 341 of the *Gay Science*, where the doctrine is presented in the form of a demon who poses the ultimate challenge to the individual concerning the nature of existence. Here Nietzsche emphasizes the responsibility in accepting or rejecting the doctrine by describing it as 'the greatest weight'. If this thought gained possession of us, Nietzsche argues, it would change us or perhaps, even crush us. The question in each and everything: 'do you desire this once more and innumerable times more?' would lie upon our actions as our greatest weight. It is this particular presentation of the thought of eternal return in terms of an existential test of the strength and courage of the will which shall govern the reading which follows.

In *Ecce Homo* the thought (*Gedanke*) of eternal return is said to be the 'fundamental conception' of *Zarathustra*, for it represents the highest formula of affirmation that is attainable.[41] In a note of 1884 the thought is referred to as the 'great cultivating thought' (*grosste züchtende Gedanke*) by which all other modes of thought will ultimately perish.[42] The idea of eternal return is so fundamental for Nietzsche because it is through the experience of this thought that he intends to educate humanity to a standpoint beyond the spirit of revenge and resentment. What is noticeable about the presentation of the thought in the context of Zarathustra's *Untergang*, however, is that, although the idea is absolutely central to the work, its importance is veiled. For example, the thought is not said to the crowd, to 'men' as such, or to the disciples, and it is not directly embraced by Zarathustra until the end of part three, and then only in his solitude. In this way attention is drawn not only to its terrifying and abysmal nature, but also to the difficulty of teaching it.[43] A note from the *Nachlass* of Autumn 1883 reveals that Nietzsche planned part three so that the thought of eternal return is not explicitly expressed by Zarathustra himself, but shows only that he is prepared for it. In part three Zarathustra's own self-overcoming is to be seen as a prefiguration (*Vorbild*) of the self-overcoming of humanity in favour of the overman.[44] The significance of the doctrine of return is twofold: it is both a teaching on time and an experience which affirms the unity of all things. I shall first approach the doctrine in the context of Zarathustra's *Untergang*; next I shall examine its nature as a teaching on the nature of time, and then, in a later section, I shall examine its significance in relation to the teaching on how one is to become what one is. The cultivating aspects of the doctrine which are to divide humanity into two – the strong and the weak – will be examined in the final chapter in a discussion of Nietzsche's conception of politics.

Part three opens with Zarathustra acknowledging that he now stands before his last summit, before 'the deed that has been deferred the longest'. He now has to ascend his most difficult path, and he recognizes that 'in the final analysis one experiences only oneself', ('The Wanderer'). He is ready to accept the destiny of the descent.

In the discourse entitled 'Of the Vision and the Riddle' (*Vom Gesicht und Räthsel*) we witness Zarathustra becoming prepared for the affirmation of the experience of eternal return. Zarathustra finds himself on a ship taking a long and dangerous journey. He addresses himself to the 'bold venturers and adventurers', teaching them that they must strive to create beyond themselves ever upward in spite of the dwarf (the Spirit of Gravity) which draws them down towards the abyss. Man, Zarathustra teaches, must overcome the temptation of pity by accepting the superiority of courage. Pity is declared to be man's deepest abyss, for as deeply as man looks into life so he deeply looks into suffering. The creative self-overcoming of life, however, depends on man not succumbing to the temptation of feeling pity for the weak, but rather rising to the demands of courage and the enhancement of life to be gained through it.[45]

At first the thought that everything returns descends upon Zarathustra in the form of a riddle and as a vision of the most solitary man. As he climbs ever higher upward on his ascent, his arch-enemy, the Spirit of Gravity, draws him down towards the abyss. The Spirit of Gravity oppresses Zarathustra and it is to him that he presents the riddle of return as his most abysmal thought. Zarathustra presents a riddle of eternity. The two stand before a gateway which has two aspects and where two paths come together: no one, Zarathustra informs the dwarf, has ever reached their end, for the two lanes go on for ever unto eternity. They merge together, however, at the gateway (*Torwegs*) at which they are standing and above which is written the word 'Moment' (*Augenblick*). Zarathustra scolds the dwarf for treating the riddle lightly when he proclaims naively: 'Everything straight lies... All truth is crooked, time itself is a circle', indicating that the thought of eternal return does not simply rest on a circular conception of time.[46] Such a conception of time can only lead to a crushing fatalism which declares 'all is in vain'. Zarathustra responds by suggesting that, if we behold the moment, we see that from its gateway a long, eternal lane runs *back*, which is eternity itself. Thus, he is led to ask the question: must not everything that can happen have already happened? Must not all things that can happen have already happened? Must not *this* gateway and *this* moment have already happened, been done, run past? Are not all things bound together to the extent that the moment even draws to it all future things?

Clearly, the thought of eternal return, if taken literally, is absurd.[47] However, if looked upon as an imaginative response to the problem of time and time's 'it was', we discover that its significance lies in the affirmation of the moment. The moment is the highest affirmation of the temporal and transient character of life which affirms the innocence of life and life's becoming. In this way the will becomes authentically temporal and authentically historical, for it affirms the innocence of becoming and no longer yearns for any revenge against time by positing an afterworld, a hereafter, a beyond, or a kingdom of ends. However, this insight is misleading if we fail to recognize that the affirmation of the moment in the thought of eternal return leads to a total dissolution of any distinction in life between form and content, for the form of life is its content (pain, suffering, joy, etc). The moment brings together past, present, and future in a moment of eternity. Eternity is neither simply a future time nor a time which lasts for ever, but the eternal now which has become visible and sensible. Moreover, if the moment is the return of the same, it must also be the return of the different, just as it is the dissolution of form and content and just as it is beyond good and evil. The 'awakening' that is the moment is not simply a present moment or a moment which glows in full presence. Once we are liberated from the illusion of seriality contained in the ordinary, everyday conception of time, we see that the experience of the moment has nothing to do with speed (it is neither short nor long); it cannot be the pure 'present' for the present only makes sense in relation to a 'past' and a 'future', but this serial conception of time becomes sublated in the experience of the moment of eternity. In other words, the experience of the moment is the experience of nothing; but by the same token, it is the experience of *everything*. The affirmation of the moment leads to the affirmation of time itself, for no single moment is self-sufficient but is connected to all the other moments of one's life. This is why, for Nietzsche, affirming one single moment entails affirming all of existence, one's own included: we recognize that it took the eternity which we are to produce the one event, and thus in the single moment of affirmation all eternity is redeemed, affirmed, and called 'good'.

After this confrontation with the Spirit of Gravity, Zarathustra begins to speak more and more softly for he becomes afraid of his own thoughts. He is presented with a horrifying vision when he sees a young shepherd writhing and choking as a heavy, black snake hangs from his mouth. Had he ever seen such disgust on a face? he asks himself. He tries to pull the snake out of the shepherd's mouth until a voice cries out to him: 'Bite! Bite!' It is the voice of his disgust and his pity, of his good and evil. He appeals to others to solve the meaning of the riddle that he has experienced and to interpret the vision of the most solitary man. 'It was a premonition: *what* did I see in this allegory? And *who* is it that must come one day?' The shepherd depicted in this parable is clearly Zarathustra himself. The vision of he who must come one day is a vision of the overman: the experience of eternal return is to provide the bridge to the over-man. The shepherd, Zarathustra says, 'is no longer a shepherd, no longer a man', but a 'transformed being, surrounded with light, *laughing*!'

The significance of this experience of the vision and the riddle in the context of Zarathustra's *Untergang* is that it shows him overcoming his disgust and pity for man and attaining the overman. He now stands triumphant having accepted his destiny. He realizes that it is for the sake of his fellow-creators and destroyers of values that he must perfect himself and become what, and who, he is: 'I have not yet been strong enough for the lion's arrogance', Zarathustra confesses, 'Your heaviness has always been fearful enough for me: but one day I shall find the strength and the lion's voice to summon you up!' ('Of Involuntary Bliss') One day each of them will undergo the experience of 'testing and recognition', to see whether they are 'masters of a protracted will'. It is for the sake of fellow-creators that Zarathustra now sets out to perfect himself by submitting to *his* ultimate testing and recognition. He must learn to love himself with 'a sound and healthy love'. The commandment to love oneself is not a commandment for today or tomorrow but is an art which is 'the finest, subtlest, ultimate, and most patient of all' ('Of the Spirit of Gravity', 2). It is at this juncture in the story of his down-going that Zarathustra recognizes the 'Way' as *his* Way. He is becoming what he is.

'Of Old and New Law-Tables' is the longest discourse in the book and immediately precedes the crucial discourse in which Zarathustra convalesces and reaches the end of his *Untergang*. In this discourse we find him sitting and waiting for the hour of his descent surrounded by old shattered law-tables and new, half-written ones. He talks to himself and tells the story of mankind to himself. When he visited men, he tells us, he found each one of them sitting on the ancient conceit that each one of them knew what was good and what was evil. He tells us that he disturbed this 'somnolence' when he taught that no one knows what good and evil are unless it be the creator. The creator is the one who creates a goal for humanity and thereby gives the earth a meaning and a future. He confesses that he is still ashamed at being a poet. However, through the teaching of parables he has taught men to recognize the unity of things (of good and evil, of freedom and necessity) and that everything is connected and necessary: the lower and the higher, the weak and the strong, the small man and the overman. 'Must there not be moles and heavy dwarfs', he asks, 'for the sake of the nimble, the nimblest?' ('Old and New Law-Tables', 2). It was out of the recognition of the unity and necessity of all things, Zarathustra reveals, that he 'picked up the word *Übermensch*', and that he taught that redemption lies in creating all that is past. Thus, he confesses, he wishes to go to men once more and give them, 'dying, my richest gift!'[48] He now seeks companions who will carry and bear a new law-table with him, undergoing the three metamorphoses, 'into the valley and fleshly hearts'. His pity is that he sees that all that is past has been merely 'handed over', and this pity leads him to having a remarkable premonition:

handed over to the favour, the spirit, the madness, of every generation that comes and transforms everything that has been into its own bridge!

A great despot could come, a shrewd devil, who with his favour and disfavour could compel and constrain all that is past, until it became his bridge and prognostic and herald and cock-crow.

This, however, is the other danger and my other pity: he who is of the mob remembers back to his grandfather – with his grandfather, however, time stops.

Thus all that is past is handed over: for the mob could one day become master, and all time be drowned in shallow waters. ('Of Old and New Law-Tables' 11)

Clearly, what we see in this passage is Nietzsche intimating at the danger that he first identified in his second untimely meditation, that the monumentalizing of the past can quite easily place history in the service of a destructive and vengeful politics of violence. Nietzsche's response in this passage is to call for 'a new nobility' who will oppose all mob-rule and all despotism and 'write anew upon new law-tables the word: "Noble"'. This new nobility will not gaze 'backward', but 'outward', outward to the land of children as 'begetters and cultivators and sowers of the future'. They shall redeem the horror and absurdity of the past by making amends to their children for being the children of their fathers. But in order to become those that they are, the sowers of the seeds of the future, they must be taught that only the best ought to rule and that 'human society' is an 'experiment' and '*not* a "contract"'.

In the discourse entitled 'The Convalescent', Zarathustra has returned to the solitude of his cave where, shortly after his return he springs up from his bed 'like a madman' and cries out in a terrible voice to his animals. Here we find Zarathustra summoning up his most abysmal thought from his depths: 'I, Zarathustra, the advocate of life, the advocate of the circle – I call you, my most abysmal thought!... My abyss *speaks*, I have turned my ultimate depth into the light!' ('The Convalescent'). Upon uttering these words Zarathustra falls down like one who is dead. He eventually comes round, pale and trembling. During this period of convalescence he is cared for only by his animals, the eagle and the serpent. They converse with him and tell him that it is time to step out of his cave after seven days of solitude. 'Has perhaps a new knowledge come to you, a bitter, oppressive knowledge?' they ask. For Zarathustra, it is his greatest danger and sickness that he has to be the first to teach the doctrine that 'the wheel of existence rolls for ever', that 'everything dies, everything blossoms anew... the ring of existence is true to itself for ever'. Moreover, 'Existence begins in every instant; the ball There rolls around every Here. The middle is everywhere. The path of eternity crooked'. He confesses to the animals that, yes, it was he who bit off the head of the snake and spat it away in the parable of the shepherd. Man is the cruellest of all animals, he tells them. But, he adds, he does not wish to slander life and to accuse man; instead, he wishes to teach man that all that is wicked in his nature must become transformed into his strength and be 'the hardest stone for the highest creator'. Man must learn to overcome the disgust he feels towards himself, not to choke on it and be tempted by the prophet who declares that all is in vain and that nothing is worth while. But can Zarathustra overcome the disgust arising from the realization that if everything returns, then so must the small man return eternally, that is, the man of whom he is weary?

It is at this moment in part three that Zarathustra is subjected once again to the thought of eternal return, this time related to him by his animals who tell him that it is his destiny to become the teacher of this doctrine. If he were to die now, the animals ask, what would he say? He would teach, they declare, the eternal return of all things, which on his behalf they, as advocates of Zarathustra, utter as follows:

I shall return with this sun, with this earth, with this eagle, with this serpent – *not* to a new life or a better life or a similar life:

I shall return eternally to this identical and self-same life, in the greatest

things and in the smallest, to teach once more the eternal recurrence of all
things,

to speak once more the teaching of the great noontide of earth and man,
to tell man of the overman once more.

I spoke my teaching, I broke on my teaching: thus my eternal fate will
have it – as prophet do I perish!

Now the hour has come when he who is going down shall bless himself.
Thus – *ends* Zarathustra's down-going.

It is thus not Zarathustra but his animals who relate the final version
of doctrine of eternal return and who inform him that his down-
going is over and has reached its end. The reason for this, I would
argue, is that Zarathustra cannot himself declare that his down-
going is at an end because, in order for him to become what *he* is, *we*
must become those that we are too. In other words, his testing and
recognition is dependent on our testing and recognition. Zarathustra
is the lawgiver who has shown us that '*the* Way' does not exist, but
that in order to attain the overman one must undergo and go across
the bridge of eternal return. I shall return to this point in the section
on how one is to become what one is, for what this point shows is that
the eternal return represents a version of the categorical imperative.

Part three closes with Zarathustra talking to his 'over-soul' and
ends with Zarathustra composing a song to eternity, to the ring of
return, singing 'all joy wants eternity'. In 'Of the Great Longing' he
teaches his soul to say '"today" and "once" and "formerly" and to
dance the dance over every Here and There and Over-there'. In
'The Second Dance Song' and 'The Seven Seals' Zarathustra has
the revelation that the wisdom of eternity (life itself) is woman:
'Never yet did I find the woman by whom I wanted children, unless
it be this woman, whom I love: for I love you, O Eternity!'

It is evident that the major part of Zarathustra's experience of his
Untergang consists in his coming to learn, to know, to experience, and
will the eternal return. With the affirmation of this doctrine life,
conceived as will to power, receives its highest affirmation (*Bejahung*).
Through the moment the notion confronts us with the totality of our
existence. The peculiar challenge the thought presents lies in the
question that confronts the person who experiences the thought in all
its abysmal and terrifying nature. Can I accept the destiny of my
being in such a way that I can also accept the necessity of my past
because, as a creator of the future, I willed it? The thought of eternal
return thus teaches a new will. It teaches the individual to creatively

will that existence which hitherto it has willed only blindly and unknowingly. The only manner in which existence can be redeemed is through the recognition and test of its totality, which takes place through the eternity of the moment; hence the testing question of eternal return: does the will have the courage and strength to repeat its existence again and again in its entirety? How well-disposed to life would the will have to be to answer this question in the affirmative? What is transformed in this willing is not the past itself, which would be impossible, but rather its significance. To accept the moment implies accepting the innocence of all that has led to it, and all that which comes from it.[49]

It is important to appreciate what exactly we are being asked to affirm in the thought of eternal return. One commentator has raised a decisive question concerning the possible full ramifications of the experiment of return.[50] The question to be considered, and it is one which anyone who undergoes the experience of return must pose at some point, is whether any person of the twentieth century could affirm the eternal return of the moment of Auschwitz and love that unconditionally. Would any decent human being not will the return of their lives *minus* the horrors and catastrophes of the mad world we live in, in which hundreds die every day through starvation, poverty, disease, and torture? Would we not have to be God (and a sick one at that) to be able to affirm unconditionally the eternalizing of such moments as these? But the question is misplaced, for it misunderstands the nature of Nietzsche's teaching. With this thought of return Nietzsche is trying to teach us something fundamental about the nature of life, something that is crucial to its future growth, development, and overcoming. It operates essentially on two levels. Firstly, it educates us about the nature of time, through teaching the affirmation of the moment, by showing us that no moment is self-sufficient, and that in willing one moment we will all moments because every moment is an exemplification of the becoming and perishing which characterize time. Secondly, it educates us about the nature of human action, for in willing the thought of return we are not being asked to will the literal return of the moments of life but only the innocence of their momentariness. This does *not* mean that we simply turn our back on the horrors and tragedies of the past; on the contrary, what the eternal return shows is that the awakening of oneself to the moment points one beyond the single, self-sufficient moment to an act of redemptive, creative willing. Thus, the horrors of the past should serve to inspire one, neither to take revenge on the present for the sake of the past, nor to ignore and neglect the past, but to perform a future act which is so creative that it is capable of redeeming, and making amends for, all that is past. It is thus not a question of assuming the absurd vantage point of a god, but of simply being, and overcoming when necessary, what we are: human, all too human, and which is the site of a struggle between innocence and revenge, joy and despair, good and evil, the old and the new, the virtuous and the vicious, the tragic and the comic, and so on. What is necessary is that we learn to become those who we are by giving style to our character, and by recognizing that the only law of life is that of self-overcoming. The thought of eternal return is designed to liberate us from the spirit of revenge by showing us how to create innocently and affirmatively, and in doing so redeeming everything that is past. The past needs to be neither ignored nor forgotten, but recognised and then affirmed as a condition of any future willing.

The affirmation contained in the experience of eternal return represents Nietzsche's attempt to overcome the spirit of revenge and to provide a solution to the problem of history – that is, the problem of the past and how humanity can create anew without guilt, remorse, or resentment. The importance of this teaching on redemption for understanding Nietzsche's political thought – or, for understanding his thought as a whole for that matter – can hardly be underestimated.

PART IV: THE RETURN OF THE OVERMAN

Georg Simmel was one of the first commentators to argue that the two principal teachings of *Thus Spoke Zarathustra* must be viewed as fundamentally at odds with each other in that, where the overman demands that we continually aim to create the new, the doctrine of eternal return contains the crushing thought that the same will return eternally.[51] In recent years this view has been most forcefully argued for by Erich Heller who provocatively suggests that the contradiction shows that Nietzsche desires to escape from 'transience, oblivion, the inarticulate'.[52] A way out of this apparent contradiction has been suggested by two commentators, Laurence Lampert and Daniel Conway, who have put forward the argument that we should read the story of Zarathustra's descent as one in which the teaching of the overman is progressively and decidedly abandoned by Zarathustra in favour of the eternal return. I consider this interpretation, however, to be untenable. Moreover, it becomes unnecessary once we appreciate that there exists no contradiction between the two doctrines, but rather only a fundamental, if admittedly difficult and puzzling, entwinement (though Heller's provocation must haunt us like a shadow casting a deep, perhaps terrible, darkness over Nietzsche's thought). In order to defend the view that the principal doctrines of Zarathustra are compatible I shall draw on material from the *Zarathustra Nachlass*.

An analysis of part four, which Nietzsche added to the book in the winter of 1884–5 after thinking the story was complete, shows that he did not have Zarathustra progressively abandon the vision of the overman in favour of that of eternal return. In this part we see that the vision of the overman returns – a return which is quite in order when one considers the full implications of the teaching of eternal return! It is worthwhile to note, for example, that whereas in the book it is stated, in the context of a test of Zarathustra's strength, that the *small man* will return eternally (the man of whom Zarathustra is weary), there is a passage in the *Nachlass* in which Nietzsche states that the overman too shall return eternally (the man of whom he is hopeful).[53] Part four begins with several years having passed over Zarathustra's soul. Sitting on a stone in front of his cave overlooking seas and abysses, his hair grown white, he is asked by his animals whether he is seeking happiness. But he replies that he aspires after his work, not after happiness. 'I am "he"', he declares cyptically, a taskmaster who once bade himself '"Become what you are!"' He is still waiting for signs that it is time for his descent, for as yet he does not go down, as he must, to men. Instead, 'men must now come *up* to me'. His destiny speaks neither of 'Today', nor of 'Never', for it has time and patience, sure in the conviction that the destiny must come one day: 'What must come one day and may not pass by?' he asks, and replies: 'Our great Hazar, our great, far-off empire of man, the thousand-year empire of Zarathustra' ('The Honey Offering'). Again he is tormented by the prophet of doom who teaches that all is in vain: 'It is all one, nothing is worthwhile, the world is without meaning, knowledge chokes' ('The Cry of Distress'). Zarathustra confesses to the prophet that the ultimate sin reserved for him, and to which the prophet has descended to seduce him to, is pity. Indeed, in a *Nachlass* note from Autumn 1883

Nietzsche actually has Zarathustra die by being overwhelmed by pity for man, after having demonstrated the truth of the eternal return and the overman.[54] It is out of this confrontation with the prophet of doom that Zarathustra hears the cry of distress of the 'Higher Man' (*höhere Mensch*). The prophet tries to seduce Zarathustra from making a descent to the higher man by saying that such a visit would be pointless. But Zarathustra replies by admitting that he too is something of a prophet.

In the discourses which follow the confrontation with the prophet, Zarathustra embarks on a search for the higher man and has a series of encounters with a number of key symbolic characters, including two kings to whom he speaks about the rabble and the rule of the powerful, and about peace as a means to new wars; the 'conscientious man of the spirit' who tells Zarathustra that he is 'the great leech of conscience' ('The Leech'): the 'sorcerer', a trembling old man who wails and suffers from bad knowledge and bad conscience; the 'old pope' who is retired from service on account of God's death; and the the 'ugliest man' who warns Zarathustra against his ultimate sin and who tells him that the God who saw everything had to die because man could not endure such a witness. In the encounter with the 'voluntary beggar' Zarathustra comes across a person who seeks knowledge of 'rumination' from the cows, and liberation from man's great affliction, that of 'disgust'. Here Zarathustra proclaims himself as 'the overcomer of the great disgust'. Out of disgust with the rich the voluntary beggar has thrown away great riches and declares that the hour has come 'for the great, evil, protracted, slow rebellion of the mob and the slaves'. The beggar, however, sees only greed and envy in the mob and unlearns the distinction between 'rich and poor', and flees far away to the blessed cows, for it is the cows, not the poor, who shall inherit the earth.

In 'The Greeting' we find Zarathustra at home in his cave holding court with all those who had passed by that day. All have ascended to discover who Zarathustra is, and whether he still lives, or whether he has been devoured by solitude. He addresses the personages gathered as the 'higher men' and declares that it is not for them that he has been waiting. The higher men are only bridges whom even higher men must step over. These are not the men for Zarathustra because each one is still suffering from God and his death, each one is possessed of great longing and great disgust which cannot transfigure itself into an innocent, creative willing for it still clings, not to man, but to God. In 'The Last Supper' Nietzsche has Zarathustra declare: '"I am a law (*Gesetz*) only for my own, I am not a law for all".' There is then a discourse devoted to the theme of the 'Higher Man' in which once again Zarathustra summons up his vision of the overman: 'Very well! Come on, you Higher Men! Only now does the mountain of mankind's future labour. God has died: now *we* desire – that the overman shall live'. ('Of the Higher Man', 2). In section 3 of the discourse Zarathustra, far from abandoning the vision of the overman, speaks of it as his 'paramount and sole concern – *not* man, not the nearest, not the poorest, not the most suffering, not the best'. Again, Zarathustra informs us that what he loves in man is that he is a going-across and a going-down, that he who despises himself also reveres himself, for he wishes to transfigure and overcome himself. The 'masters of the present' are those who wish only to preserve man. Thus, the higher men, Zarathustra teaches, must overcome 'the petty virtues, the petty prudences...the miserable ease, the "happiness of the greatest number"'. Does man possess the courage to overcome himself? he asks. Does he know that in order to overcome himself he must 'grow better and more evil', that 'the most evil is necessary for the overman's best' ('Of the Higher Man', section 5). In 'Of Science' Zarathustra teaches that if fear is humanity's 'original and fundamental sensation', then equally original and fundamental to its nature and its pre-history is 'courage', which he defines as 'adventure and joy in the unknown and the unattempted'.

Zarathustra eventually grows suspicious of the interest of the higher men in him, for he realizes that their desire to affirm themselves is little more than the Yea-saying of the ass who does not know how to say Nay. In 'The Awakening' the higher men all become pious again and begin praying to God. In 'The Ass Festival' we find them worshipping God in the belief that it is better to worship a dead God than no God at all. It is the ugliest man who has awakened God again: if he admits that it was he who killed God, is it not the case with gods, that 'death is always only a prejudice'? Zarathustra turns and addresses the ugliest man, the 'unutterable creature' whose sublimity hides its ugliness. Whether God lives or is dead, the ugliest man says to Zarathustra, the one thing he has learned from him is that he who kills most thoroughly kills not by anger but by laughter. In 'The Intoxicated Song' Nietzsche has an amazing thing happen: the ugliest man sings the song of eternity. Zarathustra leads the ugliest man by the hand and shows him his 'nocturnal world' which lies next to his cave. Zarathustra declares that he is happy with the higher men for they have become joyful again, and he respects their happiness and silence. At this point the ugliest man speaks to the assembly of higher men with the message of eternal return: 'For the sake of this day – *I* am content for the first time to have lived my whole life ... it is not enough that I testify only this much. It is worthwhile to live on earth: one day, one festival with Zarathustra has taught me to love the earth'. 'Was *that* – life?' he will say to death, 'Very well! Once more!' The affirmation of the ugliest man transforms the higher men.

It is not long, however, before the higher men suffer from their recovery and break out again in a cry of distress. Zarathustra leaves them raising the question of his own identity (is he a prophet? A dreamer? A drunkard? An odour and scent of eternity? *What* is he?) and by teaching the song of eternity:

Did you ever say a Yes to one joy? O my friends, then you said Yes to *all* woe as well. All things are chained and entwined together, all things are in love.

if you ever wanted one moment twice ... then you wanted *everything* to return!

you wanted everything anew, everything eternal, everything chained, entwined together ... ('The Intoxicated Song', 10)

In the last discourse entitled 'The Sign', Zarathustra realizes that the higher men are not his 'rightful companions' and that it is not for them that he waits in his mountains. He hears the 'gentle, protracted roar of a lion' and interprets it as the sign that his hour has come. He has overcome his pity for the higher man and now aspires after his work, for the lion has come and the children are near. Zarathustra prepares himself for the great noontide by departing from his cave, 'glowing and strong, like a morning sun emerging from behind dark mountains'.

The significance of part four and of the fact that Nietzsche added another part to the story after considering it complete, is that it discloses further the nature of his teaching of the overman, namely that Zarathustra's teaching must undergo public testing and recognition. The overman is simply that humanity which has overcome itself – overcome nihilism, the death of God, etc. – through the affirmation of the moment contained in the test of the eternal return, which releases the will from the metaphysics of the hangman and restores innocence to life, time, and becoming. Going-down and perishing 'we' will experience the hour of our loneliest loneliness and cross the bridge of the eternal return to the overman. We have seen that the overman returns in each part of the story of Zarathustra's *Untergang* after its first dramatic appearance in the prologue. Conway's contention that the overman disappears from view after part two cannot be sustained, since, as has been shown, the vision of the overman plays a key role in part three, namely in the discourse on old and new law-tables, and in the crucial discourse on convalescence where Zarathustra learns the truth of eternal return and affirms it, and in the added part four in the context of Zarathustra's overcoming of the higher men; indeed in the discourse on the higher man Zarathustra declares that the overman is his 'paramount and sole concern', which is hardly the sentiment of someone who has abandoned his 'pride and joy'.[55] Throughout the story the 'ideal' of the overman remains the same. What does change and evolve, however, are our expectations of the vision as we learn its true nature through the test of the eternal return, that is the experiment or test out of which the overman is born. 'We' learn that the overman is not simply the future which lies far off in the distance, but that is that which is constituted in the willing experience of the eternal return – remember also, that it is significant that it is not Zarathustra who relates the thought of return but his animals, that is – 'we'? But how can the new be created if everything returns exactly the same? Does not Zarathustra himself declare that there has *never* yet been an overman? Must this not mean, therefore, that once we appreciate the full implications of the teaching of eternal return, that the overman is *never* attainable?

In his major study of *Thus Spoke Zarathustra* Laurence Lampert seeks to persuade us that the 'provisional teaching' of the overman is rendered obsolete by the 'definitive teaching' of the eternal return. Failure to appreciate this point, he argues, constitutes what is perhaps the greatest single cause of the widespread misinterpretation which surrounds Nietzsche's teaching.[56] His argument is interesting and brilliantly perceptive in suggesting that because the eternal return opposes any teaching on the linearity of time (which is not strictly true or accurate) it constitutes a teaching opposed to any notion of the eschatological fulfilment of time. In other words,

Zarathustra stands against any prophetic religion which posits a notion of progress, and in which history is construed in terms of a future settlement and resolution of the past (a day of judgement, a kingdom of ends, socialism, etc.). What this entails is an abandonment of the vision of the overman, for it too rests on discredited notions of progress and redemption. This is a potent argument, and it may be that there are good reasons for rejecting Nietzsche's notion of the overman, but if there are they are *not* contained in the story of Zarathustra's *Untergang*. It is possible to reconcile the teaching of the overman and that of eternal return, I would argue, by appreciating the relation between our everyday, ordinary conception of time which rests on seriality, and the notion of time contained in the thought of eternal return, which is that of the eternity of the moment. The affirmation of the moment contains within it the sublation, not only of the past and the future, but also of the 'present'. It thus contains within it a sublation of any opposition between notions such as 'old' and 'new', 'same' and 'different'.[57] What is perhaps most difficult to appreciate about the thought of the moment is its sheer unreality, its uncanniness. However, I think it is important to appreciate that Nietzsche himself understands the birth of the overman out of the experience of the eternal return, for in this experience it becomes immaterial whether the overman has once existed or, as Zarathustra says, has never existed. Why? Because the moment of creation has neither remorse for the past nor anxiety towards the future – it is *innocent*. In affirming the eternal return of the moment we are not affirming the literal return of every moment of the past, but simply the moment's momentariness, which is the very nature of time. We are thus affirming all time. Thus, when Zarathustra says there has never yet been an overman, this 'never yet' refers to the literal future that is dependent on a serial conception of time – precisely that which the thought of eternal return overcomes. This is the great paradox of the overman, that we seek with it perhaps something monumental, fantastic, and superhuman, but in truth it lies before us, if only we could become those that we *are*. This also defines precisely the paradox of Zarathustra's whole teaching of redemption.

For these reasons I concur with those commentators who have argued that the two main teachings of Zarathustra are not incompatible. Wolfgang Müller-Lauter, for example, argues that the overman is the one who represents the highest intensity of the will to power, for in him are conjoined the past, present, and future in the moment of eternity.[58] The overman thus affirms in equal measure everything what was, is, and will be, for every moment is the same in that it contains pain and joy, suffering and pleasure, etc. But because each moment is new and eternal, it is also unique. The Zarathustra *Nachlass* is important because it shows how Nietzsche's thinking on his principal teachings and their presentation developed. It is clear that he envisages Zarathustra as a teacher and a lawgiver who descends to human beings in order to teach them that they must endeavour to overcome themselves. Zarathustra is to teach the overman in terms of a humanity which has the courage and strength to affirm life despite its terrifying, abysmal, and questionable character, to say, 'Was that – life? Then once more!' This is Nietzsche's conception of a Dionysian, tragic celebration of life as it is without subtraction, selection, or addition, but life affirmed as will to power, as the eternally self-creating and self-destroying. However, the teaching of eternal return modifies the original teaching of the overman in showing precisely through what experience of time a new humanity is to arise from.[59] In a note from June–July of 1883 Nietzsche has Zarathustra forget himself, and 'out of the overman he teaches the return: the overman *endures it* and *employs it as means of discipline*'.[60] In a note from the Summer/Autumn of 1883 Nietzsche writes: 'First the lawgiving. After the prospect of the overman the theory of return is now in an awesome way bearable'.[61] These notes show that Nietzsche is led to the overman because he requires the vision of a type of 'man' who can endure the terrifying and abysmal thought of eternal return. A note from the Summer/Autumn of 1884 shows that Nietzsche envisages the overman as emerging from the down-going and going-across experienced in the test of eternal return. Here Nietzsche says that, in order to endure the thought of the eternal return one needs 'freedom from morality...uncertainty, experimentalism...abolition of the concept of necessity as something to be suffered, abolition of the "will"', and finally, '*greatest enhancement of the consciousness of strength in man,* as of that which creates the overman'.[62]

The dangers of the vision of the overman stem from Nietzsche's attempt to arrive at what he considers to be a new conception of politics in the notion of 'great politics' (which is far from being new, but is thoroughly Machiavellian). The paradox of Nietzsche's thinking on the problem of history and the fate of humanity is that, although the eternal return teaches us how to affirm life and to recognize the unity of all things, and from which emerges the vision of the over-man, this vision of a transformed humanity must also be consciously *willed* in order to be brought into existence and in order for nihilism to be effectively and decidedly overcome. It is at this juncture in his thought that Nietzsche is in most danger of succumbing to the spirit of revenge and resentment, the spirit which must control time, which must not let go and let being become, but which must impose being on becoming as the 'supreme will to power'[63] – that is, the unnameable, which Zarathustra names 'will to power', and the good and the just name 'lust to rule' ('Of Three Evil Things'). This spirit manifests itself, I shall argue in the next chapter, in Nietzsche's thinking on great politics in which history is to be subjected to control and planning, and its accidental nature put to an end. There is nothing, however, in *Zarathustra* which merits such a critical reading; it is only after *Zarathustra*, notably in *Beyond Good and Evil* and the *Nachlass* of this period, that Nietzsche translates his teachings on the overman and eternal return into a Machiavellian-inspired politics of controlled violence. Thus, the question emerges: to what extent does the vision of the overman become in Nietzsche not only his consolation (it makes life bearable), but his revenge against life also?

The significance of Nietzsche adding part four after having initially thought that the work was complete after three acts or parts, is that it shows, through the meeting with the higher men, and through the remarkable experience of eternal return undergone by the ugliest man, that Zarathustra's teaching must be made public in order for its authenticity to be tested and recognized. The teaching of 'how one becomes what one is' through the experience of eternal return must be subjected to testing and recognition, otherwise it becomes indistinguishable from self-deception and condemned to solipsism. Each one of us must undergo the experience of eternal return, and each person's experience of it will be new, unique, and incomparable. Zarathustra becomes who he is when *we* become what we are. But that is the question: who are 'we'? Thomas Pangle poses an important question when he asks whether, at the end of Zarathustra's *Untergang*, there is simply the eternal return of individuals who will one day establish the new nobility he calls for, or simply the return of the solitary Zarathustra with his hopes and fears.[64] This is a decisive question to raise, but if read correctly the two aspects of the question reveal themselves to be two sides of the same coin. For who is Zarathustra? Is he a seducer? A prophet? A ploughshare? A good man or an evil man? A poet? Or a buffoon? In other words, the fate of Zarathustra and his *Untergang* is inseparable from *our* fate, and from *our* becoming what we are.

HOW ONE BECOMES WHAT ONE IS

One of the most important aspects of the teaching of eternal return is the way in which it aims to educate the abstract willing ego about the nature of action. For Nietzsche the notion of 'free' will is an illusion, since it is only after an action has been performed – one that is largely unconscious and the result of a multiplicity of drives and affects competing with each other for dominion – that we can say to ourselves, 'yes, I willed it!' In section 19 of *Beyond Good and Evil*, for example, Nietzsche points out that when we will we believe that will and action are one. It is this basic belief which leads us to ascribing the success of the willing to the 'will' itself, and thereby we allow ourselves to enjoy a sensation of power which accompanies success. In order to be able to declare 'I willed it!' to action, it is necessary that one learns how to become what one is. To learn to 'will one's own will', as in the child in *Thus Spoke Zarathustra*, does not mean that we have to become the heroic originators of our actions in the world (such an enormous delusion is more likely to be the sign of an impotent will than a powerful one), but rather that we identify ourselves with what we are and have become. The end is to overcome the spirit of revenge; the means to attain this end is the 'willing' of the eternal return.

Several commentators, notably Georg Simmel and Gilles Deleuze, have recognized that the thought of eternal return has a similar structure to Kant's formulation of the categorical imperative: we should will our action in such a way that in willing it we can will its eternal return. Construed in this way the eternal return becomes the means by which we are able to test the quality of any action, feeling, or thought. As Simmel notes, if we imagine that no moment of our life will ever be over once and for all, then this thought adds a new weightiness to our attitude towards life and must lead to our cultivating the 'will to self-responsibility' Nietzsche speaks of.[65] Deleuze construes the eternal return as a selective kind of categorical imperative which breeds strength and nobility. Eternal return is a selective ethical principle in that what returns is not the 'same', that is the actual content of one's willing, but only the form of willing (the returning). In this way the will selects that which it wishes to return and that which it does not. What does not return, Deleuze argues, are the reactive forces, namely, all that is sick, base, weak, and lowly.[66]

There are, however, major problems with any attempt to interpret the eternal return in terms of a revision of Kant's categorical imperative, as the two notions are dissimilar in so many key aspects that any straightforward or simple comparison becomes untenable. The notion of the categorical imperative, for example, presupposes a divided moral consciousness, an 'I' forever striving to be the 'we'. In aiming to be autonomous it is not possible in Kant's framework to appeal to one's psychological or existential condition, as is the case with the eternal return, as this would be to subject the act of willing to heteronomy. But one of the aims of the thought of eternal return is to overcome this self-negating spirit of the cruel self by teaching how one is to become what one is in a way which overcomes the opposition of what one 'is' and what one 'ought' to be. This interpretation of Nietzsche's notion of eternal return, however, only makes sense in the context of his notion of giving style to one's character. Situating the test of eternal return in this context is revealing in that it shows that Nietzsche construes the task of becoming what we are, not in any moral terms, but in purely artistic ones, and this is what constitutes the fundamental difference between Nietzsche and Kant's thinking on autonomy and self-mastery.[67] There are problems with Deleuze's reading despite its attempt to give the thought of eternal return a critical edge. For a start, his emphasis on selectivity would subject the thought to the metaphysical oppositions it is trying to overcome (notably, between active and reactive). The thought of eternal return is designed to affirm the unity of all things; its fundamental teaching is that everything is entwined and that one thing grows out of another – good from evil, active from reactive, etc. In willing the eternal return, therefore, one is willing the return of everything, but for the sake of creativity, which means that the reactive returns only in order to be sublimated into the active. The same applies to the eternal return of human types: the return of the overman, for example, requires the return of the small man, for it is only out of this 'pathos of distance' that the higher and nobler is possible. Moreover, although the willing in the eternal return appears to have a similar structure of 'universalizability' to that of the categorical imperative, the universal aspect of the thought of return is quite different. I shall demonstrate this point by drawing on a fascinating passage from Nietzsche's *Nachlass* in which he conceives eternal return in terms of an alternative doctrine to socialism. First, however, it is necessary to show the context in which Nietzsche's formulation of the doctrine in this *Nachlass* passage can be best appreciated.

Bernd Magnus, one of the most astute commentators on Zarathustra's teachings, raises the question of what we are being asked to contemplate in the thought of eternal return. Far from liberating the will, he suggests, the thought might serve to deflate it, for it asks us to contemplate the actuality that in life we will simply repeat previous moments and there will be nothing new or different in it. Thus, instead of leading to a creative willing, the thought results in a fatigue of the will, as it finds itself completely overwhelmed by the prospect of the burden of the past repeating itself eternally. It thus serves to debilitate action, and to think otherwise is little more than an act of bad faith. How are we, Magnus asks, to experience the psychological pressure of choosing and creating our eternally returning future self, without experiencing a radical deflation once we realize that our present self has already been chosen eternally, and has already been constrained?[68] The way out of this difficulty, he suggests, is to recognize that eternal return is not true factually but only hypothetically. The aim of the teaching is to change our attitude, and, since the value of life cannot be judged, it can only be evaluated in terms of its 'symptoms'.

It is necessary to appreciate the full paradoxical nature of Nietzsche's teaching on how one becomes what one is. For in becoming what we are, we are constantly reforming that which we are and have become. There is thus no supreme moment of absolute insight or of total vision, even though Nietzsche's reflection on the moment might suggest otherwise. Alexander Nehamas has argued that Nietzsche's teaching on becoming what one is rests on a complicated relationship between discovery and creation, between imposing laws and being constrained by them.[69] One could go further by stressing that becoming what one is involves exceeding what one is, stretching the limits, and not having a clue what one is. In other words, we need to grasp the aporetic nature of law and of self-legislation: does the self exist prior to its law or through its (self) creation? Nehamas interprets Nietzsche's doctrine of self-creation in terms of our readiness to accept responsibility for everything that we have done, and to recognize that everything that we have done actually constitutes what we are. But to become what one is, Nehamas points out, is not to reach a determinate or fixed state, to stop 'becoming'. Moreover, becoming what one is by accepting responsibility for it and by affirming everything that has been, is not to be construed as a moral task, for the realization of character (of what one is) is beyond the moral judgement of good and evil. In section 290 of the *Gay Science*, for example, where Nietzsche discusses what it means to give style to one's character, he makes it clear that the task of self-overcoming is not a moral one: 'In the end', he writes, 'when the work is finished, it becomes evident how the constraint of a single taste governed and formed everything large and small. Whether this taste was good or bad is less important than that it was only a single taste!'[70] The task of becoming what one is, is far from being a superhuman task (it only appears so to the slothful self or to the individual who wishes everyone to be the same as in a slave morality), for we are not being invited to assume the role of God or a supreme judge who has a total view on the world and their existence in it. The question is whether we are able to view our life, *including* its accidents, mistakes, blunders, and so on, as a fate, thus becoming what we are, and cultivating a will to self-responsibility.

In posing the question of the return of the same, however, Nietzsche is not simply asking us whether we would or would not do the same things again, since there is no room for choice if the doctrine is taken literally as a scientific hypothesis. Rather, he is asking us whether our will *wishes* to do the same things all over again.[71] As Nietzsche declares in section 341 of the *Gay Science*, such a thought would either change us, or crush us, for it asks how *well-disposed* towards life we would have to be to affirm the eternal return of all the moments of our life (and in affirming one we affirm all). The thought thus contains the possibility opened up by Magnus that its contemplation could lead to self-resignation and self-flagellation. But it could also lead to self-affirmation and to a strengthening and enhancement of the will. Only the eternal return, in fact, opens up the possibility of change, for it teaches that one can even will that which has formed one, namely the past, by *becoming* what one is. In other words, what one 'is' is not something static or fixed for all time and beyond redemption. The eternal return enables change to take place by enabling the will to distinguish between what is significant and what is insignificant in its life and being. It is thus a thought which cultivates strength and weakness, both within the individual and between human types; it establishes an order of rank, an aristocracy in the body of the self and in the body politic.[72]

In the passage in the *Gay Science* on character, Nietzsche says that one thing is necessary in becoming what one is, and this is that a human being should feel satisfied with themselves, for 'whoever is dissatisfied with himself is continually ready for revenge, and we others will be their victims'. Nietzsche's model of the emancipated self becomes that of the person who can attain 'power over itself' by freely subjecting itself to the constraint of style. Resistance to such self-imposition is considered by him to be one of the main signs of the resentful individual. It is at this point that it is possible to appreciate precisely where his thinking differs from Kant's in the formulation of the categorical imperative. Like the categorical imperative, the thought of eternal return has a universal character or form, but unlike the categorical imperative it does not posit a universal content. However, it might be argued in response that the categorical imperative too is a purely formal doctrine, for it has no determinate content. But the key point is that, although the categorical imperative is indeed formalistic, its willing does *presuppose* that the actions the autonomous will is to will are universal in content: always will in such a way that the maxims of your actions are capable of being universalized into universal natural laws. The eternal return, however, provides the form of universality only in the act of returning, whereas what returns (the actual content) and is willed to be returned cannot be universal, since each life (each becoming) is unique. In this respect the thought is genuinely beyond good and evil, for what the will holds to be 'good', and what it holds to be 'evil', is to be created by each unique and incomparable sovereign individual. This is not solipsism, as it presupposes that one becomes what one is by undergoing self-overcoming in the sphere of public testing and recognition.

A passage from Nietzsche's *Nachlass* of 1881 is helpful in clarifying this point of contrast between Nietzsche and Kant in that it clearly shows that Nietzsche designed the thought of eternal return in terms of an educative principle which would rival some of the most important social and political doctrines of his day, one of the most important for him being that of socialism, and which he saw in terms of a politics of envy and 'the tyranny of the superficial'.[73] The passage is thus significant in revealing a major, if neglected, aspect of the teaching of eternal return.[74] In the passage Nietzsche first comments on the 'delusion' (*Wahn*) of socialism, and then offers his own teaching. It runs as follows:

The political delusion, at which I smile in just the same way as my contemporaries smile at the religious delusion of earlier times, is above all *secularization*, belief in the world and a deliberate ignoring of the 'beyond' and the 'afterworld'. Its goal is the well-being of the transient individual: which is why its fruit is socialism, i.e. *transient* individuals who desire to encompass their happiness through socialization and who have no reason to wait, as do human beings with eternal souls and eternal becoming and future self-improvement. My teaching says: the task is to live in such a way that you must wish to live again – you will *in any case*! To he whom striving gives the highest feeling, let him strive; to he whom repose gives the highest feeling, let him rest; to he whom ordering, following, and obedience give the highest feeling, let him obey. Only *may* he become aware of *what* gives him the highest feeling and that he draws back before nothing! For eternity is at stake![75]

The significance of this passage is that it indicates in what sense we are to understand the eternal return as a transformative doctrine. The possibility of the eternal return of every moment impresses upon the will a new and weighty responsibility which is designed to encourage it to find contentment and satisfaction with itself by becoming what it is. Thus, what it 'is' and has been becomes recognized as what it is and has been for the first time, and in so doing it becomes transformed: what is and has been lazy, servile, cowardly, loving, generous, and powerful *before* the will wills the eternal return, is no longer the same laziness, servility, cowardice, love, generosity, and powerfulness *after* it has been willed in the experience of eternal return and the will has become what it is.[76] The passage clearly shows that Nietzsche's thought aims in the direction of a politics beyond resentment and the spirit of revenge. The question is, however, does his thought attain it?

CHAPTER 6

Bending the bow: great politics, or, the problem of the legislator

Our conclusion, then, is that political society exists for the sake of noble actions, and not of living together.

Aristotle, *The Politics*, Book III

Grant me from time to time – if there are divine goddesses in the realm of beyond good and evil – grant me the sight, but *one* glance of something perfect, wholly achieved, happy, mighty, triumphant, something still capable of arousing fear! Of a man who justifies *man*.

Nietzsche, *On the Genealogy of Morals*, I, 12

Uncanny is human existence without a meaning: a buffoon could be fatal to it.

Nietzsche, *Thus Spoke Zarathustra*, Prologue.

Recent years have seen the emergence of a number of important studies of Nietzsche's politics, a subject which for a long time attracted only the most superficial of attention and analysis. The question of Nietzsche's politics still remains a disquieting one however. In its cult of great leadership and contempt for the mass of humanity it is seen by many commentators to prefigure a fascist style of politics.[1] The question has been raised as to what extent Nietzsche's overt, aristocratic politics necessarily and logically follow from his philosophy of power and his insights into the modern age, notably the event of the death of God and the advent of nihilism.[2] Whatever politics one derives from Nietzsche's profound insights into the nature of the modern malaise, it is surely important to consider why Nietzsche himself drew the political conclusions and cultivated the political arguments that he did from his insights into the problem of civilization.

Nietzsche's own politics are best understood, I would argue, in the context of his preoccupation with the problem of civilization and the paradoxes which result from his thinking on this problem. Nietzsche's attempt to *solve* the problem of history leads him to embrace a Machiavellian-inspired immoral politics, which recognizes no limits, and which believes it is able to justify its own despotism through the cultivation of a higher and nobler humanity which, in the creative hammer it will bring to bear down on mankind, will redeem the whole past of humanity. In this vision of politics we do not see merely a prefiguration of a fascist politics – Hitler can hardly be described, as some commentators have been tempted to do, as the embodiment of Nietzsche's model of the emancipated human being who has transcended the attitude of resentment and the spirit of revenge – but of the politics of the twentieth century. For it is perhaps the tragedy of Nietzsche's genius that he saw more clearly than any other thinker of the modern period that modernity would be the era of great wars and of great politics dominated by a war of spirits and ideologies. 'The time for petty politics is over', Nietzsche informs us, in his most explicitly political work which immediately followed the publication of *Zarathustra*, *Beyond Good and Evil*: 'the next century will bring with it the fight for the dominion of the earth – the *compulsion* to great politics'.[3]

Nietzsche's thinking on politics, therefore, is best seen as an attempt to understand how the conditions can be cultivated for man to undergo further development and advancement in the epoch of the death of God and the advent of nihilism. His preoccupation with politics is thus neither accidental nor peripheral to his concerns, but can be seen to arise in a very fundamental sense from his teaching on redemption and from his reflections on the destiny of the soul. An important aspect of the attempt to think through the problem of nihilism is the need to develop an understanding of how new values can be created and fashioned through the conjunction of philosophical legislation and political power. In section 203 of *Beyond Good and Evil*, for example, Nietzsche argues that, once we recognize that the democratic movement which dominates modern politics is not only a form of the decay of political organization, but equally a form of the decay of man, then the only way forward is 'toward new *philosophers*', that is:

toward spirits strong and original enough to provide the stimuli for opposite valuations and to revalue and invert 'eternal values' toward forerunners, toward men of the future who in the present tie the knot and constraint that forces the will of millenia upon *new* tracks. To teach man the future of man as his *will*, as dependent on a human will, and to prepare great ventures and over-all experiments of discipline and cultivation by way of putting an end to that gruesome dominion of nonsense and accident that has so far been called 'history'.

The *Nachlass* of 1885 is littered with Nietzsche's thoughts on the new type of philosopher that is needed to legislate new values, and he makes it clear that the one who declares 'thus it *shall* be', can arise only in conjunction with a ruling caste as its highest spiritualization.[4]

For Nietzsche, it is only out of the '*degeneration*' of man that it is possible to envisage tremendous possibilities for his future, a future which is to be created through performing great sacrifices and great experiments on the present. This position stands Nietzsche in marked contrast to Rousseau, and explains why he is so much more sanguine than Rousseau in accepting the inevitability of the terror and wars which must necessarily come in the wake of great politics. What inspires Nietzsche's thinking here is his belief that a future creative willing can, if it produces a higher nobility, even redeem all the pain and suffering of the past (and present). This is what Nietzsche means, for example, when he tells us that he looks forward to a new, tragic age in which 'the highest art in saying Yes to life, tragedy, will be reborn when humanity has weathered the consciousness of the hardest but most necessary wars *without suffering from it*'.[5] The translation, by Nietzsche, of his teaching on redemption into the political realm also explains why, in *Ecce Homo*, for example, he is able to declare that 'the question concerning the *descent (Herkunft)* of moral values' is the most fundamental of all questions since 'it is crucial for the *future* of humanity' (my emphasis).[6] Thus, his thought seeks to prepare 'a moment of the highest self-examination for humanity, a *great noontide (Mittag)* when it looks back and far forward', and emerges from the dominion of accidents and priests. Nietzsche's justification of a politics of controlled violence, through the redemptive act of a future creative willing which redeems all that has been and is, is ironic if one recalls the manner in which Nietzsche criticizes the bloodthirsty revolutions which he believes Rousseau's thought serves to inspire: but then, for Nietzsche, this is the politics of envy and revenge, not those of the noble will to power and of justice.

Nietzsche is adamant throughout his writings, from the early unpublished essay on the Greek State to the writing of *Beyond Good and Evil*, that it is only an aristocratic form of commonwealth that is able to *justify* such terrible but noble sacrifices and experiments. In a note of 1885–6, for example, Nietzsche speaks of the breeding of a master race who will constitute the future 'masters of the earth', and who will be a 'new tremendous aristocracy, based on the severest self-legislation' which employs 'democratic Europe as its most pliant and supple instrument for taking control of the destinies of the earth'. 'Enough', says Nietzsche, 'the time is coming when politics will have a different meaning'.[7] Nietzsche thus envisages the masters of humanity as 'artist–tyrants' in which the political leader – the prince – works upon man as an artist works upon stone. In section 225 of *Beyond Good and Evil*, Nietzsche says that in man 'creature and creator are united'. Man is material, chaos, excess, and nonsense; but he is also the form-giver and creator, the hardness of the hammer. It is only through the 'discipline of great suffering' that man can be enhanced into ever, new and higher forms. But, Nietzsche wishes to ask, if this suffering induces pity in us for the 'creature in man', for that which must be formed and broken, should we not also respect that pity which is the converse of this and which resists it as 'the worst of all pamperings and weaknesses?' And thus, Nietzsche concludes, 'it is pity *versus* pity'. In the end, however, it is necessary to learn that all the 'higher problems' have nothing to do with pleasure, pain, or pity; for the philosopher to think otherwise is no more than a piece of 'naiveté'.

Nietzsche understands his politics as being neither individualistic nor collectivistic. Even the former, he argues, 'does not recognize an order of rank and would grant one the same freedom as all'. As for his own conception of the political, Nietzsche informs us that his thinking 'does not revolve around the degree of freedom that is granted to the one or to the other or to all, but around the degree of *power* that the one or the other should exercise over others or over all'. The decisive question is to what extent 'a sacrifice of freedom, even enslavement, provides the basis for the emergence of a *higher type*'.[8] In its 'crudest form', the question of great politics is to what extent one could '*sacrifice the evolution of mankind* to help a higher species than man to come into existence'. According to Nietzsche, the only justification that can be given of the homogenization of modern European man through the dominion of democratic politics is that it should serve a 'higher sovereign type', one which is not simply a master race whose only task is to rule, 'but a race with its own sphere of life, with an excess of strength for beauty, bravery, culture, manners to the highest peak of the spirit; an affirming race that may grant itself every luxury'.[9] In a note from the *Nachlass* of the Autumn of 1887 the overman is identified as the model of this higher type. Nietzsche's note is revealing in showing precisely how he understood the vision of the overman in terms of the evolution of the human type. He tells us that, in opposition to the 'dwarfing and adaptation of man to a specialized utility, a reverse movement is needed', which consists in producing a 'synthetic, summarizing, justifying man' who requires the 'opposition of the masses' as his pathos of distance. The 'exploitation' of the masses by the higher aristocracy of the future, considered as the maximum point in the exploitation of man so far, justifies itself only on account of those for whom this exploitation (*Ausbeutung*) has meaning. The kind of thinking he wishes to combat with this notion of the overman, Nietzsche tells us, is the 'economic optimism' of the modern age which rests on the delusion that the 'increasing expenditure of everybody must necessarily involve the increasing welfare of everybody'.[10]

It is in sections 257 and 258 of *Beyond Good and Evil* that Nietzsche provides us with his conception of aristocratic politics. 'Truth is hard', we are told in section 257. What is this truth? It is the truth which reveals that:

Every enhancement of the type 'man' has so far been the work of an aristocratic society – and it will be so again and again – a society that believes in the long ladder of an order of rank and differences in value between man and man, and that requires slavery in some sense or other. Without that *pathos of distance* which grows out of the ingrained difference between strata – when the ruling caste constantly looks afar and looks down upon subjects and instruments and just as constantly practices obedience and command, keeping down and keeping at a distance – that other, more mysterious pathos could not have grown up either – the craving for an ever widening of distances within the soul itself... in brief, simply the enhancement of the type 'man', the continual 'self-overcoming of man', to use a moral formula in a supra-moral (*über moralischen*) sense.[11]

An aristocracy becomes corrupt – Nietzsche's example is that of France at the beginning of the Revolution – when it demotes itself to a 'mere function' and throws away its privileges. For it is, Nietzsche informs us, the 'essential characteristic of a good and healthy aristocracy that it experiences itself *not* as a function (whether of the monarchy or the commonwealth) but as their *meaning* and highest justification'. What this means for Nietzsche is that a healthy aristocracy is one which gaily accepts with a clear (not bad) conscience 'the sacrifice of untold human beings who, *for its sake*, must be reduced and lowered to incomplete human beings, to slaves, to instruments'. It has to be the 'fundamental faith' (one could almost say a 'natural law') of an aristocratic society that society does not exist for society's sake but 'only as the foundation and scaffolding on which a choice type of being is able to raise itself to its higher task and to a higher state of *being*'.[12]

For Nietzsche, therefore, the philosophers of the future who are to assume the guise of philosopher–legislators should address themselves to the 'great task and question' which is approaching humanity inexorably as a terrible fate: 'how shall the earth as a whole be governed? To what end shall "man" as a whole – and no longer as people or a race – be raised and trained.'[13]

It is in the context of a conception of an aristocratic cultivation of man, and the formulation of a notion of great politics, that we can appreciate the role that the notion of eternal return plays in Nietzsche's political thought. In a note from 1884 Nietzsche argues that 'a doctrine is needed powerful enough to work as a breeding agent' which will strengthen the strong and paralyze the world-weary.[14] Nietzsche's notes of this period are scattered with drafts and plans for a work in which he would put forward the teaching of eternal return in terms of a philosophy beyond good and evil that is to be placed in the service of a great politics. A note from the Winter of 1883/4, for example, refers to a 'book of prophecy' in which the teaching of return is to be presented, and its theoretical presuppositions and consequences stated. In addition there is to be a proof (*Beweis*) of the doctrine, a guide to the means of how to endure it, and an examination of its role in history as a 'mid-point' (*Mitte*). The thought is to lead to the 'foundation of an oligarchy over peoples and their interests: education to a universally human politics (*allmenschlichen Politik*)'.[15] Eternal return is construed as the 'great cultivating thought' which will introduce a new order of rank and a 'new Enlightenment'.[16] It is interesting to note that Nietzsche originally conceived *Beyond Good and Evil* in terms of a 'preface to a Philosophy of Eternal Return'.[17]

Perhaps the most important aspect of understanding Nietzsche's political thought in its attempt to construe an aristocratic politics that envisages the creation of a new higher type, an overman, through the cultivation of the test of eternal return, is that it is compelled to rely on a politics of force in order to imagine how the overman can be willed and created. One of the most revealing notes from the Zarathustra *Nachlass* is one from the Autumn of 1883 in which Nietzsche states: 'It is not enough to propound a teaching:

one has also to *forcibly change* men so that they will accept it! –
Zarathustra finally grasps this.'[18] Nietzsche's thinking on great
politics thus revolves around a problem that has been of great
importance in the history of political thought from Plato to
Machiavelli and Rousseau, namely the problem of the legislator or
lawgiver. In Greek thought the legislator is the archetype of the
political hero, and the symbol of what uninhibited greatness might
achieve. He is the figure who suddenly appears in order to save the
life of the polis from disintegration and decay, and to re-establish it
on a fresh foundation.[19] Nietzsche's notes from the period of
Zarathustra are full of thoughts on the nature of the lawgiver
(*Gesetzgeber*), and the notion provides an important point of contrast
between Rousseau and Nietzsche in their ethical and political
thinking.[20]

While drawing attention to the fundamental difference between
Rousseau and Nietzsche in their conceptions of the problem of
civilization, this study has also shown that it is possible to locate a
common problem at the centre of their thinking on the formation
and deformation of the human animal, namely, the problem of
history. If man has become a social and political animal through a
historical labour of culture, but this process of development has
resulted in a corrupt and degenerate civilization, then the question
arises – still appreciating the fact that the way in which each
construes the meaning and significance of this corruption and
degeneration is quite different – as to how humanity is to undergo a
process of transfiguration and learn the meaning of its self-
overcoming. Central to both in thinking through this problem is the
notion of a legislator who is to play the role of the agent and
instigator of reform. However, an examination of precisely how the
two conceive the precise role and status of the legislator reveals some
important differences in their thinking.

In Rousseau the legislator is the great human being who devises
the particular set of laws for a people, a *nomothetes* like Solon in
Athens, or Numa in Rome. It is his task not to legislate as such, but
rather to create the conditions under which civil association can take
place (which is why 'lawgiver' is probably a better term to use than
legislator). It is the legislator who devises the laws which will educate
human beings about citizenship, and who prepares the ground on
which the particular will can be brought into conformity with the
general will. For the successful realization of this task the lawgiver

requires superhuman powers and attributes. For Rousseau the role of the lawgiver is to bring about a political community which requires that he is capable of transforming human nature in such a way that each individual, who is by nature a complete and solitary whole, becomes part of a greater whole upon which it is totally dependent for its existence as a moral being. The lawgiver is not to be confused with a Hobbesian sovereign, since he has no legislative power at all; his role is what Nietzsche would call 'extra-moral'.

Rousseau identifies a number of problems with his construal of the lawgiver as the educator who will transform individuals into virtuous citizens. In particular, he notes that two incompatible things can be identified with the task of lawgiving. Firstly, it is both an enterprize too difficult for human powers, and one which requires for its execution an authority which is not an authority (it has no legitimate power). Secondly, he notes what he calls 'a difficulty that deserves special attention', and refers to the problem facing the wise who attempt to educate the herd by speaking their own language and, as a result, end up with their teaching not being understood. In order for human beings to fully understand and appreciate the wisdom of the lawgiver, they would have to be, *before* the lawgiving, what they are to *become* by means of it. Without recourse to either force or reason, therefore, and since he lacks power and the herd lack reason, the lawgiver must possess superhuman powers of perception and persuasion so that he can constrain human beings without doing violence to them, and persuade without indoctrinating them. Rousseau notes that in all ages the creators of peoples and nations have had recourse to a notion of divine intervention in order to credit the gods with their own wisdom, and in this way to persuade people to submit to the laws of the State. Rousseau acknowledges his debt to Machiavelli for this insight into the problem of the lawgiver.

In a note from 1885 Nietzsche remarks that 'law-giving moralities' are the 'principal means by which man can be fashioned according to the pleasure of a creative and profound will'.[21] The great lawgiver calls upon law, religions, and customs in order to bend man's will in a new direction. In section 61 of *Beyond Good and Evil*, Nietzsche states that the philosopher–lawgiver, that is the one who has 'the most comprehensive responsibility and conscience for the over-all development of man', will 'make use of religions for his work of cultivation and education, just as he will make use of whatever political and economic conditions are at hand'. For the vast majority of human beings, who exist only for service and as instruments, religion, Nietzsche argues, serves to give 'an inestimable contentment with their situation and type, manifold peace of the heart, an ennobling of obedience.'

One of the most interesting passages in Nietzsche's work, where he discusses the lawgiver, is in section 57 of the *Anti-Christ*. In section 55 of that work Nietzsche had pointed out that words such as the 'Law', the 'will of God', and the 'sacred book' stand for the conditions under which the priest and shepherd of mankind comes to power and maintains power. It is the concept of the 'holy lie' which we find common to Confuscius, the law-book of Manu, Mohammed, Christianity, and Plato. The justification of the holy lie is found in the end that it serves; thus, Nietzsche objects to Christianity because it means do not serve 'holy' (noble) ends. A law-book, Nietzsche informs us, never reveals the utility of the law, or of the reason for it and the casuistry which went into its making, for if it did it would undermine the mysterious (the sacred) basis of its divine authority. Thus, the two most important things a law-book places in its service are 'revelation' and 'tradition'. The former gives the illusion that the source of laws lies not in a human, but in a divine, origin, while the latter gives the illusion that the laws are eternal and have existed from time immemorial. The chief purpose of the holy lie is to make the law unconscious so that it becomes *instinct*. The order of rank existing in society is to be conceived in terms of a natural law over which 'no arbitrary caprice, no "modern idea" has any power'.[22] Every healthy society, argues Nietzsche, is built on the order of 'three types of man of divergent physiological tendency which mutually condition one another'. It is nature, not Manu, which separates the three types as the spiritual (the élite), the muscular, and the mediocre (the majority). The spiritual ones find their strength in the severest self-legislation and constraint. They rule 'not because they want to but because they *are*'. The second rank are the guardians of law, the 'noble warriors' and 'kings' who judge and uphold the law. 'In all this', Nietzsche says, 'there is nothing capricious, nothing "artificial"'... The order of castes, *order of rank*, only formulates the supreme law of life itself'. The order of rank is necessary not only for the preservation of society, but for 'making possible higher and higher types – *inequality* of rights is the condition for the existence of rights at all. A right is a privilege'. When reflecting on this model of society we should not, Nietzsche argues, underestimate the privileges of the mediocre, for responsibilities increase as we approach the heights. It is thus a privilege for them to have so few responsibilities. 'A high culture', as Nietzsche calls it, can only be conceived along the lines of a pyramid in which society is divided into a noble élite and a mediocre majority. Thus to be 'a public utility, a cog, a function, is a natural vocation…it is the kind of *happiness* of which the great majority alone are capable'. Nietzsche concludes this discussion of the ancient natural lawgiving moralities by criticizing the 'socialist rabble' for undermining the worker's instinct and feeling of contentment with himself. Socialism is based on the fundamental delusion that justice is to be reached through equality and the establishment of equal rights. But, Nietzsche argues, such a demand for equality by the socialists is merely the expression of the envy and vengefulness they share with Christians and anarchists.[23]

All the problems which Rousseau identifies with the task of the lawgiver are present in Nietzsche's understanding. But where Nietzsche's understanding differs is in recognizing that, with the death of God and the advent of nihilism, the problem of the legitimacy of the legislator's task takes on a whole new problematical dimension, for there can be no honest recourse to the divine to legitimate it. For Nietzsche, modern politics is characterized by an attitude of moral hypocrisy among those who wield political power. Instead of having the strength and courage to stand up and be independent, to have the *will* to command and rule, they choose instead to hide their impotence behind slogans such as 'servants of the people' and 'instruments of the common weal'. These leaders protect themselves from their bad conscience by claiming that they are merely executors of higher commands (of ancestors, of divine laws, and of God, etc.) However, with the death of God it becomes sheer dishonesty and mendacity for any political power to claim divine sanction for its rule.[24]

Nietzsche's insight into the problem of the legislator in the modern age is clearly apparent in his discussion of Plato. In its confluence of philosophy and politics Nietzsche's conception of the philosopher–legislator reveals an obvious close link with Plato's conception of the philosopher–king. Nietzsche's model of social order is also built on clearly identifiable Platonic lines. However, Nietzsche's insight into the crisis of legitimacy of the modern age leads him to refine his affinity with Plato. For he argues that Plato's politics give expression neither to eternal verities about the human condition, nor to absolute truths about the nature of political life; rather, Plato's politics give expression to Plato's own particular will to power concerning the good and just polity. It is the will to power behind the creation of values which is concealed by all founders of religions and by great philosophers in their attempt to construct an image of man based on so-called eternal truths about human nature. Thus, the question which concerns Nietzsche most, and disturbs him because he knows that an inadequate understanding of it could lead to unscrupulous, ignoble, and vengeful despotic regimes assuming power, is that of which kind of justification of existence is possible in the age of the death of God and nihilism. Thus, for example, he informs us that hitherto the legislators of humanity – philosophers and religious teachers – have concealed from themselves the fearfulness which faces the legislator in the greatness of his task, either by speaking of the good in terms of the 'good-in-itself', as in Plato, or by speaking of the good in terms of the commands of God, as in Mohammed. However:

As soon as these two means of comfort, that of Plato and that of Mohammed, have fallen away and no thinker can relieve his conscience with the hypothesis of a 'god' or 'eternal values', the task of the legislator of values rises to a new fearfulness never yet attained. From then on, those elect on whom the suspicion of having such a duty begins to dawn, try to see if they cannot, 'at the right moment', elude it, as their greatest danger...Many may indeed succeed in eluding it: history is full of the traces of men who have eluded this task...Usually, however, there came to these men of fate that redeeming hour...in which they *had* to do what they did not even 'want' to do – and the deed of which they had hitherto been most fearful fell easily and unsought from the tree, as an involuntary deed, almost as a gift.[25]

In thinking through the problem of the legislator, however, Nietzsche sacrifices what for Rousseau constitutes the most important question of politics in the modern age, that of legitimacy. For Nietzsche, this is a necessary consequence of the task of the revaluation of values and of the self-overcoming of morals, in that an aristocratic cultivation cannot rely on notions of social justice in order to legitimate its authority and rule. But here we encounter the fundamental problem of Nietzsche's political thought: if God is dead, if political rule can no longer be based on divine sanction, *and* if he is compelled to sacrifice the peculiar modern question of legitimacy (of 'rights', of equality, liberty, justice, etc.), then by what means can Nietzsche legitimate his great politics at all? This must lead us to asking how adequate, and how coherent, Nietzsche's conception of politics is in response to the problems his political thought has identified and the solutions it has offered.

It is evident that unlike Rousseau, Nietzsche's conception of the task of the lawgiver is one which has recourse to force and violence in order to impose its creative will on humanity. Nietzsche of course would argue that, in conceiving of the lawgiver's task as a non-violent one, Rousseau was simply guilty of duplicity and of concealing the Machiavellian basis of his own plebeian-inspired politics of envy and resentment. But the failure of Nietzsche's political thought is that it does not recognize that the question of legitimacy is equally crucial to its own concern with aristocratic rule. For perhaps the key question concerning Nietzsche's vision of politics is to what extent the breeding of an aristocratic discipline and cultivation is possible without at the same time giving rise to a politics of resentment. Given that the aim is to produce greatness by rendering the majority, in Nietzsche's own words, 'incomplete human beings', it is difficult to see how Nietzsche's aristocrats could maintain their rule without recourse to the deployment of the most oppressive instruments of political control and manipulation. Michael Haar, however, has attempted to defend Nietzsche's politics from such a reading. Nietzsche's rule of the overman does not rest on a politics of domination, he argues, but rests on what he calls a 'nonviolent Caesarism', which is to be conceived in terms of the 'tyranny' of the artist.[26] A note from the *Nachlass of* 1883 would seem to lend much support to Haar's argument. In it Nietzsche writes:

Morality hitherto has had its boundaries within the species: all moralities hitherto have been utilized *first and foremost* to give to the species unconditional durability: *if and when* this has been achieved the goal can be set higher.

One movement is unconditional: the levelling of humanity, the great anthills, etc...

The *other* movement: my movement: is, on the contrary, the enhancement of all antitheses and chasms, abolition of equality, the creation of men of superior power.

The former produces the last man. My movement the overman.

The goal is *absolutely not* to conceive the latter as masters of the former. But: two types and species are to exist side by side – separated as far as possible; *like the gods of Epicurus the one paying no heed to the other*.[27]

However, by failing to address the question of legitimacy on the level of social justice and the 'right of subjectivity', as Hegel described the right of modern individuals to self-determination,[28] it is impossible to see how this dual rule of the overman and last man could be maintained except through ruthless forms of political control. Nietzsche's conception of a peaceful co-existence between the two, of a settlement and discipline between the two classes which will not lead to either a politics of vanity or one of envy and revenge, strikes me as being both utopian and naive, especially in the absence of any discussion on the need for individual rights and social justice.

In one of the first and finest attempts to take Nietzsche's politics seriously and examine them intelligently, Tracy Strong argued that Nietzsche's model of a noble politics was that of the Greek *agon*, in which the private and public realms of existence are united, and in which politics exists in order to promote greatness in culture.[29] In Greek political thought as Nietzsche conceives it, the State is construed as an Apollonian institution by which the powerful and joyous but ultimately frenzied and dangerous, Dionysian forces of life are harnessed into culture. The most important political institution is the *agon*, or contest, in which this Dionysian chaos and energy, that conceals a desire for domination and violence, is healthily refracted in order to bring about the political stability and continuity that is a prerequisite for creating culture. But what this means is that the State and politics do not exist for themselves, but rather only as the arena in which human beings compete creatively in order to produce a high culture. Politics becomes degenerate when it is no longer an *arena* of power, but has become an *instrument* of power in the hands of men who use it for purely private ends. The excellence of the Greek State for Nietzsche, on Strong's reading, is that it provided a political space through the contest in which men could compete in argument and debate just as they did in games. Turning to modern politics, however, Nietzsche sees modern democracy undermining the agonistic basis of the State, and imposing a spurious universality and equality on human beings through cultivating a nationalist and racist politics. As Strong points out, unlike those who see the main achievement of modern politics in terms of its production of the autonomous individual, Nietzsche finds modern man to be a mere isolate and atom, not a full, complete personality. The politics of the weak become a politics of compassion which conceals the vanity of the weak who do not have the strength and pride to stand alone.

That Nietzsche's appreciation of the Greek *agon* represents a critique of liberal political culture on his part is evident in his discussion of the *agon* in the early unpublished essay on *Homer's Wettkampf* written in 1872. Here Nietzsche argues that fundamental to Hellenic national pedagogy is the idea that every natural gift must develop itself by means of the contest. This means that selfishness (*Selbstsucht*) is indeed valued, but only to the extent that in the arena of the contest it is bridled and channelled so that it ends up serving the needs of the common good. Thus, Nietzsche argues that selfish deeds can only be judged good or evil in terms of the ends they pursue. He writes: 'To the ancients the aim of an agonistic education (*agonalen Erziehung*) was the welfare of the whole, of the civic society (*staatlichen Gesellschaft*)'. An appreciation of the Greek *agon* leads Nietzsche to arguing that individuals in antiquity were freer than individuals in modern times because their aims and goals in life were more tangible and actually attainable. 'By comparison', he writes, 'modern man is everywhere hampered by infinity, like the swift-footed Achilles in the allegory of the Eleate Zeno: infinity impedes him, he cannot even keep up with the tortoise.'[30] If Nietzsche is to be accurately described as an individualist in his ethical and political thinking, then it is of a decidedly aristocratic kind. His argument against liberal political culture is that, far from fostering authentic types or forms of sovereign individuality, it leads to conformity in social life, and that it is based on a vacuous ethical pluralism and relativism. It has no notion of an 'order of rank' either amongst the passions and virtues or amongst the various members of the social whole.

In the unpublished essay of 1871 on the *Greek State* Nietzsche criticises what he calls modern 'liberal optimism' for reducing political existence to a merely prudential level (fear, insecurity, and rational self-interest), and he defends an ethical conception of the State which draws its main inspiration from Plato. The Greeks, Nietzsche argues, were the 'political men in themselves' for whom each human being only had dignity in so far as it was a conscious, or unconscious, tool of genius. Plato erred simply in the fact that under the influence of Socrates he conceived the genius in terms of the man of knowledge and not the artist. What is interesting about Nietzsche's conception of the State in this essay is that it tries to argue that the need for a strong, powerful warlike State has its basis in nature. Nature expresses herself through the necessity of the State and its iron hand which demands tremendous sacrifices and duties of the individual. Looking at modern political theories (liberalism and socialism are explicitly referred to) Nietzsche sees a total emasculation of the Greek conception of political life. Today, he notes, individuals esteem the State only to extent that it does not interfere with their private lives, and only insofar as its interests coincide with theirs.

For Nietzsche, the rise of socialism and the demand for equality have to be seen in the context of the evolution of society into an atomistic culture. He opposes the modern drive towards equality because he sees it as something fundamentally selfish in which society rests on an individualistic basis, and culture becomes reduced to the pursuit of private gains. There exists no great co-ordinating, unifying force, and no longer will any great sacrifices and great experiments be made and conducted, for modern politics is the rule of the mediocre who have no time or inclination for such sacrifices and experiments. This explains why Nietzsche regards the democratic movement as not only a 'form of the decay of political organization', but equally as a form of the decay of the type 'man'. The establishment of equality on an individualistic basis does not lead to the reign of virtue, but to the rule of an anarchistic mob. Socialism for Nietzsche is primarily to be understood in terms of a *reaction* to the atomization of society, not as something qualitatively new and different.[31] For Nietzsche socialism represents a form of the decay of the political in that it sees the role of society to be, not one of producing culture and great, noble human beings ('higher types'), but one of making as many 'isolates' or atoms as possible and giving each one of them 'freedom'.

Tracy Strong's emphasis on the importance of the notion of the *agon* in Nietzsche's early political thought draws our attention to the substantive basis which underlies Nietzsche's critique of the democratic movement and suspicion towards modern politics and its preoccupation with the question of legitimacy. However, he ignores, I believe, an important aspect of Nietzsche's interest in the *agon*. A note from the *Nachlass* of 1881 reveals that part of the attraction of the Greek *agon* for Nietzsche lies in its role of *depoliticization*, of diverting attention from the State. Nietzsche writes:

The Greek lawgivers promoted the *agon* as they did so as to divert the idea of competition away from the State and thus acquire political quietude… Reflection on the State was to be diverted through agonal excitation – people were to be occupied with gymnastics and poetry.[32]

In other words, the promotion of agonal competition, by diverting people's attention into non-political matters, served to conceal the noble lie (the order of rank) on which the State was based. Nietzsche sees the primary function of the *agon* as non-, even, anti-political. This is quite a different understanding from Rousseau's agonal general will, whose goal is to construct a democratic politics of virtue in which all have the opportunity to develop their political faculties.

Nevertheless, even if we recognize the fact, as we must, that Nietzsche's model of the ideal aristocratic society rests on enslavement and force, it is still possible to see a substantive basis behind his lack of interest in the question of political legitimacy. For Nietzsche, the modern preoccupation with the question of legitimacy, with the grounds of political obligation in consent and in 'will', is a sign that the cohesion and unity of society have gone; it is a sign of political decay for it reveals that an anti-cultural individualism, attained through the pursuit of an egalitarian politics, has come to dominate political life. As Nietzsche points out in a crucial passage in the *Gay Science*, today we moderns are no longer '*material for a society*'.[33] Thus, as Strong astutely notes, there 'can be no Nietzschean *Contrat social*, because the unity of philosophy and politics...which would correspond to it does not (yet) exist'.[34] However, while this is a perceptive observation, it must also be appreciated that in Nietzsche's vision of politics there could *never be* a social contract, because the basis of social contract is an individualistic one which would undermine the whole aristocratic nature of society as he conceives it. Moreover, as Rousseau recognized, no one who is given the chance will voluntarily consent to social slavery. Let us not forget that Nietzsche's model of an aristocratic society rests on both violence and lies, even if he claims it to be a creative kind of force and a lie that serves noble ends.

It is interesting to note that, in the writings prior to his vision of the overman, Nietzsche, in the writings of his middle period, shows a surer, more insightful grasp of the realities of modern political life than perhaps at any other time in his intellectual career. In a remarkable passage in *Daybreak*, for example, Nietzsche looks forward to what he calls a 'future lawgiving', which can only be described as Rousseauian in its vision of a lawgiving founded on the idea that the individual declares to itself that 'I submit only to the law I myself have given in great and small things'.[35] In other words, the only basis of a legitimate political authority is that which resides in the autonomous 'will' (the 'will' here is simply a metaphor which

locates and identifies the source of the individual's unique identity).
In section 224 of *Human, All Too Human* Nietzsche puts forward a
conception of a living community founded on good, sound customs
and common, habitual principles, which comes very close to
Rousseau's vision of a general will. However, regarding the issue of
government, as opposed to that of community, Nietzsche states in
this passage that he agrees with Machiavelli that 'so far as the State
is concerned' the actual form of government signifies little, for the
fundamental problem of politics, of statecraft, is that of 'duration'
and stability In section 276 of the same work Nietzsche also states
that any great culture is only possible by creating a society which
rests on a 'harmony and concord between contending parties', and
which develops through an 'overwhelming assemblage of the other
powers, but without the need to suppress them or clap them in
irons'. In section 438 of *Human, All Too Human* Nietzsche acknowledges that if the purpose of modern politics is to be that of
making life 'endurable for as many as possible, then these as many-
as-possible are entitled to determine what they understand by an
endurable life'. However, 'this feeling of self-determination', while
being encouraged, must not be allowed to dominate the political
sphere completely, for there must also be a space for those who wish
to 'refrain from politics, and to step aside a little'. In section 441
Nietzsche seems to recognize that modern social life makes
aristocratic rule impossible in that it removes the feeling of
subordination on which such rule depends:

Subordination, which is so highly rated in the military and bureaucratic
state, will soon become as unbelievable to us as the closed tactics of the
Jesuits already are…It is bound to disappear because its foundation is
disappearing: belief in unconditional authority, in definitive truth; even in
military states it cannot be generated even by physical compulsion, for its
origin is the inherited adoration of the princely as of something superhuman
(*übermenschlichem*). – In *freer* circumstances people subordinate themselves
only under conditions, as the result of a mutual contract (*gegenseitigen
Vertrages*), thus without prejudice to their own interests.

In section 450 Nietzsche considers what he takes to be the new
constitutional form of politics, that of the unity of government and
people, which characterizes the modern period. Traditionally, he
argues, the relationship between government and people has been
construed in terms of that between a stronger and higher power and
a weaker and lower one, between a commanding and an obeying
power. It is thus necessary, he argues, to take issue with the view that

the attainment of government as the organ of the people is the fuel which has motored history, and to encourage 'caution and slow evolution', for such a view can become fanatical and intolerant.

In his thinking on the political in this period, Nietzsche sees the crucial development in modern social life to be the decline of religion and the rise of a democratic form of politics which is based on distrust of all government and of social discipline. Since religion serves to appease the individual soul in times of loss and fear, it contributes to the permanence of government, as it is able to provide the suffering of individuals with meaning, even during unstoppable, universal misfortunes such as famine and war. Tutelary government and the preservation of religion necessarily go together. However, when religion begins to decline, the sacred foundations of the State are also shaken, and democratic impulses in the form of a secularized Christianity express themselves. A government dominated by these impulses ceases to be a sacred mystery and becomes transformed into a mere instrument of the popular will, which culminates in a distrust of all forms of government and social control (in anarchism). With the rise of democratic politics in the modern world Nietzsche sees both negative and positive possibilities. Whatever the results of this development prove to be, we should not, Nietzsche argues, confuse the emancipation of the private person in the modern polity with the emancipation of the 'individual':

Disregard for and the decline and *death of the State*, the liberation of the private person (I take care not to say: of the individual), is the consequence of the democratic conception of the State; it is in this that its mission lies. When it has performed its task – which like everything human bears much rationality and irrationality in its womb – when every relapse into the old sickness has been overcome, a new page will be turned in the storybook of humanity in which there will be many strange tales to read and perhaps some of them good ones... The belief in a divine order in the realm of politics, in a sacred mystery in the existence of the State, is of religious origin: if religion disappears the State will unavoidably lose its ancient Isis veil and cease to excite reverence. Viewed from close to, the sovereignty of the people serves to banish the last remnant of magic and superstition from this realm of feeling; modern democracy is the historical form of the *decay of the State*.[36]

Nietzsche goes on to argue, in this passage, that the qualities of prudence and self-interest which have informed the creation of the modern polity should be cultivated further, as they represent the best developed of human qualities. He argues that if the State is no longer

equal to the demands of these qualities then something more suited
to their existence will have to be invented. In his writings of this
period, however, Nietzsche rejects both liberalism and socialism as
political ideologies which could fulfil this role of replacing the
religious-founded State. In contrast to a morality founded on strong
customs and an ethos of community, liberalism celebrates the
freedom of the private person, not of the individual (who, for
Nietzsche, means nothing apart from the whole to which it belongs),
and ends up producing social conformism through cultivating a
timid herd morality. Nietzsche opposes socialism at this point in his
intellectual development on account of what he sees as its naive
dreaming of bringing about a social order in which everyone will be
provided with the good, the true, and the beautiful. Socialism, he
argues, rests on an optimism concerning the 'good man', which it
believes is awaiting to appear from behind the scenes if only it was
possible to abolish the old order and set man's so-called natural
drives free. Socialism represents the emergence of a new despotism,
since it requires more executive power than any previous political
regime in order to enact its programme of revolution, and guarantee
the complete subjugation of all citizens to its control of all levels of
social existence. Because it is attempting a revolutionary transformation of society, socialism requires more political power to be
concentrated in the hands of the State than any previous power.
Moreover, since it acknowledges no recourse to divine authority or
religious sanction to support its political claims (other than that
provided by the inexorable march of history), socialism is compelled
to invent its own religious sanctity (perhaps in the form of 'scientific
socialism') and to employ the most extreme forms of political
terror.[37]

In the work of his middle period, Nietzsche places himself on the
side of caution, moderation, and enlightenment. In section 452 of
Human, All Too Human, for example, he argues that what modern
existence requires is not 'a forcible redistribution of property but, a
gradual transformation of mind: the sense of justice must grow
greater in everyone, the instinct of violence weaker'. However, the
similarity between Nietzsche's critical description of socialism as a
form of politics that must have recourse to deception and terror, and
the later construal of his own aristocratic conception of great politics
is striking. In his later writings, Nietzsche's estimation of the
principal features of modern politics is not so subtle, for where in the

writings of the middle period he recognizes the ambiguity and potentiality of the rise of democratic politics for cultivating a *new* social and political sensibility, in his later writings, such as *Beyond Good and Evil*, for example, Nietzsche adopts a purely Machiavellian conception of power and of politics, and reduces the rise of democratic politics and the cry for justice to the physiological– psychological expression of the weak and impotent in their struggle against the noble and powerful. He does this by showing the origins of democracy to lie in Christianity, and by portraying the democratic sensibility as little more than the expression of the spirit of resentment injected into history by the slave rebellion in morals. Democracy is no longer seen as a possible alternative to an antiquated aristocratic order, but its significance is seen to lie solely in its potential as a breeding ground for tyrants (understood in the sense of great spiritual leaders). The key to understanding why Nietzsche should revert to his earlier aristocratism can be found in a passage from the early, unpublished essay on the Greek State. The major argument of this essay is that slavery represents the very essence of a high, noble culture: this is a truth which is presented as a cruel, hard, but necessary truth. The passage is crucial for understanding Nietzsche's relationship to Rousseau's political thought. Nietzsche argues as follows:

If culture (*Kultur*) really depended on the will (*Belieben*) of a people, if ineluctable powers were not at work here, which are law and boundary to the individual, then disdain for culture, the glorification of poverty of the spirit, the iconoclastic destruction of the claims of art would be more than a rebellion of the oppressed masses against dronelike individuals; it would be the cry of compassion knocking down the walls of culture; the drive of justice, for equality of suffering, would swamp all other ideas.[38]

This passage shows that, for Nietzsche, a choice must be made in the end between the needs and claims of a noble culture whose goal is art, and those of a democratic one whose goal is justice and compassion, for the two cannot be reconciled and unified: we must have one or the other, or rather, we must have one at the expense of the other. But this choice is as unacceptable in its starkness as the one presented to us by Hobbes between absolutism and anarchism.

Rousseau's politics would easily fall prey to the power of Nietzsche's critique of politics in the modern age were it the case that he advocated a simple politics of pity. But his politics have to be recognized to be more than this. Rousseau's starting-point is the corruption and degeneration brought about by the rule of inequality – not the inequality of social rank and merit which he recognized as necessary to any society, but that of material inequality – which corrupts rich and poor alike, leading to the politics of vanity, on the one hand, and the politics of envy and resentment on the other. Rousseau's desire for a social contract, which would establish the reign of virtue and a new kind of social discipline based on the rule of law and the protection of individual liberty, is a desire to transcend the corrupting effects of both of these forms of degenerative politics. Thus, like Nietzsche, Rousseau regards modern society as a form of the decay of the political in which the State has become a mere instrument for the pursuit of private ends, and which has released the private person, but has not produced the citizen who enjoys and practises moral freedom. Rousseau's importance lies in the fact that he grounds political legitimacy not simply on a notion of consent (which is passive obligation) but in a notion of self-legislation which transcends the narrow self of bourgeois society, and which presupposes an *active* obligation.

As Judith Shklar points out in what is, in my opinion, one of the finest essays ever written on Rousseau, Rousseau's insight into the corrupting effects of inequality is based on an acutely felt personal experience. Thus, Rousseau's 'fateful decision' to turn his private life into a public statement, which would serve as an indictment of modern society, was grounded in his belief that his existence was of great political significance for modern human beings.[39] Rousseau speaks and writes as a 'universal victim', a victim for 'all' *or* 'none'. The identification between human beings, which is to take place for Rousseau through the formation of a general will, is not simply based on pity for what is weak and lowly in mankind, but rather on a desire for freedom, for will to power in the sense of a will to grow and develop, to become what one is but which has been repressed and put down by the brutal and brutalizing suppression of the poor by the rich. Rousseau's political vision is inspired by the thought that the individual must not submit merely to the accidents of its birth, but must rebel and attain the strength and greatness which the capricious, illegitimate rule of, not merely the strong, but the rich, deny it. This is indeed, as Judith Shklar has pointed out, the politics of one who is downtrodden and outcast. But it is also the politics of one who has recognized the fundamental political problems of modern social existence.

In the end Rousseau's vision of politics has to be seen not simply as a politics of pity, but as the politics of justice in the modern period. Although he did a great deal to advertise pity as a means of creating new bonds of solidarity, he was well aware of its deficiencies if used as a social force. Pity is a fleeting, capricious sentiment. In nature pity is innocent, but in society it can corrupt and result in an excessive *amour-propre*. As Shklar points out, pity cures us of cruelty and envy, but it also creates new ties of dependence in which 'the feeble cling to their benefactors without gaining strength, while the latter soon feel intolerably burdened by the objects of their generosity'.[40] Rousseau, himself, for example admitted in his *Reveries* that he was too weak and inconsistent to endure the obligations which he had assumed by his casual acts of kindness. The socially ambiguous nature of pity means for Rousseau that it cannot served as a basis on which to construct a politics. Rather, this can only be provided by justice, which lies in the establishment of objective, neutral, and impersonal social rules of conduct that are to be administered compassionately but fairly in accordance with recognizable and agreed ethical principles. As Shklar writes, for Rousseau 'we need duty and justice that depend on law, not sentiment, which reduces the weak to suffering clients'.[41] We need compassion to bring us together by overcoming the conditioning of the accidental social position we are born into (that is, rich or poor), but once this solidarity has been forged we can only establish politics on the basis of justice. The aim of justice is to make the individual independent. Both compassion and vanity are inadequate in society for forming enduring, peaceful and harmonious social bonds. *Contra* Nietzsche, Rousseau shows that an opposition between 'commanding' and 'obeying' is not a natural feature of political life, but is one which can be overcome through the formation of a democratic polity in which none obey because all command. But Rousseau's vision of the just polity only makes sense to the extent that we can conceive of a mode of ethical existence in which the 'I' and the 'We' are one, and not opposed.

The principal weakness of Rousseau's thought is that it rests on an untenable distinction between the natural and the artificial which leads him to putting forward a completely ahistorical solution to the problem of civilization that he has posed. In his formulation of the general will, for example, what we find being constructed is an abstract and static will which can only preserve its moral purity by purging society of dissent and of the spirit of rebellion (of change) which is fundamental to its continual enhancement and overcoming. Rousseau's political thought is paradoxical for having disclosed to us the deeply historical nature of the human condition, he then closes off history by constructing a vision of society in which change and development are deemed to be undesirable and socially destructive.

In its attempt to translate its vision of redemption into a political one, Nietzsche's thought reveals its own mode of resentment towards history. For it too does not allow becoming to become, but seeks to take control of 'the gruesome accident' which constitutes history, in order to bend the bow of history and shoot it in another direction. As Leo Strauss has pointed out, for Nietzsche the fact that modern human beings are fragmentary and defective cannot be on account of any fixed nature, but is to be understood as no more than an inheritance of the past, of history as it has developed so far. Nietzsche envisages a historical redemption of this accidental inheritance through a courageous and noble 'great politics', which will play the role of producing a future nobility whose creation will redeem the entire past. But if our nature is not something given or fixed, then it has to be created and willed. This, as Strauss points out, is the real meaning of the doctrine of eternal return conceived as a political teaching: 'The return of the past, of the whole past, must be willed, if the over-man is to be possible.'[42] And yet, by making the remarkable educative teaching of eternal return serve the role of cultivation in the breeding of a renewed, aristocratic political order, Nietzsche renders the real existential significance and import of that teaching obsolete and impotent, for it becomes reified into a natural law, it becomes a matter of (religious) belief when, as Zarathustra asks us, of what account and consequence is belief? Again, this point serves to show the deficiency and inadequacy of Nietzsche's aristocratic conception of politics which must rely on force, fraud, and deception in order to maintain the stability and continuance of its rule. When translated into a principle of great politics the eternal return serves the same role in Nietzsche's political thought as that of the ancient noble myth.

It is however, I would argue, only Rousseau's vision of a democratic polity which can make such an ethical discipline of the individual freely possible. Where Nietzsche's aristocratism falls back on social coercion and the use of controlled political violence in order to bring about the reign of the overman – the weak, or 'poor', as

Rousseau points out to us, and as Nietzsche appreciated, will not voluntarily subject themselves to social slavery (hence the impotence of the eternal return in Nietzsche's conception of an aristocratic politics without *imposing* it from above) – a democratic polity inspired by Rousseau's concern with justice would enable there to be a political space which would serve as the arena, as the *agora*, in which the strength and weakness of individuals, their courage and compassion, along with the experience of the agony and tragedy of existence, could test themselves out, be recognized as such a testing, and constantly overcome themselves. It is thus necessary to supplant Nietzsche's exclusively aesthetic appreciation of the experience of the Dionysian – of the oneness of human beings with nature and with each other – with a *political* one, and one which lies in the vision of a tragic, but courageous and compassionate democracy.

In his thinking on the nature of the political, Nietzsche shares the delusion which has served to inspire the politics of the modern age, namely, the belief that it is possible to gain control of the historical process and to subject it to the mastery of the human will. As Erich Heller has argued in a remarkable insight, the doctrine of eternal return is 'the extreme *epic* philosophy to the point of grandiose absurdity, a cosmic therapy against the terror of the passing of every moment'.[43] Out of this epic moment there is to emerge the beautiful (not sublime) vision of the man who justifies all of time, the over-man. In the meantime we 'forerunners' are to sacrifice the present and ourselves, and to engage in a wild experimentalism in the hope and promise of producing the great redeeming man who 'must come one day'.[44]

The main conclusion to be reached in this study of Nietzsche's moral and political thought is that the relation between ethics and politics in Nietzsche is an antinomical one. There exists a deep incompatibility between the historical insights of his inquiry into the problem of civilization, and the political vision he develops in response to the particular historical problematic of nihilism. For his great politics do not address the major cause of the rise of the metaphysics of resentment, namely, the experience of political alienation. On the one hand, it has been shown that in the story of Zarathustra's down-going the question of the creation and legislation of new values is presented phenomenologically in a manner which ensures that Zarathustra's teaching is not imposed in terms of a new metaphysics. On the other hand, it has been shown that in the conception of great politics, where philosophy and politics come together to establish the vigorous reign of the overman, Nietzsche presents us with an aristocratic will to supremacy which rests on a politics of force and which stands in conflict with the ethical import of Zarathustra's down-going. In the story of Zarathustra's down-going the emphasis is on the ethics of courage and commitment; in the conception of great politics, however, the emphasis is on force and belief. Nietzsche's justice is only for the strong: the weak (even if they be poor and oppressed?) must perish.

Both Rousseau and Nietzsche seek a transfiguration of liberal political culture which is deeply paradoxical. It is clear that both regard liberalism as a political culture which rests on an atomistic individualism that makes impossible a genuinely agonistic culture able to promote either virtue or greatness. Rousseau is important, I would argue, because he so clearly sees that the major problem facing modern human beings is their existence as bourgeois individuals. The great paradox of his thought is that in order to undergo such a fundamental moral transformation modern human beings would have to be *before* the law what they should *become* by means of it. Nietzsche's moral and political thought partakes of the same paradox. He too demands a politics of transfiguration in which modern individuals (*Mensch*) are to elevate themselves through a process of 'going-down' and 'going-across' to higher tasks and to higher responsibilities (the *Übermensch*). But the conditions – namely, a tragic culture – which would serve to cultivate such individuals are absent in modern liberal societies. As Nietzsche says in section 354 of *The Gay Science*, the problem is that 'we' are no longer *material* for society. The most important difference between Rousseau and Nietzsche concerning a politics of transfiguration is that, in contrast to Rousseau, Nietzsche gaily accepts and affirms the fundamentally immoral nature of the legislator's task. Nietzsche is indeed, as he proclaimed himself to be, the immoralist *par excellence*.

An examination of the meaning of Nietzsche's portrait of himself as '*contra* Rousseau' appears to leave us with a straightforward choice between the politics of pity and those of will to power, with both claiming to have justice on their side, and to be speaking the 'voice of nature'.

Conclusion

The evil, the unhappy, and the exceptional human being – all these should also have their philosophy, their good right, their sunshine! Pity is not needed for them...not confession, conjuring of souls, and forgiveness of sins. But a new *justice* is what is needed!

Nietzsche, *The Gay Science*, section 289.

It cannot be doubted that Rousseau, who portrayed himself not without a certain degree of immodesty, as the philosopher of modern humanity's misery and unhappiness, experienced and suffered from tremendous bouts of resentment in his life. Rousseau tried to subject the problem of civilization – the problem whether man progresses through it – to the cold scrutiny of the dispassionate philosopher, and ended up presenting a damning indictment of the moral bankruptcy of modern civilization. It is history which cultivates and disciplines the human animal, transforming a limited and stupid creature into a moral and rational one. Rousseau's attitude to history, however, is deeply ambiguous. On the one hand, he laments the rise of the reign of vanity and resentment which has been created by the decadent and corrupt rule of the rich over the poor, while, on the other hand, he recognizes that it is only by undergoing the process of social development that the human animal can become a moral being capable of the highest freedom, that of moral liberty. Rousseau finds himself caught in a trap, for he recognizes that there can be no question of 'going back' and yet, because he regards degeneration as the law of time, as an inevitable consequence of the ruthless nature of becoming, he cannot see a way forward. Is everything simply in vain? Do we stand condemned? Rousseau saw himself as a victim of a corrupt society, and spectacularly located the sources of resentment amongst the oppressed and the downtrodden in the iniquitous economic and political structures of modern society.

There have been several psychological studies of Rousseau's life in an attempt to discredit his critique of civilized humanity. Nietzsche is interesting because he locates the source of Rousseau's failure in his moralism and romanticism. For Nietzsche, Rousseau is the perfect example of a moral hypocrite because, in seeking to expose the hypocrisy of a corrupt society, his own quest for authenticity leads him to advocate subterfuge and deception. Denying the legitimacy of the use of force, but not that of subterfuge, Rousseau becomes an advocate of the very hypocrisy he despises and regards as the genesis of all human vices and evil.[1] In a passage in *Daybreak*, Nietzsche notes perceptively that Rousseau could only ever find true happiness in solitude, for it is only here that he can freely practise *evil*:

'Only the solitary man is evil!' cried Diderot: and Rousseau at once felt mortally offended. Which means that he admitted to himself that Diderot was right. It is, indeed, a fact that, in the midst of society and sociability every evil inclination has to place itself under great restraint, don so many masks, lay itself so often on the Procrustean bed of virtue, that one could well speak of a martyrdom of the evil man. In solitude all this falls away. He who is evil is at his most evil in solitude.[2]

Rousseau began his intellectual life by painting for humanity a portrait of civilization which would condemn it in its own eyes, and he ended his life being perceived, by the humanity he once called a herd of happy slaves, as a buffoon. In this context one can appreciate why Nietzsche was so concerned, not only as a matter of intellectual conscience, but also as a matter of personal integrity, to present Zarathustra's identity in terms of a series of open question marks, and to present his teaching for 'all' and 'none'.

One could respond to a purely psychological reading of Rousseau by arguing that it simply fails to confront the major problem which Rousseau identified with the modern polity, that of the question of political legitimacy, which is a question about the nature of the just society, and how to prevent the modern degeneration of the political to the level of an economic battle between rich and poor. Despite the blatant inadequacy of Rousseau's own formulation of the general will with its tyrannical implications, the question he poses about justice in relation to the modern polity remains fundamental to grasping the dilemmas and conflicts of modern societies.

A key question, which emerges from reflection on the spirit of rebellion as it is revealed in the tragic life of Rousseau, is whether the desire for justice is motivated only by the base sentiment of revenge, that is, whether it is simply a façade behind which the weak individual conceals his own inadequacy and blames the other – society – for all his ills, and which he identifies with the ills of the world, which is certainly how Nietzsche reads Rousseau, or whether it represents a genuine desire for a new social and existential order. In his classic study of human revolt, Camus argued in a recognizably Rousseauian vein that the spirit of rebellion can only exist in a social order where a theoretical equality conceals tremendous factual inequalities. In an effort to disentangle the spirit of rebellion from that of resentment, Camus argues that, where resentment is envious and covetous, the mainspring of revolt is 'superabundant activity and energy'; where the resentful envy that which they do not possess, the rebellious set out to defend that which they believe in; where resentment represents an 'evil secretion, in a sealed vessel, of prolonged impotence', rebellion removes the seal and allows the whole being to come into play. Resentment is passive, where rebellion is active.[3] Is this not the spirit of Rousseau, of one whose life represents, in spite of its dreadful hypocrisy and pitifulness, an attempt to defend that which modern civilization is bent on destroying, namely, respect and dignity for human (but not only human) life? In the end, Camus argues, we must be vigilant in our rebellion, for it is necessary to know the limits of one's own transgression of the law. The act of rebellion cannot simply be identified with a struggle for individual rights, because the affirmation implicit in every act of revolt reaches out to something which transcends the individual and removes it from its solitude. Thus, the act of rebellion has to be founded on human solidarity and political love, but as soon as this solidarity and love are destroyed then the act of rebellion becomes an accomplice to a murderous terror:

In contemplating the results of an act of rebellion, we shall have to say, each time, whether it remains faithful to its first noble promise or whether, through lassitude or folly, it forgets its purpose and plunges into a mire of tyranny or servitude.[4]

Nietzsche's response to the problem of history is a fascinating and highly instructive one, which is prepared to descend into dangerous abysses and ascend to great, icy heights. He develops a kind of amoral theodicy in which 'life' and history become one because both are immoral.[5] This standpoint of beyond good and evil enables him, he believes, to overcome Rousseau's impasse on the problem of civilization, for the way forward simply lies in the further cultivation of evil. The fact that history cannot unequivocally be read as the story of the progressive evolution of man into a moral being presents no great problems for Nietzsche. Consider, for example, the following highly revealing passage from *Human, All Too Human*:

The voice of history. – In general history *seems* to furnish the following instruction regarding the production of genius: mistreat and torment men – thus it cries to the passions of envy, hatred, and contest – drive them to the limit, one against the other, nation against nation, and do it for centuries on end; then perhaps, a spark as it were thrown off by the fearful energy thus ignited, the light of genius will suddenly flare up; the will, made wild like a horse under the rider's spur, will then break out and leap over into another domain. – He who became aware of how genius is produced, and desired to proceed in the manner in which nature usually does in this matter, would have to be exactly as evil and ruthless as nature is.[6]

Nietzsche's thinking on the problem of history, however, operates in terms of an abstract, prejudicial notion of life, as will to power, and as self-overcoming, in which the past that becomes history is neither atoned for in a future act of redemption, nor simply forgotten, but ignored. This is evident in Nietzsche's reduction of the cry of the oppressed to the physiological expression of a slave rebellion which is full of resentment against the strength and nobility of the powerful. Is not Nietzsche's faith in the overman that of a blind and trusting fatalism which believes that out of good there will always emerge a deeper, more profound evil? The use and abuse of Nietzsche's writings and ideas by the principal actors in the catastrophic events of the twentieth century would seem to validate such a claim. For even if Nietzsche cannot be labelled a fascist (and such a description is an injustice in my opinion), it cannot be denied – indeed, it must not be denied, but pondered upon and agonized over – that Nietzsche's political thought freely opens up the possibility for such an abuse. If a buffoon could be fatal to humanity undergoing the experience of nihilism, then Nietzsche's Machiavellian conception of great politics, which posits no limits to the economy of violence to be used in man's further cultivation and enhancement, provides the human beings full of revenge and resentment with all that they need in order to justify their tyrannical rule. Thus, in the course of history, Nietzsche's noble vision of the reign of the overman became transmuted into the rule of a herd of sub-men. But, it could be asked, by failing to address the crucial questions raised by a major figure of the modern age, like Rousseau, concerning the nature of legitimate and just power, did not Nietzsche simply encourage this abuse of his political thought?

Nietzsche, as I have shown, construes justice as will to power in quite a remarkable way. Justice is not only beyond good and evil, it is also beyond the claims of weakness and compassion. But the coherence of this standpoint is negated by Nietzsche himself in his conception of a possible redemption through a great politics which aims to harness the forces of history in order to produce the overman. If the claim of the strong is to be legitimated as the claim of a just will to power, is not the cry of the oppressed also to be recognized as the voice of a just will to power? Nietzsche rejects the idea of establishing the legitimacy of political authority or sovereignty in terms of a social contract, as this, he believes, is to subject the strong, independent, and powerful human being to a contract which only serves the fears and insecurities of the weak who desire a social order which promotes conformity and timidity. Thus, the modern social contract amounts to little more than a slave revolt in morals. But in spite of the trenchant nature of much of Nietzsche's critique of modern politics, his thought ultimately rests on an abstract, unmediated opposition between 'life' and history: life is governed by the law of self-overcoming, and is on the side of the noble and the powerful, while history is the triumph of resentment and impotence, and represents the march to power of the weak and the base. The way out of this impasse for Nietzsche is, as Camus was one of the first to recognize, to demand *obedience to nature* ('life' as will to power) in order to *subjugate history*.[7] It is perhaps a great irony – and tragedy – of Nietzsche's attempt to suppress history in the name of a higher justice (the panoramic will to power) that it commits the same errors and follies of a monumentalistic reading of history which he warned against in his untimely meditation on history. By forgetting and neglecting key aspects of the past Nietzsche allows his thought to be abused by the foolhardy and the fanatical. His vision of great politics, and of the cultivation of the overman, inspired not simply gifted egoists and great visionaries, but also the impotent and the indolent.

It is tempting, but ultimately profoundly mistaken, I would argue to interpret Rousseau's demand for justice as no more than concealed resentment, and to construe his proclaimed love of humanity as a need to love something universal, in order to avoid loving anybody in particular. Rousseau's failure lies in him being unable to achieve the kind of marriage of knowledge and life which he sought throughout his tempestuous life. But his failure is instructive, for, as Nietzsche wrote in one of his more dispassionate reflections on the nature of Jean-Jacques, which could equally apply to Nietzsche's own life, 'the fairest virtue of the great thinker is the magnanimity with which, as a man of knowledge, he intrepidly, often with embarrassment, often with sublime mockery, and smiling – offers himself and his life as a sacrifice'.[8] As a man of knowledge, as a moral hypocrite, as a failed life punctuated by moments of awful resentment and paranoia, but equally as an advocate of justice and freedom, Rousseau speaks to all of us – *or* he speaks to none of us. Similarly, the sacrifices of Nietzsche's own life to the cause of tragic thinking, are equally instructive in showing the great risks that one faces as a lawbreaker, and the dangers that result from the attempt to create the new by denying that one's creation of the new can be restricted by the recognition of moral limits. Nietzsche's vision of the overman is not inspired by a notion of the end or 'ends' (*Zwecken*) of history, whether it be a kingdom of ends, or the just society. Instead he sacrifices everything, including our desire for freedom and emancipation, to the cause of a higher justice that proclaims itself to be beyond good and evil. Every mind that finds itself 'solitary and agitated', Nietzsche says, in section 14 of *Daybreak*, is consumed by doubt, in particular by the doubt of belief in itself, for, if one has 'killed the law', then the law 'anguishes' one 'as a corpse does a living man: if I am not *more* than the law I am the vilest of all men'. To break the law one must not only be equal to it but greater than it. But for Nietzsche to become what he was, meant that his life ended in the ultimate knowledge of madness. In Nietzsche's vision we do not find any redemption at all, but only the eternal return of the struggle between the will to power of the strong and the weak, of masters and slaves, of the justice that claims to be beyond resentment, and of the resentment that masquerades as justice. Nietzsche seeks not an end to history, but the rebirth of a tragic culture in which people have the strength and the will to live to the extent that they can *will* the eternal return of the nihilistic conditions of their human existence, and gaily affirm that life ultimately has no meaning and is without justification. Nietzsche invites us to engage in wars, in combat, and in struggle so as to create the new and the unique, but to emerge from the contest without suffering from it, for this can only lead to guilt and to the frightful unleashing of destructive energies. What we require, therefore in this vision is to re-establish the 'discipline of great suffering', as Nietzsche puts it in section 225 of *Beyond Good and Evil*. Man is both 'creature' and 'creator', that is, he is both material, excess, chaos, and clay; but he is also creator, form-giver, and 'hammer hardness'. The test of courage is whether one has the strength to affirm the creator in man, or whether one succumbs to weakness by feeling pity for the creature in man. To affirm the creative potentialities of man, and to create the new by affirming the nihilistic and tragic conditions of existence, it is necessary for Nietzsche that we learn how to overcome the problem of civilization as posed by Rousseau. The way *he* does, as I have shown, is by overcoming pity for the creature in man, and cultivating courage for the creator in man. The question for *us*, however, is whether Nietzsche's conception of the task of the self-overcoming of morality in terms of a position that is '*contra Rousseau*' does not present us with a false and spurious opposition which forces us to make an unnecessary and unacceptable choice between freedom and greatness, between pity and will to power.

In their finest and stillest hour both Rousseau and Nietzsche show us that the way of liberation lies through a self-education in which we organize and discipline the chaos we are by thinking back to our true needs, and recognize that the unity of willing, thinking, and doing can only be achieved through human solidarity. We must strive to create the new through a creation which does not forget or ignore the horrors and sufferings of the past, but redeems the past and all that was by recognizing that it is a condition of any future creative willing that it must engage in a labour of self-overcoming, for only a buffoon thinks the past can be jumped over. But Nietzsche is right in pointing out that, in order to achieve an emancipatory, creative willing, it will be necessary to affirm the paradoxes associated with the task of self-overcoming by recognizing the tragic conditions of a creative human existence. For, in order to be humane, we may have to be cruel, in order to be just we may have to discriminate, and in order to be moral we will be forced to appear immoral. But what is our end? And what are our means? Where are our brethren who will carry the new law-tables we have created into the valley, and engrave them onto the compassionate and courageous hearts of men and women? The lion has roared, my child is near, but who are 'we'?

Notes

INTRODUCTION

1 Rousseau, *OC* III, p. 7; tr. *DAS*, p. 5.
2 Nietzsche, *KSA* I, p. 334; tr. *UADH*, section 10.
3 On the 'liberal addiction towards social conformity' see S. S. Wolin, *Politics and Vision. Continuity and Innovation in Western Political Thought*, Boston, Little Brown and Co., 1960, p. 343.
4 Nietzsche, *KSA* I, p. 146; tr. *D* section 163.
   Nietzsche's writings are ambiguous on the precise sense in which he understands the term 'civilization', for there are places when he uses two separate words to indicate the same process, '*Cultur*' and '*Civilisation*', and there are places when he speaks of the relationship between the two in terms of an opposition. A distinction between the two can be made by saying that the former refers to the educative process by which the human animal is cultivated and disciplined, which is the focus of the second essay of the *Genealogy of Morals* where Nietzsche examines what he regards as the fundamental problem concerning the evolution of man, that of breeding an animal which is able to make promises and which takes place through what Nietzsche calls 'the morality of custom'. The latter, on the other hand, can be taken to refer to cultural and technological progress which contains the idea of moral refinement. In Freud civilization is synonymous with society and his use of the term has the same meaning which Nietzsche ascribes to *Cultur*. '*Civilization*' (*Kultur*), Freud writes, 'describes the whole sum of achievements and the regulations which distinguish our lives from those of our animal ancestors and which serve two purposes – namely to protect men against nature and to adjust their mutual relations.' See S. Freud, *Civilization and Its Discontents*, Middlesex, Penguin, 1985, p. 278. In his critique of Rousseau, Nietzsche uses the term 'civilization' in the same sense as Rousseau as denoting the opposite of a 'natural', pre-social and pre-civil state. A key passage for understanding his position is from the *Nachlass* of Autumn 1887 where he speaks of the relationship between '*Cultur*' and '*Civilisation*' as an antagonistic one, namely where the high points of culture have always been times of corruption, the periods when the 'taming' (*Zähmung*) of the human animal was being

carried out have been, conversely, times of intolerance against bold and independent natures. See Nietzsche, *KSA* xii (*Nachlass* 1885–7), 9 [142], p. 416.

5 See Nietzsche, on 'How the "Real World" at last became a Fable', part four of *Twilight of the Idols*. On the connection between Rousseau and Christianity see Nietzsche, *KSA* xi (*Nachlass* 1884–5), 25 [130], p. 48.

6 L. Strauss, 'Three Waves of Modernity', in Strauss, *Political Philosophy, Six Essays*, ed. H. Gilden, Indianapolis, Bobbs-Merrill, 1975, pp. 81–98, pp. 81–2.

7 L. Gossman, 'Time and History in Rousseau', *Studies in Voltaire and the Eighteenth Century*', 30 (1964), pp. 311–49, pp. 348–9.

8 *Ibid.*, p. 344.

9 See Nietzsche, *KSA* v, p. 399; tr. *OGM* iii, section, 24.

10 Gossman, 'Time and History in Rousseau', p. 345.

11 *Ibid.*, p. 339.

12 Strauss, 'Three Waves of Modernity', p. 94.

13 Nietzsche, *KSA* vi, p. 150; tr. *TI* 'Expeditions of an Untimely Man', section 48.

14 Rousseau, *OC* iii, p. 133; tr. *DI*, p. 46.

15 Rousseau *OC* i, p. 1046; tr. *RSW*, p. 88.

16 *Ibid.*, p. 1047; tr. p. 89.

17 Nietzsche, *KSA* vi, pp. 96–7; tr. *TI* 'The Four Great Errors', section 8.

18 Nietzsche, *KSA* x (*Nachlass* 1882–4), 8 [19], pp. 340–1; tr. *WP* 787.

19 Nietzsche, *KSA* ii, pp. 24–5; tr. *HAH*, section 2.

20 Nietzsche, *KSA* vi, p. 293; tr. *EH* 'Why I am so clever', section 9.

21 Nietzsche, *KSA* v, pp. 405–6; tr. *OGM* iii, section 26.

22 Nietzsche, *KSA* v, pp. 157–8; tr. *BGE*, section 224.

23 In his essay of 1841 on 'History', which Nietzsche was familiar with, Emerson argued that the writing of history was in need of an 'ethical reformation'. See R. W. Emerson, *Selected Essays*, ed. L. Ziff, Middlesex, Penguin, 1982, pp. 149–75, p. 172.

24 Nietzsche, *KSA* i, pp. 248–9; tr. *UADH*, section 1.

25 *Ibid.*, p. 249; section 1.

26 *Ibid.*, p. 255; section 1.

27 *Ibid.*, p. 319; section 9.

28 *Ibid.*, p. 330; section 10.

29 *Ibid.*, p. 269; section 3.

30 *Ibid.*, p. 250; section 1.

31 Nietzsche, *KSA* i, pp. 374–5; tr. *SE*, section 4.

32 Nietzsche, *KSA* vi, p. 264; tr. *EH* 'Why I am so wise', section 1: 'The good fortune of my existence, its uniqueness perhaps, lies in its fatality: I am, to express it in the form of a riddle, already dead as my father, while as my mother I am still living and becoming old'. It is 'this dual descent' from the highest and the lowest rung on the ladder of life ('at the same time a *decadent* and a *beginning*'), writes Nietzsche, which provides him with a subtler sense of smell for the signs of ascent and

decline than any other human being before him: 'I am the teacher *par excellence* for this – I know both, I am both'. His genius, we might say, is in his nostrils.

1. NIETZSCHE CONTRA ROUSSEAU

1 See especially *D* section 163, and *KSA* xii (*Nachlass* 1885–7), 9 [125], p. 409, 9 [146], p. 421; tr. *WP* 99 and 98. The earliest study of the relationship can be traced to Herbert Kramer, *Nietzsche und Rousseau*, Leipzig, R. Noske, 1928. Kramer's dissertation provides a biographical monograph together with a terse account of Nietzsche's scattered remarks on Rousseau, and is altogether lacking in critical acumen. An earlier attempt to examine the relationship from the perspective of the concerns of political theory, which focuses on the problem of the legislator, can be found in I. Forbes, 'Rousseau and Nietzsche: The Philosopher as Legislator', unpublished MA thesis, University of Adelaide, 1979. For an interpretation of Nietzsche's philosophy in terms of its inheritance of the Rousseauian–Kantian tradition of moral philosophy see B. Yack, *The Longing for Total Revolution. Philosophic Sources of Discontent from Rousseau to Marx and Nietzsche*, New Jersey, Princeton University Press, 1986. For an interpretation of Nietzsche's reading of Rousseau in the wider context of his reading of French writers and culture see, W. D. Williams, *Nietzsche and the French*, Oxford, Basil Blackwell, 1952. In his recent study, *Immediary Lost. Construction of the Social in Rousseau and Nietzsche* Copenhagen, Akademisk Forlag, 1988, Lars-Henrik Schmidt focuses on the theme of the 'overcoming of metaphysics' in both thinkers.

2 It is interesting to note that Nietzsche's criticism of 'modernity' is centred on a critique of politics. In section 39 of 'Expeditions of an Untimely Man' in *Twilight of the Idols*, for example, Nietzsche criticizes modern democracy for not cultivating the instincts amongst its citizens out of which strong and vibrant institutions can grow: 'Whenever the word "authority" is so much as heard one believes oneself to be in danger of a new slavery'.

3 Nietzsche, *KSA* ii, pp. 533–4; tr. *AOM*, section 408. The eight thinkers Nietzsche groups together into four pairs are Epicurus and Montaigne, Goethe and Spinoza, Plato and Rousseau, Pascal and Schopenhauer.

4 For Nietzsche on Rousseau's moral fanaticism see *D* preface, section 3; on the French Revolution as a modern slave revolt in morals see *OGM* i, section 16.

5 K. Löwith, *From Hegel to Nietzsche*, tr. D. E. Green, London, Constable, 1964, p. 260.

6 For Nietzsche's understanding of decadence in the context of the problem of nihilism see *KSA* xiii (*Nachlass* 1887–89), 14 [86], pp. 264–5; tr. *WP* 43.

7 See Nietzsche, *BT*, section 3 and *GS* section 91. A fragment from the *Nachlass* of the beginning of 1884 suggests that Nietzsche was also

familiar with Rousseau's novel, *La Nouvelle Héloïse*. See *KSA* xi (*Nachlass* 1884–5), 25 [197], p. 66.

8 See Nietzsche, *KSA* ii, pp. 650–2; tr. *WS*, section 216. On Rousseau's influence on Kant see E. Cassirer, *Rousseau, Kant, and Goethe. Two Essays*, Connecticut, Archon Books, 1961. For a comparative reading of their moral and political thought see S. Ellenburg, 'Rousseau and Kant: principles of political right', in R. A. Leigh (ed.), *Rousseau After Two Hundred Years*, Cambridge, Cambridge University Press, 1982.

9 Although William's study, *Nietzsche and the French*, is an instructive one in many respects, it is guilty of doing what Nietzsche warns against in *GS*, section 228, namely of mediating between two resolutely independent thinkers by making them identical. See Williams, *Nietzsche and the French*, especially p. 9 and pp. 170–1. Like Williams, Bernard Yack equates Nietzsche's critique of civilization with Rousseau's in a way which ignores the subtle but crucial points of difference between them. See Yack, *The Longing for Total Revolution*, especially p. 24 and p. 311.

10 See J. W. Chapman, *Rousseau. Totalitarian or Liberal?* (1956), New York, Ams Press, 1968, and J. L. Talmon, *The Origins of Totalitarian Democracy*, London, Secker and Warburg, 1952.

11 For readings of Nietzsche as a moral (or, rather, amoral) individualist see H. S. Kariel, 'Nietzsche's Preface to Constitutionalism', *Journal of Politics*, 25 (May 1963), pp. 211–225; J. S. Colman, 'Nietzsche as Politique et Moraliste', *Journal of the History of Ideas*, 27 (Oct–Dec. 1966), pp. 549–74; J. P. Stern, *Nietzsche*, Glasgow, Collins, 1978, pp. 76–84.

12 The classic study of the antinomies of modern thought is to be found in Georg Lukács's study, originally published in the 1920s, *History and Class Consciousness*, tr. R. Livingstone, London, Merlin Press, 1971, pp. 110–149. The Oxford English Dictionary defines an antinomy as a contradiction in a law, or between two laws, a conflict of authority, and a paradox.

13 I borrow this characterization of individualism from S. Ellenburg, *Rousseau's Political Philosophy*, Ithaca, Cornell University Press, 1976, p. 35.

14 C. B. MacPherson, *The Political Theory of Possessive Individualism*, Oxford, Oxford University Press, 1962, p. 4.

15 Of course, it is important to recognize that in both Rousseau and Nietzsche women are excluded from the creative task of self-legislation. In spite of this exclusion, however, and in spite of Nietzsche's notorious views on women, a number of feminists have argued that his thought has dimensions – namely a mode of thinking which celebrates difference and otherness – which can be used to fruitful effect for articulating a radical feminist political practice, namely one which goes beyond the limited egalitarianism and universalism of the women's liberation movement. See, for example, R. Diprose, 'Nietzsche, Ethics, and Sexual Difference', *Radical Philosophy*, 52 (Summer 1989), pp. 27–33.

16 For Nietzsche's devaluation of community see *BGE* section 284. On

Nietzsche's ethical thought as solipsistic see A. MacIntyre, *After Virtue. A Study in Moral Theory*, London, Duckworth, 1981, pp. 103–114, and T. B. Strong, 'Nietzsche's Political Aesthetics' in M. A. Gillespie and T. B. Strong, *Nietzsche's New Seas*, Chicago, Chicago University Press, 1988, pp. 153–74.

17 Nietzsche, *KSA* I, p. 37; tr. *BT*, section 3. Compare *KSA* VII (*Nachlass* 1869–74), 9 [85], p. 305.

18 *Ibid.*, p. 34; tr. section 2.

19 *Ibid.*, pp. 29–30; tr. section 1.

20 For a discussion of Nietzsche's depoliticization of the Dionysian in his early writings see P. Bergmann, *Nietzsche, 'the Last Anti-political German'*, Bloomington, Indiana University Press, 1987, pp. 86–7.

21 *KSA* I, p. 123; tr. *BT*, section 19.

22 *Ibid.*, p. 117; tr. section 18.

23 *Ibid.*, p. 133; tr. section 21.

24 *Ibid.*, p. 47; tr. section 5.

25 *Ibid.*, p. 17; tr. 'Attempt at a Self-Criticism' (1886), section 5.

26 See, for example, Rousseau, *OC* IV, p. 857; tr. *E*, p. 437: 'the eternal laws of nature and of order do exist'. For Nietzsche on 'the lie of the ethical world-order' (*die Lüge der sittlichen Weltordnung*) see *KSA* VI, p. 195; tr. *AC*, section 26. As R. Grimsley points out in his Introduction to *Du Contrat social* (Oxford University Press, 1972, p. 69), Rousseau's political thought is linked up with a fundamental belief that although social life is an artifice, not nature, it depends on a proper understanding of human nature and its relationship with God and the eternal moral order he has created. On this point see also the excellent study by M. Viroli, *Jean-Jacques Rousseau and the 'Well-Ordered Society'*, Cambridge, Cambridge University Press, 1988, especially, pp. 17–24. As Viroli points out in this study, for Rousseau truth and knowledge are not simply human conventions, but consist in the recognition of an order and a reality which already exists in things. Needless to say, Nietzsche's embracing of a conventionalist approach to questions of truth and knowledge could not make his position more dissimilar from such a realist view.

27 On this point see M. Haar, 'Nietzsche and Metaphysical Language', in D. B. Allison (ed.), *The New Nietzsche*, Cambridge, Mass.: MIT Press, 1985, pp. 20–1.

28 See Rousseau, *OC* III, p. 142; tr. *DI* p. 54. See Nietzsche, *KSA* I, p. 334; tr. *UADH*, section 10. See also *KSA* I, p. 362; tr. *SE*, section 3.

29 Nietzsche, *KSA* I, pp. 384–5; tr. *SE*, section 6.

30 *Ibid.*, p. 334; tr. *UDHL*, section 10.

31 On Nietzsche's reading of Mill see K. Brose, 'Nietzsches Verhältnis zu J. S. Mill', *Nietzsche-Studien*, 3 (1974), pp. 152–74. Nietzsche's library contained a complete German edition of Mill's works.

32 On Nietzsche and Tocqueville see U. Marti, 'Nietzsches Kritik der Französischen Revolution', *Nietzsche-Studien*, 19 (1990), pp. 312–26.

33 Nietzsche, *KSa* I, p. 345; tr. *SE*, section 2. Compare Rousseau *OC* 3, p. 22, tr. *DAS*, p. 18: 'We cannot reflect on the mores (*les moeurs*) of mankind without contemplating without pleasure the picture of the simplicity which prevailed in earliest times. This image may be justly compared to a beautiful coast, adorned by the hands of nature; towards which our eyes are constantly turned, and which we see receding with regret'. The notion of mores or customs is an important one in the ethical thought of both Rousseau and Nietzsche.

34 See Nietzsche, *KSA* I, pp. 384–5; tr. *SE*, section 6. Compare *KSA* VI, p. 106; tr. *TI*, 'What the Germans Lack', section 4.

35 *Ibid.*, p. 365; tr. section 4.
For Nietzsche's later critique of the State see the section on 'The New Idol' in part one of *Thus Spoke Zarathustra*. Nietzsche's critique of the State as a totalitarian institution is misdirected if applied to thinkers like Rousseau and Hegel who aim to revive in the modern world the Greek conception of man as a political animal, that is, the idea that the human animal only becomes fully human when it becomes a social being. For Aristotle, only a beast or a god could live outside of society. Rousseau and Hegel's modern conception of man as a political animal differs from antiquity in an important respect, namely, that it is applicable to all, irrespective of social rank or class and is philosophically grounded on the primacy of the individual, which explains why the notion of the *will* assumes such an importance in their respective deductions of the principles of political right, for it is the 'will' which represents the unique nature of the human animal and which accounts for its sense of responsibility and obligation. Thus, for example, in his *Philosophy of Right* Hegel offers an exposition of the political, of 'right', in terms of the principle of the will first articulated by Rousseau. In his essay, 'The "Warrior Spirit" as an Inlet to the Political Philosophy of Nietzsche's Zarathustra', *Nietzsche Studien*, 15 (1986), pp. 140–179, p. 145, Thomas Pangle rightly points out that Nietzsche's thought draws an important distinction between a concrete 'people' (*Volk*) and an abstract 'State'. Whereas the former notion refers to the customs and mores of a communal body which is very close to Rousseau's model of political virtue, the latter notion refers to the cold, distant authority of the modern bureaucratic State. It is possible, therefore, to interpret Nietzsche's critique of Hegel, or of what he regards as the Hegelian cult of the State, as a critique of the view that a renewed ethical life (*Sittlichkeit*) is in any way attainable through the institutions and machinery of the modern State.

36 *Ibid.*, p. 365; tr. section 4.
37 *Ibid.*, p. 400; tr. section 6.
38 *Ibid.*, p. 388.
39 *Ibid.*, p. 363; tr. section 3.
40 *Ibid.*, p. 369; tr. section 4.
41 *ibid.*, pp. 370–1; tr. section 4.

42 Nietzsche, *KSA* VI, pp. 151–2; tr. *TI*, 'Expeditions of an Untimely Man', section 49.
43 *Ibid.*, pp. 150–1; tr. section 48.
44 W. Kaufmann, *Nietzsche. Philosopher, Psychologist, and Anti-christ*, Princeton, Princeton University Press, 1974, p. 155.
45 Nietzsche, *KSA* II, p. 299; *HAH*, section 463.
46 This critique of the politicization of the Dionysian runs throughout Nietzsche's writings. It is mistaken, therefore, to view his political thought in terms of advocating any return to a pagan aristocracy of blond beasts. On the notion of the 'blond beast' in Nietzsche see D. Brennecke, 'Die blonde Bestie. Vom Missverständnis eines Schlagworts', *Nietzsche-Studien*, 5 (1976), pp. 113–45.
47 See Nietzsche, section 48 of 'Expeditions of an Untimely Man' in *Twilight of the Idols* where he defines justice in Aristotelian terms as equality for equals and inequality for unequals. In Rousseau, equality is not simply a moral ideal but a juridical condition of the just polity.
48 On Taine's reading of Rousseau see A. Horowitz, *Rousseau, Nature, and History*, Toronto, Toronto University Press, 1987, p. 13. The correspondence between Nietzsche and Taine began in October 1886 when Taine wrote to thank Nietzsche for sending him a copy of *Beyond Good and Evil*. In *BGE* 254 Nietzsche refers to Taine as the greatest living historian. Nietzsche first read him on the Revolution in 1878–9. See *KSA* VIII, 39 [8], p. 577. For Nietzsche on Benjamin Constant see *KSA* VII (*Nachlass*, 1868–74), 29 [179], pp. 705–6, and *KSA* XIII, 11 [305], p. 130.
49 See Marti, 'Nietzsches Kritik der Französischen Revolution', p. 326.
50 *Ibid.*, pp. 318–19.
51 Nietzsche, *KSA* XIII, 15 [53], p. 444.
52 I. Kant, 'Conjectural Beginning of Human History', in Kant, *On History*, ed. L. W. Beck, Indianapolis, Bobbs-Merrill, 1963, pp. 53–69, p. 60. For Rousseau's influence on Kant and Hegel in their conception of a philosophy of history see R. Polin, *La politique de la solitude. Essai sur Jean-Jacques Rousseau*, Paris, Editions Sirey, 1971, chapter six, especially pp. 243–54.
53 Kant is of the conviction that any opposition between nature and culture in Rousseau's thought can be overcome by recognizing that the problematic of the second discourse on the origin of inequality is resolved in the two works of 1762, *Émile* and the *Social Contract*. We need to construe culture in terms of an education in which the development of humanity considered as a *moral species* ends the conflict between the natural and the moral. Culture is our second nature, the 'ultimate moral end of the human species'. See Kant, 'Conjectural Beginning of Human History', p. 63.
54 Nietzsche, *KSA* III, pp. 14–15; tr. *D* preface, section 3.
55 Nietzsche, *KSA* XIII, 15 [30], p. 424; tr. *WP* 765: 'It was Christianity that first invited the individual to play the judge of everything and

everyone; megalomania almost became a duty: one has to enforce *eternal* rights against everything temporal and conditioned! What of the State! What of society! What of historical laws! What of physiology! What speaks here is something beyond becoming, something unchanging throughout history…a *soul*!'

56 G. W. F. Hegel, *Philosophy of Right*, tr. T. M. Knox, Oxford, Oxford University Press, 1967, paragraph 258. Having made this comparison between Rousseau and Hegel, however, it has also to be recognized that the dialectical and speculative presentation of 'right' which Hegel develops in the *Philosophy of Right* contains a critique of the natural law tradition which posits the fiction of isolated individuals being brought together through the artificial device of a social contract. Thus, in paragraph 256, for example, Hegel says that when we reach the end of the presentation we should recognise that, although he has followed the natural law tradition by beginning with a notion of 'will' (the abstract individual) and culminating in a notion of 'right' (the State as ethical life), the State is really the beginning and not the end of political thinking.

57 See Nietzsche, *KSA* v, p. 288; tr. *OGM* I, 16. See also *BGE*, sections 199, 244–45, 256. For an examination of the influences on Nietzsche's Napoleon *Bild* (mainly Taine and Stendhal) see U. Marti, 'Der Plebejer in der Revolte – Ein Beitrag zur Genealogie des "Höheren Menschen"', *Nietzsche-Studien*, 18 (1989), pp. 550–73.

58 Nietzsche, *KSA* vi, p. 273; tr. *EH*, 'Why I am so wise', section 6.

59 Nietzsche, *KSA* ii, p. 349; tr. *HAH*, section 617.

60 J. Starobinski, *Jean-Jacques Rousseau. Transparency and Obstruction* (first published 1957, revised 1971), tr. A. Goldhammer, Chicago, Chicago University Press, 1988, p. 34.

61 See G. W. F. Hegel, *Phenomenology of Spirit*, tr. A. V. Miller, Oxford, Oxford University Press, 1978, paragraph 658.

62 Rousseau, *OC* i, p. 1018; tr. *RSW*, p. 56.

63 *Ibid.*, p. 1058; p. 103.

64 Starobinski, *Rousseau. Transparency and Obstruction*, p. 39, draws attention to the paradox of Rousseau's career as a writer. In Rousseau we see a transformation of a literary life into a heroic destiny. He wishes to free life from the vicissitudes of literature, 'to set forth in *writing* a philosophy…based on the rejection of literature'. W. H. Blanchard, *Rousseau and the Spirit of Revolt. A Psychological Study*, Ann Arbor, University of Michigan Press, 1967, pp. 248–51, argues that Rousseau's writings are propelled by a fear of the female. Thus, in his thought, society is conceived along masculine lines (transparent, simple, uncomplicated), while luxury and superfluity (the 'feminine') are detested. He admires Spartan discipline because here social graces are replaced by pure physical exercise. Blanchard sees Rousseau's work as characterized by a conflict between a desire for simplicity and the recognition of the inherent complexity of social existence. Rousseau's

ambivalence towards writing is evident in the disgust he expresses for
his own work in the later part of his life. Through writing he discovers
that pure virtue cannot be his primary motivation, and he is thus faced
with the painful task of coming to terms with his own loss of innocence.
On this problem of writing in Rousseau see also J. Derrida, *Of
Grammatology*, tr. G. C. Spivak, Baltimore, John Hopkins University
Press, 1976. In section 5 of 'Why I write such good books' in *Ecce Homo*
Nietzsche describes himself as the 'first psychologist of the eternally
feminine'. For an exploration of the extent to which Nietzsche writes
with the hand of woman see J. Derrida, *Spurs. Nietzsche's Styles*, tr. B.
Harlow, Chicago, Chicago University Press, 1979.

65 For Nietzsche on Mirabeau see *OGM* I, section 10 and *GS*, section 95.
   For a comparison of Mirabeau and Rousseau see *KSA* IX (*Nachlass
   1880–82*), 15 [37], p. 647.

66 Nietzsche, *KSA* I, pp. 312–13; tr. *EH*, 'The Birth of Tragedy', section 3.

67 Nietzsche, *KSA* I, p. 12; tr. *BT*, 'Self-Criticism', section 1.

68 Nietzsche, *KSA* I, pp. 18–19; tr. *BT*, 'Self-Criticism', section 5.

69 The Oxford English Dictionary defines 'machiavellian' as deceitful,
   perfidious, and cunning action. For further insight see J. Leonard,
   'Public versus Private Claims. Machiavellianism from Another Perspective', *Political Theory* 12:4 (November 1984), pp. 491–506.

70 See Niccolò Machiavelli, *The Prince* (1513–14), tr. G. Bull, Middlesex,
   Penguin, 1981, chapter 18.

71 The classic study of Machiavelli as a teacher of evil is Leo Strauss's
   Thoughts on Machiavelli, Seattle, University of Washington Press, 1969.
   Two studies which explore Nietzsche's relation to Machiavelli at length
   are B. H. F. Taureck, *Nietzsche und der Faschismus. Eine Studie über
   Nietzsches politische Philosophie und ihre Folgen*, Hamburg, Junius Verlag,
   1989, and N. Prostka, *Nietzsches Machtbegriff in Beziehung zu den
   Machiavellis*, Münster, Lit. Verlag, 1989. Taureck sees Nietzsche's
   political thought as decidedly Machiavellian, and argues that it is this
   aspect of his thought which provides the link between Nietzsche and a
   fascist politics.

72 Nietzsche, *KSA* XII, 9 [145], p. 419; tr. *WP*, section 776.

73 See Wolin, *Politics and Vision*, pp. 195–99.

74 *Ibid.*, p. 214.

75 See Nietzsche, *BGE*, section 28, and *TI*, 'What I Owe to the Ancients',
   section 2.

76 Nietzsche *KSA* XII, 9 [147], pp. 421–22; tr. *WP*, section 311.

77 *KSA* XII, 9 [140], p. 415; tr. *WP*, section 308.

78 *KSA* XIII, 11 [54], pp. 24–7; tr. *WP*, section 304. Compare *KSA* XII, 10
   [14], p. 461. Both of these fragments carry the heading 'Ein tractatus
   politicus Von Friedrich Nietzsche' (not given by Kaufmann). It is a
   tractatus, Nietzsche says, not for the ears of '*Jedermann*'.

79 See the Introduction to Machiavelli's *Discourses* by Bernard Crick, tr.
   L. J. Walker, Middlesex, Penguin, 1983, p. 58. *Virtù* is primarily a role-

related concept; the *virtus* differ fundamentally from the Christian virtues which all human beings, irrespective of rank, are capable of exhibiting. See T. Ball, 'The Picaresque Prince. Reflections on Machiavelli and Moral Change', *Political Theory*, 12:4 (November 1984), p. 425. In *BGE*, section 284 Nietzsche lists *his* four virtues as 'courage, insight, sympathy, and solitude'. Compare *D*, section 556.

80 Nietzsche, *KSA* XIII, 15 [113], pp. 471–4; tr. *WP*, section 351.

81 Nietzsche *KSA* XII, 10 [2], pp. 453–4; tr. *WP*, section 1021.

82 *Ibid.*, 10 [5], pp. 456–7; tr. section 1017.
An interesting passage for understanding the grounds of Nietzsche's opposition to Rousseau's sentimentalism and moralism regards nature, is the following from the early unpublished essay of 1872 *Homer's Wettkampf* ('Homer's Contest'), in *KSA* I, pp. 783–92, 783: 'When we speak of *humanity* there lies at bottom the idea that the human is that which is separate and distinct from nature. But in reality there is no such distinction: the "natural" qualities and the properly called "human" ones have grown up inseparably together. In his highest and noblest capacities man is nature and carries within himself her awful double character. The generally considered terrible and inhuman capacities are even perhaps the fertile soil out of which alone all humanity can grow forth in feelings, actions, and works'.

83 See Rousseau *OC* III, p. 247; tr. *DPE*, p. 123, and *SC* book III, chapter VI. For a comparison of Rousseau and Machiavelli see M. Viroli, 'Republic and Politics in Machiavelli and Rousseau', *History of Political Thought*, 10:3 (1989), pp. 405–20.

84 Rousseau, *SC* IV, VIII, and Machiavelli, *Discourses* II, 2. Compare Nietzsche, *KSA* XIII, 15 [110], pp. 469–71; tr. *WP*, section 246: 'What is "virtue" and "charity" in Christianity if not just this mutual preservation, this solidarity of the weak.'

85 See L. McKenzie, 'Rousseau's Debate with Machiavelli in the *Social Contract*', *Journal of the History of Ideas*, 43 (April–June 1982), pp. 209–28.

86 *Ibid.*, p. 224.

87 Viroli, *Rousseau and the 'Well-Ordered Society'*, p. 418.

88 Nietzsche, *GSt.* in *KSA* I, pp. 764–77, p. 770.

89 Nietzsche, *KSA* VI, pp. 136–9; tr. *TI*, 'Expeditions of an Untimely Man', section 37.

90 Nietzsche, *KSA* VI, p. 251; tr. *AC*, section 61.

91 Nietzsche, *KSA* III, p. 146; tr. *D*, section 163.

92 Nietzsche, *KSA* XII, 9 [185], p. 449; tr. *WP*, 123. A major influence on Nietzsche at this time in his thinking on the problem of civilization and the way he construes it in terms of an opposition between the spirit of Voltaire and that of Rousseau was Ferdinand Brunetière's *Études critiques sur l'histoire de la litterature Françoise* of 1887. See E. Kuhn, 'Cultur, Civilisation. Die Zweideutigkeit des "Modernen"', *Nietzsche-Studien*, 18 (1989), pp. 600–27.

93 *KSA* XII, 9 [35], pp. 350–1; tr. *WP*, section 22.
94 *Ibid.*, 10 [23], pp. 468–9; tr. *WP*, section 110.
95 *Ibid.*, 5 [71], pp. 211–12; tr. *WP*, section 5.
96 *Ibid.*, 10 [192], p. 571; tr. section 6.
97 Nietzsche, *KSA* VI, p. 373; tr. *EH*, 'Why I am a destiny', section 7.
98 Nietzsche, *KSA* XII, 5 [71], pp. 214–15; tr. *WP*, section 55.
99 Nietzsche, *KSA* XI, 25 [178], pp. 161–2; tr. *WP*, section 94.
100 Nietzsche *KSA* XII, 9 [178], p. 440; tr. *WP*, section 95.
101 *Ibid.*, 9 [184], pp. 447–9; tr. section 100.
102 *Ibid.*, 10 [53], pp. 482–4; tr. section 120.
103 *Ibid.*, 9 [146], p. 421; tr. section 98.
104 See V. Gerrantana, 'The Citizen of Geneva and the Seigneur of Ferney', *New Left Review*, 111 (September–October 1978), pp. 66–77, p. 68.
105 Nietzsche, *KSA* XIII, 14 [75], pp. 225–6; *WP*, section 40.
106 *Ibid.*, 12, 10 [22], p. 468; tr. section 112.
107 *Ibid.*, 9 [142], p. 416; section 121.
108 *Ibid.*, 9 [125], p. 409; tr. section 99.
109 P. Heller, 'Nietzsche in his relation to Voltaire and Rousseau', in J. C. O'Flaherty (ed.), *Nietzsche and the Classical Tradition*, North Carolina, Chapel Hill, 1976, pp. 51–88, p. 59.
110 Nietzsche, *KSA* XII, 9 [184], pp. 447–9; tr. *WP*, section 100.
111 *Ibid.*, 9 [125], p. 409; tr. section 99.
112 Nietzsche, *KSA* V, p. 169; tr. *BGE*, section 230.
113 *Ibid.*, pp. 21–2; tr. section 9.
114 Nietzsche, *KSA* III, pp. 468–9; tr. *GS*, section 109.
115 Nietzsche, *KSA* XI, 27 [60], p. 289; tr. *WP*, section 983.
116 *Ibid.*, 12, 10 [5], pp. 456–7; tr. section 1017.
117 P. Heller, 'Nietzsche in his relation to Voltaire and Rousseau', p. 68.
118 See Rousseau, *SC* III, IV and V on the merits and demerits of aristocracy and democracy.
119 On Rousseau's influence on the French Revolution see I. Fetscher, *Rousseaus politische Philosophie. Zur Geschichte des demokratischen Freiheits-begriffs*, Frankfurt, Suhrkamp, 1975, pp. 258–307; J. Miller, *Rousseau. Dreamer of Democracy*, New Haven, Yale University Press, 1984, pp. 132–65.
120 See Rousseau, *SC* II, XII.
121 See section 221 of *WS* for Nietzsche's pitting of the spirit of the 'Enlightenment' against that of 'revolution'.
122 See T. M. Kavanagh, *Writing the Truth. Authority and Desire in Rousseau*, Berkeley, University of California Press, 1987, p. 143.
123 See, for example, Rousseau *OC* IV, p. 249; tr. *E*, p. 8: 'A Spartan mother had five sons with the army. A Helot arrived; trembling she asked his news: "Your five sons are slain.". "Vile slave, was that what I asked you? We have won the victory." She hastened to the temple to render thanks to the gods. That was a citizen'.
124 Kaufmann, *Nietzsche*, p. 418.

2. CIVILIZATION AND ITS DISCONTENTS:
ROUSSEAU ON MAN'S NATURAL GOODNESS

1 See B. Yack, *The Longing for Total Revolution. Philosophic Sources of Discontent from Rousseau to Marx and Nietzsche*, New Jersey, Princeton University Press, 1986, especially ch. 3.

2 For a useful account of the conflicting interpretations of Rousseau's political thought see J. Merquior, *Rousseau and Weber. Two Studies in the Theory of Legitimacy*, London, Routledge, 1980, pp. 35–56.

3 I appreciate that some readers will find the description of Hobbes as an early liberal somewhat odd. However, here I am simply following a fairly well-established tradition of commentary which includes such diverse thinkers as Leo Strauss, Sheldon Wolin, and Richard Tuck. In his study, *Hobbes*, Oxford, Oxford University Press, 1989, pp. 72–3, Tuck argues that if liberalism can be regarded as the political doctrine which considers rights, as distinguished from duties, to be the most important fact of political life, and which views the prime function of the State to be the protection of these rights, then Hobbes can justifiably be described as the founder of liberalism.

4 At the conclusion of the work Rousseau identifies himself as neither a philosopher nor a wise man, but as a simple 'common man' who does not seek glory but obscurity, who need not build his happiness on the opinion of others but can find it solely within himself, and who will not instruct mankind in the discharge of its duties but confine himself to discharging his own. And yet we know that Rousseau's self-portrait is a disingenuous one, for was not the essay written in order to win a prize to be awarded on the basis of the informed opinions of certain academicians? Rousseau's art is a subtle one. His discourse sets out to show that the sciences are responsible for the corruption of culture before one of Europe's most learned societies, and to praise the virtue of ignorance to a famous academy and reconcile contempt for study with respect for the learned. The effect of Rousseau's method is quite remarkable, for it makes the only valid criterion of the truthfulness of his work to be a moral one. Thus, the academicians are invited to judge the value of their own scholarly pursuits in terms of the standards of virtue which Rousseau defends. Who could deny the power of Rousseau's insight that in the study of virtue itself, that 'sublime science of simple souls', we discover its principles 'are graven on every heart'? In other words, Rousseau is asking the academicians to examine their own hearts, provided they have one. See Rousseau, *OC* III, p. 30, tr. *DAS*, p. 26. For further discussion see R. D. Masters, *The Political Philosophy of Rousseau*, New Jersey, Princeton University Press, 1968, pp. 209–12.

5 Rousseau, *OC* III, p. 133; tr. *DI*, p. 46. Rousseau's distinction between philosophic readers and vulgar ones informs his use of footnotes and the audience they are aimed at, namely his philosophic readers. Vulgar readers have neither the time nor the patience for labouring over footnotes (vulgar readers of this book will obviously miss this point). See

his '*Advertissement*' in Notes on *OC* III, p. 128 (not included in the Cole translation which I guess is appropriate given that it is an edition intended for *every* man).

6 Rousseau, *OC* III, p. 123; tr. *DI*, p. 39.

7 *Ibid.*, p. 123; tr. p. 38.

8 Rousseau simplifies Hobbes's argument here, for Hobbes recognizes that 'wickedness' is a moral term which only has a settled meaning in a social context in which there is a sovereign to fix the conventions of right and wrong, good and bad, and so on. See Hobbes, *Leviathan* (1651), Middlesex, Penguin, 1981, ch. 13: 'The Desires, and other Passions, are in themselves no Sin. No more are the Actions that proceed from those Passions 'til they know a law that forbids them'. Rousseau's point seems to be that in Hobbes's depiction of the state of nature human beings wilfully inflict unnecessary (superfluous we might say) pain and suffering on others.

9 M. F. Plattner in his study, *Rousseau's State of Nature*, DeKalb, Northern Illinois University Press, 1979, develops an account of the state of nature in Rousseau's works in terms of an actual historical state, with the result that the notion is deprived of its philosophical import and ambiguous status.

10 Rousseau, *OC* III, p. 133; tr. *DI*, p. 45.

11 See Nietzsche, *KSA* v, p. 317; tr. *OGM* II, section 13: 'all concepts in which an entire process is semiotically concentrated elude definition; only that which has no history is definable'.

12 Rousseau, *OC* III, p. 132; tr. *DI*, pp. 44–5.

13 On this point see J. C. Hall, *Rousseau. An Introduction to his Political Philosophy*, London, Macmillan, 1973, p. 29.

14 Hobbes, *Leviathan* ch. 13.

15 *Ibid.*, ch. 14.

16 G. H. Sabine and T. L. Thorson, (eds.), *A History of Political Theory*, Illinois, Dryden Press, 1973 (fourth edition), p. 431.

17 See I. Kant, *Groundwork of the Metaphysic of Morals*, tr. H. J. Paton, New York, Harper and Row, 1964, pp. 69–71, and pp. 108–113.

18 Indeed, as Benjamin Constant was one of the first to point out, Rousseau's theory of sovereignty is structurally the same as Hobbes's, with the 'only' difference being that Hobbes assigns undivided power to an individual sovereign (a prince), whereas Rousseau places it in the hands of a collective sovereign (the people). See Merquior, *Rousseau and Weber*, pp. 28–9.

19 Wolin, *Politics and Vision*, Boston, Little Brown and Co, 1960, p. 264.

20 The classical source of the debate on the status of natural law in Rousseau is R. Derathé's, *Jean-Jacques Rousseau et la Science Politique de son Temps* (originally published 1950), Paris, 1979, pp. 132–48.

21 See L. Strauss, *Natural Right and History*, Chicago, Chicago University Press, 1953, pp. 266–70.

22 Rousseau, *OC* III, pp. 152–3; tr. DI, pp. 65–6.

23 Strauss, *Natural Right and History*, p. 271.
24 Rousseau, *OC* III, p. 125; tr. *DI*, p. 41.
25 *Ibid.*
26 *Ibid.*, p. 219; tr. p. 66.
27 See A. Horowitz, *Rousseau, Nature, and History*, Toronto, Toronto University Press, 1987, pp. 94–5 and p. 110. Nietzsche gives a good account of the nature of vanity in section 89 of *Human, All Too Human* and shows precisely where a distinction between temperate *amour-propre* and excessive *amour-propre* is to be made. He argues that only where the good opinion of others is important to someone apart from advantage or the desire to give pleasure do we speak of vanity. It is the 'mighty habituation to authority', which is 'as old as mankind itself', that impels a human being to depend on an external authority for their belief in themselves. Through the opinion of others we seek to confirm the opinions we have formed about ourselves. The vain person gives pleasure to itself in this regard, however, at the expense of others, either by seducing those others to a false opinion of itself, or by aiming at a good opinion that is painful to others by, for example, arousing envy.
28 Nietzsche, *KSA* V, pp. 50–1; tr. *BGE*, section 32.
29 Rousseau *OC* III, pp. 219–20; tr. *DI*, p. 66.
30 Rousseau *OC* III, p. 156; tr. *DI*, p. 68.
31 *Ibid.*, p. 156; tr. p. 69.
32 Even if a similarity between the two is recognized on this point, it remains the case that Nietzsche regards phenomena such as cruelty and revenge to be as essential and as formative to the development of the human animal as those of pity or compassion.
33 Rousseau, *OC* IV, pp. 503–4; tr. *E*, p. 182.
34 *Ibid.*, pp. 505–6; tr. p. 184.
35 See Masters, *The Political Philosophy of J. J. Rousseau*, p. 48.
36 N. J. H. Dent offers a good defence of Rousseau's account of pity in his study, *Rousseau. An Introduction to his Psychological, Social and Political Theory*, Oxford, Basil Blackwell, 1988. See especially pp. 75–6, p. 97, pp. 119–122.
37 See J. Locke, *Two Treatises of Government* ed. P. Laslett, Cambridge, Cambridge University Press, 1988.
   Except in the preface to the second discourse, the notion of conscience is not discussed at all in either the *Discourse on Inequality* or the *Social Contract*. In *Émile* the notion plays an important role and serves to support the major argument on which Rousseau's political theory is based, that man is naturally good. For an account which argues that conscience is not a suprahistorical source of value in Rousseau see Horowitz, *Rousseau, Nature, and History*, pp. 43–6, pp. 139–46.
38 The account provided here draws on that given by L. Colletti in his essay 'Rousseau as Critic of "Civil Society"', in his *From Rousseau to Lenin*, tr. J. Merrington, London and New York, New Left Books, 1972, pp. 152–3.
39 Rousseau, *OC* III, p. 171; tr. *DI*, p. 83.

40 *Ibid.*, pp. 176–8; tr. pp. 87–9.
41 *Ibid.*, pp. 179–80; tr. p. 91.
42 *Ibid.*, p. 192; tr. p. 104.
43 See J. Charvet, *The Social Problem in the Philosophy of Rousseau*, Cambridge, Cambridge University Press, 1974, pp. 2–3, p. 26. For insight into this question see also A. Skillen, 'Rousseau and the Fall of Social Man', *Philosophy*, 60 (1985), pp. 105–21.
44 Rousseau, *QC* III, pp. 169–70; tr. *DI*, pp. 81–2.
45 Rousseau, *OC* IV, p. 493; tr. *E*, p. 175.
46 See Dent, *Rousseau*, pp. 21–4, pp. 55–6. Colletti, *From Rousseau to Lenin*, p. 164, suggests that Rousseau's thought is susceptible to a double reading, to a reading which argues that he desires a return to pre-social man and to one which argues that his main concern is with defining a legitimate society, because he confuses a critique of specific social relationships (civil society conceived as market capitalism) with a critique of social relationships *per se*, and thus a critique of a specific form of society becomes a critique of society in general.
47 Rousseau, *OC* III, p. 175; tr. *DI*, p. 87.
48 *Ibid.*, p. 193; tr. p. 105.
49 *Ibid.*, pp. 193–4; tr. p. 105.
50 *Ibid.*, p. 207; tr. p. 112.
51 Horowitz, *Rousseau, Nature, and History*, p. 165.
52 See Masters, *The Political Philosophy of Rousseau*, p. 11. This paradoxical education of Emile is echoed by Marx in his early conception of the revolutionary role of the proletariat conceived in terms of a class of civil society that is also not of civil society. See K. Marx, *Early Writings*, tr. R. Livingstone, Middlesex, Penguin, 1975, pp. 256–7.
53 Horowitz, *Rousseau, Nature, and History*, p. 240.
54 Masters, *The Political Philosophy of Rousseau*, pp. 154–55.
55 On the unity of politics and ethics see Rousseau, *OC* IV, p. 524; tr. *E*, p. 197: 'Society must be studied in the individual and the individual in society; those who wish to treat politics and morals separately will never understand either'. Translation slightly modified.
56 Horowitz, *Rousseau, Nature, and History*, p. 36.
57 *Ibid.*, p. 46.
58 *Ibid.*, pp. 31–2.

3. SQUARING THE CIRCLE: ROUSSEAU ON THE GENERAL WILL

1 Rousseau, *SC*, book I, chapter I.
2 On this point see Ronald Grimsley's Introduction to the edition of *Du Contrat Social* published by Oxford University Press, 1972, p. 15. For an account of the different versions of the *Social Contract* see J. C. Hall, *Rousseau. An Introduction to his Political Philosophy*, London, Macmillan, 1973, pp. 56–61.

3 Rousseau, *SC* I, I.

4 As R. D. Masters notes in his *The Political Philosophy of Rousseau*, New Jersey, Princeton University Press, 1968, p. 322, Rousseau's principle of legitimacy is enforced by an unlimited right of revolution. Rousseau's anarchism manifests itself in that he makes the individual the arbiter of society's obligation towards him or her. Thus, the individual's surrender of natural liberty is not an unconditional one but rather takes the form of a deposit with the community to be resumed once the remainder of the moral-collective body commits the slightest abuse of power. On this point see K. F. Roche, *Rousseau, Stoic and Romantic*, London, Methuen, 1974, p. 65. No doubt it was this kind of observation which determined Hegel's belief that Rousseau's thought on the principles of political right made political society impossible for as soon as it is established it will be easily destroyed.

5 *SC* I, IV.

6 *Ibid.*

7 *Ibid.*

8 For a good account of these points see A. Horowitz, *Rousseau, Nature, and History*, Toronto, Toronto University Press, 1987, pp. 183–93.

9 See Rousseau, *OC* III, pp. 281–9, tr. Cole, in *The Social Contract and Discourses*, London, Dent, 1973, pp. 155–62.

10 *OC* III, pp. 288–89; tr. *GSHR*, pp. 161–2.

11 *Ibid.*

12 *Ibid.*

13 *SC* I.

14 M. Viroli, *Rousseau and the ' Well-Ordered Society'*, Cambridge, Cambridge University Press, 1988, p. 119.

15 *Ibid.*, p. 124.

16 *Ibid.*, p. 128.

17 *Ibid.*, p. 9.

18 Rousseau, *SC* I, VII.

19 A classic study of the roots of modern totalitarianism is J. L. Talmon's *The Origins of Totalitarian Democracy*, London, Secker and Warburg, 1952. See also Hegel's critique of the notion of the general will in his *Phenomenology of Spirit*, tr. A. V. Miller, Oxford, Oxford University Press, 1977, in the section entitled 'Absolute Freedom and Terror', pp. 355–64.

20 Rousseau, *SC* II, I.

21 See Grimsley, Introduction to *Du Contrat social*, p. 23. Whereas in English and German power/*Macht* denotes both the *capacity* to do something and the actual *exercise* of this capacity, in French power is denoted by two different words, *puissance* (capacity, potential) and *pouvoir* (act, exercise).

22 Rousseau, *SC* II, IV.

23 *Ibid.*

24 *Ibid.*, II, II.

25 On this point see Rousseau's letter to Mirabeau – the father of the one who was to become prominent in the French Revolution – in J. Hope Mason, *The Indispensable Rousseau*, London, Quartet Books, 1979, pp. 276–80, p. 280: 'I do not see any tolerable compromise between the most austere democracy and the most perfect Hobbesism'.

26 Rousseau, *OC* III, p. 252; tr. *DPE*, pp. 127–8.

27 Rousseau, *SC* II, III.

28 See footnote 1 to *SC* II, III.

29 *Ibid.*, 11, IV.

30 *Ibid.*

31 See J. N. Shklar, *Men and Citizens. A Study of Rousseau's Social Theory*, Cambridge, Cambridge University Press, 1969, p. 204.

32 See Viroli, *Rousseau and the 'Well-Ordered Society'*, pp. 4–5.

33 Rousseau *SC* I, VII.

34 See Nietzsche, *BGE*, section 32. For Nietzsche on the morality of custom see *HAH*, sections 95, 97, 99, and *D* sections 9, 14, 16, 18.

35 See Rousseau, *OGM* II, section 2.

36 Rousseau, *SC* I, VIII.

37 See F. M. Barnard, 'Will and Political Rationality in Rousseau', in J. Lively and A. Reeve (eds.), *Modern Political Theory from Hobbes to Marx*, London, Routledge, 1989, p. 136.

38 See J. Merquior, *Rousseau and Weber. Two studies in the Theory of Legitimacy*, London, Routledge and Kegan Paul, 1980, p. 62 and his conclusion.

39 Shklar, *Men and Citizens*, p. 184.

40 In making such a distinction I have been inspired in part by Agnes Heller's distinction between a static conception of justice and a dynamic one in her book *Beyond Justice*, Oxford, Basil Blackwell, 1989.

41 See Merquior, *Rousseau and Weber*, pp. 60–1.

42 See Rousseau, *SC* IV, II.
   To be fair, Rousseau's argument does not amount to a straightforward majoritiaranism. In the same section he makes the stipulation that if the majority is to articulate the general will then this presupposes that 'all the qualities of the general will still reside in the majority: when they cease to do so, whatever side a man may take, liberty is no longer possible'. The question which immediately arises from this qualification, however, is: who is to decide whether or not all the qualities of the general will do indeed reside in the majority?

43 See Nietzsche, section 38 of 'Expeditions of an Untimely Man' entitled 'My conception of freedom' in *Twilight of the Idols*.

44 See Nietzsche, *GS*, section 335.

45 Viroli, *Rousseau and the 'Well-Ordered Society'*, p. 129.

46 See W. E. Connolly, *Political Theory and Modernity*, Oxford, Basil Blackwell, 1988, p. 60.

47 *Ibid.*

48 *Ibid.*, p. 251; tr. p. 127.

49 Rousseau, *SC* II, VI.

50 *Ibid.*

51 *Ibid.*

52 Rousseau has in mind figures such as Moses, Solon of Athens, the legendary Lycurgus of Sparta, and Numa of Rome. See Rousseau, *OC* III, p. 956; tr. *The Government of Poland*, tr. W. Kendall, Indianapolis, Hackett Publishing Co., 1985, pp. 5–6.

53 Viroli, *Rousseau and the 'Well-Ordered Society'*, p. 189.

54 Rousseau *SC* II, VII.

55 *Ibid.*

56 *Ibid.*

57 *Ibid.* See Machiavelli, *Discourses*, I, II, tr. L. J. Walker, Middlesex, Penguin, 1983.

58 See Nietzsche 'The "Improvers" of Mankind', section 5 in *Twilight of the Idols*.

59 See Nietzsche *KSA* II, pp. 95–6; tr. *HAH*, section 99: 'Morality is preceded by *compulsion*, indeed it is for a time still compulsion...Later it becomes custom, later still voluntary obedience, finally almost instinct: then, like everything that has for a long time been habitual and natural, it is associated with pleasure – and is now called *virtue*'.

60 See J. Starobinski, *Jean-Jacques Rousseau. Transparency and Obstruction*, tr. A. Goldhammer, Chicago, Chicago University Press, 1988, p. 30.

61 Horowitz, *Rousseau, Nature, and History*, p. 166.

62 *Ibid.*, p. 168.

63 See Marx, 'Theses on Feuerbach' number III in K. Marx and F. Engels, *The German Ideology*, ed. C. J. Arthur, London, Lawrence and Wishart, 1977. Compare, Nietzsche, *KSA* VI, pp. 107–8; tr. *TI*, 'What the Germans Lack', section 5.

64 This is the view taken by Lionel Gossman in his essay 'Time and History in Rousseau', *Studies in Voltaire and the Eighteenth Century*, 30 (1964), pp. 311–49, p. 344.

65 Horowitz, *Rousseau, Nature, and History*, p. 45, note 13, argues that the impasse is largely a personal one which does not necessarily coincide with a theoretical one.

66 See L. Strauss, *Natural Right and History*, Chicago, Chicago University Press, 1953, p. 264.

4. NIETZSCHE'S DIONYSIAN DRAMA ON THE DESTINY OF THE SOUL

1 Nietzsche, *KSA* V, p. 410; tr. *OGM*, III, section 27. The reader should be aware that Nietzsche uses the expressions '*Selbstaufhebung*' and '*Selbstüberwindung*' interchangeably when speaking of the law of self-overcoming. There is thus a tension in Nietzsche's conception between the 'sublation' (*Aufhebung*) and 'preservation' of morality and its 'conquest' and 'destruction' (*Überwindung*).

2 See Y. Yovel, 'Nietzsche and Spinoza: *amor fati* and *amor dei*', in Y. Yovel (ed.), *Nietzsche as Affirmative Thinker*, Dordrecht, Martinus Nijhoff, 1986, pp. 183–204, p. 189.

3 For Nietzsche on the idea of a 'philosophy of right' (*Philosophie des Rechts*) see *KSA* x (*Nachlass* 1882–4), 8 [13], p. 334 and *KSA* xi (*Nachlass* 1884–5), 42 [8], p. 697. For Nietzsche on the 'natural bellum omnium contra omnes' see *GSt* in *KSA* i, pp. 764–77, p. 772. For Nietzsche's justification of society in terms of producing 'a choice type of being', see *KSA* v, pp. 206–7; tr. *BGE*, section 258.

4 Nietzsche *KSA* iii, p. 12; tr. *D*, preface 3.

5 On the paradoxes of Nietzsche's 'immoral', 'extra-moral' and 'amoral' critique of morality see, V. Gerhardt, 'Die Moral des Immoralismus. Nietzsches Beitrag zu einer Grundlegung der Ethik', in Günter Abel and Jorg Salquarda (eds.), *Krisis der Metaphysik*, Berlin and New York, Walter de Gruyter, 1989, pp. 417–47.

6 Nietzsche *KSA* xii, 5 [58], p. 206; tr. *WP*, section 404.

7 Nietzsche, *KSA* vi, p. 367; tr. *EH*, 'Why I am a destiny', section 3.

8 Nietzsche, *KSA* iii, p. 579; tr. *GS*, section 345. Compare *BGE*, section 11.

9 Nietzsche *KSA* ii, pp. 103–6; tr. *HAH*, section 107.

10 *Ibid.*

11 *Ibid.*, p. 75; tr. section 56.

12 Nietzsche, *KSA* xii, 9 [13], p. 344; tr. *WP*, section 706.

13 *Ibid.*, xiii, 11 [72], pp. 35–6; tr. section 708.

14 *Ibid.*

15 *Ibid.*, 11, 25 [484], p. 141.
For an instructive reading of the importance of this conception of justice in Nietzsche's work see M. Heidegger, *Nietzsche. Volume Three. The Will to Power as Knowledge and as Metaphysics*, tr. J. Stambaugh, D. F. Krell, and F. A. Capuzzi, San Francisco, Harper and Row, 1987, pp. 137–50 and pp. 235–55. Heidegger's reading is an idiosyncratic one in that he argues (p. 141) that the notion of justice in Nietzsche operates neither simply as a legal, nor simply as a moral, one, but as the 'metaphysical name for the *essence* of truth.' Clearly, Nietzsche's notion of justice is 'metaphysical' in the sense in which Heidegger claims, but it is also of great significance for appreciating that Nietzsche explicitly seeks a notion of legality and of morals which transcends the narrow horizon of bourgeois right.

16 *Ibid.*, 11, 26 [425], pp. 264–5. See J. Stevens, 'Nietzsche and Heidegger on Truth and Justice ', *Nietzsche-Studien*, 9 (1980), pp. 224–39, p. 232.

17 Nietzsche, *KSA* xi, 26 [149], p. 188.

18 See Nietzsche, *KSA* xiii, 14 [121], p. 301, tr. *WP*, section 688: 'Spinoza's law of "self-preservation" ought really to put a stop to change: but this law is false, the opposite is true. It can be shown that every living thing does everything it can not to preserve itself but to become *more*.'

19 *Ibid.*, 14 [79], p. 259; tr. *WP*, section 635: 'The will to power not a being, not a becoming, but a *pathos* – the most elemental fact from which a becoming and effecting first emerge.'
20 Nietzsche, *KSA* v, pp. 315–16; tr. *OGM* II, section 12.
21 *Ibid.*, pp. 33–4; tr. *BGE*, section 19.
22 *Ibid.*
23 Nietzsche, *KSA* II, pp. 99–100; tr. *HAH*, section 107.
24 Kaufmann's reason for preferring the title 'On the' over that of 'Towards the Genealogy of Morals' – that in no other title does Nietzsche deploy *Zur* or *Zum* to mean 'toward' – is not very persuasive. See his Introduction to his co-translation of *OGM*, pp. 4–5.
25 By 'English psychologists' it is fairly certain that Nietzsche has in mind thinkers like Hobbes, Locke, Hume, Bentham, Mill, Shaftesbury, and Spencer. D. S. Thatcher has suggested that Nietzsche may be referring to W. E. H. Lecky's *History of European Morals* of 1869, which mentions the writers listed above in the first chapter and which Nietzsche read in a hostile spirit. See D. S. Thatcher, 'Zur Genealogie der Moral: Some Textual Annotations', *Nietzsche-Studien*, 18 (1989), pp. 587–600, p. 588. For some useful background information on the text see C. P. Janz, *Friedrich Nietzsche, Biographie*, Carl Hanser Verlag, München, 1978, vol. II, pp. 541–52, and for useful information on sources see the editors' commentary to volumes I–XIII of the *Kritische Studienausgabe* in *KSA* xiv, pp. 377–82.
26 Thatcher believes that either 'Toward the Genealogy of Morals' or 'The Genealogy of Morals: A Contribution' expresses more faithfully Nietzsche's intentions than 'On the Genealogy of Morals'. See his essay 'Zur Genealogie der Moral', pp. 598–99. I myself, however, prefer the 'innocence' of 'On the...', which should be read as denoting both a contribution to an existing subject *and* an attempt to redefine that subject.
27 See Nietzsche, *KSA* v, pp. 288–9; tr. *OGM*, pp. 55–6.
28 Nietzsche, *KSA* vi, pp. 350–1; tr. *EH*, 'Beyond Good and Evil'.
29 This is the mistake made, in my opinion, by Howard Caygill in his essay, 'Affirmation and Eternal Return in the Free-Spirit Trilogy' in K. Ansell-Pearson (ed.), *Nietzsche and Modern German Thought*, London, Routledge, 1991. Caygill's essay is an original attempt to try and show that the doctrine of eternal return entails an abandonment or suspension of that of the will to power in Nietzsche's thought. The 'authentic' Nietzsche thus lies in the 'yea' of eternal return (1880–2 and *Zarathustra*) and not in the 'nay' of the will to power (*Beyond Good and Evil* and after). A similar argument can be found in H. Arendt, *The Life of the Mind. Volume Two: Willing*, London, Secker and Warburg, 1978.
30 Nietzsche, *KSA* v, pp. 248–9; tr. *OGM*, preface, section 2.
31 Nietzsche, *KSA* vi, p. 368; tr. *EH*, 'Why I am a destiny', section 4.
32 Nietzsche, *KSA* v, pp. 254–5; tr. *OGM*, preface, section 7.
33 *Ibid.*, pp. 255–6; tr. preface, section 8.

34 *Ibid.*, pp. 254–5; tr. preface, section 7. See *GS*, section 1, for Nietzsche on 'the comedy of existence' in which he envisages the coming together of wisdom and laughter to form a new 'gay science'.

35 Nietzsche's *Nachlass* of the Autumn of 1887 contains a plan for a second polemic which would consist of a further three essays and culminate by reflecting on the significance of the '*Eintritt in das tragische Zeitalter von Europa*'. See Nietzsche, *KSA* XII (*Nachlass* 1885–7), 9 [83], pp. 377–8.

36 Nietzsche, *KSA* V, pp. 124–5; tr. *BGE*, section 202.

37 Nietzsche, *KSA* V, pp. 105–7; tr. *BGE*, section 186.

38 *Ibid.*, p. 253; tr. *OGM*, preface, section 6.

39 Nietzsche, *KSA* VI, pp. 352–3; tr. *EH*, 'On the Genealogy of Morals'.

40 Nietzsche, *KSA* V, pp. 249–50; tr. *OGM*, preface, section 3.

41 Nietzsche, *KSA* III, pp. 140; tr. *D*, section 148.

42 G. Deleuze, *Nietzsche and Philosophy*, tr. H. Tomlinson, London, Athlone Press, 1983, p. 166.

43 J. Habermas, 'The Entwinement of Myth and Enlightenment: Re-reading *Dialectic of Enlightenment*', *New German Critique*, 26 (1983), pp. 13–30, p. 27.

44 M. Foucault, 'Nietzsche, Genealogy, and History' in Foucault, *Language, Counter-Memory, and Practice*, tr. D. F. Bouchard and S. Simon, Oxford, Basil Blackwell, 1977, p. 142.

45 Nietzsche, *KSA* V, pp. 313–15; tr. *OGM* II, section 12.

46 On this point see D. C. Hoy's essay, 'Nietzsche, Hume, and the Genealogical Method' in Y. Yovel (ed.), *Nietzsche as Affirmative Thinker*, Dordrecht, Martinus Nijhoff, 1986, pp. 20–39.

47 Nietzsche, *KSA* XII, 2 [189–90], pp. 160–1; tr. *WP*, section 254.

48 On the question of the relativistic nature of Nietzsche's genealogical project see Hoy, 'Nietzsche, Hume, and the Genealogical Method', pp. 33–6. For an affirmation of the relativism of that project see S. Kemal, 'Some Problems of Genealogy', *Nietzsche-Studien*, 19 (1990), pp. 30–43.

49 See J. Pizer's highly informative essay, 'The Use and Abuse of "Ursprung": On Foucault's Reading of Nietzsche', *Nietzsche-Studien*, 19 (1990), pp. 462–78, p. 469.

50 *Ibid.*, p. 473.

51 It might be useful to readers if I identify all the references to 'origin' in the text (as far as I have been able to detect them), especially as Kaufmann translates *Ursprung*, *Herkunft*, and *Entstehung* all as 'origin' throughout his translation of the text.
Preface, section 2: '*Herkunft* of moral prejudices'.
Preface, section 3: '*Ursprung* of good and evil'.
Preface, section 5: '*Ursprung* of morality'.
I, section 1: '*Entstehungsgeschichte der Moral*'.
I, section 2: '*Herkunft* of the concept of good'.
'*Ursprung* of good'.
'*Ursprung* of the opposition "good" and "bad"'.
I, section 3: '*Herkunft* of good'.

i, section 4:	'all questions of *Herkunft*'.
i, section 13:	'*Ursprung* of good'.
ii, section 2:	'*Herkunft* of responsibility'.
ii, section 4:	'*Herkunft* of guilt'.
ii, section 6:	'*Entstehung* of the moral-conceptual world'.
ii, section 8:	'*Ursprung* of the feeling of personal obligation'.
ii, section 11:	'*Ursprung* of justice'.
ii, section 12:	'*Ursprung* of punishment'.

This section is without doubt the most crucial one in the whole book for understanding the nature of Nietzsche's genealogical inquiry into the origin of morals. Nietzsche makes an important distinction not only between '*Ursprung*' and '*Zweck*', but an equally important one between the inquiry into the *Ursprung* of something and an *Entstehungsgeschichte*. The latter, he argues, is ahistorical in that it confuses the evolution of something into a purpose with its origin. It thus lacks a genuine historical sense.

ii, section 16: '*Ursprung* of the bad conscience' (appears twice).
ii, section 17: the same.
ii, section 18: '*Herkunft* of the moral value of the "unegoistic"'.
ii, section 23: '*Herkunft* of the "holy God"'.
iii, section 4: '*Herkunft* of a work'.

52 See J. Minson, *Genealogies of Morals, Nietzsche, Deleuze, Foucault, and the Eccentricity of Ethics*, New York, St Martin's Press, 1985, p. 77.

53 On this point see Gary Shapiro's essay 'Nietzsche *contra* Renan', *History and Theory*, 21 (May 1982), pp. 193–222, p. 203.

54 Nietzsche, *KSA* iii, pp. 349–50; tr. *GS* preface (to the second edition), section 3.

55 *Ibid.*, pp. 351–2; tr. preface, section 4.

56 *Ibid.*, p. 352. Baubo, according to Walter Kaufmann's footnote on this section in his translation, represents in Greek mythology a primitive female demon who was originally depicted as the personification of the female genitals.

57 An instructive account of the use and abuse of metaphor in Nietzsche can be found in P. Cantor, 'Friedrich Nietzsche: the Use and Abuse of Metaphor', in D. S. Miall (ed.), *Metaphor, Problems and Perspectives*, Brighton, Harvester Press, 1982, pp. 71–89.

58 Nietzsche, *KSA* v, pp. 258–9; tr. *OGM* i, section 2.

59 Nietzsche, *KSA* iii, pp. 373–4; tr. *GS*, section 2.

60 Nietzsche, *KSA* v, p. 259; tr. *OGM* i, section 2.

61 *Ibid.*, pp. 261–2; tr. i, section 4.

62 *Ibid.*, pp. 262–3; tr. i, section 5.

63 For recent scholarship on Nietzsche on the Jewish question see J. Golomb, 'Nietzsche's Judaism of Power', *Revue des études juives*, 148 (July–December, 1988), pp. 353–85, and M. F. Duffy and W. Mittelman, 'Nietzsche's Attitude Toward the Jews', *Journal of the History of Ideas*, 49:2, (April–June 1988), pp. 301–17.

64 Nietzsche, *KSA* v, p. 267; tr. *OGM* I, section 7.

65 *Ibid.*, pp. 270–1; tr. I, section 10.

66 *Ibid.*, p. 273.

67 *Ibid.*

68 *Ibid.*, p. 276; tr. I, section 11.

69 *Ibid.*, pp. 269–70; tr. I, section 9.

70 *Ibid.*, p. 210; tr. *BGE*, section 260.

71 *Ibid.*, p. 212.

72 Nietzsche, *KSA* v, pp. 279–80; tr. *OGM* I, section 13.

73 *Ibid.*

74 Nietzsche, *KSA* v, p. 269; OGM I, section 8.

75 *Ibid.*, pp. 285–8; tr. I, section 16.

76 *Ibid.*, p. 267; tr. I, section 7.

77 *Ibid.*, pp. 264–5; tr. I, section 6.

78 *Ibid.*, p. 272; tr. I, section 10.

79 *Ibid.*, p. 276–7; tr. I, section 11.

80 Ibid., p. 288; tr. I, section 17.

81 *Ibid.*, pp. 109–10; tr. *BGE*, section 188.

82 See M. Foucault, 'Technologies of the Self', in Luther H. Martin *et al.*, *Technologies of the Self. A Seminar with Michel Foucault*, London, Tavistock, 1988, pp. 16–50.

83 The extent of von Ihering's influence on Nietzsche's legal and political thinking is seriously underestimated by D. S. Thatcher in his essay on 'Zur Genealogie der Moral: Some Textual Annotations', p. 592. By contrast see H. Kerger, *Autorität und Recht im Denken Nietzsches*, Berlin, Duncker and Humblot, 1988.

84 Von Ihering (1818–92) was widely regarded as the most encyclopaedic mind in German law in the nineteenth century. His jurisprudence is a unique mixture of English utilitarianism, classical economic thought, and Kantian moral philosophy. For further insight into von Ihering's jurisprudence see the various Introductions to the English translation of the fourth German edition of the first volume of his *Der Zweck im Recht*, *Law As A Means to An End*, tr. I. Husik, New York, Augustus M. Kelley, 1968. In addition to the areas of influence which I discuss here, von Ihering's book also contains a major analysis of egoism and altruism and of the phenomenon of asceticism or self-denial, as well as placing at the centre of its inquiries 'the problem of the will in the living being' and a 'concept of life' – a great deal of this material would have exerted a major influence on Nietzsche.

85 For Nietzsche's notes on von Ihering see *KSA* x, 7 [69], pp. 265–6.

86 See the excerpt from von Ihering's book in C. Morris (ed.), *The Great Legal Philosophers. Readings in Jurisprudence*, Philadelphia, University of Pennsylvania Press, 1971, pp. 397–418, p. 402.

87 *Ibid.*, p. 405.

88 *Ibid.*, p. 406.

89 *Ibid.* Compare Nietzsche, *HAH*, section 452.

90 *Ibid.*, p. 407
91 *Ibid.*, p. 413
92 *Ibid.*, p. 417.
93 Although I have retained the Kaufmann/Hollingdale translation of this phrase and passage, readers should note that nowhere in sections 1 or 2 (in section 2 it appears five times) of the second essay of the *Genealogy* does Nietzsche deploy the notion of *Recht* ('right'). Instead he uses the modal auxiliary verb *dürfen* as in *man darf versprechen* (literally translated as 'one may – or may be allowed to – make promises'). Thus, it is important to bear in mind that when Nietzsche speaks of this 'right' to make promises – and one could argue that to be allowed to do something is to have a 'right' to do that something – he means a 'right' in the sense of a privilege bestowed upon the individual by society and by his peers, which he bears as his 'mark of distinction'.
94 Nietzsche, *KSA* v, pp. 293–4; tr. *OGM* ii, section 2.
95 For Nietzsche's conception of the individual as a historical product of certain cultural forces compare *KSA* ix (*Nachlass* 1880–2), 11 [287], pp. 551–2.
96 Nietzsche, *KSA* v, pp. 294–5; tr. *OGM* ii, section 3.
97 Nietzsche, *KSA* iii, p. 32; tr. *D*, section 18.
98 *Ibid.*, pp. 21–2; tr. section 9.
99 Nietzsche, *KSA* iii, p. 563; tr. *GS*, section 335.
100 *Ibid.*, pp. 475–6; tr. section 117.
101 Nietzsche, *KSA* v, pp. 293–4; tr. *OGM* ii, section 2.
102 *Ibid.*, p. 294.
103 Nietzsche, *KSA* iii, pp. 384–5; tr. *GS*, section 13.
104 Nietzsche, *KSA* v, p. 300; tr. *OGM* ii, section 6.
105 *Ibid.*, pp. 297–8; tr. ii, section 4.
106 *Ibid.*, pp. 300–1; tr. ii, section 6.
107 *Ibid.*, pp. 165–6; tr. *BGE*, section 229: 'We should reconsider cruelty and open our eyes... Almost everything we call "higher culture" is based on the spiritualization of *cruelty*, on its becoming more profound: this is my proposition. That the "savage animal" has not really been "mortified"; it lives and flourishes, it has merely become – divine'.
108 *Ibid.*, pp. 305–6; tr. *OGM* ii, section 8.
109 *Ibid.*, p. 306.
110 *Ibid.*, pp. 311–12; tr. ii, section 11.
111 *Ibid.*, p. 309; tr. ii, section 10.
112 *Ibid.*, pp. 302–3; tr. ii, section 7.
113 *Ibid.*, pp. 322–3; tr. ii, section 16.
114 *Ibid.*, p. 324; tr. ii, section 17.
115 *Ibid.*, p. 323; tr. ii, section 16.
116 *Ibid.*, pp. 324–7; tr. ii, sections 17 and 18.
117 *Ibid.*, p. 327; tr. ii, section 19.
118 *Ibid.*, pp. 330–1; tr. ii, 21. Compare the account of the death of God given in *GS*, section 125.

119 *Ibid.*, p. 324; tr. ii, section 17.
120 Nietzsche, *KSA* v, pp. 335–6; tr. *OGM* ii, section 24.
121 *Ibid.*, p. 336.
122 Nietzsche, *KSA* v, pp. 408–10; tr. *OGM* iii, section 27.
123 *Ibid.*, p. 409.
124 Michel Haar makes a good point in his essay 'Nietzsche and Metaphysical Language', in D. B. Allison, *The New Nietzsche*, Cambridge, Mass.: MIT Press, 1985, p. 19, when he argues that any genealogy (whether it be of reason, science, metaphysics, etc.) should be viewed in terms of a genealogy of morals 'since the ethical ideal is the archetype and source of every ideal, and especially of truth. Things are true or false only inasmuch as they are good or evil'.
125 Nietzsche, *KSA* v, pp. 410–11; tr. *OGM* iii, section 27.
126 *Ibid.*, pp. 411–12; tr. iii, section 28.
127 It is important to be aware of the multi-faceted nature of the descent or down-going we are about to examine in the figure of Zarathustra. The German *Untergehen* has three meanings, namely, to descend, to set (as in the setting of the sun), and to be destroyed or to go under and perish. *Untergang* should be treated in the same way.

5. ZARATHUSTRA'S DESCENT: ON A TEACHING OF REDEMPTION

1 Nietzsche, *KSA* iii, p. 571; tr. *GS*, section 342.
It is only in recent years that *Thus Spoke Zarathustra* has been subjected to any systematic, scholarly study in the Anglo-Saxon world. The best study to date in my opinion is that by Laurence Lampert entitled *Nietzsche's Teaching*, New Haven, Yale University Press, 1987. See also H. Alderman, *Nietzsche's Gift*, Athens, Ohio University Press, 1977, and K. Higgins, *Nietzsche's Zarathustra*, Philadelphia, Temple University Press, 1987. Three important essays on the text are M. Heidegger, 'Who is Nietzsche's Zarathustra?' tr. B. Magnus, in D. B. Allison (ed.), *The New Nietzsche*, Cambridge, Mass.: MIT Press, 1985, pp. 64–80; D. W. Conway, 'Solving the Problem of Socrates. Nietzsche's *Zarathustra* as Political Irony', *Political Theory*, 16:2 (May 1988), pp. 257–80; and R. B. Pippin, 'Irony and Affirmation in Nietzsche's *Thus Spoke Zarathustra*', in M. A. Gillespie and T. B. Strong (eds.), *Nietzsche's New Seas*, Chicago, Chicago University Press, 1988, pp. 45–71. Important German studies of the text include, W. Resenhofft, *Nietzsches Zarathustra Wahn. Deutung und Dokumentation zur Apokalypse des Übermenschen*, Herbert Lang, Bern, and Peter Lang, Frankfurt am Main, 1972; A. Bennholdt-Thomsen, *Nietzsches 'Also sprach Zarathustra' als Literarisches Phaenomen*, Frankfurt, Atheaneum, 1974; S. F. Oduev, *Auf den Spuren Zarathustras. Der Einfluss Nietzsches auf die bürgerliche deutsche Philosophie*, Köln, 1977 (first published in Russian).
As R. J. Hollingdale points out in his Introduction to the Penguin

edition, the book represents the resolution of a long-sustained intellectual (and emotional) crisis in Nietzsche's life. For useful background information and for information on sources see C. P. Janz, *Friedrich Nietzsche. Biographie*, München, Carl Hanser Verlag, 1978, II, pp. 211–34, and volume XIV of the *Kritische Studienausgabe*, pp. 279–344. Also highly useful is Mazzino Montinari's essay 'Zarathustra vor *Also sprach Zarathustra*' in his collection *Nietzsche lesen*, Berlin and New York, Walter de Gruyter, 1982, pp. 79–92.

2 *Ibid.*, pp. 564–5;. tr. section 337.

3 Nietzsche *KSA* VI, p. 367; tr. *EH*, 'Why I Am A Destiny', section 3. See also a note written in early 1884 on Zarathustra the Persian prophet in *KSA* XI (*Nachlass* 1884–5), 25 [148], p. 53.

4 Nietzsche, *KSA* IX (*Nachlass* 1880–2), 15 [8], p. 636 and 15 [17], p. 642. See also 9, 12 [78–9], p. 590.

5 Nietzsche, *KSA* III, pp. 259–60; tr. *EH*, preface, section 4.

6 Nietzsche, *KSA* III, pp. 369–72 and pp. 635–7; tr. *GS*, sections 1 and 382.

7 Nietzsche, *KSA* IV, pp. 343–5 and pp. 348–9; tr. *EH*, 'Thus Spoke Zarathustra', sections 6 and 8.

8 Nietzsche, *KSA* III, pp. 635–7; tr. *GS*, section 382 (Nietzsche quotes this passage in *EH*, 'Thus Spoke Zarathustra', section 2).

9 Nietzsche, *KSA* VI, pp. 369–70; tr. *EH*, 'Why I am a destiny', section 5. Nietzsche's notion of the *Übermensch* is deliberately intended to be an ambiguous one which is parasitic upon the meaning we give to 'man' (*Mensch*) and on our definition of the human. Depending on its context and on the perspective of the human individual receiving the teaching, it could mean a type that is both 'inhuman' and 'superhuman'. A key passage in this context is from the *Nachlass* of the Autumn of 1887, in which Nietzsche says that man is both '*Unthier* und *Überthier*', that in the higher human type the 'inhuman' (*Unmensch*) and the 'super-human' (*Übermensch*) belong together. Thus, 'with every growth in humanity in terms of the great (*Grösse*) and the high (*Höhe*) there also grows the deep (*Tiefe*) and the terrible (*Furchtbare*)'. See *KSA* XII (*Nachlass* 1885–7), 9 [154], p. 426. The precise meaning of the term *Übermensch* is inseparable from the reader's interpretation of the experience of Zarathustra's *Untergang*.

10 *TSZ* 'Of the Spirit of Gravity', section 2.

11 *Ibid.*
As Pippin points out in his essay 'Irony and Affirmation', pp. 60–1, it would be mistaken to infer from this teaching on the Way that Nietzsche is advocating any simple individualistic relativism.

12 As Nietzsche points out in his autobiography, *EH*, 'Why I am so wise', section 8, his whole *Zarathustra* can be read as 'a dithyramb on solitude'.

13 Nietzsche, *TSZ*, prologue, section 2. The similarities between Nietzsche's fundamental thought of eternal return and Buddhist teaching are quite remarkable. In both teachings we find an

abandonment of the willing ego in which the idea of a unified subject lying behind all action in the world and enduring through changing experiences is recognized to be an illusion, an emphasis on life as flux and becoming, a recognition that the absolute or the ultimate experience is both unnameable and immeasurable, and the affirmation of the transitoriness of life as the mark of its divinity. Nietzsche's teaching also shares with Buddhism the fact that it is not articulated as a moral law enjoined either by God or by nature. For both it is rather a question how one 'learns' to give style to one's character. For further insight see F. Mistry, *Nietzsche and Buddhism*, Berlin and New York, Walter de Gruyter, 1981, pp. 139–66.

14 On this point see the editor's comments in *KSA* xiv, pp. 256–7.

15 The term '*Übermensch*' is by no means original to Nietzsche. He was influenced by a number of sources, including Goethe's Faust and Emerson's notion of the 'Over-Soul'. For further insight see chapter 11 of W. Kaufmann's, *Nietzsche. Philosopher, Psychologist, and Anti-Christ*, New Jersey, Princeton University Press, 1974, and Marie-Luise Haase, 'Der Übermensch in *Also sprach Zarathustra* und im Zarathustra-Nachlass 1882–5', *Nietzsche-Studien*, 13 (1984), pp. 228–45, pp. 240–1.

16 W. Kaufmann, *Nietzsche*, p. 308.

17 Nietzsche, *KSA* vi, p. 300; tr. *EH*, 'Why I write such good books', section 1.

18 Nietzsche, *TSZ*, prologue, section 4.

19 *Ibid.*

20 Bernd Magnus is right to point out that if taken as a model or ideal of perfection, then the *Übermensch* is extraordinarily vague. The notion, he argues, does not denote a specific set of attributes or virtues, but a certain attitude towards life and the world – it is one which can not only endure, but affirm its eternal return. See B. Magnus, 'Perfectibility and Attitude in Nietzsche's *Übermensch*', *Review of Metaphysics*, 36 (March 1983), pp. 633–59.

21 See Haar, 'Nietzsche and Metaphysical Language', pp. 24–8.

22 Pippin, 'Irony and Affirmation', p. 52.

23 Lampert, *Nietzsche's Teaching*, p. 24.

24 See W. Müller-Lauter, *Nietzsche. Seine Philosophie der Gegensätze und die Gegensätze seiner Philosophie*, Berlin and New York, Walter de Gruyter, 1971, pp. 140–1.

25 Heidegger, 'Who is Nietzsche's Zarathustra?', pp. 66–7.

26 Nietzsche, *TSZ*, 'Of the Priests'.

27 *Ibid.*, prologue, section 5.

28 *Ibid.*, section 9.

29 *Ibid.*

30 Nietzsche, *KSA* vi, p. 198; tr. *AC*, section 27.

31 *Ibid.*, pp. 207–8; tr. section 35.

32 Nietzsche, *TSZ*, 'Of the Gift-Giving Virtue', section 3.

33 Nietzsche's use of the phrase the '*Grosser Mittag*' (the great noontide), which also closes the book, refers back to the ancient representation of

midday as the time of supreme revelation (an 'awakening') understood as a moment of stillness.

34 Nietzsche, *TSZ*, 'Of the Gift-Giving Virtue', section 3.

35 *Erlösung* also translates as 'deliverance' or 'salvation'. Daniel Conway has argued that Nietzsche is being merely ironic in offering a teaching of redemption for our desire for salvation is itself characteristic of a nihilistic attitude towards life. See D. W. Conway, 'Overcoming the *Übermensch*: Nietzsche's Revaluation of Values', *Journal of the British Society for Phenomenology*, 20:3, (October 1989), pp. 211–24. A key insight into Nietzsche's thinking on this problem of redemption can be found in a note from the beginning of 1884 in *KSA* 11 25 [290], p. 85. In this note Nietzsche poses the thought of eternal return as 'the great test' and declares that whoever is brought to destruction when faced with the proposition that 'there is no redemption' should 'die out'.

36 See R. Small, 'Eternal Recurrence', *Canadian Journal of Philosophy*, 13:4, (December 1983), pp. 585–605, p. 598.

37 *Ibid.*, p. 599.

38 P. Klossowski, 'Nietzsche's Experience of the Eternal Return', in D. B. Allison, *The New Nietzsche*, Cambridge, Mass.: MIT Press, 1985, pp. 107–20, p. 115.

39 For Nietzsche on the difference between the same (*Gleiche*), and the similar (*Ähnliche*), see *KSA* ix (*Nachlass* 1880–2), 11 [166], p. 505. One of the best accounts of what Nietzsche might mean by speaking of the eternal return of the *same* is that given by Mark Warren in his *Nietzsche and Political Thought* (a study, it has to be noted, in which an examination of the significance of *Thus Spoke Zarathustra* for cultivating an understanding of Nietzsche's political thought is completely absent), Cambridge, Mass.: MIT Press, 1988, pp. 196–203. On p. 201, for example, Warren illuminates its meaning by suggesting that the notion of 'the same' in the thought of eternal return is a quality of experience, and as such cannot be regarded in terms of a fixed essence. The quality of 'sameness' denotes our relation to the world, it is 'a cognitive stance that we take toward existence... In this case, identity is never closed or exclusive; it is never metaphysically guaranteed because it constantly must be constructed and reconstructed'.

40 For insight see J. Krueger, 'Nietzschean Recurrence as a Cosmological Hypothesis', *Journal of the History of Philosophy*, 16 (1978), pp. 435–44. Bernd Magnus has pointed out that it is only in the *Nachlass* that Nietzsche experiments with the idea of eternal return in terms of a scientific hypothesis, while the normative import of the notion is emphasized in virtually every work Nietzsche wrote for publication after 1881. See Magnus, 'Nietzsche's Eternalistic Counter-Myth', *Review of Metaphysics*, 26:4 (June 1973), pp. 604–16. Alexander Nehamas has argued that the presentation of the doctrine in psychological or existential terms does not presuppose the validity of the cosmological hypothesis. See his, 'The Eternal Recurrence', *Philosophical Review*, 89:3 (June 1980), pp. 331–56.

41 Nietzsche, *KSA* VI, p. 335; tr. *EH*, 'Thus Spoke Zarathustra', section 1.
42 Nietzsche, *KSA* XI, 26 [376], p. 250; tr. *WP*, section 1053. See also *KSA* XI, 34 [129], p. 463.
43 On this point see L. Lampert, 'Harold Alderman, *Nietzsche's Gift*', in *International Philosophical Quarterly*, 18:4 (December 1978), pp. 471–81. See also his essay, 'Zarathustra and His Disciples', *Nietzsche Studien*, 8 (1979), pp. 309–33.
44 Nietzsche, *KSA* X (*Nachlass* 1882–4), 16 [63], p. 520.
45 In a note from the Summer of 1883 Nietzsche says that the Way runs between two dangers: to attain the height one faces the danger of 'pride' (*Über-Muth*) and to avoid sinking into the abyss one faces the danger of 'pity' (*Mitleid*). See Nietzsche, *KSA* X, 13 [1], p. 439.
46 Robin Small has produced some of the most important writing on this question of whether eternal return posits a circular or linear understanding of time. In the essay, 'Nietzsche, Dühring, and Time', *Journal of the History of Philosophy*, 28:2 (1990), pp. 229–50, he argues that the doctine that every event occurs not just once but an infinite number of times presupposes three theses about the nature of time. Firstly, and straightforward, that time must be *infinite*, for nothing can occur an infinite number of times without taking an infinite amount of time to do so (assuming a finite period of time between one occurrence and another); secondly, and less straightforward, that time must be *linear* and not circular, as is commonly supposed, as circular time is finite (no two occurrences within it could be separated by more than a certain period of time); and thirdly, that time and the events within time must be distinct (there could be no return unless the same event returns at different times). This could explain why Nietzsche has Zarathustra rebuff the dwarf when it interprets the doctrine of eternal return as meaning that time must be a circle (this is to turn it into a hurdy-gurdy song, Zarathustra says). Thus, one might say that the set of events that returns represents a circle, but not the time in which they do so. There is thus freedom *in* necessity. Zarathustra has to reject the dwarf's rendition of eternal return as supposing time to be a circle, since such a view leads to the fatalistic and resignatory belief that all is in vain. If one subscribes to the dwarf's reading of eternal return as resting on a circular conception of time, then on this conception there can be no escape from the infinite repeatability of one's deeds, and indeed, all would be in vain.
47 The doctrine of return represents in many ways Nietzsche's attempt to formulate a form of conscious innocence, for it rests on a curious dialectic of memory and forgetfulness. In order to create anew one must have innocence, a willing which takes place in the moment; but in order to will responsibly one must have memory. Both, strange as it may seem, are achieved through the test of eternal return: first, one must create the new innocently in the manner of the creative forgetfulness of the child and then one must test the responsibility of this creation by asking

oneself whether one is prepared to affirm the eternal return of one's creation in terms of recognizing the unity of doer and deed (one is what one does). What this shows is that what returns is not literally the 'same' (a laziness that returns is not the same laziness after it undergoes the test of return) and that in order for the doctrine of return to be effective it must presuppose the cultivation of memory, for without memory the impact of the test of return would amount to nothing, since there would be no difference between actions and states of consciousness without memory. In order words the free willing of the eternal return presupposes the breeding of an animal which has the right to make promises.

48 In the *Zarathustra Nachlass* Nietzsche frequently presents Zarathustra's *Untergang* as ending in death. In a note from the *Nachlass* of June/July 1883, for example, Zarathustra forgets himself, teaches the eternal return, which the overman then endures and uses as a means of discipline, and then 'while returning out of the vision he dies of it'. See *KSA* x, 10 [47], p. 378.

49 On the eternal return as a teaching on the significance of the past, as opposed to one which teaches the literal return of the past, see A. Nehamas, 'Eternal Recurrence', pp. 34–9.

50 See B. Magnus, 'Nietzsche's Philosophy in 1888: *The Will to Power* and the *Übermensch*', *Journal of the History of Philosophy*, 24: 1 (1986), pp. 79–98, p. 96.

51 G. Simmel, *Schopenhauer and Nietzsche*, tr. H. Loiskandl *et al.*, Amherst, University of Massachusetts Press, 1986, p. 175.

52 E. Heller, *The Importance of Nietzsche, Ten Essays*, Chicago, Chicago University Press, 1988, p. 184.

53 Nietzsche, *KSA* xi, 27 [23], p. 281.

54 *Ibid.*, 10, 16 [54], p. 517.

55 Conway, 'Overcoming the *Übermensch*', pp. 215–16.

56 See Lampert, *Nietzsche's Teaching*, p. 21, pp. 257–8.

57 Nietzsche, *KSA* ix, 11 [166], p. 505.

58 See Müller-Lauter, *Nietzsche*, pp. 140–2.

59 Pippin, 'Irony and Affirmation', pp. 54–5, speaks of the teaching of eternal return as 'deflating', not abandoning, that of the overman. But this deflation of the import of the notion of the overman only makes sense in relation to our expectations and anticipations. As I try to argue here, the teaching of eternal return, far from abandoning the vision of the overman, can be said to reveal its real nature.

60 Nietzsche, *KSA* x, 10 [47], p. 378.

61 *Ibid.*, 15 [10], p. 482. Compare 16 [86], p. 530.

62 *Ibid.*, 11, 26 [283], pp. 224–5; tr. *WP*, section 1060.

63 Nietzsche, *KSA* xii, 7 [54], pp. 312–13; tr. *WP*, section 617: 'To impress becoming with the character of being – that is the supreme will to power' (translation changed).
Hannah Arendt, *Life of the Mind, Volume Two: Willing*, London, Secker

and Warburg, 1978, pp. 168–70, argues that what Nietzsche discovers in thinking about redemption is that if the self generates power by willing, then the will whose objective is humility is no less powerful than the will whose goal is supremacy and dominion. The act of willing is an act of potency and an indication of the feeling of strength. But this leads to a contradiction between the will's factual impotence (it has no control over what it has been in the past) and this feeling of strength. Thus, the resolution of the problem of the will being unable to will backwards lies in a renunciation of the notion of the will which presupposes notions such as cause and effect, intention and goal, that rest on the illusion of a centre of human agency. I agree that the notion of eternal return does indeed entail an abandonment of the notion of the will, but I disagree that it makes the notion of life as will to power redundant, for the will in 'will to power' is not the same as that posited in metaphysics. Eternal return is the eternal return of life as eternally self-creating and self-destroying, of the ring that is beyond good and evil. The test of return is whether one can actually become what one is by affirming this conception of life which is without final resolution, reconciliation, intention, and purpose. The task is to *become* those that we *are* (will to power as freedom in necessity).

64 See T. Pangle, 'The "Warrior Spirit" as an Inlet to the Political Philosophy of Nietzsche's Zarathustra', *Nietzsche-Studien*, 15 (1986), pp. 140–79, p. 178.

65 Simmel, *Schopenhauer and Nietzsche*, p. 171.

66 See G. Deleuze, *Nietzsche and Philosophy*, tr. H. Tomlinson, London, Athlone Press, 1983, pp. 47–9, pp. 68–73.

67 Haar, 'Nietzsche and Metaphysical Language', p. 32, argues that the ethic of eternal return opposes every categorical imperative ('I should') and replaces it with an imperative of necessity ('I am constrained to') which is turned into a *love* of fate that overcomes any contradiction between freedom and determinism.

68 Magnus, 'Perfectibility and Attitude', p. 645.

69 A. Nehamas, *Nietzsche. Life as Literature*, Cambridge, Mass.: Harvard University Press, 1985, p. 174.

70 Daniel Conway in his essay 'Overcoming the *Übermensch*', pp. 213–14, has challenged the view (typified in Nehamas) that the notion of giving 'style' to one's character in terms of creating a harmonious whole represents Nietzsche's final or definitive statement on the self. He argues that the model of the self put forward in section 290 of *GS* smacks too much of Aristotelian moderation (Emersonian might be more accurate). Internal coherence or self-integration, he argues, may be a necessary condition of human greatness but it is not a sufficient condition, for genuine self-creation, like any artistic labour, must also emerge out of an excess of creative energy. Conway, I believe, is right to emphasize this point. However, while recognizing that the creation of the self is always a risk – of reason, of limits, etc. – it is also necessary to appreciate

that any 'successful' process of self-creation must presuppose a capacity for self-organization able to integrate the chaos that one is into a coherent whole (as in Nietzsche's late depiction of Goethe). The risk of this process is the total disintegration of the self as in madness.

71 Nehamas, *Nietzsche. Life as Literature*, p. 151.
72 See *WP*, section 660 for Nietzsche on 'the body as a political structure'.
73 Nietzsche, *KSA* XI, 37 [11], p. 586; tr. *WP*, section 125.
74 Magnus, 'Perfectibility and Attitude in Nietzsche', p. 647, quotes only the second half from 'My teaching' onwards.
75 Nietzsche, *KSA* IX, 11 [163], pp. 504–5. Compare IX, 11 [188], p. 515.
76 This is a reformulation of a point made by A. Lingis, 'The Will to Power', in D. B. Allison, *The New Nietzsche*, Cambridge, Mass.: MIT Press, 1985, pp. 37–64, p. 60.

6. BENDING THE BOW: GREAT POLITICS, OR THE PROBLEM OF THE LEGISLATOR

1 In a reappraisal of Walter Kaufmann's evisceration of Nietzsche's thought one commentator speaks of the 'embarrassingly political Nietzsche'. See W. H. Sokel, 'The Political Uses and Abuses of Nietzsche in Walter Kaufmann's Image of Nietzsche', *Nietzsche-Studien*, 12 (1983), pp. 436–42.
2 One of the most important studies to date is M. Warren, *Nietzsche and Political Thought*, Cambridge, Mass.: MIT Press, 1988. For a critical appreciation of Warren see my essay, 'Nietzsche: A Radical Challenge to Political Theory?' *Radical Philosophy* 54 (1990), pp. 10–19. Bruce Detwiler has recently argued that Nietzsche's 'ethical nihilism' allows him to become 'the first avowed philosophical atheist of the far Right', and, like many previous commentators, he argues that Nietzsche's aestheticization of the political has distinct affinities with fascism. See B. Detwiler, *Nietzsche and the Politics of Aristocratic Radicalism*, Chicago, Chicago University Press, 1990. For some recent important German studies on Nietzsche's politics see H. Ottmann, *Philosophie und Politik bei Nietzsche*, Berlin and New York, Walter de Gruyter 1987; B. H. F. Taureck, *Nietzsche und der Faschismus. Eine Studie über Nietzsches politische Philosophie und ihre Folgen*, Hamburg, Junius Verlag, 1989; K. Brose, *Sklavenmoral. Nietzsches Sozialphilosophie*, Bonn, Bouvier Verlag, 1990.
3 Kaufmann translates '*grossen Politik*' as 'large-scale politics'. In section 208 of *BGE*, Nietzsche places his political hopes on the menace of Russia leading to European States responding by creating one European will and a new caste to rule Europe.
4 See, for example, Nietzsche, *KSA* XI (*Nachlass* 1884–5), 36 [17], pp. 517–19. See also 11, 35 [24], pp. 518–19; 37 [7], p. 580; 38 [11], pp. 609–10.
5 Nietzsche, *KSA* VI, pp. 313–14; tr. *EH*, 'The Birth of Tragedy', section 4.

6 *Ibid.*, pp. 330–1; tr. *EH*, 'Daybreak', section 2.

7 Nietzsche, *KSA* xii (*Nachlass* 1885–7), 2 [57], pp. 87–8; tr. *WP*, section 960.

8 Nietzsche, *WP*, section 859.

9 Nietzsche, *KSA* xii, 9 [153], pp. 424–6; tr. *WP*, section 898.

10 *Ibid.*, 10 [17], pp. 462–3 (Autumn 1887); tr. *WP*, 866. Compare 13, 11 [413], p. 191 (November 1887–March 1888). The latter is the last note on the overman to be found in Nietzsche's *Nachlass*. A truncated version found its way into *The Anti-Christ* (section 4).

11 The original note of section 257 of *BGE*, which is much longer than the published version, can be found in *KSA* xii, 2 [13], pp. 71–4.

12 Nietzsche, *KSA* v, p. 206; tr. *BGE*, section 258.

13 Nietzsche, *KSA* xi, 37 [8], pp. 580–3; tr. *WP*, section 957.

14 *Ibid.*, 25 [211], p. 69; tr. *WP*, section 862.

15 *Ibid.*, 10, 24 [4], p. 645; tr. *WP*, section 1057.

16 *Ibid.*, 11, 26 [243], pp. 212–13.

17 *Ibid.*, 26 [325], pp. 235–6; 27 [58], p. 289; 27 [80–2], pp. 295–6; 29 [40–1], p. 346; and 34 [191], p. 485.

18 *Ibid.*, 10, 16 [60], p. 519.

19 See S. S. Wolin, *Politics and Vision. Community and Innovation in Western Political Thought*, Boston, Little Brown and Co., 1960, p. 53.

20 See, for example, Nietzsche, *KSA* x, 18 [50], p. 579.

21 *Ibid.*, 11, 37 [8], pp. 580–3; tr. *WP*, section 957.

22 Nietzsche, *KSA* vi, pp. 241–4; tr. *AC*, section 57.

23 *Ibid.* Compare *BGE*, section 212: 'Today..."equality of rights" could all too easily be turned into equality in violating rights...into a common war on all that is rare, strange, privileged, the higher man, the higher soul, the higher duty, the higher responsibility...'

24 Nietzsche, *KSA* v, pp. 119–20; tr. *BGE*, section 199.

25 Nietzsche, *KSA* xi, 38 [12], pp. 611–13 (this note contains the original draft of section 211 of *BGE* on the philosopher as a lawgiver). The translation in section 972 of *WP* is a conflation of two separate notes from the *Nachlass* which appear in *KSA* xi as numbers 38 [12], pp. 611–13 and 26 [407], pp. 258–9.

26 M. Haar, 'Nietzsche and Metaphysical Language', in D. B. Allison, *The New Nietzsche*, Cambridge, Mass.: MIT Press, 1985, p. 26.

27 Nietzsche, *KSA* x, 7 [21], p. 244. I am grateful to R. J. Hollingdale for his help in translating this passage.

28 See Hegel, *Philosophy of Right*, tr. T. M. Knox, Oxford, Oxford University Press, 1967, paragraph 124. For Hegel the 'right of subjectivity' is the principal difference between antiquity and modern times.

29 T. B. Strong, *Friedrich Nietzsche and the Politics of Transfiguration*, Berkeley, University of California Press, 1975, pp. 192–202.

30 Nietzsche, *Homer's Wettkampf*, in *KSA* i, pp. 789–90.

31 *Ibid.*, pp. 206–7.

32 Nietzsche, *KSA* IX, 11 [186], pp. 514–5.

33 Nietzsche, *KSA* III, p. 597; tr. *GS*, section 356. In this passage Nietzsche argues that 'our good socialists' are unaware of the extent of the problem created by this situation in which human beings are no longer 'material for society'. Because of this ignorance they seek to create a 'free society' out of 'wooden iron' (*hölzernen Eisen*), which in German is a proverbial contradiction in terms.

34 Strong, *Nietzsche and the Politics of Transfiguration*, p. 189.

35 Nietzsche, *KSA* III, p. 160; tr. *D*, section 187.

36 Nietzsche, *KSA* II, pp. 302–7; tr. *HAH*, section 472.

37 *Ibid.*, pp. 307–8; tr. section 473.

38 Nietzsche, *KSA* I, *Gst*, p. 768.

39 J. N. Shklar, 'Jean-Jacques Rousseau and Equality', *Daedalus*, Summer (1978), pp. 13–25, p. 14.

40 *Ibid.*, p. 23. Compare Hannah Arendt, *On Revolution*, London, Faber and Faber, 1963, pp. 83–94. On p. 85 Arendt writes that taken as the 'spring of virtue' pity 'has proved to possess a greater capacity for cruelty than cruelty itself'. Arendt argues that if Rousseau introduced compassion into political theory, it was Robespierre who introduced it into the market-place with a vengeance.

41 *Ibid.*

42 L. Strauss, 'Three Waves of Modernity', in Strauss, *Political Philosophy. Six Essays*, ed. H. Gilden, Indianapolis, Bobbs-Merrill, 1975, p. 97.

43 E. Heller, *The Importance of Nietzsche. Ten Essays*, Chicago, Chicago University Pres, 1988, p. 185.

44 For some of the terrifying, eschatological aspects of Nietzsche's conception of great politics see one of the last notes he ever wrote in *KSA* XIII (*Nachlass* 1887–9), 25 [1], pp. 637–8.

CONCLUSION

1 On Rousseau's alleged psychosis see W. H. Blanchard, *Rousseau and the Spirit of Revolt. A Psychological Study*, Ann Arbor, University of Michigan Press, 1967, pp. 217–27.

2 Nietzsche, *KSA* III, p. 293; tr. *D*, section 499.

3 A. Camus, *The Rebel*, tr. A. Bower, Middlesex, Penguin, 1971, p. 23.

4 *Ibid.*, pp. 27–8.

5 It is interesting to note that in a *Nachlass* note of the 1880s Nietzsche actually acknowledges that his thinking ends in a theodicy, namely, in an absolute affirmation of the world, but for the reasons which have previously led humanity to deny it. This affirmation of the world as the 'actually achieved highest possible ideal' is what Nietzsche means by describing his Dionysian philosophy of life in terms of a 'pessimism of strength'. It is the mark of the highest culture that humanity no longer needs a 'justification of ills' because it is strong and brave enough to take pleasure in the terrible, the ambiguous, and the seductive. See *WP*,

section 1019 and the 1886 'Attempt At A Self-Criticism' to the *Birth of Tragedy*, especially section 1.

6 Nietzsche, *KSA* II, p. 195; tr. *HAH*, section 233.

7 Camus, *The Rebel*, p. 71. Camus draws an instructive comparison between Marx and Nietzsche by suggesting that, where Marx's thought posits the subjugation of nature in order to obey history, Nietzsche's thought posits the subjugation of history in order to ensure that nature (immoral, beyond good and evil) is obeyed.

8 Nietzsche, *KSA* III, p. 276; tr. *D*, section 459.

Bibliography

This bibliography includes all the works cited in the notes as well as a number of essays and studies I have found useful in preparing this book.

Abel, G. *Die Dynamik der Willen zur Macht und die ewige Wiederkehr*, Berlin and New York, Walter de Gruyter, 1984.

Abel, G. and Salaquarda J. (eds.), *Krisis der Metaphysik*, Berlin and New York, Walter de Gruyter, 1989.

Alderman, H., *Nietzsche's Gift*, Athens, Ohio University Press, 1977.

Allison, D. B. (ed.), *The New Nietzsche*, Cambridge, Mass.: MIT Press, 1985.

Ansell-Pearson, K., 'The Exoteric Philosophy of Friedrich Nietzsche', *Political Theory*, 14:3 (1986), pp. 497–505.
'Nietzsche's Overcoming of Kant and Metaphysics: From Tragedy to Nihilism', *Nietzsche-Studien*, 16 (1987), pp. 310–40.
'Nietzsche: A Radical Challenge to Political Theory?' *Radical Philosophy*, 54 (1990), pp. 10–19.
'Nietzsche the Rebel', *The Jewish Quarterley*, 139 (1990), pp. 27–32.
'The Significance of Michel Foucault's Reading of Nietzsche: Power, the Subject, and Political Theory', *Nietzsche-Studien*, 20 (1991), pp. 267–84.
'Nietzsche on Autonomy and Morality: the Challenge to Political Theory', *Political Studies*, 34:2 (June, 1991), pp. 270–87.
'Nietzsche and the Problem of the Will in Modernity', in K. Ansell-Pearson (ed.), *Nietzsche and Modern German Thought*, London, Routledge, 1991, pp. 165–92.

Ansell-Pearson, K. (ed.), *Nietzsche and Modern German Thought*, London, Routledge, 1991.

Arendt, H. *On Revolution*, London, Faber and Faber, 1963.
The Life of the Mind. Volume Two: Willing, London, Secker and Warburg, 1978.

Aristotle, *Politics*, tr. S. Everson, Cambridge, Cambridge University Press, 1988.

Ball, T., 'The Picaresque Prince. Reflections on Machiavelli and Moral Change', *Political Theory*, 12:4 (1984), pp. 521–36.

Barnard, F. M. 'Will and Political Rationality in Rousseau', in J. Lively and A. Reeve (eds.), *Modern Political Theory from Hobbes to Marx*, London, Routledge, 1989, pp. 129–49.

Bennholdt-Thomsen, A., *Nietzsches 'Also sprach Zarathustra' als Literarisches Phaenomen*, Frankfurt, Athenaeum, 1974.

Bergmann, P., *Nietzsche. The 'Last Anti-political German'*, Bloomington, Indiana University Press, 1987.

Bergoffen, D. B., 'Why A Genealogy of Morals?' *Man and World*, 16 (1983), pp. 129–38.

Bernstein, J. Andrew, *Nietzsche's Moral Philosophy*, London and Toronto, Associated University Presses, 1987.

Blanchard, W. H., *Rousseau and the Spirit of Revolt. A Psychological Study*, Ann Arbor, University of Michigan Press, 1967.

Blanchot, M., 'Nihilism. The Limit of Experience', in D. B. Allison (ed.), *The New Nietzsche*, Cambridge, Mass.: MIT Press, 1985, pp. 121–9.

Blitz, M., 'Nietzsche and Political Science: The Problem of Politics', *Symposium*, 28:1 (1974), pp. 74–86.

Blondel, E., 'Nietzsche: Life as Metaphor', in D. B. Allison (ed.), *The New Nietzsche*, Cambridge, Mass.: MIT Press, 1985, pp. 150–76.

'Nietzsche's Style of Affirmation: The Metaphors of Genealogy', in Y. Yovel (ed.), *Nietzsche as Affirmative Thinker*, Dordrecht, Martinus Nijhoff, 1986, pp. 132–47.

Bloom, H. (ed.), *Friedrich Nietzsche*, New York, Chelsea House Publishers, 1987.

Brandes, G., *Friedrich Nietzsche*, London, Heinemann, 1914.

Brennecke, D., 'Die blonde Bestie, Vom Missverständnis eines Schlagworts', *Nietzsche-Studien*, 5 (1976), pp. 113–45.

Brose, K., *Geschichtsphilosophische Strukturen im Werk Nietzsches*, Frankfurt am Main, Peter Lang, 1973.

'Nietzsches Verhältnis zu J. S. Mill', *Nietzsche-Studien*, 3 (1974), pp. 152–74.

Sklavenmoral. Nietzsches Sozialphilosophie, Bonn, Bouvier Verlag, 1990.

Buddhist Scriptures, selected and translated by Edward Conze, Middlesex, Penguin, 1959.

Bueb, B., *Nietzsches Kritik der praktischen Vernunft*, Stuttgart, Ernst Klett Verlag, 1970.

Camus, A., *The Rebel*, tr. A. Bower, Middlesex, Penguin, 1971.

Cantor, P., 'Friedrich Nietzsche: the Use and Abuse of Metaphor', in D. S. Miall (ed.), *Metaphor. Problems and Perspectives*, Brighton, Harvester Press, 1982, pp. 71–89.

Cartwright, D. E., 'Kant, Schopenhauer, and Nietzsche on the Morality of Pity', *Journal of the History of Ideas*, 45 (January–March 1984), pp. 83–98.

Cassirer, E., *The Question of Jean-Jacques Rousseau*, tr. P. Gay, Bloomington, Indiana University Press, 1954.

Rousseau, Kant, and Goethe, Two Essays, Connecticut, Archon Books, 1961.

Caygill, H., 'Affirmation and Eternal Return in the Free-Spirit Trilogy', in K. Ansell-Pearson (ed.), *Nietzsche and Modern German Thought*, London, Routledge, 1991, pp. 216–40.

Chapman, J. W., *Rousseau. Totalitarian or Liberal?*, New York, Ams Press, 1968.

Charvet, J., *The Social Problem in the Philosophy of Rousseau*, Cambridge, Cambridge University Press, 1974.

Cobban, A., *Rousseau and the Modern State*, London, Allen and Unwin, 1964.

Colletti, L., *From Rousseau to Lenin*, tr. J. Merrington, London and New York, New Left Books, 1972.

Colman, J. S., 'Nietzsche as *Politique et Moraliste*', *Journal of the History of Ideas*, 27 (1966), pp. 549–74.

Connolly, W. E., *Political Theory and Modernity*, Oxford, Basil Blackwell, 1988.

Conway, D. W., 'Solving the Problem of Socrates. Nietzsche's *Zarathustra* as Political Irony', *Political Theory*, 16:2 (1988), pp. 257–80.

'Overcoming the *Übermensch*: Nietzsche's Revaluation of Values', *Journal of the British Society for Phenomenology*, 20:3, (October 1989), pp. 211–24.

Cranston, M. and Peters, R. S. (eds.), *Hobbes and Rousseau: A Collection of Critical Essays*, New York, Doubleday, 1972.

Cropsey, J. and Strauss, L. (eds.), *History of Political Philosophy*, Chicago, Chicago University Press, 1987 (third edition).

Dannhauser, W. J., 'Friedrich Nietzsche' in J. Cropsey and L. Strauss (eds.), *History of Political Philosophy*, Chicago, Chicago University Press, 1987, pp. 829–51.

Deleuze, G., *Nietzsche and Philosophy*, tr. H. Tomlinson, London, Athlone Press, 1983.

'Nomad Thought', in D. B. Allison (ed.), *The New Nietzsche*, Cambridge, Mass.: MIT Press, 1985, pp. 142–50.

Dent, N. J. H., *Rousseau. An Introduction to his Psychological, Social and Political Theory*, Oxford, Basil Blackwell, 1988.

Derathé, R., *Jean-Jacques Rousseau et la Science Politique de son Temps* (1950), Paris 1979.

Derrida, J., *Of Grammatology*, tr. G. C. Spivak, Baltimore, Johns Hopkins University Press, 1976.

Spurs. Nietzsche's Styles, tr. B. Harlow, Chicago, Chicago University Press, 1979.

'Otobiographies. The Teaching of Nietzsche and the Politics of the Proper Name' in H. Bloom (ed.), *Friedrich Nietzsche*, New York, Chelsea House Publishers, 1987, pp. 105–34.

Detwiler, B., *Nietzsche and the Politics of Aristocratic Radicalism*, Chicago, Chicago University Press, 1990.

Diprose, R., 'Nietzsche, Ethics, and Sexual Difference', *Radical Philosophy*, 52 (1989), pp. 27–33.

Donnellan, B., *Nietzsche and the French Moralists*, Bonn, Bouvier Verlag, Herbert Grundmann, 1982.

Duffy, M. F. and Mittelman, W., 'Nietzsche's Attitude Toward the Jews', *Journal of the History of Ideas*, 49:2 (April–June 1988), pp. 301–17.

Ellenburg, S., *Rousseau's Political Philosophy*, Ithaca, Cornell University Press, 1976.

'Rousseau and Kant: principles of political right', in R. A. Leigh (ed.), *Rousseau after two hundred years*, Cambridge, Cambridge University Press, 1982.

Emerson, R. W., *Selected Essays*, ed. L. Ziff, Middlesex, Penguin, 1982.

Fetscher, I., *Rousseaus politische Philosophie. Zur Geschichte des demokratischen Freiheitsbegriffs*, Frankfurt, Suhrkamp, 1975.

Fischer, K. R., 'Nazism as a Nietzschean Experiment', *Nietzsche-Studien*, 6 (1977), pp. 116–122.

Forbes, I., 'Rousseau and Nietzsche: The Philosopher as Legislator', unpublished MA thesis, University of Adelaide, 1979.

Foucault, M., 'Nietzsche, Genealogy, and History' in Foucault, *Language, Counter-Memory, and Practice*, tr. D. F. Bouchard and S. Simon, Oxford, Basil Blackwell, 1977.

Power/Knowledge. Selected Writings and Interviews 1972–77, ed. C. Gordon, Brighton Harvester Press, 1980.

'Technologies of the Self' in Luther H. Martin et al. *Technologies of the Self. A Seminar with Michel Foucault*, London, Tavistock, 1988, pp. 16–50.

Fralin, R., 'Rousseau and Community: the role of custom in social change', *History of Political Thought*, 7:1 (1986), pp. 131–51.

Freud, S., *Civilization and Its Discontents*, Middlesex, Penguin, 1985.

Gerhardt, V., 'Das "Princip des Gleichgewichts". Zum Verhältnis von Recht und Macht bei Nietzsche', *Nietzsche-Studien*, 12 (1983), pp. 111–33.

'Die Moral des Immoralismus. Nietzsches Beitrag zu einer Grundlegung der Ethik', in G. Abel and J. Salaquarda (eds.), *Krisis der Metaphysik*, Berlin and New York, Walter de Gruyter, 1989, pp. 417–47.

Gerrantana, V., 'The Citizen of Geneva and the Seigneur of Ferney', *New Left Review*, 111 (1978), pp. 66–77.

Gillespie, M. A. and Strong, T. B. (eds.), *Nietzsche's New Seas*, Chicago, Chicago University Press, 1988.

Golomb, J., 'Nietzsche's Phenomenology of Power', *Nietzsche-Studien*, 15 (1986), pp. 289–305.

'Nietzsche's Judaism of Power', *Revue des études juives*, 147 (July–December 1988), pp. 353–85.

Gossman, L., 'Time and History in Rousseau', *Studies in Voltaire and the Eighteenth Century*, 30 (1964), pp. 311–49.

Haar, M., 'Nietzsche and Metaphysical Language', D. B. Allison (ed.), *The New Nietzsche*, Cambridge, Mass.: MIT Press, 1985, pp. 5–37.

Haase, Marie-Luise, 'Der Übermensch in *Also sprach Zarathustra* und im Zarathustra-Nachlass 1882–85', *Nietzsche-Studien*, 13 (1984), pp. 228–45.

Habermas, J., 'The Entwinement of Myth and Enlightenment: Rereading *Dialectic of Enlightenment*', *New German Critique*, 26 (1983), pp. 13–30.

Hall, J. C., *Rousseau. An Introduction to his Political Philosophy*, London, Macmillan, 1973.

Hamacher, W., '"Disgregation of the Will": Nietzsche on the Individual and Individuality' in H. Bloom (ed.), *Friedrich Nietzsche*, New York, Chelsea House Publishers, 1987, pp. 163–93.

Hegel, G. W. F., *Philosophy of Right*, tr. T. M. Knox, Oxford, Oxford University Press, 1967.

Phenomenology of Spirit, tr. A.V. Miller, Oxford, Oxford University Press, 1977.

Heidegger, M., 'Who is Nietzsche's Zarathustra?' tr. B. Magnus, in D. B. Allison (ed.), *The New Nietzsche*, Cambridge, Mass.: MIT Press, 1985, pp. 64–80.

'The Word of Nietzsche: "God is Dead"', in Heidegger, *The Question Concerning Technology and Other Essays*, tr. W. Lovitt, New York, Harper and Row, 1977.

Nietzsche. Volume One. The Will to Power as Art, tr. D. F. Krell, London, Routledge, 1979.

Nietzsche. Volume Two. The Eternal Recurrence of the Same, tr. D. F. Krell, New York, Harper and Row, 1985.

Nietzsche. Volume Three. The Will to Power as Knowledge and as Metaphysics, tr. J. Stambaugh, F. A. Capuzzi, D. F. Krell, San Francisco, Harper and Row, 1987.

Nietzsche. Volume Four. Nihilism, tr. F. A. Capuzzi, San Francisco, Harper and Row, 1982.

Heller, A., *Beyond Justice*, Oxford, Basil Blackwell, 1989.

A Philosophy of Morals, Oxford, Basil Blackwell, 1990.

Heller, E., *The Importance of Nietzsche. Ten Essays*, Chicago, Chicago, University Press, 1988.

Heller, P., 'Nietzsche in his relation to Voltaire and Rousseau', in J. C. O'Flaherty (ed.), *Studies in Nietzsche and the Classical Tradition*, North Carolina, Chapel Hill, 1976, pp. 51–88.

Higgins, K., *Nietzsche's Zarathustra*, Philadelphia, Temple University Press, 1987.

Hobbes, T., *Leviathan*, Middlesex, Penguin, 1981.

Hollingdale, R. J., *Nietzsche. The Man and his Philosophy*, London, Routledge and Kegan Paul, 1965.

Horowitz, A., *Rousseau, Nature, and History*, Toronto, Toronto University Press, 1987.

Houlgate, S., *Hegel, Nietzsche, and the Criticism of Metaphysics*, Cambridge, Cambridge University Press, 1986.

Hoy, David C., 'Nietzsche, Hume, and Genealogical Method', in Y. Yovel (ed.), *Nietzsche as Affirmative Thinker*, The Hague, Martinus Nijhoff, 1986, pp. 20–39.

Ihering, Rudolf von, *Law as a Means to an End*, tr. I. Husik, New York, Augustus M. Kelley, 1968.

Janz, C. P., *Friedrich Nietzsche: Biographie*, 3 vols. München, Carl Hanser Verlag, 1978.

Jaspers, K., *Nietzsche. An Introduction to his Philosophical Activity*, tr. C. F. Wallraff and F. J. Schmitz, Tucson, University of Arizona Press, 1965.

Kant, I., *Critique of Pure Reason*, tr. N. K. Smith, London, Macmillam, 1950.
On History, tr. L. W. Beck, Indianapolis, Bobbs-Merrill, 1963.
Groundwork of the Metaphysic of Morals, tr. H. J. Paton, New York, Harper and Row, 1964.

Kariel, H. S., 'Nietzsche's Preface to Constitutionalism', *Journal of Politics*, 25 (1963), pp. 211–25.

Kaufmann, W., *Nietzsche. Philosopher, Psychologist, and Antichrist*, New Jersey, Princeton University Press, 1974 (fourth edition).

Kaulbach, F., *Sprachen der ewigen Wiederkunft*, Würzburg, Königshauser und Neumann, 1985.

Kavanagh, T. M., *Writing the Truth. Authority and Desire in Rousseau*, Berkeley, University of California Press, 1987.

Kemal, S., 'Some Problems of Genealogy', *Nietzsche-Studien*, 19 (1990), pp. 30–43.

Kerger, H., *Autorität und Recht in Denken Nietzsches*, Berlin, Duncker and Humblot, 1968.
'Normativität und Selektivität der "Willens-Kausalität" bei Nietzsche', *Nietzsche-Studien*, 19 (1990), pp. 81–112.

Kimmerle, G., *Die Aporie der Wahrheit. Anmerkungen zu Nietzsches 'Genealogie der Moral'*, Tübingen, Konkursbuchverlag, 1983.

Klossowski, P., 'Nietzsche's Experience of the Eternal Return', in D. B. Allison (ed.), *The New Nietzsche*, Cambridge, Mass.: MIT Press, 1985, pp. 107–20.

Kramer, H., *Nietzsche und Rousseau*, Leipzig, R. Noske, 1928.

Krell, D. F. and Wood, D. (eds.), *Exceedingly Nietzsche. Aspects of Contemporary Nietzsche-Interpretation*, London, Routledge, 1988.

Kreuger, J. 'Nietzschean Recurrence as a Cosmological Hypothesis', *Journal of the History of Philosophy*, 16 (1978), pp. 435–44.

Kuenzli, R. E., 'The Nazi Appropriation of Nietzsche', *Nietzsche-Studien*, 12 (1983), pp. 428–35.

Kuhn, E., 'Nietzsches Quelle des Nihilismus-Begriff', *Nietzsche-Studien*, 13 (1984), pp. 253–79.
'Cultur, Civilisation. Die Zweideutigkeit des "Modernen"', *Nietzsche-Studien*, 18 (1989), pp. 600–27.

Lampert, L., 'Heidegger's Nietzsche Interpretation', *Man and World*, 17 (1974), pp. 353–78.
'Harold Alderman, *Nietzsche's Gift*', *International Philosophical Quarterly*, 18:4 (1978), pp. 471–81.
'Zarathustra and His Disciplies', *Nietzsche-Studien*, 8 (1979), pp. 309–33.

Nietzsche's Teaching, New Haven, Yale University Press, 1987.

Leigh, R. A. (ed.), *Rousseau after two hundred years*, Cambridge, Cambridge University Press, 1982.

Leonard, J., 'Public versus Private Claims. Machiavellianism from another Perspective', *Political Theory*, 12:4 (1984), pp. 491–506.

Levine, A. M., *The Politics of Autonomy. A Kantian Reading of Rousseau's Social Contract*, Amherst, University of Massachussetts Press, 1976.

Lingis, A., 'The Will to Power', in D. B. Allison (ed.), *The New Nietzsche*, Cambridge, Mass.: MIT Press, 1985, pp. 37–64.

Lively, J. and Reeve, A. (eds.), *Modern Political Theory from Hobbes to Marx*, London, Routledge, 1989.

Locke, J., *Two Treatises of Government*, ed. P. Laslett, Cambridge, Cambridge University Press, 1988.

Love, N. S., *Marx, Nietzsche, and Modernity*, New York, Columbia University Press, 1986.

Löwith, K., *Nietzsches Philosophie der ewigen Widerkunft des Gleichen*, Stuttgart, 1956.

From Hegel to Nietzsche, tr. D. E. Green, London, Constable, 1964.

Lukács, G., *History and Class Consciousness*, tr. R. Livingstone, London, Merlin Press, 1971.

Luke, T. W., 'On Nature and Society: Rousseau versus the Enlightenment', *History of Political Thought*, 5:2 (1984), pp. 211–43.

MacAdam, J. L. '*The Discourse on Inequality*' and '*The Social Contract*', in J. Lively and A. Reeve (eds.), *Modern Political Theory from Hobbes to Marx*, London, Routledge, 1989, pp. 113–29.

Machiavelli, N., *The Prince*, tr. G. Bull, Middlesex, Penguin, 1981. *Discourses*, tr. L. J. Walker, Middlesex, Penguin, 1983.

MacIntyre, A., *After Virtue. A Study in Moral Theory*, London, Duckworth, 1981.

MacPherson, C. B., *The Political Theory of Possessive Individualism*, Oxford, Oxford University Press, 1962.

Magnus, B., 'Nietzsche's Eternalistic counter-Myth', *Review of Metaphysics*, 26:4 (1973), pp. 604–16.

Nietzsche's Existential Imperative, Bloomington, Indiana University Press, 1978.

'Eternal Recurrence', *Nietzsche-Studien*, 8 (1979), pp. 362–77.

'Perfectibility and Attitude in Nietzsche's *Übermensch*', *Review of Metaphysics*, 36 (March 1983), pp. 633–59.

'Nietzsche's Philosophy in 1888: *The Will to Power* and the *Übermensch*', *Journal of the History of Philosophy*, 24:1 (1986), pp. 79–98.

Man, P. de, *Allegories of Reading. Figural Language in Rousseau, Nietzsche, Rilke, and Proust*, New Haven, Yale University Press, 1979.

Marti, U., 'Der Plebejer in der Revolte – Ein Beitrag zur Genealogie des "Höheren Menschen"', *Nietzsche-Studien*, 18 (1989), pp. 550–73.

'Nietzsches Kritik der Französischen Revolution', *Nietzsche-Studien*, 19 (1990), pp. 312–36.

Marx, K., *Early Writings*, tr. R. Livingstone, Middlesex, Penguin, 1975.

Marx, K. and Engels, F., *The German Ideology*, ed. C. J. Arthur, London, Lawrence and Wishart, 1977.

Masters, R. D., *The Political Philosophy of Rousseau*, New Jersey, Princeton University Press, 1968.

McKenzie, L., 'Rousseau's Debate with Machiavelli in the *Social Contract*', *Journal of the History of Ideas*, 43 (April–June, 1982), pp. 209–28.

Melzer, A. M., 'Rousseau and the Problem of Bougeois Society', *American Political Science Review*, 74:4 (December 1980), pp. 1019–1034.

Merquior, J., *Rousseau and Weber. Two studies in the Theory of Legitimacy*, London, Routledge and Kegan Paul, 1980.

Miall, D. S. (ed.), *Metaphor. Problems and Perspectives*, Brighton, Harvester Press, 1982.

Mill, J. S., *On Liberty*, ed. S. Collini, Cambridge, Cambridge University Press, 1989.

Miller, J., *Rousseau. Dreamer of Democracy*, New Haven, Yale University Press, 1984.

Minson, J., *Genealogies of Morals. Nietzsche, Deleuze, Foucault, and the Eccentricity of Ethics*, New York, St Martin's Press, 1985.

Mistry, F., *Nietzsche and Buddhism*, Berlin and New York, Walter de Gruyter, 1981.

Montinari, M., *Nietzsche lesen*, Berlin and New York, Walter de Gruyter, 1982.

Morris, C. (ed.), *The Great Legal Philosophers. Readings in Jurisprudence*, Philadelphia, University of Pennsylvania Press, 1971.

Müller-Lauter, W., *Nietzsche. Seine Philosophie der Gegensätze und die Gegensätze seiner Philosophie*, Berlin and New York, Walter de Gruyter, 1971.

'Nietzsches Lehre vom Willen zur Macht', *Nietzsche-Studien*, 3 (1974), pp. 1–60.

Nehamas, A., 'Eternal Recurrence', *Philosophical Review*, 89:3 (June 1980), pp. 331–56.

Nietzsche. Life as Literature, Cambridge, Mass., Harvard University Press, 1985.

Oduev, S. F., *Auf den Spuren Zarathustras. Der Einfluss Nietzsches auf die bürgerliche deutsche Philosophie*, Köln, 1977.

Ottmann, H., *Philosophie und Politik bei Nietzsche*, Berlin and New York, Walter de Gruyter, 1987.

Pangle, T. L., 'The Roots of Contemporary Nihilism and Its Political Consequences', *Review of Politics*, 45 (1983), pp. 45–70.

'The "Warrior Spirit" as an Inlet to the Political Philosophy of Nietzsche's Zarathustra', *Nietzsche-Studien*, 15 (1986), pp. 140–79.

Pippin, R. B., 'Nietzsche and the Origin of the Idea of Modernism', *Inquiry*, 23 (1983), pp. 151–80.

'Irony and Affirmation in Nietzsche's *Thus Spoke Zarathustra*', in M. A. Gillespie and T. B. Strong (eds.), *Nietzsche's New Seas*, Chicago, Chicago University Press (1988), pp. 45–71.

Pizer, J., 'The Use and Abuse of "Ursprung": On Foucault's Reading of Nietzsche', *Nietzsche-Studien*, 19 (1990), pp. 462–78.

Plato, *The Republic*, tr. H. D. P. Lee, Middlesex, Penguin, 1970.

Plattner, M. F., *Rousseau's State of Nature*, DeKalb, Northern Illinois University Press, 1979.

Polin, R., *La politique de la solitude. Essai sur Jean-Jacques Rousseau*, Paris, Editions Sirey, 1971.

'Nietzsche und der Staat – oder die Politik eines Einsamen', in H. Steffen (ed.). *Nietzsche. Werk und Wirkungen*, Gottingen, Vandenhoeck and Ruprecht, 1974, pp. 27–45.

Prostka, N., *Nietzsches Machtbegriff in Beziehung zu den Machiavellis*, Münster, Lit. Verlag, 1989.

Riley, P., *Will and Political Legitimacy*, Cambridge, Mass., Harvard University Press, 1982.

Roche, K. F., *Rousseau. Stoic and Romantic*, London, Methuen. 1974.

Rosen, S., 'Nietzsche's Revolution', in S. Rosen, *The Ancients and the Moderns, Rethinking Modernity*, New Haven, Yale University Press, 1989.

Rosenhofft, W., *Nietzsches Zarathustra Wahn. Deutung und Dokumentation zur Apokalypse des Übermenschen*, Herbert Lang, Bern and Peter Lang, Frankfurt am Main., 1972.

Röttges, H., *Nietzsche und die Dialetik der Aufklärung*, Berlin and New York, Walter de Gruyter, 1972.

Sabine, G. H. and Thorson, T. L. (eds.), *A History of Political Theory*, Illinois, Dryden Press, 1973 (fourth edition).

Schacht, R., *Nietzsche*, London, Routledge, 1983.

Scheier, Claus-Artur, *Nietzsche's Labyrinth. Das ursprünchliche Denken und die Seele*, Freiburg, Alber, 1985.

Scheler, M., 'Ressentiment' in R. C. Solomon (ed.), *Nietzsche: A Collection of Critical Essays*, New York, Doubleday, 1973, pp. 243–58.

Schmidt, Lars-Henrik, *Immediacy Lost. Construction of the Social in Rousseau and Nietzsche*, Copenhagen, Akademisk Forlag, 1988.

Schutte, O., *Beyond Nihilism. Nietzsche without Masks*, Chicago, Chicago University Press, 1984.

Shapiro, G., 'Nietzsche contra Renan', *History and Theory*, 21 (May 1982), pp. 193–222.

Shklar, J. N., *Men and Citizens. A Study of Rousseau's Social Theory*, Cambridge, Cambridge University Press, 1969.

'Subversive Genealogies', *Daedalus*, 101:1 (1972), pp. 129–54.

'Jean-Jacques Rousseau and Equality', *Daedalus*, Summer (1978), pp. 13–25.

Simmel, G., *Schopenhauer and Nietzsche*, tr. H. Loiskandl *et al.*, Amherst, University of Massachusetts Press, 1986.

Skillen, A., 'Rousseau and the Fall of Social Man', *Philosophy*, 60 (1985), pp. 105–21.

Small, R., 'Eternal Recurrence', *Canadian Journal of Philosophy*, 13:4 (December 1983), pp. 585–605.
'Absolute Becoming and Absolute Necessity', *International Studies in Philosophy*, 21 (1990), pp. 125–34.
'Nietzsche, Dühring, and Time', *Journal of the History of Philosophy*, 28:2 (1990), pp. 229–50.
Sokel, W. H., 'The Political Uses and Abuses of Nietzsche in Walter Kaufmann's Image of Nietzsche', *Nietzsche-Studien*, 12 (1983), pp. 436–42.
Solomon, R. C., *Nietzsche. A Collection of Critical Essays*, New York, Doubleday, 1973.
'A More Severe Morality. Nietzsche's Affirmative Ethics', *Journal of the British Society for Phenomenology*, 16:3 (1985), pp. 250–67.
Stambaugh, J., *Nietzsche's Thought of Eternal Return*, Baltimore, John Hopkins University Press, 1972.
'Thoughts on Pity and Revenge', *Nietzsche-Studien*, 1 (1972), pp. 27–36.
Starobinski, J., *Jean-Jacques Rousseau. Transparency and Obstruction*, tr. A. Goldhammer, Chicago University Press, 1953.
Steffen, H. (ed.), *Nietzsche, Werk und Wirkungen*, Gottingen, Vandenhoeck and Ruprecht, 1974.
Stern, J. P., *Nietzsche*, Glasgow, Collins, 1978.
Stevens, J., '*Nietzsche and Heidegger on Truth and Justice*', *Nietzsche-Studien*, 9 (1980), pp. 224–39.
Strauss, Leo, *Natural Right and History*, Chicago, Chicago University Press, 1953.
Thoughts on Machiavelli, Seattle, University of Washington Press, 1969.
'Three Waves of Modernity', in Strauss, *Political Philosophy. Six Essays*, ed. H. Gilden, Indianapolis, Bobbs-Merrill, 1975, pp. 81–98.
Strong, T. B., *Friedrich Nietzsche and the Politics of Transfiguration*, Berkeley, University of California Press, 1975 (second edition, 1989).
'Nietzsche's Political Aesthetics', in M. A. Gillespie and T. B. Strong (eds.), *Nietzsche's New Seas*, Chicago, Chicago University Press, 1988, pp. 153–74.
Talmon, J. L., *The Origins of Totalitarian Democracy*, London, Secker and Warburg, 1952.
Taureck, B. H. F., *Nietzsche und der Faschismus. Eine Studie über Nietzsches politische Philosophie und ihre Folgen*. Hamburg, Junius Verlag, 1989.
Thatcher, D. S., 'Zur Genealogie der Moral. Some Textual Annotations', *Nietzsche-Studien*, 18 (1989), pp. 587–99.
Tuck, R., *Hobbes*, Oxford, Oxford University Press, 1989.
Viroli, M., *Rousseau and the 'Well-Ordered Society'*, tr. D. Hanson, Cambridge, Cambridge University Press, 1988.
'Republic and Politics in Machiavelli and Rousseau', *History of Political Thought*, 10:3 (1989), pp. 405–20.
Voegelin, E., 'Nietzsche, the Crisis and the War', *Journal of Politics*, 6 (1944), pp. 177–211.

Warren, M., *Nietzsche and Political Thought*, Cambridge, Mass., MIT Press, 1988.
Williams, W. D., *Nietzsche and the French*, Oxford, Basil Blackwell, 1952.
Wolin, S. S., *Politics and Vision. Continuity and Innovation in Western Political Thought*, Boston, Little Brown and Co., 1960.
Wood, D., 'Nietzsche's Transvaluation of Time', in D. F. Krell and D. Wood (eds.), *Exceedingly Nietzsche. Aspects of Contemporary Nietzsche-Interpretation*, London, Routledge, 1988, pp. 31–63.
Wuthenow, R. R., 'Die Grosse Inversion: Jean-Jacques Rousseau im Denken Nietzsches', *Neue Hefte für Philosophie*, 29 (1989), pp. 60–79.
Yack, B., *The Longing for Total Revolution. Philosophic Sources of Discontent from Rousseau to Marx and Nietzsche*, New Jersey, Princeton University Press, 1986.
Yovel, Y. (ed.), *Nietzsche as Affirmative Thinker*, Dordrecht, Martinus Nijhoff, 1986.
  'Nietzsche and Spinoza: *amor fati* and *amor dei*', in Y. Yovel (ed.), *Nietzsche as Affirmative Thinker*, Dordrecht, Martinus Nijhoff, 1986, pp. 183–204.
Zuckert, C., 'Nietzsche on the Origins and Development of the Distinctively Human', *Polity*, Fall (1983), pp. 48–71.
  'Nietzsche's Re-reading of Plato', *Political Theory*, 13:3 (1985), pp. 213–38.

Index

279